Lawyers as Peacemakers

J. Kim Wright

Lawyers as Peacemakers

Practicing Holistic, Problem-Solving Law

J. Kim Wright

Defending Liberty
Pursuing Justice

Cover design by ABA Publishing.

The materials contained herein represent the opinions and views of the authors and/or the editors, and should not be construed to be the views or opinions of the law firms or companies with whom such persons are in partnership with, associated with, or employed by, nor of the American Bar Association, unless adopted pursuant to the bylaws of the Association.

Nothing contained in this book is to be considered as the rendering of legal advice, either generally or in connection with any specific issue or case; nor do these materials purport to explain or interpret any specific bond or policy, or any provisions thereof, issued by any particular franchise company, or to render franchise or other professional advice. Readers are responsible for obtaining advice from their own lawyers or other professionals. This book and any forms and agreements herein are intended for educational and informational purposes only.

Printed in the United States of America.

14 13 12 11 10   5 4 3 2 1

Library of Congress Cataloging-in-Publication Data

Wright, J. Kim
    Lawyers as peacemakers : practicing holistic, problem-solving law / J. Kim Wright.
      p. cm.
    Includes index.
    ISBN 978-1-60442-862-9
    1. Attorney and client—United States. 2. Conflict management—United States.
3. Dispute resolution (Law)—United States. I. Title.

    KF311.W75 2010
    340.023'73—dc22

                                                            2010011171

Discounts are available for books ordered in bulk. Special consideration is given to state bars, CLE programs, and other bar-related organizations. Inquire at Book Publishing, ABA Publishing, American Bar Association, 321 North Clark Street, Chicago, Illinois 60654-7598.

www.ababooks.org

Advance Praise for *Lawyers as Peacemakers*

"Lawyers as Peacemakers follows the ABA's tradition of publishing cutting-edge books that meld the goals of helping lawyers develop practices that provide competent, profitable, client-centered services and increasing the public's access to justice. Building on the new paradigm shift of increasing a consumer-oriented, nonadversarial approach as pioneered by mediation, unbundling, and Collaborative Law, Kim Wright challenges lawyers to encourage peace, healing, conciliation, and sustainable human relationships within heartfelt client connections and needed new service products. Perhaps most important, to prevent career burnout and encourage lawyer self-care, this book is a must read just for its tips on how to balance important, stimulating careers while maintaining a meaningful personal and home life. This book can truly help make peacemaking your life's work."

—Forrest (Woody) Mosten, author of *Collaborative Divorce Handbook, Mediation Career Guide, Unbundling Legal Services,* and *Complete Guide to Mediation,* recipient of the ABA "Lawyer as Problem-Solver" Award, ABA Lifetime Legal Access Award, and 2009 ABA Frank Sander Co-Lecturer

"The legal profession is transforming before our eyes, moving from an 18th century to a 21st century jurisprudence that recognizes how human beings are wired biologically to behave and that places the needs of clients squarely in the center of our efforts as lawyers. In this emerging jurisprudence, as the over-arching purpose of our professional work shifts from winning legal victories to providing meaningful conflict resolution services for our clients, what kind of person the lawyer *is* matters equally as much as the power of the lawyer's intellect.

"When legal historians and sociologists begin writing the story of how this transformation of a profession was wrought, the publication by the American Bar Association of J. Kim Wright's remarkable book will surely be seen as a defining event. Wright devotes a chapter to describing important new vectors in the practice of law: restorative justice, therapeutic jurisprudence, collaborative law, and other modalities. But the heart of Wright's information-rich book illuminates and provides guidance not so much about what lawyers do as about who we are and who we can be: emotionally and physically healthy, self aware, and reflective professionals with a strong sense of values and ethics, working as humanistic conflict resolution specialists toward the highest purpose of the law—healing breaches in the social fabric."

> —Pauline H. Tesler, co-founder of the International Academy of Collaborative Professionals, co-editor of the journal *The Collaborative Review,* fellow of the American Academy of Matrimonial Lawyers, author of *Collaborative Law: Achieving Effective Resolution in Divorce without Litigation,* and in August 2002, was co-recipient (with Stu Webb) of the first American Bar Association "Lawyer as Problem Solver" award

"The depth and breadth of Wright's work cannot be overstated. As I grew into my position on the bench I attempted to research resources and like-minded colleagues, and it was no mean task. Wright pulls the information together skillfully, and envisions this tome as a tool in bringing integrity, balance, and peace to the practice of law; I agree. And it is a tool both for the attorney, and for the judge. The practical guide she provides for the professional moving in that direction is icing on the cake."

> —Kathryn Carter, Retired District Magistrate Judge, District Court of Cloud County, Kansas, and President, Renaissance Lawyer Society

"Kim Wright has crafted a balanced template of possibility for those lawyers who feel ready to bring an enheartened awareness into their lives and their work. This book points the way to a new paradigm for lawyers, one that is meaning-based and congruent with the burgeoning consciousness movement in society-at-large. It should be mandatory reading in law school and beyond. Wonderful."

> —Jeff Brown, LL.B.,[author of *Soulshaping: A Journey of Self-Creation.*

"By the time I had read the first chapter, I knew that this would be a book that I would keep with me at all times as an attorney. And it is a book I will keep giving out to my attorney friends as well."

> —Amanda Hibler, 2L, Sandra Day O'Connor School of Law, Arizona State University

"'What do you call 50 lawyers on the bottom of the ocean?' A 'very yesterday' bad joke, that's what! In *Lawyers as Peacemakers,* Kim Wright has produced a meaty and readable resource on how an ethic of care can become a canon of legal practice. Some, like myself, will be attracted by its emphasis on Therapeutic Jurisprudence—humanizing the law through reliance on insights from psychology and related social sciences. Others will be attracted by the book's holistic approaches and its spiritual side. The end result, however, should be

a bench and bar that better serves society, and a legal profession composed of counselors, leaders, and peacemakers."
—David B. Wexler, Professor of Law and Director, International Network on Therapeutic Jurisprudence, University of Puerto Rico, and Distinguished Research Professor of Law and Professor of Psychology, University of Arizona

"This book is well grounded, not 'airy-fairy,' fluffy, feel good stuff. It has substance and is full of possibility. Kim Wright is a very strong example of a 'Gravitational Core' of a conversation—whereby the conversations that constitute 'restorative justice' etc. find her, and the more they find her, the more mass there is, and thus more conversations tend to find her. Gravitational Cores are the stewards and shepherds of conversations—much like a star starts is a mass of gas that gathers, builds mass, and eventually becomes something that brings light to the absolute darkness of the universe—or at least a portion of it—knowing that it is not the person that brings the light, but the conversation."
—Scott Wolf, Performance and Leadership Consultant at Sunergos Consulting

"In *Lawyers as Peacemakers*, Kim Wright chronicles the expansion of the legal profession beyond adversarial assumptions and adjudicatory habits. Kim shares numerous examples of how lawyers can make, and are making, positive differences in the world. *Lawyers as Peacemakers* is a breath of fresh air for a legal profession overdue for change."
—James Melamed, co-founder of Resourceful Internet Solutions (RIS) and Mediate.com, founder of The Mediation Center in Eugene, Oregon, former Executive Director of the national Academy of Family Mediators, and professor of Mediation at the Pepperdine University School of Law's Straus Institute for Dispute Resolution.

"When I met Kim Wright at the beginning of the new millennium, my work had felt for too long like I'd been sweating my way through the legal profession jungle trying to hack out an untraveled swath. I was practicing law using terms like 'preventive intervention' and 'client legal education' in an effort to minimize legal intrusions for my clients, when it seemed many around me were glad for them—and the billable hours they represented—to just get bigger. Kim came into the jungle from a different direction, bringing the comforting relief of recognition, and her own sharp blade and determination to clear the trail. I learned for the first time I was not alone in my thinking. Helping co-found Renaissance Lawyer Society with her was a privilege, and an opportunity to make the path wider and more definite. Reading *Lawyers as Peacemakers* and supporting its creation has been like watching a great symphony being composed. Turns out there is a harmony of voices in our profession—caring, committed professional lawyers who also understand that the work is not about issues or cases or parties, but about people, and how the law impacts and affects them. And Kim is committed to meeting them all and sharing their humanist approach with the world. Kim's brilliance and commitment to this profession has allowed her, often at great sacrifice, to assemble the first comprehensive look at how law is being practiced to heal and create peace among people. I am grateful for the resources she has assembled, and am hopeful for the profession and the scores of lawyers to come who will benefit from knowing about them."

—Dolly M. Garlo, RN, JD, PCC is President of *Thrive!!*© Inc.
(www.AllThrive.com) and Founder of Creating Legacy™
(www.CreatingLegacyNetwork.com)

"Wright's book is a beautiful and palpable illustration that will bring a more dignified and effective approach to American jurisprudence. Reading this book will benefit us all and is a must read for lawyers, judges, clients, and the general community, as reading this book enhances our humanity."

—Sunny Schwartz, Esq, Program Administrator, San Francisco Sheriff's
Department and author of *Dreams from the Monster Factory: A Tale of
Prison, Redemption, and One Woman's Fight to Restore Justice to All*

"I knew the moment I met her that Kim Wright was 'one of my people.' This book just confirms for me that everything I thought I knew about her was true. Kim is a true visionary with a real heart for justice.

"I highly recommend her book to anyone with a different vision of how conflicts can be resolved, using all of the intelligences and many alternative tools to bring about real and meaningful change in people's lives."

—Linda Warren Seely, Director of Pro Bono Projects,
Memphis Area Legal Services, Inc.

"The legal profession is in a deep malaise, with practitioners experiencing increased dissatisfaction, distress, and burnout. In this provocative book, a leading figure in the reform movement describes and illustrates the alternative modes of practice and related developments and techniques that have been emerging in recent years, and profiles some of their leading innovators and practitioners. Therapeutic jurisprudence, preventive law, holistic law, creative problem solving, such developing alternative dispute resolution techniques as collaborative law and transformative mediation, restorative justice, problem-solving courts, unbundled legal services, legal coaching and others are brought to life. An engaging book that can transform your practice and increase both professional and client satisfaction."

—Bruce J. Winick, Silvers and Rubenstein Distinguished Professor of Law, Director, Therapeutic Jurisprudence Center, Professor of Psychiatry and Behavioral Sciences, University of Miami

"Kim Wright has compiled a treasure trove of ideas and wisdom for lawyers who want to use their heads and hearts to help clients in humanistic ways. This book not only provides guidance for serving clients but, equally as important, also in helping lawyers make their own true paths in life."

—John Lande, Isidor Loeb Professor and Director, LL.M. Program in Dispute Resolution, University of Missouri School of Law

"What would you like to know to enhance the ability of a lawyer to become a peacemaker? Well, Kim Wright, in *Lawyers as Peacemakers*, provides the answers, resources and inspiration to achieve that result. Kim brings her first-hand knowledge of the subject from her extensive travels and her sharing of collaborative dialogues with those with special expertise. Kim's approach is directed both to the external tools and the internal ones required to reach creative solutions. It is a joy to experience this rich book."

—Stuart Webb, founder of collaborative law, has appeared on the *CBS Evening News* and in *The New York Times* and *The Wall Street Journal*, and in August 2002, was co-recipient (with Pauline Tesler) of the first American Bar Association, "Lawyer as Problem Solver" award.

"Author-lawyer Kim Wright's inspired book, *Lawyers as Peacemaker*, overflows with glowing stories of real lawyers who 'took the road less travelled' and found that 'it made all of the difference.' Wright may well be the Oprah of the Emerging Legal World; like the media star, she generously shares her own journey as lawyer and social entrepreneur, and then invites us to join her road trip across America to meet those who inspired her with their innovations in law practice, personal philosophies, and justice reforms. Wright's passion for high professional ideals shines on every page. An entertaining book on trends in law practice trends is unique. This one, like a collection of precious short stories, can be enjoyed in a weekend, or in short doses. If you teach law and want a book for law students, jam-packed with resources and uplifting stories, put it on your syllabus. If you are a practicing lawyer and have only 30 minutes a day to do something 'for you,' then this book might just save your life."

—Cheryl Conner, Founder, New Prospects Collaborative, Boston, former law professor and Asst. U.S. Attorney

"In the last 50 years, there have been extraordinary shifts in science, technology, and medicine, shifts that have prompted us to question our fundamental beliefs and perspectives. We now find ourselves experiencing a shift in the American legal system led by thousands of lawyers across the United States who seeking to more clearly define the true meaning of justice.

"*Lawyers as Peacemakers* by J. Kim Wright articulates a new vision of law and invites the reader to consider new ways of practicing law, utilizing not only the powers of intellectual reasoning, but the even more powerful characteristics of heart and soul. Wright draws us into a conversation about the foundational thinking that birthed our legal system and asks us to consider a more holistic and integrative approach to the practice of law, an approach that will ultimately transform the American legal system into one that is more human and life-affirming."

—MaryLynn Schiavi, Writer\Producer of the Emmy
Award-winning "Matter and Beyond" television series

"In *Lawyers as Peacemakers*, Kim Wright uses her gifts of collection and connection to create and display a showcase of what being a lawyer is really about. For those who thought law school would be a great way to make a difference in the world but came out the other side unsure of how a J.D. really helps, this book is a must-read. For those who struggle to balance their fractured personal and professional selves, this book is a must-read. Kim has created a compendium, a hands-on guide, and, most importantly, a voice of acceptance for holistic law."

—Gretchen Duhaime, J.D., Founder, Practicing on Purpose LLC

FOREWORD

M ARTIN E. P. SELIGMAN, Fox Leadership Professor of Psychology at the University of Pennsylvania, is often credited with founding the field of positive psychology. Dr. Seligman frequently points out that the social sciences developed without "an engineering." The physical sciences had an engineering to serve as the foundation for the science. In other words, physics and chemistry developed after centuries of efforts to create results in the real world that those sciences could both describe and assist. Thus, the dome that Flippo Brunelleschi designed in the 15th century for the Cathedral of Florence is amazing partially because neither the mathematics nor the science of the time could explain or predict his success. Even in modern times, engineering can run ahead of science. For example, not even the successful architect in the competition to design the Sydney Opera House knew how his design would be built when construction began; he finally worked out a successful approach only after the foundation had been completed!

Perhaps, however, Dr. Seligman's assertion is not completely correct. Long before the formal sciences of psychology, sociology, and linguistics began to develop, societies were calling on their wisest, their most culturally attuned, and their best communicators to resolve disputes. Over time, techniques were devised that would allow the resolution of many disputes in ways that created a sense of fairness and justice and allowed the disputants to remain part of the society. These wise, culturally attuned, and articulate individuals began to record these resolutions, and from them developed codes of conduct and decision making to enable both more consistent dispute resolution and the negotiation of agreements to minimize the chance of disputes.

While the raw material for much of the development of law—disputes and crimes—might be perceived as "negative," the purpose of the law is "positive": to enable and encourage cooperation, collaboration, and creativity for the good of the individual and society. Perhaps, therefore, it is not surprising that, just as alchemy produced many positive advancements for society even before it was transformed into the science of chemistry, law has also been advancing in positive directions even while social sciences were only beginning to unravel the mechanisms and theorems that would explain the success of these efforts and point the way toward future steps. This book speaks clearly to the development of that "engineering."

Law is an extraordinarily demanding area of human endeavor. Lawyers are called upon to deal regularly with aspects of our life together in society that most individuals only rarely encounter. These aspects include:

- **Zero-sum conflicts**—conflicts in which gains by one party can only come at the expense of the other party.

- **Values conflicts**—conflicts in which values widely endorsed in our society are represented by different parties in the conflict. Therefore, these widely endorsed values will not resolve the conflict.
- **Necessary evils**—actions requiring effort and skill that create physical or psychological pain or distress for another person but that are undertaken in service to a greater good.
- **Rule-based thinking**—application of rules to reach results that may be in conflict with a more holistic assessment of the situation.
- **Adversarial communication style**—a default option of advocacy statements, as opposed to those emphasizing inquiry.
- **Negative legal cultures**—professional lives lived within organizations where "how we do things around here" has been shaped by the preceding factors and the low positive-to-negative emotional ratios resulting therefrom.

Each of these aspects of legal practice exacts a price from the lawyer physically, psychologically, and in relationships.

Zero-sum conflicts and necessary evils both generate high levels of negative emotions. Extended periods with high levels of negative emotions can cause physical damage ranging from reduced immune response to deterioration in the cardiovascular system. Chronic depression can even lead to a significant loss of mass in the frontal cortex of the brain. Negative emotions also cause us to think less broadly and be less likely to establish connections with other people.

Values conflicts can also create negative emotions, and they have the additional cost of frequently causing lawyers to partially detach from those values due to the constant conflict between values that lawyers witness in their practices. Because these are values that other members of society find admirable and elevating in others, the cost to lawyers from detachment is decreased respect and lowered interest in close relationships.

Rule-based thinking requires lawyers to utilize energy-intensive and inefficient conscious processes to overrule the results of efficient and virtually effortless unconscious thought processes. This is a form of self-regulation. Self-regulation is much like a muscle. Strenuous self-regulatory efforts frequently leave lawyers' self-regulation reserves depleted. When a challenging interaction with another lawyer, a client, or a family member comes along while the lawyer is still in a depleted state, the depleted lawyer may react in a way that creates a long-term negative dynamic in the relationship.

Finally, adversarial communication styles and negative legal cultures increase the likelihood of interactions between lawyers that increase negative emotions and decrease the chance of redirecting the relationship in a more positive direction. Recently, David Maister, a well-known international consultant to professional services firms, has admitted that, contrary to his claims for decades, lawyers are different from other professionals and law firms are much harder to manage than other businesses. While he simply suggests that something in the training and experience of lawyers accounts for this, the previous outline makes it easy to understand how this could be the case.

For those feeling both the motivation and the ability to move toward ways of practicing law that minimize the impact of negative factors, this book will help by describing approaches and practices you can use to achieve such results. Further, the stories of those who have achieved new ways of practicing in the past can increase the confidence of those embarking on the journey. However, some may need a bit of additional help to create energy and momentum for the journey. Some of the practices contained in this book will directly increase energy and motivation. For example, mindfulness meditation has been shown to have significant and broad positive consequences. Some readers, however, may need a bit more, or a different place to start.

It is easy to believe that our emotions and moods are strictly the result of our circumstances in life. Such a belief contributes to what I call the "Fluffy Fallacy." The Fluffy Fallacy assumes that emotions and moods (and even relationships!) are "fluffy" and do not have significant effects on what we accomplish in life. Further, this fallacy assumes that emotions and moods, even if they are important to outcomes, can only be changed by changing outcomes. In this view, you have to change the circumstances of your life—city, spouse, job, etc.—in order to change your emotions and moods.

Such a view may be the least accurate way of understanding the relationship between our thoughts, our emotions, and the circumstances of our lives. A broad variety of research evidence now indicates that not only are positive emotions necessary to the broad, creative, collaborative thinking necessary to change our circumstances, but also that such positive emotions can be generated by relatively simple practices that are easy and enjoyable to do. We now know that it is possible to generate positivity through a variety of research-tested activities. It is within the power of each of us to increase the ratio of positive to negative emotions in our lives and thus generate the energy, creativity, and collaboration necessary to move forward on meaningful goals. We work with our thoughts and emotions first, then find ways to affect the circumstances of our lives so that it is easier to maintain a positive emotional balance.

In the appendix, I have provided "Five Paths to Positivity." Each path is a research-based action you can take to increase the level of positive emotions and energy in your life. Most will also serve to decrease negative emotions.

The combination creates the necessary ratio of positive to negative emotions to allow you to move forward in efforts to reshape your practice in more satisfying and sustainable directions. You might want to start implementing some or all of these Paths to Positivity even as you're reading the stories and possibilities contained in this wonderful book. Your effort to create a more positive balance in your life and law practice is a good thing not only for you, but for your colleagues, clients, family, and community, and for the role of law in society. All the best to you as you take the first steps into what could be an exciting new chapter in your life in law.

> David N. Shearon, JD, MAPP
> Executive Director of the Tennessee
>   Commission on Continuing Legal
>   Education and Specialization, and
>   of the Tennessee Lawyers' Fund
>   for Client Protection
> Nashville, Tennessee
> November 2009

CONTENTS

CHAPTER ONE
A FUNDAMENTAL SHIFT OF MIND AND INTEGRATION OF HEART INTO LAW   1

CHAPTER TWO
VECTORS, MODELS, APPROACHES, PROCESSES, AND LENSES OF THE SHIFT IN LAW   21

CHAPTER THREE
MAKING THE TRANSITION   87

CHAPTER FOUR
MULTIDIMENSIONAL HOLISTIC WELL-BEING   131

CHAPTER FIVE
EXPANDING THE LAWYER'S TOOLBOX: SKILLS THAT WORK IN ANY PRACTICE   213

PUTTING OUR SKILLS TO WORK IN THE WORLD   297

AFTERWORD   305

APPENDIX A: POSITIVE PSYCHOLOGY: FIVE PATHS TO POSITIVITY   307

ACKNOWL-
EDGMENTS

WITH DEEP THANKS to my collaborators and contributors:

Michael Matthews, my business partner, dear friend, and wonderful and wise teacher, who constantly listens to me and holds space better than anyone I've ever known.

Editor and friend Sheila Boyce, for her willingness to step on my toes when it was called for, and ABA Editor Erin Nevius, for actually liking what I had to say.

Karen Werve Grant and Michael Grant, great writers and friends, who stepped up to work on the profile vignettes.

Eileen Dunn, Jane Faulkner, and Jill Dahlquist, who helped take care of the parts of me that are not my mind.

Elizabeth Roach, who balanced a new baby, a job, and researching the resources.

Kathryn Carter, who balanced taking care of her new grandbaby and researching the resources.

Lockey White, who balanced motherhood, looking for a job, and researching the resources.

Amanda Hibler, who saved us lawyers from the perils of researching law reviews.

Marni Pilafian, who volunteered to share research she'd collected over many years of hard work, then found herself editing more than 50 pages of resources at 2 a.m.—thanks for your willingness to take on the impossible.

Donna Boris, who looked for a job and balanced her new role as a stepparent to express her commitment to healing in the law.

Dave Shearon, for the Foreword and many conversations that set the context of the book.

Thanks to Leslie Rawls, Kali S. Tara, Jeff Brown, Irene Leonard, Stewart Levine, Melissa Cole Essig, Annabelle Berrios, Dolly Garlo, Michael King, Susan Daicoff, Pat Sullivan, Jill Breslau, Gretchen Duhaime, Lorenn Walker, Theresa Beran Kulat, Debra Bruce, Janet Smith Warfield, Irene Leonard, Stefani Quane, Alexis Martin Neely, Kevin Houchin, Kay Pranis, Kathleen Clark, Gretchen Rubin, Jennifer Foster, Gary Harper, Carl Michael Rossi, Doris Tennant, Cheryl Stephens, Jennie Winter, Mike Zeytoonian, Scott Rogers, Moira McCaskill, and the Center for Understanding in Law, Forrest (Woody) Mosten, Sheila Boyce, Donna Boris, Kevin Houchin, Robert Hall, Mila Tecala, Azim Khamisa, Aba Gayle, John Lande, David Hoffman, Maureen McCarthy and Zelle Nelson, University of Kansas School of Social Welfare Strengths Institute, Andrea Schneider,

Michael Hunter Schwartz, Julie Sandine, Jane Faulkner, and any others I've missed for their contributions.

To Dolly Garlo and Robert Keeley who provided a warm and comfortable place to spend winters and our other hosts and hostesses in our twenty-seven state tour, who all exemplified hospitality; our donors and supporters on the tour; and the over 100 amazing lawyers who allowed us to interview them.

My parents, who are always there in any way they can be, even when our views are very different, and my kids, who first gave me the reason to transform the world.

My sister, Kathy Marshall and her family, who put me up and put up with me while I wrote the book, sitting like a lump in the chair in their den day after day.

The thousands of lawyers who have talked with me, sparked my imagination, and inspired me for the past ten years.

And the late Forrest Bayard, without whom I would never have become a lawyer.

 **PREFACE**

I DIDN'T GO TO LAW SCHOOL to be a lawyer, at least not to represent any-one else. When I began classes at the University of Florida in 1987, I was married and we had a blended family of seven children (ages 2 to 16) living at home. From the beginning, I wanted the skills and knowledge, but didn't really expect to practice law. My politically active husband was often involved in civil disobedience and, with all those kids, we were often in custody court. One of the kids had some contact with the juvenile criminal court. We figured it was cheaper for me to go to law school than for us to hire lawyers all the time.

While I was in law school, we went through our own divorce. There was a nasty and divisive custody battle, which ended with my youngest daughter living with me—along with her oldest sister (my step-daughter) and later her step-brother. With that taste of the adversarial system, I was more convinced that law school wasn't a match for my mom-oriented personality. In 1989, I passed the Georgia bar exam in my last semester, graduated, and passed the Florida bar. I did not practice law.

Instead, at first I ran a domestic violence program and later moved to a state (North Carolina) where I had not taken the bar exam. But in November 1993, I was blessed to meet Forrest Bayard, a Chicago lawyer who inspired me to consider a new way of practicing law that focused on helping couples divorce while looking out for the best interests of their children. I was assisting with "Wisdom," a course offered by Landmark Education. Forrest, a participant visiting from Chicago, stood up to introduce himself to the group. He talked about how he practiced law with the goal of having divorcing clients still be friends at the end of the process, about granting dignity and respect to every-one in the process. I'm sure the sky opened, the angelic hosts sang, the birds and butterflies flew, and flowers burst into bloom as he talked. I immediately signed up for the next NC bar exam, took it, and passed it in February 1994.

By 1995, I was practicing law in a small town in North Carolina, doing what has been called "door law"—whatever walks in the door. I was dealing with my own clients in a holistic, caring manner but had not yet extended that attitude to the opposing parties. My first custody trial went well from the adver-sarial legal perspective—that is, my client won custody of the child. I enjoyed the competition of the battle and was pleased at the result, at first. Soon I saw that winning was not the end of the case. My client, her ex-husband, and their son remained embroiled in conflict. They were all miserable and fought about every little thing—notes in the backpack, being five minutes late, the visitation schedule, etc. The trial had failed to bring the peace that was needed for them to move forward. Not long after that, I "won" another custody case. Again, the "game" of the competition was exhilarating. I did everything I'd learned to do in law school. After the trial, my client, an extremely dedicated mother, told me that she would give up custody of her children before she would ever go through another trial.

I began to research other options, contacting Forrest for his ideas. Soon, I discovered Stu Webb, a Minnesota lawyer who had created a process called "collaborative law," and I became familiar with mediation. I began working with a coach to create a statement of my life purpose, I signed up for several transformational education programs, and I began to focus my work as a lawyer on peacemaking. Soon, my practice was redesigned and renamed the Divorce & Family Law Center. I took on fewer litigation cases. I hired a mediator, counselor, and social worker to round out my holistic staff. At the time, my practice was so cutting-edge that I was in frequent contact with the North Carolina State Bar to make sure that I was not in conflict with the ethical rules. (Since then, others have been able to design similar practices. I like to think that I broke the ground.)

After practicing holistically for several years, it was time for another transition. By then I had remarried. It was 1999 and the world was nervous about Y2K. My computer-professional husband was offered a stable job in a technology company in Portland, Oregon, and we moved. Not being a member of the Oregon Bar, I began to look for my next project. My sister was a teacher of web design, and with her help, I'd had the first lawyer website in North Carolina. I had recently become acquainted with the International Alliance of Holistic Lawyers (IAHL) and realized there were many kindred spirits who saw law as a healing, peacemaking profession, but most were not aware of what others were doing. I decided to find them and to create my own website where we could all find each other.

In 2000, I put nearly 400 pages of information onto the Web: www .renaissancelawyer.com. At the time, I'd been doing some coaching, and part of my motivation for building the site was related to my coaching practice. Little did I know! There were many lawyers who were hungry for the information. My little homemade site began to draw significant traffic. Within a few months, the Renaissance Lawyer Society had grown from the website—100 founding members signed on immediately. An introductory tele-class filled the conference line. I found myself in the role of a leader.

Over the next few years, I published in a number of legal journals, spoke to thousands of lawyers, appeared in the media, trained, taught workshops, and led retreats. I coached many lawyers in creating their own peacemaking practices and in starting collaborative practice groups. I attended, planned, and hosted many conferences. I served as a family mediator. Thousands of lawyers contacted me by e-mail and telephone. Almost all began the conversation by saying, "I thought that I was alone and then I saw your article, website . . . ."

Once, I talked to two different lawyers who worked at a single large law firm who told me that no one there would understand. It turned out that they worked down the hall from each other and, luckily, finally each granted me permission to share that information with the other.

Those who had been my heroes became my colleagues. They asked me to edit and comment on their books. We spoke together, sought each other out at conferences, and served on planning committees together. I was interviewed by journalists and authors of several books. In 2003, the *Christian Science Monitor* described a "movement" in the law.

In 2003, I returned to North Carolina to create my own law practice. In a few short years, collaborative law had grown from an idea with a handful of followers into a movement. I wanted to personally try out all of the approaches I was writing and coaching about, to have each of them as part of the most cutting-edge law practice I could create. My practice, Healers of Conflicts Law & Conflict Resolution Center, became a laboratory for the work of collaborative law, holistic law, therapeutic jurisprudence, and problem-solving approaches. Besides co-creating a collaborative practice group, I was involved in restorative justice, facilitating the healing process in complex cases of severe violence. I became a trainer in both restorative justice and collaborative law. I chose colleagues who practiced spiritual estate planning. With preventive law in mind, we drafted agreements using plain, understandable language.

In 2007, several conferences showcased various aspects of a different view of law. For example, that fall Washburn University Law School hosted a conference on Humanizing Legal Education where 50 law schools were represented. The International Academy of Collaborative Professionals conference was attended by more than 600 professionals from a dozen countries. And in Memphis, a conference called Lawyers as Peacemakers reached a mainstream audience hungry for a more holistic, healing approach to resolving legal problems. It seemed that we'd reached a new level of acceptance of the ideas of peacemaking and healing in law. Because I had hundreds of contacts with innovators, I liked to think that I had a unique vantage point that allowed me to see what was missing, what the next stages and steps would be, and to take actions that would move us forward.

As it turned out, the expansion of the movement outpaced anyone's ability to track and report about it. The many intimate conversations I had with hundreds of lawyers, judges, law professors, and law students engaged in out-of-the-box peacemaking and healing practices inspired me to want to share them. I knew that so many still thought they were alone—that their ideas, challenges, struggles, and joys were not shared by others—while I knew there were thousands of like-minded lawyers who just didn't have a way to connect with each other, and that doing so would strengthen them all. I was constantly being asked to connect cutting-edge lawyers with each other and I was the one who was a common denominator among the different models. It seemed that I was the one who ought to be reporting about it. I began to develop a Web portal, http://www.cuttingedgelaw.com, that would be a platform for sharing stories and connecting kindred spirits.

THE ROAD TRIP

At an international restorative justice conference in Texas in 2007, I was amazed by the diversity of stories I was hearing. There were retired judges, law students, lawyers, and law professors who had somehow managed to create a satisfying niche for themselves in restorative justice. I asked one of the conference assistants to drive me to a store where I could buy a video camera, and I spent the weekend pointing it at people, recording their stories. Later, I took that same camera with me to Harvard Negotiation Insight Initiative's summer program and to the Humanizing Legal Education conference in Kansas. While the stories were fabulous, my camera work was not. I needed a video editor and camera person!

Michael Matthews

About that time, my housemate and I were co-hosts of the annual holistic law conference in Asheville. During the conference, several people stayed at our house. One of the visitors was my housemate's non-lawyer friend who was coincidentally visiting from out of town that weekend. Michael Matthews is a renaissance man. He has been a cowboy, a truck-driver, a commercial construction superintendent, a crisis intervention counselor and a teacher of wilderness skills to at risk and gifted teens. Among his many previous careers and talents, Michael edited and did other post-production work on a documentary that was included in the first Asheville Film Festival. He had already spent years traveling around the country and is one of those competent men who has a broad range of other useful talents. He is a counselor and healer with a soft heart and good mind. When we met, he had just experienced one of those meltdowns in life where everything seemed to come to an end all at once. He was one of those rare people who had been successful in network marketing and had been living on the proceeds of his marketing business for several years. That income stream came to a sudden halt about the same time that he had pneumonia and tendonitis in his shoulder. The tendonitis prevented him from performing his fallback jobs of finish carpentry and massage therapy. In the midst of all that, his father had a stroke and Michael went home to help his parents until his father died. Michael was looking for a new direction.

One evening, shortly after the holistic law conference, I put on my "coach hat" and had a conversation with Michael. In typical coach fashion, I asked him, "If you could do anything you wanted, what would you do?" Michael was quick to answer, "I'd travel around the world and make a documentary about people making a difference." He'd been especially impressed with the holistic lawyers he'd met during the conference and saw them as kindred spirits who were working for healing and world transformation. He, like many people, was surprised to hear about this movement in the law but quickly realized the power of it all. With law being the foundation of societal structures, transforming law could indeed transform the world. We became fast friends and, eventually, business partners.

We spent a couple of months planning our journey. I gave up my home and office in February 2008, taking a house-sitting position for a few weeks while I finished my adjunct teaching. I had a list of a hundred people who I thought were representative of the movement, and I mapped them out, using a display board with string and colored pins, Google maps, and mileage estimates. We planned to interview these people and make a documentary about this movement within the legal profession with clips from each video.

When we left, we thought we were going to travel for a long time—two or three months—so we wanted to be smart about handling logistics. We did a trial run from Asheville to Detroit for the 2008 International Alliance of Holistic Lawyers conference in mid-May. We took way too much stuff with us and spent the week feeling crowded by the pile in the back seat of my Honda CRV. Many of our systems broke down—we came back realizing we had to get a new mailing address and storage. We returned to Asheville to regroup then left again on June 4, 2008.

Our first destination: Jacksonville Beach, Florida, and our first interview on the tour was, appropriately, Susan Daicoff, who had first introduced me to the connections between many holistic practice approaches at the 1999 IAHL conference. Professor Daicoff is a great example of a holistic lawyer. The youngest student ever admitted to the University of Florida Law School, she graduated with honors, then went on to get her LLM in tax from New York University and her master's in clinical psychology from the University of Central Florida. Daicoff has an impressive list of achievements and publications. Since 1991, she has been researching and writing in the areas of psychology of lawyers, lawyer personality, lawyer distress and dissatisfaction, professionalism, and ethical decision making by lawyers. Her book, *Lawyer, Know Thyself,*

© Michael Matthews

Susan Daicoff

synthesized 40 years of empirical research on law-yers' personality traits and related these findings to professionalism and lawyer well-being. Her research focuses on a "comprehensive law movement" that seeks a healthier way to resolve legal matters. A pro-fessor of law at Florida Coastal School of Law in Jacksonville, Florida, she teaches contracts, profes-sional responsibility, and a course on law as a heal-ing profession. She has an active spiritual life and is the mother of two children. Daicoff also expresses her musical creativity as a member of three bands; she is a songwriter and regularly performs. Before our interview, we attended her performance at a bar association event. It was a perfect start to our adventure. (An article by Susan Daicoff about her work appears in Appendix B.)

As I write this in November 2009, Michael and I are still on the road. We've now interviewed more than 100 leaders and pioneers. One benefit to doing these interviews has been meeting all sorts of people who are doing this kind of work. We've had dinner with fascinating lawyers who are struggling with transitioning their practices to peacemaking. We've shared stories of the perils and rewards of operating outside the box.

During our interviews with the pioneers and heroes of this movement, we have been encouraged and inspired by their bravery and creativity. There was no therapeutic jurisprudence until Bruce Winick and David Wexler spoke it into being. Stu Webb created collaborative law because a tough litigation case had cost him his best friend. Judge Ginger Lerner Wren started her men-tal health court on her lunch hour because she believed that it was a critical human rights issue that mentally ill people should not be locked up in jail because they were sick. Judge Tracy McCooey spends every Saturday morning at a quilting circle with drug court defendants because it is the way she can make the biggest difference in helping their recovery. Week after week, I read about problem-solving court graduates who say "it saved my life" so often it could be a cliché. Judges like Peggy Hora, Cindy Lederman, Steve Leifman, and Jeri Beth Cohen made those courts possible. There was no consensus, generally no funding at the beginning, and no acceptance for new ideas. Each of these courageous practitioners took a stand for the evolution of our culture, for what they believed in and were called to action to accomplish. They took a stand for their own integrity, taking advantage of what their position as judges allowed them to do. Law students like Meredith Blount and Randy Lang-ford didn't believe those who said law students couldn't make a difference.

Meredith pioneered a group on well-being at Vanderbilt, and Randy started a restorative justice program at his law school.

In dozens of interviews, I've heard, "I went to law school to change the world." Many of us shared those early goals, but somewhere along the way we have gotten lost and separated from those aspirations. We've convinced ourselves that we were idealistic and therefore foolish. As we've fed our cynicism, our profession has lost the confidence of the people. Some would say that many lawyers have lost their own souls. It's no secret that addiction, suicide, depression, and cynicism are rampant among lawyers.

Along the way, those of us who have explored these new approaches to the practice of law have become convinced that we're onto something. Positive psychology supports our belief that a purposeful practice based on our values will add to our happiness. Several people have validated our hypothesis that the legal profession is at a crossroads of evolution. We aren't just misfits and weirdos. We're pioneers in a movement.

This book is for those lawyers who thought they were alone and for the ones who already know that they are not. It is for the ones whose stories have been told and the ones whose stories should have been told. It is an introduction to a movement, a way of practicing law, a way of being in the world.

J. Kim Wright, JD
Publisher and Managing Editor
Cutting Edge Law, Inc.
www.CuttingEdgeLaw.com
November 2009
Somewhere on the road

INTRODUCTION

W̲HEN I STOPPED LITIGATING CUSTODY CASES, I found myself in an unfamiliar place. I had never been one to "count coup." Clients would sometimes call and ask my paralegal how often I won my custody cases, hoping to get the edge by choosing a winning lawyer, but neither of us kept track. We were focused on the client's needs, not the win, we told them. I remember a client who once came to me because she said I had won every trial against her husband's lawyer. I wondered how she knew that—who was keeping score. Later, faced with the raised eyebrows of litigators who clearly assumed that I had given up trial work because I was a loser, I had to make sure they knew I had consciously chosen my new peaceful path.

While always pointing out that litigation damages families and should be a last resort, I also made sure that I let my fellow lawyers know that in six years of family law trial practice, I only really lost one case. Over the years, I have found myself in the same conversation with many other peaceful pioneers; we don't want our peaceful paths to be judged as "less than." Still, in law school, competition is so inculcated into our beings that we may at one moment be apologetic or defensive about our peace-making roles, then the next, feel guilty for taking that stance. If litigation is such a terrible thing for families, how can we be proud that we were good at it?

In my conflict resolution training self-assessment exercises, I once identified myself as an "accommodator" with a heavy dose of "conflict avoider." In looking at my role as a lawyer, I have had to ask myself whether I am using the legal system to avoid conflict. I have wondered whether I gave up trial work to avoid the battle. Recently, I realized a new perspective. I had the experience of sharing a conflict with a fellow lawyer. The content of the conflict involved all the drama of hurt feelings, money on the table, reputations at stake, and the future of our relationship on the edge. From past experience, I knew my opponent to be a resolver of conflict, so I expected he would offer to sit down and talk out the issues, and to seek an amicable settlement. Not so. He rebuffed my offers of sitting down at the table and it seemed we were headed for court.

And then I saw something for myself. Although my opponent had training in mediation, he preferred the formal rules of gentlemanly behavior in the courtroom over the raw emotion of face-to-face contact. As law students, we were trained in a model of conflict resolution that is indirect. In litigation, lawyers don't sit face to face and work out their issues. They speak to a neutral third party at a high table, dressed in a dark robe. There are strict rules governing their conduct. They send impersonal discovery requests to the other party's representative. They often prepare lengthy written arguments or take depositions within closely constrained environments, following well-defined rules. The process is designed to remove the conflict and emotion from the process and especially from the courtroom. Litigators are typically uncomfortable when their clients cry or show strong emotion (unless, of course, they do so at the proper dramatic moment). Clients and witnesses enter the courthouse by going through security. Armed bailiffs keep the peace.

In contrast, peace-making lawyers wade right into the emotional fray. Strong feelings are everywhere. There are few rules, and those that exist are created by the participants. People cry. They get angry. Without the physical and emotional distance provided by the ritual dance of courtroom procedure, resolving conflict becomes a contact sport. Our interactions are unpredictable. We aren't limited to the predetermined solutions allowed by law. When a collaborative lawyer walks into the room for a four-way meeting, she doesn't know what will happen next. Compared to that, litigation is calm and predictable. Litigation is actually playing it safe.

Sometimes it is appropriate to rely on the safety and structure of a court. The adversarial system was a huge improvement over jousting and dueling. Jousting and dueling were an improvement over tribal warfare. We all know that there are people who ought to be searched before they engage in a conflict. And there are some conflicts that need to be decided by a judge. Not everyone considers the best interests of their opponent along with their own. Some cases are far too important to be resolved in a lawyer's office. I am fond of saying that if I am falsely accused of a crime, I want the best trial lawyer in town to defend me. If my neighbor is dumping toxic waste into the river above me, I want it stopped; I am not interested in spending time to collaborate and perhaps compromise. Rosa Parks had a cause far too important to be settled with the bus company's representative in some law office.

However, there is an old saying that "if a hammer is your only tool, every problem begins to look like a nail." Because lawyers have been seen only as litigators and law schools have focused on training law students in litigation skills, lawyers have until recently focused on litigation as the tool to resolve most conflicts. Within the past few years, there has been an explosion of new approaches to practicing law that offer lawyers alternative tools for dispute resolution. While predispute and dispute avoidance work have long been part of transactional legal practice, these notions have now gained footing in many other areas of law.

Professor Susan Daicoff calls these new approaches "comprehensive law." Others have coined terms like "visionary lawyering," "holistic law," "transformational lawyering," "integrative law," "creative lawyering," "community lawyering," and so on. When I wrote about the movement in 1999, I called it a "renaissance" and have heard (and even sometimes used) "renaissance lawyering" to describe a broad range of related approaches and models. Because

Daicoff was a math major, she chose a mathematical term for the different approaches and called them "vectors," referring to their direction and magnitude. Each vector is a bit different from the others, but all have common characteristics. All of these new approaches are sensitive to the needs, values, and highest good of the client, society, and legal professionals. Like their mathematical namesakes, vectors are solutions to problems, using many different approaches, skills, and creative thought.

Whether they refer to themselves as holistic lawyers, integrative lawyers, or conscious lawyers—or prefer no label at all—they are all talking about much the same thing: an orientation toward law practice that shuns the rancor and blood-letting of litigation whenever possible; seeks to identify the roots of conflict without assigning blame; encourages clients to accept responsibility for their problems and to recognize their opponent's humanity; and sees in every conflict an opportunity for both client and lawyer to let go of judgment, anger, and bias to grow as human beings. In order to do this, lawyers who practice holistically set as their goal not only to resolve conflicts, but also to heal the rifts that keep people in pain and denial.

—*Steven Keeva,* Transforming Practices

Initially, each of the new options developed independently with its own name and focus, often in different practice areas. For example, collaborative law became a popular option in family law, and restorative justice became a recognized alternative to retributive justice in criminal law. Many lawyers were responding to their unhappiness in the profession and looking for new options. Some were looking out for client needs and using creative problem-solving skills to develop new approaches, while others were focused on their own quality of life. Some were trained in a particular skill that set them off in a new direction. Some incorporated their personal development work into their law practices. Many of the new approaches began when one lawyer began to practice differently and then shared the ideas with colleagues. By whatever name, each of these new approaches offers support for transforming the legal profession by developing techniques for serving other important needs besides the litigation of rights-based disputes. Because the approaches go by so many names, I usually just refer to "the movement." I sometimes also express it as an inquiry: "What if lawyers were peacemakers, problem-solvers, and healers of conflicts?"

Not Just a Shift in How We Practice

Many lawyers appropriately point out that law school did not teach them to practice this messy, chaotic form of law. No one told them how to walk into a room full of angry people and help them talk to each other about the most sensitive issues. We were not prepared to sit with a mother whose child has been killed or has killed another child. No one told us how to manage a schedule full of client emergencies when we don't have time for a bathroom break.

My friend and business partner, Michael, has taught wilderness survival skills. For Michael, surviving in the woods is the perfect metaphor for surviving in life. In the woods, survival seems like it is about our physical survival. In the world, our goals, aspirations, possibilities, and commitments are always at stake. Ignoring your basic needs in the wilderness will kill you. Ignoring your deepest needs and values, spending your days focused on energy-draining activities, puts your life and everything you stand for at risk. Looking at many of the grave statistics of lawyer distress, it is easy to conclude that our lives are at stake.

Michael talks about stepping back and looking with "expanded vision." This means not focusing on being lost, on the things that you don't have. Step back and notice what resources are all around you. There are edible plants in the woods if you just know where to look. You can pull those leaves and branches together into a shelter to stay warm. On our full-time travel adventures over the past two years, this ability of his has often come in handy. As a lawyer, by inclination or training, I tend to look for problems and notice what we don't have. Will we run out of money? We don't have a place to stay two weeks from now. That grant didn't come through. Often, I'm obsessing over whether we have a workable plan for next month rather than enjoying the present moment.

At such times, Michael reminds me to stop, take a breath, step back, and shift my awareness. What do we have? What resources can I see with the broader vision? When I step back, I can see that I am fine in that moment. I have everything I need in that moment. The bigger picture is that I love what I do and feel very privileged to do it. I have a wonderful, supportive, and loving community. I always have food to eat. I love my car and have only six more payments before it is paid off. As I shift, suddenly I see more possibilities for whatever challenge I'm facing. I realize that there is nothing I need that is not available in my community. I can choose from many different options.

This book is an invitation to step outside the rules and constraints of the structured legal system and adopt a more expanded and holistic vision. It isn't going to change your circumstances by some miracle, but I hope it will

change your perception of them. The old worries will be there—but they'll be surrounded by new possibilities and possible solutions.

> I already pretty much understand what I do, what I like about it, and what I'm getting out of it. I have thought about what I don't like and what makes me uncomfortable but I'm not sure that I have really considered too much of the deeper stuff. I believe a lot of lawyers do what we do by deliberately anesthetizing ourselves against thinking about what is unjust about how we practice law. The money makes up for the injustice we participate in. . . . It has already occurred to me that I want to at least know more about how things could be different. I want to have a grip on what each alternative is, how it works, whether I might fit into it, and how I would get there.
>
> —*Sheila Boyce*

Some people might want to read this book from cover to cover, but I've written it with the idea that most of us don't have time for that. It is a resource book, a reference, a possible source of inspiration on those days when you would rather be doing something (anything?) else. It is a guide to a holistic approach to law that includes the lawyer's well-being and the best interests of the client and society. As your guide, I've traveled through the territory I'm telling you about. I've coached many lawyers through the same territory. I haven't mastered it all, but I think I have some ideas to share with you. I share them with the intention of easing your journey.

This book includes a section about taking care of ourselves. Perhaps you are so resigned on that topic that you resolve to skip it altogether. I, too, live in the real world of being a lawyer and I work with lawyers all the time. I know it is a challenge and I have some actual experience with everything I will share with you. It helped me. Maybe it will help you if you try it out as something other than an intellectual exercise that you talk yourself out of.

As lawyers have invented and discovered new ways of practicing, they've needed to redesign their practices and acquire new tools, most of which were not taught in law school. Many of these tools and practice designs are useful for any of the approaches and models. For example, the skills I use with a collaborative divorce are very similar to the skills I use when sitting down to a meeting between a murderer and the family of his victim. Both situations call for extremely good listening skills, compassion, and empathy. I have to hold space for conflicting views and help the participants express strong emotions in a peaceful context. I could utilize the same skills within a corporate setting—in fact, I sometimes do help businesses with organizational issues using those very same skills.

As I've met lawyers who are new to these peacemaking approaches, I've been asked many questions about where to start, what to do, and how to make a living with these new ideas. I've watched newly trained and inspired lawyers expand like blooming flowers, opening to new ideas and soaking up whatever they can to quench their thirst for more knowledge and creative expression. I've also talked to lawyers who were skeptical and cynical about whether they could actually transform their practices. Some chose to leave law rather than tackle the seemingly monumental task of shifting their practices. When coaching clients, I've wrestled with these same issues and found solutions as I've created my own practice. This book attempts to answer the questions and address the objections that I hear most often.

When I began the Renaissance Lawyer website, I captured almost every idea and mentioned almost everyone who was doing transformational work (as I defined it then). Ten years later, it is impossible for me (or anyone) to keep track of all the developments. For this book, a team of researchers helped me with identifying key resources. As I put the finishing touches on the book, several significant law review articles came in my e-mail and had to be incorporated into the content. I apologize in advance for the obvious resources I've missed, especially those written or produced by my friends who think I should have their books and articles always at the ready. They're probably right, but with the hundreds of thousands of resources currently available, I hope they will forgive my errors and omissions. As I write this, the CuttingEdgeLaw.com site includes several thousand files that are news reports, events, publications, and articles. They couldn't all possibly fit into this book, and my memory isn't reliable enough to recall them all.

Some of what I have written here will be controversial. Some people will think I have gone too far and that I may have alienated some people. They will be right. Some will think that I haven't gone far enough in describing the paradigm shift and that I have alienated different people. They will also be right. I will be accused of bringing my spiritual beliefs into my work, and some will criticize that. They will probably not realize that I want them to bring *their* beliefs into their work, too. And some won't understand the difference between freely practicing my beliefs and imposing them on others through laws. Like any print publication, this work will be dated as soon as it is published. Please consider this book as part of a conversation that has been going on for a long time. Some people have been in it for many years and some are new to it. We're all coming in in the middle.

Mostly, my perspective is as a practicing lawyer. I do my research on the Internet with Google. I am allergic to law review articles and not particularly intellectual. I'm interested in how to do things, in getting the information I need to move forward. I have written this book for people like me. If you are looking for more, there are plenty of academic articles, books, and resources listed in the Resources section.

A FINAL WORD OF INTRODUCTION

I've talked to enough lawyers to think that I know what we all have in common, even when I can't quite articulate it. Whether it was Perry Mason, Atticus Finch, Thurgood Marshall, Robert F. Kennedy, Nelson Mandela, Sandra Day O'Connor, Katherine Hepburn, or Reese Witherspoon in *Legally Blonde*, there was someone who inspired us. We saw the law as a path to making a difference. We all get frustrated with endless discovery, moving money from one corporate balance sheet to another, clients who just want to be right, and the stress of everyday practice emergencies. We all want more from life, and doing something different against the mass of the legal system can seem impossible. We've been jerks and we've faced jerks on the other side of a case. It is time for us to talk about all this. It is time to bring integrity, balance, and peace to the profession and give us the gift of our *selves*. It is time to wake up, to consciously live our lives and create our legacies. This book is an invitation to inquire into all of that, to learn together, to evolve the legal system so it works for everyone. You may not embrace everything in this book, and some of it may offend or even scare you. Take what works and try out other ideas. Step outside the box and create a practice that works for *you* and your clients.

What *if* lawyers were peacemakers, problem-solvers, and healers of conflicts?

A FUNDAMEN-
TAL SHIFT OF
MIND AND
INTEGRATION
OF HEART
INTO LAW

*The interdependency of humankind, the
relevance of relationship, the sacredness of
creation is ancient, ancient wisdom.*
                    —*Rebecca Adamson*

CHAPTER ONE

WHEN I was practicing law back in the 1990s and looking for alternatives to litigation, my office mate, Bob Martin, told me about the International Alliance of Holistic Lawyers (IAHL). For a couple of years, I ignored the organization and reinvented the wheel of holistic law on my own.

By 1999, I'd created a cutting-edge holistic law practice in Graham, North Carolina. Called the Divorce and Family Law Center, the practice included two lawyers, a mediator-counselor, two social work interns, two paralegals, and several law student interns focused on creating holistic, out-of-court settlements. After many interactions, the North Carolina Bar and I had worked out a plan that fit within ethical guidelines, allowing an interdisciplinary approach to divorce. I had the first law website in North Carolina. I had consulted with a feng shui consultant about my office design and we sometimes cleansed the office by burning sage. I took high-level personal development seminars, some of which were only offered in San Francisco. I thought I was way out there, out of the box, on the cutting edge, so when I got the invitation to the IAHL conference, I decided it was a good time to go. I imagined being the star of the show. As a further attraction, the conference was held in Hawk's Cay in the Florida Keys in November! For weeks, my desk held the photograph of the island, surrounded with blue water, as a beacon.

I think I spent most of the conference in shock, from the first time we all stood in a circle and held hands on Thursday night to the consensus board meeting on Sunday afternoon. I'd never experienced anything like it. Compared with these seasoned holistic lawyers, I was mainstream, maybe even conservative. One couple combined yoga and law to help their clients resolve conflict. There were lawyers who were channeling and doing energy work and talking about spiritual and emotional issues that were foreign to me. I remember telling Jill Dahlquist that she scared me. My world had exploded with possibility, and there were so many new ideas. I didn't know what to think, and I wasn't sure what to do with it all. I was tempted to climb back into my comfortable box.

Somehow, through the shock, I was able to hear the presentations about the peacemaking approaches. Susan Daicoff, an associate professor of law at Florida Coastal School of Law, presented her research on lawyer distress, lawyer personality traits, and the emergence of a trend she'd come across. She found that some lawyers were breaking out of the mold and creating new ways of practicing law. She noticed that these lawyers expressed higher satisfaction and fulfillment with the practice of law. Daicoff referred to the shift as "comprehensive law."

What we are doing in our legal system is not working. Clients are unhappy with their lawyers, with the system, and with the outcomes of the process. Lawyers are extraordinarily unhappy or even impaired. Nonlegal dispute resolution mechanisms in society have failed and society is depending on litigative processes to resolve conflict. As a result, society in general is suffering from the effects of law's overly adversarial, other-blaming, position-taking, and hostile approach to conflict resolution. Perhaps in response to these developments, a number of alternative approaches to law practice are emerging to replace the old, outmoded monolithic system. All of these approaches attempt to optimize the well-being of the people involved in each legal matter and acknowledge the importance of concerns beyond simply strict legal rights. This more "comprehensive" form of legal practice is illustrated by ten converging "vectors" . . .

—*Professor Susan Daicoff*

Professor Daicoff compares the evolution in law to medicine's recent embrace of parts of alternative medicine and integrative medicine. The change began with early mediation and alternative dispute resolution programs that have now been integrated into traditional legal practices.

The IAHL included everything Daicoff talked about under the umbrella of holistic law, encompassing the notion of law as a healing profession. Some have adopted terms like "therapeutic jurisprudence," "preventive law," "restorative justice," "law and healing," "collaborative law," "creative problem-solving," "transformational law," and "procedural justice" as specific expressions of comprehensive law. "Integrative law" has also been suggested as an umbrella term.

In fact, there is a good-natured ongoing debate among the leaders about what to call the collection of approaches, models, theories, and practice developments that I call "the movement." My collaborative colleague, Chris Craig, talks about resolving a divorce as being like trying to put socks on an octopus. Characterizing this movement feels like that. Like the octopus, it is in constant motion. Creativity and adaptability are cornerstones of why the movement exists. Each leg of the movement operates independently. However, unlike an octopus, the movement has an unlimited number of expressions and many interrelationships, not just eight.

For example, restorative justice is generally utilized in the criminal context, but Ken Jaray in Colorado has created a form of restorative mediation for personal injury cases, bringing issues like apology and forgiveness to torts. Therapeutic jurisprudence has spawned many different problem-solving courts. Collaborative law was invented by Stu Webb, a holistic lawyer.

Some of the approaches spring from philosophical or theoretical considerations of the role of the lawyer in society. Therapeutic jurisprudence is like a lens through which we can examine the therapeutic or nontherapeutic impact of any action in the legal profession. Holistic law can describe one vector or philosophy of practice, or a collection of some or all of the philosophies. In this book, I've had to make some decisions about how to organize the material. Some of you will suggest that I could have organized it in different ways. I agree.

Like obscenity, most of us in the movement recognize it when we see it. Each of us talks about it in different terms, with different viewpoints and terminology. We generally agree whether something is aligned with the movement or not, and we distinguish common characteristics representing retreat from what are increasingly being considered the negative aspects of the adversarial process that have become the darlings of the media and sensationalized talk shows. Famous trials like those of O.J. Simpson, Michael Jackson, Amanda Knox, and most celebrity divorces, plus television show hosts like Maury Povich, Jerry Springer, and myriad other media role models of conflict exacerbation do not represent the highest good of society or humankind.

The new approaches add more cooperative, comprehensive, humanistic, healing, and even spiritual aspects to the traditional forms of law practice being taught and utilized in the profession. They are focused on optimizing well-being for all the involved parties by expressly seeking to eliminate brutal and contentious adversarial approaches to advocacy and problem solving, as well as endeavoring to avoid legal problems altogether. Rather than defining problems only as legal concerns—strict legal rights and obligations demarcated by the boundaries of published statutes and judicial opinions—these more comprehensive approaches include humanistic values such as overall well-being, relationships, feelings, needs, resources, meaning, values, and psychological goals; an idea that is often described by the term "rights plus."

"These visionary approaches tend to spring from 'the heart stuff,' qualities like collaboration, healing, restoration, peace-building, and human connection," says Stella Rabaut, a Kirkland, Wash., attorney who facilitates retreats on law as a healing profession—qualities the legal profession has always considered soft or suspect. It's not that the "head stuff" must disappear; on the contrary, analytical skills and legal knowledge are crucial. But "there has to be more recognition of the human, relational aspects," she says. "It's not either/or. It's both/and."

—*As quoted by Barbara Stahura*

There is more to this movement than just doing all the right things or creating labels and ways of talking about what we do. We often talk about a paradigm shift.

THE PARADIGM SHIFT

A "PARADIGM" is a worldview, a set of beliefs about what is real and true. A paradigm shift involves a shift in the framework of our beliefs, of how we view the world. This shift isn't about just doing something differently; it is a shift in the entire context for what we do. Our worldview shapes what we see and what is important to us. Paradigm shifts often occur suddenly because of a discovery or new theory, like the change in perspective that occurred when mankind realized that world is not flat after all. It often starts with a reexamination of what we previously believed and knew to be true.

Originally a scientific term coined in 1962 by Thomas Kuhn, a *paradigm shift* refers to a shift in thinking such as the shift from Newtonian physics to Einstein's theory of relativity. If (like me), you didn't actually take physics and have always been a little fuzzy about it, there are other examples. The invention of the printing press was a paradigm shift in information technology. The introduction of the Internet was another.

A paradigm shift is often difficult to explain to someone who hasn't experienced one. This is not a judgment about whether people who have experienced a paradigm shift are better than those who have not. Before I was a parent, many people tried to explain what it would be like. No one could have prepared me for the moment when I first held Bryan in my arms. While the hormones of childbirth might have had some impact on how I felt, they didn't explain the enduring and profound shifts that continue 32 years later. I didn't just have a new person living in my house—*everything* changed that day. My concerns were different. I was not the same person. The world was not the same world. I wasn't wrong before I was a parent; I was just in a different paradigm.

Marketers caution against using the term "paradigm shift" because it has been overused. The paradigm shifts of new laundry detergents don't quite communicate the power the term was intended to convey. My editor cringed and begged me to use another term, but it *is* the term that is used in the movement. We even considered making up a new term or using a common word in a different way. I researched the term and the ideas for days, hoping to find a better way to talk about the change of consciousness that must occur in a paradigm shift. I found some interesting attempts and will share many of them here, but in the end I returned to "paradigm shift" because it is the most fully descriptive term of the message I want to convey.

We lawyers really like to be able to quantify and explain things in concrete, scientific, rational terms. Many of us are wary of anything that is out of the ordinary. In teaching us to think like lawyers, law school discouraged our thinking about anything that was emotional, mystical, or spiritual. It wasn't relevant. In this movement, in life, those qualities matter a lot and are extremely relevant. In reality, the law has gone through many paradigm shifts. The representative nature of jousting created a new reality for people who were used to tribal warfare. Common law created new expectations of consistency. I believe we are at the doorstep of yet another such advancement in the practice of law, a new paradigm.

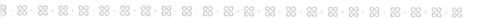

Society made a big advancement by requiring symbolic battle rather than actual battle, by introducing a system of litigation where the sides presented their claims before a member of the elite, who decided the winner. Law school assumes this is the environment for the practice of law, where lawyers either do battle to resolve problems or assist their clients in pursuing their interests in a way that prevents battles from occurring. But always the underlying assumptions are that litigation might happen, so the best thing is to try to foresee any possible future troubles, keep your information and often your intentions confidential, and if you do get drawn into battle you do whatever it takes to win. Business people incorporated to protect themselves from liability. Now we have this huge, unwieldy and inhumane system where he who has the most money has the most influence, profits are everything, and millions of people go without vital necessities even in the midst of plenty. Millions more spend their lives in prison. Lawyers and judges are the linchpins to this system. The fundamental assumption is that we are separate and apart and potentially in conflict with each other, that there is not enough to go around, and that the strong (and smart) person must be well defended. If someone commits a crime, the proper reaction is to convict, then separate, punish, and deprive that person for some period of time. At some point thoughtful people will look at this and start to question, first the outcomes, which seem so obviously unsatisfactory, then the underpinnings and assumptions that keep them in place. In particular, lawyers find themselves jaded and dissatisfied with what they do with their time and their energy.

This is the vital question! I think this is the one central difference between the old and new paradigms; whether humanity is a whole, integrated organism and each person is entitled to being treated with love and compassion, or whether each person is separate and entitled to pursue his or her own egoistic interests to the detriment of others or without regard for the effect on others. Feminine vs. masculine worldview. It's more than just making lawyers happier and better adjusted; it's changing the relationship between citizens and jurisprudence.

Seems to me that the vectors, as you call them, have to do with application of the new thinking to different areas of the law. Restorative justice has to do with correcting structural issues in the criminal justice and penal systems. Therapeutic jurisprudence and problem solving courts deal with new approaches to the structure and role of the judicial system. Mediation, collaborative law, and holistic law are not structural changes but are alternative problem solving/problem avoidance techniques that are applicable to almost every area of legal practice. Modifications to legal education address issues of preparing incoming practitioners for a new universal legal model.

Those who are ready to forge something new have started by questioning the existential environment surrounding the legal system. What if we aren't all separate and at odds with each other? What if the corrections system, with its focus on retribution, is ultimately dehumanizing and damaging to all of us? Maybe litigated divorces are bad for both kids and parents. Maybe pot smokers don't belong in prison. Maybe sending a wrongdoer to prison doesn't make the victim whole and doesn't stop crime. Maybe litigators are excited and energized by the process of doing battle yet still question whether their efforts are meaningful in the larger human picture. Maybe we will always have problems and disputes and accidents and crimes but there is a better way to address these problems than suiting up in armor and hacking away at each other, symbolically or otherwise. But how do we get from here to there? And what is "there" when we get there? Do we try to modify the existing structure or dismantle it entirely? What new training is needed for lawyers and judges? How will the expectations of legal clientele need to change? How will the money part work? What new structures and institutions need to be constructed?

—E-mail from Sheila Boyce to author

⚯ · ⚯

THE ADVERSARIAL PARADIGM

In law school, we were exposed to the adversarial paradigm in overt and subtle ways. The competition started when we applied and vied for a seat in the class, continued with the fight for grades and rank, and extended into law practice. We're trained in the skills of litigation, in drawing fine distinctions that focus on the differences between people. We debate positions rather than engage in dialogue focused on understanding each other. Urban legends tell of law students using razor blades to cut critical pages out of research books. We hide the ball. We watch our backs. The political discourse and nightly news are adversarial and focused on sound bites and positions. The view is of a world where individuals protect their rights, territory, property, and selves from other individuals. In this paradigm, we are separate and our needs and values are at odds with each other.

THE OTHER PARADIGM

I think the paradigm shift comes in two parts: external and internal. The external shift is the process of learning about a new way to approach dispute resolution (collaborative law, mediation; in general, a nonadversarial and interest-based approach), training in those ways and practices, committing to make them a part of our toolbox as conflict resolution advocates or facilitators, becoming engaged in that community of like-minded practitioners and applying these processes and practices to actual cases.

But the second part of the shift is the more profound part that follows these prerequisite steps above, and that is when we have internalized these processes and approaches so that they become natural and aligned with who we are philosophically and in our souls and how we approach our roles as solvers of problems and peacemakers. When this internal paradigm shifts happens within us, it becomes increasingly difficult to go back to the old, adversarial litigation-type models. Approaching disputes first from the nonadversarial, interest-based door then also becomes easier and flows much more naturally from within us. We find ourselves speaking, acting, and working with a much deeper conviction, passion, and grasp of what it is we are doing. Not only is the approach now different, but we are also different. To transform the way disputes are resolved, we have to first be transformed ourselves.

—*Michael Zeytoonian*

There are other words that I can use to describe the new paradigm: "partnership," "systems," "oneness," "unity consciousness," and "teamwork" are all characteristic of the paradigm, but none of these words captures everything I'm talking about. Even after ten years in this movement, I'm not sure how to label this paradigm. That is why I often just call it "the movement." Perhaps it is because labels are about separation and individuality. This paradigm is about connection and community. It recognizes that we are all part of a system, that our well-being is interconnected. Labels are fixed; the movement is dynamic, organic, flexible. It acknowledges our humanity but calls for the best in each of us.

⚿ · ⚿

It would be helpful if we began with a systems view of the world, which is holistic and much more dynamic than the Newtonian perspective we often begin with. Complex organisms (the divorcing parties and their children, not to mention extended families), constantly moving and changing, are a part of and actors in an incredibly complex ecosystem (not just in the environmental movement sense).

—*George Collis, CFP, CDFA, from an e-mail*
on the Collaborative Law Listserv

⚿ · ⚿

THE NEW PARADIGM ILLUSTRATED

> *Integrity is the key to understanding legal practice. Law's empire is defined by attitude, not territory or power or process.*
> —Ronald D. Dworkin

THE DIFFERENCES in the paradigms are best illustrated rather than explained. Here are two stories of victim–offender dialogue:

In 1993, 47-year old Elaine Myers was on her way home from a late night class, a 57-mile drive down the Washington coast. Elaine was a much-loved wife, sister, aunt, and friend who hosted a local radio show on gardening and was a potter. On that dark road, Susie Cooper was on her way home from a night of partying when she crossed the centerline. Twenty-five-year-old Susie was drunk. Elaine was killed instantly. Susie was critically injured. When she woke to learn that she had killed Elaine, she said she wanted to die; but she did not. Angry and grief-stricken, David, Elaine's husband of 27 years, said he wanted to cut Susie into little pieces. Elaine's sister, Betty, a hospice doctor, said she'd never cried so much. Betty's ten-year-old daughter, Aileen, had a close relationship with her aunt, and she went with the family to view the mangled wreck of the two cars. Aileen saw toys in Susie's car and asked if Susie was somebody's mom. The thought of Susie's children touched Elaine's father, 80-year-old Peter Serrell.

A few weeks earlier, Peter had heard a talk about restorative justice and victim–offender dialogue at his church. He contacted the speaker and asked if he could help him meet the woman who killed his daughter. The speaker, Marty Price, a lawyer turned mediator, arranged to meet with Peter. Over the course of nine months, Marty worked intimately with Peter to heal his grief, to arrange for Susie to meet with him, and to help the patriarch deal with the anger and grief of the rest of the family. Eventually, the family members each recognized that Peter was getting value from the preparations for mediation and that each might gain some closure and value from meeting with Susie. David had been afraid that he could not control his anger and would attack Susie, but eventually even he became interested in the healing prospects of meeting with her. It helped everyone that Susie was remorseful and wanted to make amends for her actions. She pled guilty to vehicular homicide to save the family from the stress of a trial, and admitted that she was an alcoholic.

The family arranged to meet with Susie in a hotel conference room. David had been concerned that Susie would be outnumbered and made sure that she found a trusted friend to support her in the process. (This was Marty's cue that David was ready for the meeting.) Each family member told Susie about Elaine and their loss. Peter told her that he had asked for the meeting to help him feel, through the pain of losing his daughter, as though he could do something positive. He told her that something positive would be a chance for Susie to rebuild herself and become a true mother to her children. Elaine's mother talked about her own pain and how the loss of Elaine had affected her husband so deeply that she felt she'd lost them both. Each family member shared their anger and pain. Susie apologized. Everyone cried and cried.

At the end of the tearful process, Susie had agreed to get her high school equivalency diploma, to stop drinking, to attend Alcoholics Anonymous (AA), and to make up for the loss by being a better person and parent. At sentencing, Betty read a statement. "There is no way she can provide a wife for David or a sister for me. The only restitution she can make is a lifelong commitment to a daily effort toward making the world a better place in exchange for her having survived the crash. She is not required to complete the job of repairing the world, but she must not be excused from starting and continually working at the job. Reform means that she must create a new form of herself—to emerge as a sober person, a thoughtful and considerate person, a contributor. If she can do all of these, I can forgive."

Marty later wrote, "The victims and offender each became allies in the healing of the other." While Susie was in prison, the family visited her and wrote letters. They supported Susie in achieving her goals. Miraculously, so intimate was their bond of healing, the Serrells virtually adopted Susie Cooper. For years, they appeared together on panels for victim–offender mediation and were interviewed by the media. They were even featured on an ABC 20/20 program. Before Peter died in 2009, he said that that work with Susie Cooper ranked with his children as his most treasured legacy.

Contrast that with the following:

A few years ago, Dr. Phil put out the word that he was looking to be educated in victim–offender dialogue. Several trainers offered to advise him, but as far as I know, no one actually did. A few weeks later, we saw the show. In many ways, what they did looked like a victim–offender dialogue. A man who had killed his wife was brought face-to-face with their daughter, many years later. The daughter had been a small child when the murder occurred; she was now grown to young adulthood. Dr. Phil was there to "facilitate" their conversation. The daughter had apparently been on a previous show and expressed interest in talking with her father. Dr. Phil found the father, recently released from prison, living in a flop house and abusing drugs. He convinced the father to enter a rehab program, promising he could see his daughter. At the time of the show, the man had been clean for less than two months, and his sobriety was still on shaky ground.

Dr. Phil's idea of facilitating the conversation involved loudly attacking and shaming the father/offender and exacerbating the anger and devastation of the daughter. At one point, the man fled the stage and Dr. Phil and his cameras followed him backstage. In spite of all this, the father was unyielding in his commitment to telling his daughter how sorry he was, how much he loved her. The daughter clearly wanted to reconnect with her father and to understand what had happened all those years before.

In the restorative justice paradigm, it was a disastrous confrontation. Although it appeared that the techniques of restorative justice were being applied to this situation, how the people producing the show were *being* about the whole thing was *not* consistent with restorative justice.

NEW PARADIGM: NEW CHALLENGES, SKILLS, AND OPPORTUNITIES

THE SHIFTING of paradigms isn't a prescription for resolving all problems, and it isn't about singing "Kumbaya" and everything being sweetness and light. Although sometimes the old problems do become irrelevant as we redefine our worldviews, new issues arise in the new paradigm. Transitions between paradigms can be awkward and even uncomfortable. When the printing press was invented, new ways of distributing books had to be created. Scribes were no longer needed for copying documents by hand. We can only imagine that they must have been concerned about their transitional unemployment. I'm sure many people did not consider the printing press to be progress.

Legal education, like the law in general, is slow to change. Although it is now commonly accepted that negotiation skills and conflict resolution skills are important skills for lawyers, they are still not required classes. In the adversarial culture of law school, there is confusion about how to classify courses that teach students how to listen to their clients and give them advice. For the most part, these subjects are taught under the umbrella of alternative dispute resolution (ADR).

15

I am sure that no area of the law would self-describe as stagnant, and that every area of the law is dynamic in at least some ways. Within environmental law, though, I am confident that climate change and carbon emissions play a significant role in a modern curriculum—but few faculty who have been teaching in the field for very long would have come into the academy with this as their academic focus. Similarly, in the ADR world, most scholars to date have entered as specialists in arbitration, mediation, or negotiation. Twenty years from now (well within the tenures of faculty being hired today), the real action in ADR could very well be dispute systems design, new governance, collaborative law, or cooperative law.

—Michael Moffit

Context for the Legal Paradigm Shift

The adversarialism in the legal profession has occurred in the context of an individualistic society. It is the same adversarialism that brought us Jerry Springer, Maury Povich, and reality television.

Stories of how the legal system is broken have stirred professionals, including many lawyers, to pursue alternative modes of dispute resolution. The villain is an "adversarial" system that dehumanizes both the people and the professionals caught up in the web of the legal process. The traditional lawyer is cast as the epitome of a mean-spirited, competitive, warrior-type, who practices without mercy. This popular and simplistic view conveniently avoids observing how the legal system merely reflects the views of the larger culture regarding conflict. Nonetheless, many lawyers describe themselves as "recovering attorneys," as if practicing law had been a crime.

—Robert Benjamin, "The 'Truthiness' Virus Has Infected the Conflict
Management Field," Mediate.com

The shift in the law also isn't occurring in a vacuum. Society is experiencing a paradigm shift that is much bigger than the law—the 2009 Nobel Prize in Economics went to an expert in cooperation, and the Nobel Peace Prize went to a lawyer-president who talks about diplomacy, dialogue, and peacemaking. There are many explanations of the shift with many theories attempting to provide models of it: spiral dynamics, cultural creatives, integral consciousness, spiritual transformation, etc.

I am the first to acknowledge that in attempting to address these questions we are exploring the frontiers of human knowledge, and that whatever is said here is only a beginning. But this is the story of my personal journey in search of the answers to those questions, and of my inner transformation along the way. I invite you to take that journey with me. Along the way, you will meet some of the people who are leading the renaissance now occurring in many disciplines, philosophy, physics, neurobiology, leadership theory, and organizational learning. These people are breaking the boundaries between disparate disciplines and transforming them at their further reaches–where for me they all converge, leading to a deeper understanding of how human beings, both individually and collectively, might develop the capacity to see what wants to emerge in this world and thus have the opportunity to shape the future instead of simply responding to the forces at large.

—*Joe Jaworski*, Introduction to Synchronicity,
the Inner Path to Leadership

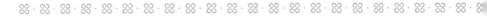

A Paradigm of Consciousness, Relationships, and Connection

Though I enjoyed many aspects of my work, I found it too constraining after my consciousness was raised. I felt that I was suffocating, so it seemed fortuitous that an early retirement offer was made just when I was trying to figure out a way to move.
—*Patricia Clayton, lawyer who now also leads workshops on spirituality, from an e-mail to the author*

Patricia's words echo something I've heard from many others. For some, the shift in practice did not feel like a choice they made but one that was thrust upon them when they could no longer do things the old way. And for these people, the paradigm shift is not an intellectual conversation. It is experiential. It is a knowing that changes everything. This shift occurs at a very personal level but is larger than one person.

At first I thought that this energy was just the next step on my own journey. But it soon made known to me that it was not personal, but belonged to a whole new beginning. With power and speed it swept away years of spiritual conditioning, and brought with it a quality of fun and pure joy that I knew I had always been waiting for. Mercilessly, laughingly, it began to change my life, my way of thinking, my way of relating. This energy is alive, demanding change and needing to be lived in the midst of life. And it has a quality of oneness that brings with it a stamp of divine presence.

—*Llewellyn Vaughan-Lee*

On the last day, in the final minute of the last interview, Father Thomas Keating summarized the journey: "The spiritual journey is the realization—not just the information but the real interior conviction—that there is a higher power or God. Or, to make it as easy as possible for everybody: there is an Other; second step: to try to become the Other; and finally the realization that there is no Other. You and the Other are One, always have been, always will be."

—*From* One: The Movie, *produced by Michigan lawyer Ward Powers*

LOVE COMING OUT OF THE CLOSET

A FEW years ago, I would never have dared to use the word "love" in a publication for lawyers. In dozens of conversations over the years, leaders in this movement have spoken it in hushed tones. What we're doing here, they say, is bringing love to law. We're acknowledging the underlying connection of all.

Peter Gabel is a graduate of Harvard Law School, has a PhD in psychology from Wright Institute and is associate editor of *Tikkun Magazine*, a former law school dean, a founder of the Critical Legal Studies movement, the co-founder of the Politics of Meaning, and co-director of the Project for Integrating Spirituality, Law, and Politics (PISLAP). In his article, "Critical Legal Studies as a Spiritual Practice," [36 Pepp. L. Rev. 515 (2009)], he says:

> . . .there was always a spiritual impulse behind the work and the politics of CLS [Critical Legal Studies]. But it is absolutely the case that CLS—or at least what came to be known as the dominant strain within CLS—refused to embrace this transcendent spiritual impulse, to stand behind it, or to speak about it. We really were motivated by love, but it was a love that dared not speak its name. And in my opinion, that is because our movement was infected with the same fear of the other that underlay the injustices that we criticized in the wider society. We were motivated by a powerful moral transcendent impulse that was an expression of what this conference is calling a Higher Law, but we would not say so, or to be honest, some of us would not say so. On this point, there was a division inside CLS, and in my opinion the wrong side carried the day—but today is another day.

CHAPTER TWO

VECTORS, MODELS, APPROACHES, PROCESSES, AND LENSES OF THE SHIFT IN LAW

Lawyers who have experienced "the shift" have created or discovered many new approaches. In this chapter, I'll talk about some of the more common expressions. Each section includes a description and a story that illustrates the innovation or talks about the innovator. Besides terming them as "vectors," Susan Daicoff speaks of them as "lenses" (through which to view law) and "processes" (ways of practicing). Ten years ago, these lenses, processes, vectors, approaches, and models were seen as very distinct from each other. Several of us have spent a lot of words to say how they are alike, and we have agreed that they had more commonalities than differences. There are still many people who see them as very distinct practices, but more often we are being asked about how they are different. People new to the movement sometimes ask how holistic law is different from therapeutic jurisprudence, why collaborative law can't be used in criminal law, etc. They don't quite get the differences because they all seem so alike.

And certainly there are some differences. To me, the image that fits is one of a wheel with many spokes. There is a common core but many different expressions, and different people are attracted to different approaches.

I've attended many holistic law conferences and have found that they are immediately warm and connective. There is a feeling of having "come home," of complete and whole acceptance. People congregate in the common areas and talk into the night about deep and intimate subjects. There is a lot of hugging. In contrast, collaborative law conferences begin with a little more formality. Some of the new attendees even show up wearing business suits at the early conference events. As they feel safer, they are soon relaxing and dancing until all hours. At restorative justice conferences, people tend to talk about their religious faith and how this work is an expression of that deep faith. There is a storytelling focus and a sense of reverence for the work. Integrating Spirituality, Law, and Politics (PISLAP) gatherings appropriately tend to be populated by political activists who've realized that their spiritual lives must be integrated into their work transforming the political structures. And so it goes.

HOLISTIC LAW

*H*OLISTIC LAW means many things to many people. For some, it is an approach or style of practice that focuses on the whole person and the whole of the problem as a way of finding more healthy and sustainable solutions to legal problems. For some, it is the practice of law as a healing profession or as a spiritual practice. To a holistic lawyer, the whole problem or picture would include more than just a focus on the "other side" and his or her contribution to the problem. The analysis often includes the lawyer's role, the client's role in the problem and solution, and the impact of the problem and solution on the community. Holistic law practitioners look inward and strive to become whole themselves in order to better assist their clients in using the legal process to find wholeness. Often, holistic lawyers include a spiritual component in their thinking, exploring the unity of purpose between the seemingly opposing parties.

Some lawyers who practice in this style view holistic law as the umbrella under which other styles or approaches fit. For example, a holistic lawyer might take a preventive law approach or a collaborative law approach as part of his or her holistic legal problem solving. (There are a number of practitioners who practice in this style, but who are not aware that the term identifies them.) Other lawyers practicing as holistic lawyers have self-identified their approach, putting "holistic law" or "holistic lawyer" on their business cards and letterhead and using the term in their marketing.

The International Alliance of Holistic Lawyers (IAHL), http://www.iahl.org, provides many opportunities for discussion of holistic law. Members of the IAHL are engaged in many visionary and transformative legal practices. The IAHL hosts an annual conference, which provides a forum for networking and support for the holistic practice of law.

& · & · & · & · & · & · & · & · & · & · & · & · & · & · & · & · & · & · & · &

Holistic law is hard to define. It often seems more a process than a particular method of practicing law. However, there seem to be some common threads among holistic lawyers, which may lead to a practical definition of holistic law. IAHL weaves these threads together and finds that many of its members are committed to "PEACELAW" as defined here:

Promote peaceful advocacy and holistic legal principles.
Encourage compassion, reconciliation, forgiveness, and healing.
Advocate the need for a humane legal process.
Contribute to peace building at all levels.
Enjoy the practice of law.
Listen intentionally and deeply in order to gain complete understanding.
Acknowledge the opportunity in conflict.
Wholly honor and respect the dignity and integrity of each individual.

—From the IAHL website, November, 2009

& · & · & · & · & · & · & · & · & · & · & · & · & · & · & · & · & · & · & · &

A Symphony Thinker in Law

Daniel Pink, author of the New York Times *best seller* A Whole New Mind, *describes lawyer Stefani Quane in his book as a "symphony thinker," who is able to see the whole from the parts.*

A Seattle family law attorney, Stefani began identifying as a "holistic attorney" as early as 1997. Her career in family law started from a disgruntled place doing insurance defense litigation. She was burned out with that litigious practice and considered going back to school for a therapist's degree, but hated the idea of starting over from scratch. Instead, she saw that being a family law and divorce attorney in many respects was like being a marriage counselor without having the added school work.

She says, "When I created my own law practice in 1997, it was quite an act of bravery to purchase and use the website name Lawlady.com. At the time, in Washington, lawyers were not allowed to use brand names for a law firm, but I reasoned that if the Bar challenged me, I would explain how it made more marketing sense than using an obscure last name that no one would remember. I also committed at the beginning to represent two people in a divorce and to never litigate a family matter. At the time, it was very disapproved of to represent two people in a divorce, but the rules of professional conduct did not 100 percent forbid it. I was willing to risk disbarment to practice in a manner I felt was more healthy and beneficial for clients. I was willing to stand up to the Washington Bar if I had to over these issues. I grew into full maturity as a lawyer at that point when I realized my legal opinions were as valid and legitimate as some JD working for the State Bar Association."

According to Stefani, "From the onset of private practice I embraced the attitude that there is nothing mandatory about a lawyer acting stilted and wearing corporate gray and working in an inhospitable tall office tower. I realized that if a client was comfortable with a more relaxed attorney, that was all that was important. The first clients I attracted were from the Seattle new age-y scene, as I was an avid seminar and workshop attendee. I would draw clients from meditation groups, yoga retreats, and readings at the local East-West Bookshop that hosts astrologers, tarot readers, and other new thought speakers and authors. These clients taught me much about divorce rituals, as this was an active and important part of their lives. Together we celebrated their divorces with 'burning vows ceremonies,' 'sacred baths on the shores of the Puget Sound,' and sage burning outside the Kent Regional Justice Center before finalizing a divorce. I knew I was ready for more career stretching when I found myself checking my watch while the divorcée explained the importance of the silver goblets she was about to bury along with her wedding ring.

"To add challenge to my career, and to offer services to clients who were less amicable or not as interested in deep, sacred closure of their marriage, I stumbled upon collaborative law. I created the first collaborative law group in Washington and eventually was instrumental in introducing many more attorneys to this way of practice. I later created Washington's first practice pod, a model other attorneys in Washington have followed. During the time of developing a collaborative law practice with other professionals, I refined my methods of incorporating ceremony and ritual so that they would appeal to even close-minded, serious, non-sacred people and people from all religions.

"I find that being conversant in the deeper imagery and the poetic or soulful aspect of life can arm an attorney to provide necessary healing and comfort to clients during the difficult journey of divorce. I particularly like the ritual of gifting clients with geodes that they can throw to the ground and crack open to find amethysts or crystals. It's an ugly rock on the outside, but inside are lovely gems. The fragments of the broken geode are like family members, with their beauty exposed, more separate but yet of the same origin. When the clients are crying and reaching the 'what is life's awfulness' point of the divorce, having a bowl of geodes handy as a gift and teaching tool is very useful.

"I'm ready for my next career adventure, being someone who likes to stay at the forefront of evolution and progress. In the recent year I've begun to send clients in very protracted, stuck cases what I call 'Come to Jesus' or 'Let's Get Clear' letters.

"Basically, after we've reached an intractable point, I like to write very intimate, detailed, and caring letters to all parties about how I see the dynamics unfolding, and what I believe will need to change before the situation will resolve. I try to be kind, but also as honest and accurate as I can about their likely future legal costs, the personal traits that must change or evolve before a settlement will likely occur, and any other patterns or themes I see playing out. The first half dozen times I sent such letters (typically written in the evening, when I'm feeling more philosophical), I worried about the response from opposing counsel, the clients, or the mediator. It's risky to be so revealing and frank, but the feedback after a certain time was always favorable. I think of these letters like a sweeter version of a closing argument, explaining the best path that could occur and result in some growth of the parties or professionals."

RESTORATIVE JUSTICE: HEALING THE HARM OF CRIME

RESTORATIVE JUSTICE is a different approach toward those involved and affected by crime than the traditional judicial system provides.

- Restorative justice helps victims, survivors, offenders, and communities to take a proactive approach to crime and engages all stakeholders involved in the healing process after a crime has been committed.
- Restorative justice can be utilized in nonviolent crimes and in crimes of severe violence, as well as with juvenile offenders.
- Restorative justice is an approach to crime that puts the victim or the victim's family first and fully acknowledges the harm caused by the offender.
- The restorative justice process facilitates the offender in taking full responsibility for his or her actions by creating a direct or indirect dialogue with the victim, the victim's family, and/or the community.
- A restorative justice approach seeks to support the victim and/or the family in expressing the harm done and fulfilling their needs as a result of the crime.

- Restorative justice is an approach that supports the community in healing from the crime.
- Restorative justice expects offenders to take full responsibility for their actions and assists them in taking steps to find solutions to help heal the harm they have caused.

Some common restorative justice techniques include:

- Victim–offender dialogue
- Circle processes
- Restorative school discipline and anti-bullying programs
- Truth and reconciliation commissions
- Community justice programs
- Family-group conferencing
- Restorative community service

DIFFERENT QUESTIONS, DIFFERENT PERSPECTIVES

Restorative justice (RJ) is not a particular program, but an approach to justice. It is a different paradigm for understanding and responding to issues of crime and justice than traditional approaches. It can take many forms, such as bringing offenders face-to-face with the victims of their crimes with the assistance of a trained mediator or facilitator.

Our traditional system of punitive/retributive justice focuses on three questions:

- Who did it?
- What laws were broken?
- What should be done to punish (or, in some cases, treat) the offender?

A restorative justice inquiry poses three very different questions:

- What harm resulted from the crime?
- What needs to be done to "make it right" or repair the harm?
- Who is responsible for the repair?

With programs in North America, Europe, Australia, New Zealand, Central and South America, Asia, and Africa, restorative justice has emerged as an international movement for justice reform. The American Bar Association (ABA) issued a formal endorsement of RJ and guidelines for the application of RJ programs and principles as early as 1994. The Criminal Justice section of the ABA has an ongoing Alternative Dispute Resolution and Restorative

Justice Committee (which recommended further expansion of mediation in criminal cases in 2009).

In the traditional judicial system of retributive justice, crime is treated as an offense against the government (e.g., *The State of Alaska v. John Doe Smith*). In contrast, instead of viewing crime primarily as a violation of law, RJ emphasizes the relational nature of crime. Crime is seen as a breach of peace and of the social contract. Restorative justice seeks to repair the harms resulting from crime to all affected parties, taking a more holistic view of "harm" that includes the secondary victims and community. Rather than punishment, RJ processes seek healing of the victims, community, and even the offender.

RJ posits that crime is both a symptom and cause of separation in society; its processes seek to reconnect people as human beings. In the RJ setting, victims become human beings instead of targets, allowing offenders to realize the human impact of their actions. In turn, offenders can become human beings instead of scary monsters, relieving the fear of the victims. The community becomes a web of connections, offering support and accountability. RJ practitioners explore ways that the community can join together to heal the harm, prevent future harm, and strengthen ties.

A review of research on restorative justice (RJ) in the UK and abroad shows that across 36 direct comparisons to conventional criminal justice (CJ), RJ has, in at least two tests each:

- substantially reduced repeat offending for some offenders, but not all;
- doubled (or more) the offences brought to justice using CJ;
- reduced crime victims' post-traumatic stress symptoms and related costs;
- provided both victims and offenders with more satisfaction with justice than CJ;
- reduced crime victims' desire for violent revenge against their offenders;
- reduced the costs of criminal justice;
- reduced recidivism more than prison (adults) or as well as prison (youths).

These conclusions are based largely on two forms of restorative justice (RJ): face-to-face meetings among all parties connected to a crime, including victims, offenders, their families and friends, and court-ordered financial restitution. Most of the face-to-face evidence is based on consistent use of police officers trained in the same format for leading RJ discussions.

These meetings have been tested in comparison with conventional criminal justice (CJ) without benefit of RJ, at several stages of CJ for violence and theft:

- as replacement of prosecution altogether (Australia and US);
- as a pre-sentencing, post-conviction add-on to the sentencing process;
- as a supplement to a community sentence (probation);
- as a preparation for release from long-term imprisonment to resettlement;
- as a form of final warning to young offenders.

—Abstract, Restorative Justice, The Evidence, Study
by Heather Strang and Lawrence W. Sherman
http://www.smith-institute.org.uk/publications/
restorative_justice_the-evidence.htm

Victim–Offender Dialogue

In victim–offender dialogue, the offender and victim face each other in a facilitated dialogue. The dialogue can include family members, neighbors, teachers, members of the community, and anyone else that either the victim or offender wants to be present. These dialogue sessions are assisted by a trained facilitator (sometimes more than one). Depending on the circumstances, there may be a long preparatory period prior to the face-to-face meeting(s).

In the face-to-face meetings, the offender talks about what happened and answers questions. Each victim tells his or her story. Family members can talk about the impact of the crime on the victim and secondary impact of the crime on others. Community members share their perspective about how having had the crime happen where they live affected their sense of safety. Crime is personalized as offenders learn the human consequences of their actions, and victims have the opportunity to speak their minds and explain their feelings to the one who most ought to hear them.

Victims report high satisfaction with the process—it gives them answers to the haunting questions that only the offender can answer. The most commonly asked questions are the following: Why did you do this to me? Was this my fault? Could I have prevented this? Were you stalking or watching me? The answers contribute to the victims' healing process and allow them to move forward. They commonly report a new peace of mind, even when the answers to their questions are worse than they had feared. One answer, even a frightening answer, is better than the hundreds of possible answers victims can imagine. Victims are never asked to forgive the offender but often spontaneously do so.

Offenders take meaningful responsibility for their actions, often by mediating a restitution agreement with the victim to restore the victims' losses in whatever ways possible. Restitution may be monetary or symbolic; it may consist of work for the victim, meaningful community service, or other actions that contribute to a sense of justice among the victim, others affected by the crime, and the offender. Offenders are generally asked to take responsibility for their actions and to apologize to the victim as part of the process.

From the perspective of the RJ practitioner, it would be tempting to say that minor crimes require less preparation than crimes of severe violence. While it is true that they sometimes do, that isn't a hard and fast rule. The sense of invasion that results from even fairly minor property crimes can be terrifying for some victims. The courage to face the person who frightened them can take a lot of support and may require counseling in preparation. The offender may require a lot of work to be ready to take full responsibility for his or her actions, no matter the severity of the crime.

Victim–offender dialogue programs have been fostering mediation between crime victims and offenders for about 40 years. The worthiness of these programs is supported by a substantial body of research. While statistics regarding offenders tend to show lower recidivism after the offender participates in such a program, there are some exceptions in some of the studies that have not yet been explained. What is consistent in the research is that victims who go through the process are overwhelmingly satisfied and report value from the process.

Most victim–offender dialogue programs limit their work to property offenses or offenses of lesser violence. The majority of programs involve juveniles. Some programs expand the application to adult offenders and crimes of severe violence, including homicides. In juvenile offenses and in minor crimes committed by adults, RJ processes may be substituted for, or be supplementary to, court action. In crimes of severe violence, RJ has seldom been a substitute for prosecution. However, in those types of cases, RJ processes have been used to create more meaningful sentencing for offenders and their victims.

In all victim–offender dialogue programs, victim participation is voluntary. Offender participation is voluntary in most programs. Victim–offender dialogue is not appropriate for every crime, every victim, or every offender. Individual, preliminary meetings between mediator and victim and between mediator and offender are essential for careful screening and assessment according to established criteria. Criteria may differ from program to program but generally follow certain guidelines. For example, offenders must be remorseful.

Victims must be safe from revictimization in the process and must be mentally and emotionally able to get value from the process. Even if the circumstances are not appropriate for mediation/dialogue in a specific offense, the resolution of most crimes can benefit from some application of RJ principles. Restorative justice isn't appropriate for every case, every victim, or every offender, but where it is appropriate, it expands the opportunities for healing and completion for all the stakeholders.

Juvenile Rock Throwers

Two boys, aged 11 and 12, admitted attacking two cars and a van by throwing rocks at them. After consulting the motorists, it was agreed that the boys should be dealt a "restorative reprimand," developed in a program by the local police. The process brought the offenders and the drivers face-to-face at a restorative justice conference, where the boys apologized for their actions and promised not to repeat the attacks.

"The boys appeared genuinely sorry and won't do anything like this again," said the driver of one of the damaged cars. The driver of the damaged van said the meeting provided a satisfactory outcome for all parties involved, including the children. The restorative justice officer observed that using the method allowed victims to communicate to the boys how distressed they were by the crime. The boys were able to face up to the consequences of their actions and to move on without receiving a criminal record.

CIRCLE PROCESS*

Another common example of restorative justice practice involves the use of the circle process. Circles are used in many situations involving groups of people with a common need. They can be used to focus on conversations, healing, sentencing after trial, support, conflict resolution, or celebration. Training is recommended for practitioners before undertaking to facilitate the use of circles, as there are often unexpected, difficult challenges for novices.

---

*This section is based upon KAY PRANIS, THE LITTLE BOOK OF CIRCLE PROCESSES: A NEW/OLD APPROACH TO PEACEMAKING, Intercourse, PA: Good Books (2005).

A *circle* is a way of bringing people together in which:

- Everyone is respected.
- Everyone gets a chance to talk without interruption.
- Participants explain themselves by telling their stories.
- Everyone is equal—no person is more important than anyone else.
- Spiritual and emotional aspects of individual experience are welcomed.

Typically, the following elements are present in circle processes:

- **Ceremony**—spiritual, emotional, physical, and mental participation. No tables are present in the meeting space. Chairs are set in a circle. The idea is to create a "sacred space." This is not business as usual. Participants are expected to drop their day-to-day "masks" and be real with each other.
- **A talking piece**—a symbolic item that is passed consecutively to individual participants in a circle, often a stick. The person holding the talking stick becomes the only speaker and holds the floor, then passes the stick around the circle when she or he is finished speaking. The use of the talking stick allows for full expression of emotions, deeper listening, thoughtful reflections, and an unhurried pace. It creates space for people who find it otherwise difficult to speak, but never requires anyone to speak. It ensures each speaker that she or he will have time to speak, reflect, and pause as necessary. The talking stick moves around the circle rather than passing across as a way to ensure everyone gets a turn, if they'd like one.
- **A facilitator or circle-keeper**—co-creates and holds the space for safety and speaking honestly and openly with respect for all. The facilitator doesn't try to move the conversation in any direction and generally doesn't speak unless he or she has the talking piece. He or she is a member of the circle and may participate as any other member.
- **Guidelines**—created by participants, thus allowing them to play a major role in designing the space. What does each person need in order to feel safe in the circle? The guidelines set out the group's promises and agreements about conduct in the circle. They are not intended to be rules that are used to judge behavior, but gentle reminders of what all the participants need.
- **Consensus decision making**—recognizes the needs and concerns of all participants. Everyone must be willing to live with a decision, although supporting the implementation of a decision does not necessarily mean that everyone in the circle will be enthusiastic about it.

- **Storytelling**—opens the listener up in ways that opinions do not. When someone states an opinion, we agree or disagree. Personal experience is not up for debate. Stories encourage connection and allow others to know us more completely. It is harder to hold anger for someone who expresses vulnerability. Hearing a story is often a way for us to better understand an experience of our own. The act of listening to someone is an expression of honor that empowers both speaker and listener.
- **Focusing on relationships**—the fundamental strength of the circle process; connects the participants as human beings. We share our stories, our values, something meaningful about us as a way of introducing ourselves to the circle. Shared vulnerability builds trust and allows the discussion to go deeper.
- **Foundational values of circles**—respect, honesty, humility, sharing, courage, inclusivity, empathy, trust, forgiveness, and love. The participants in each circle create their own values, but those listed are some of the most common.

Conducting a Circle

Like victim–offender dialogue, circle processes involve a screening process, preparation, facilitation, and follow-up. As noted previously, successful facilitators need training and experience before conducting a circle, but these are the basic considerations:

- Determining suitability. Is the process suitable, and is there time for everyone to speak? Can safety be maintained? Is there an appropriate facilitator/keeper?
- Preparation. Determine who needs to participate, and explore and become familiar with the process. Training programs are offered around the country. (See the Resources section.)
- Convening all parties:
  - Identify shared values and develop guidelines.
  - Engage storytelling to build relationships and connections.
  - Share concerns and hopes.
  - Express feelings.
  - Probe underlying causes of conflict or harm.
  - Generate ideas for addressing harm or resolving conflict.
  - Determine areas of consensus for action.
  - Develop agreement and clarify responsibilities.

- Follow-up:
  - Assess progress on agreements. Is everyone fulfilling their obligations?
  - Probe causes of any failures, clarify responsibilities, and identify next steps if failure continues.
  - Adjust agreements as needed based on new information or developments.
  - Celebrate success.

EXAMPLE: LINGERING TRAUMA IN CLEVELAND, OHIO

In 2009, Cleveland law enforcement made a grisly discovery when they found 11 bodies in a house. According to news reports, they arrested and charged Anthony Sowell (the man living in the house, an ex-con) with multiple murders. All the victims were African American women. Some of the victims could have been missing for up to five years, the Cleveland police chief told reporters; at least two of the women had not even been reported missing. Others had been reported missing but were also known to be drug users or were bipolar. A year earlier, a woman had accused the same man of trying to rape her, but the police had closed the case because they found she was not credible.

Neighbors said that there had been a lingering odor in the air for a long time. They blamed it on the local sausage factory. The sausage factory actually made several repairs to its sewer and grease traps to try to address the problem.

Entomologist Joe Keiper, whose day job is at a museum, was asked to help in estimating when the victims died by analyzing the insects on the bodies. "You drop everything you're doing," said Keiper. "I know when I go to something like this, it's just going to be very horrific, very sad. But the second you get there, everyone has their game face on. . . . You look past the emotion, you look past the normal human reaction to something that's horrifying like this. You do your job."

Neighbors were in a state of shock, and news reports indicated that they were looking for answers and healing. It was reported that there was a common perception in the community that the police department didn't take the cases seriously enough, claiming that most missing adults turn up unharmed. Activist Judy Martin said, "I have been asking Cleveland police for years to form a missing persons unit. There is no centralized office where efforts to find people are maintained. I, along with others, have always felt that we need a centralized missing persons department in Cuyahoga County."

"They don't see the system working for them," a local pastor said. "Sowell was not rehabilitated. They are not keeping a watch on him. I just feel that

when the system fails, the people give up. They give up on the system, and they give up on the God they can't see."

Sowell's brother was quoted as saying: "He deserves whatever he gets from the justice system."

Considering this example of criminal behavior and its impact on a community, let's compare the traditional criminal justice approach with the restorative justice approach.

RETRIBUTIVE JUSTICE SYSTEM

This system focuses on the following questions:

- Who did it?
- What laws were broken?
- What should be done to punish the offender?

THE RESULTS

The offender has been identified as Anthony Sowell, who lived in the house. Sowell is charged with many different crimes—among them aggravated murder, rape, felonious assault, and kidnapping. Unless he pleads guilty, he will be tried. Various family members of the victims and other community members will be called to testify as witnesses. That is likely to be the only role they will play in fashioning the outcome of the trial, and even that experience will be stressful and upsetting for them. It is unlikely that any of the people traumatized by this crime will receive much in the way of assistance in dealing with the effects on their lives. Furthermore, the distrust and suspicion that exists between the police and the community will likely continue unless someone acts to intervene. Punishment for the offender will be set at trial and is likely to include a sentence that will keep Sowell out of society for the rest of his life.

RESTORATIVE JUSTICE APPROACH

This system focuses on a different set of concerns:

- What harm resulted from the crime?
- What needs to be done to make it right or repair the harm?
- Who is responsible for the repair?

THE HARM

The women killed in the gruesome murders are clearly victims, but the harm of this crime has a much broader reach. The families and friends of the victims—as well as the family of the offender—have been affected by these awful murders. The damage also extends to loss of trust by the community in the police and the legal system. The citizens have experienced the trauma of having this crime in their neighborhood. They experience the lingering effects and possible guilt of not having addressed the odor. In addition, there are racial issues that are not addressed by removing Sowell from the neighborhood.

The police investigating at the crime scene are not immune to the effects of this crime. They are exposed to scenes no one should have to see, much less spend time exploring. At the same time, they are under attack by the community for not having done something sooner. They may feel the frustration of being burdened with the expectation that they should have more aggressively investigated the disappearances of victims who habitually cooperate in drug use or other crimes and voluntarily disappear for substantial stretches of time. They may feel that the community members have a history of not being very helpful in cooperating with them or in volunteering information, all of which makes their efforts to investigate crime seem like exercises in futility.

And there are others affected by this crime. The entomologist may be able to verbalize the process of shutting off his emotions, but what psychic harm does he sustain by doing so? A little more far-fetched perhaps, but worthy of asking, is this: What about the sausage company? Blamed for the smell, they spent money making unnecessary repairs. How have they been harmed?

WHAT NEEDS TO BE DONE AND WHO IS RESPONSIBLE?

As you can see, restorative justice takes a much broader approach to exploring the harm to all the stakeholders. The answers to the questions of what needs to be done and who is responsible are not so easy or well defined. Consider some of the tools of restorative justice and how they might apply.

VICTIM-OFFENDER DIALOGUE?

Based on what the news media have reported about the offender, victim–offender dialogue is highly unlikely in this situation, at least at this time. Offenders must admit their guilt and be willing to express remorse before a dialogue can begin. It is conceivable that Sowell could someday get to that point. Generally speaking, those offenders who participate in restorative justice programs have been convicted and imprisoned for a long time, and all their appeals are complete.

However, just because the offender cannot or will not participate in dialogue with the victim doesn't necessarily mean that the victims cannot benefit from the dialogue process. In many situations, victims and their families are able to participate in surrogate interactions with stand-in offenders who are remorseful and are willing to cooperate, often because their own victims are not able to participate in such face-to-face interactions.

CIRCLE PROCESS?

The circle process may offer some promise here. One possibility is that a very large circle of all the stakeholders (victims' families, neighbors, police officers, the entomologist, and sausage company representatives) could be convened. Each could share their own stories of how this has affected them, the fears it raises, and the trauma they've experienced. After hearing out everyone, the community could create a cooperative plan for healing. Any of the stakeholders could convene a circle, but some of the stakeholders are in a more powerful position to do so. For example, a circle convened by the police department or the City of Cleveland would have the authority and standing that would invite a higher-level discussion in the community with more opportunity for a true resolution of issues.

EXAMPLE 2: MORNING TRAGEDY

Each morning, with her four-year-old son in tow, a working mother crossed many lanes of heavy traffic to catch the bus to get to one of her two jobs at a child care center. The road is flat and straight. Signs mark city bus stops on either side of the roadway. There is no traffic light or pedestrian crossing at the intersection. One Wednesday morning, as the mother and child were crossing to catch the bus, her son broke free from her hand and ran into the path of a vehicle.

At the time it was dark, weather conditions were poor and the boy was wearing dark clothing. The responding officer immediately performed CPR on the boy, but he died of a traumatic head injury at the scene. Police did not release the name of the driver of the vehicle. One can only imagine how that person must have felt.

A neighbor said, "He was a rambunctious little fellow. He loved to run. He broke loose from her hand and ran out into the road. She couldn't move quick enough to get him." Another neighbor said, "With all that traffic on that road I wonder why there aren't more wrecks than there are."

RETRIBUTIVE OPTIONS

In this scenario, law enforcement may or may not charge the driver. If charges are filed, the grieving mother will probably have to re-experience the accident as she testifies. Whether the driver is convicted or found innocent, he or she will bear the financial cost of defense and the emotional burden of his or her part of this tragedy. If charges are filed and the driver is convicted, the driver will be punished, his or her family will experience further turmoil, and he or she will have a lifelong criminal history.

RESTORATIVE OPTIONS

A comment in the news article said: "What a precious little boy. Still praying for his mother, who must be in the darkest time of her life, the driver of the car who is probably guilt ridden, and the officer who responded and was not able to revive little Jamal. I hope the mother is able to find a new job so that she won't have to work with children for a while. That might be too painful right now. A huge pat on the back to this mother who was setting an example for her little boy of hard work and sacrifice."

The compassion evident in the comment points to the harm of this tragedy. Each of the people mentioned in this comment holds a piece of the pain of the death of this child. Whether or not the driver is charged with or punished for a crime, all of the stakeholders have been marked for life, and all need more than the retributive justice system offers them. Face-to-face confrontations are always voluntary. What if all were able to sit down and share that pain with each other with the help of a facilitator? What healing might occur for all of them?

EXAMPLE 3: UNAVAILABLE OFFENDERS

When the offender is not available or appropriate, the restorative justice process must be flexible enough to find a way to address the needs of the victims or the other stakeholders. The following is an example of addressing the victim's need for healing when a victim–offender dialogue is not possible.

Amanda contacted us because she saw a restorative justice segment on Oprah. *She wanted to talk with the man who had killed her boyfriend 18 years previously, when she was eight months pregnant. The killer was Amanda's own brother. Her brother had been immediately arrested after the killing, and his lawyer had advised him not to talk about what happened, and then Amanda had complications and gave birth to her son, so there had never been a chance for them to talk openly. Of course, she was also very angry; she not only had lost her boyfriend but her only brother, with whom she had been very close. The questions had haunted her for years. What happened? Were drugs involved? Had he found out that her boyfriend had been unfaithful to her? Was her brother defending her for some reason? Her son was now in high school and was asking the same questions that Amanda had been asking herself.*

After several conversations with Amanda, we concluded that she seemed to be an appropriate candidate for a face-to-face encounter with her brother. Her love for her brother and wish to reconnect with him overcame her anger, especially with the passage of time. Her son chose not to participate in any face-to-face meeting, but was very interested in the outcome. Amanda's mother and father expressed an interest in the outcome, too, but both had health problems and they felt they weren't up to the meeting.

Our next step was to contact the prison where her brother was incarcerated. We first talked with the chaplain, who was very helpful (within the bounds of confidentiality). He thought that the brother would be open to talking with us. We then contacted the prison authorities for permission to meet the brother face-to-face, to determine whether we could work together to prepare him for meeting with his sister. The prison had no policy in place for such visits and had concerns about our safety and Amanda's. We provided them with contact information for prisons where they have successful programs and gave them sample policies. As far as we know, they're still working on their policies. Having already waited for almost 18 years, Amanda is still waiting patiently.

I offer this particular example because I've found that it is not atypical in murder cases. There are many steps in screening all the participants, working with the prisons, and then preparing all the participants for meeting face-to-face. Because it is voluntary, at any point in the process anyone involved can call the whole thing off. Preparation for victim–offender dialogue in cases of severe violence can take a very long time. The facilitator must be sure that the participants are going to be successful and must protect the victim from revictimization.

There can be many reasons why an offender is not available to meet with a victim. It may be that a particular offender denies responsibility for the crime, or that he or she admits the crime but is not remorseful. In some situations, such as Amanda's, the prison is willing to allow the meeting but needs time to put the proper procedures in place before it can move forward; in other cases, prisons simply won't allow a meeting. Perhaps the offender has died. Or, a victim may want a meeting but not be quite ready to face his or her particular offender. There are restorative justice processes that can be applied that focus on healing the victim but do not involve making contact with the offender. It can be very helpful to a victim simply to meet with an RJ practitioner.

Facilitator/Victim Meeting When the Offender Is Unavailable

If the offender is unavailable due to death, unsuitability, or lack of access, there are many processes that can still help the victims. Surrogate offenders may stand in. A facilitator can help the victim voice his or her pain and concerns. Lorenn Walker, a restorative justice expert and lawyer in Hawaii, provides this type of practice. Before a restorative event, the facilitator talks with victims about what to expect in the meeting, which is held at a place and time convenient for them. The facilitator asks victims if they want to bring supporters with them to the meeting. Most of the victims in her project chose to meet alone with the facilitators, and most meetings are held at the victims' homes. Lorenn describes the process used in her program:

> Victims are asked a series of open-ended questions, presented below. The questions are not followed in every case. The list of questions is still a work in progress. The initial questions address the issue of how the victims have coped with the aftermath of the crime:
>
> - How have you managed to get through this so far?
> - Who or what has been most helpful in dealing with this terrible situation?
>
> Facilitators may use subsequent questions to help the victims tell their stories:
>
> - What happened?
> - How has the crime or crisis affected you?
> - What has been the hardest thing about what happened?
> - How have others who are close to you been affected?
> - How have they responded?
> - What would you want those responsible for what happened to you to know about your experience?
> - What is needed to help you deal with some of your hurt and pain?
> - How might others help?
> - What things can you do that might also help?
> - What can others learn from your experience?
> - Can you think of anyone else who also has experienced the same or a similar event?
> - How have others dealt with the same or similar crises or crimes?
> - What other crises or crimes have you experienced in the past?
> - How did you deal with those crimes or crises in the past?

A written plan can be created at the meeting, stating the goal or goals the victim has developed. After the initial meeting, the victims are offered the option of additional meetings. Most victims in Lorenn's project chose to meet only once.

Bringing a Better Balance to the Victim–Offender Equation

©Michael Matthews

David Lerman

It was in the mid-1990s, says David Lerman, an assistant district attorney in Milwaukee, that he began "to feel some frustration with the normal course of business."

In the course of his work, Lerman repeatedly encountered situations where "victims of crime were still being treated as pieces of evidence, and in the court process, people were not having certain questions answered, were not being satisfied by the court process, because, after all, the court process was paramount to the human side of the situation."

Lerman decided to work to bring better balance to that equation, acknowledging that conflict will forever be the heart of the process, but taking the position that conflict is, after all, created by humans who, if given the opportunity by prosecutors, can also be a meaningful force in the resolution of the conflict. And not only meaningful, but positive—it can restore social relationships, which Lerman sees as the key principle in restorative justice.

"Crime or harm or wrongdoing is an offense against relationships," he says, meaning the relationship of the victim, the offender, and the community. "Through the legal system, we so often look at it as an offense against rules, or statutes." Those two views, in the justice system, can exist side-by-side, Lerman believes. "There are times it is appropriate," he says. "The justice system needs to be wiser with different tools."

Today, Lerman is a leader of the restorative justice movement in Wisconsin and a director of the district attorney's Community Conferencing Program in Milwaukee. "Restorative justice, broadly speaking, is about participation, democracy, and getting people involved," Lerman says. "We want to focus on the needs of the victim and what are the obligations of the offender. We want to do that in a process that is collaborative, where all the people who have a stake in the situation are involved."

Lerman uses the circle practice in criminal cases, in the Community Conferencing Program, and in a district attorneys' collaboration with the Milwaukee Public Schools specifically targeting sale of marijuana cases. It was at the end of a school session that a young student suggested the activity be given a special name: "Unheard Voices."

"That phrase," Lerman says, "the notion of having the opportunity, of having everyone at the table share their stories, a collaborative process, is huge. His phrase rings in my head."

—Profile by Michael Grant based on an interview of David Lerman at:
http://www.cuttingedgelaw.com/video/david-lerman-prosecutor
-restorative-justice-pioneer

THERAPEUTIC JURISPRUDENCE: LAW AS A HEALING PROFESSION

*T*HERAPEUTIC JURISPRUDENCE (TJ) is a holistic, interdisciplinary perspective that focuses on the law's impact on the emotional and psychological health of the participants, clients, lawyers, and judges. It is a context for the legal system that can be applied to almost any practice and incorporated into other holistic approaches. Some would argue that most (if not all) of the vectors that comprise the emerging legal paradigm discussed in this book are actually forms of TJ. The baseline goal in TJ is to bring sensitivity into law practice. It focuses on listening to participants with an awareness of the psychological and emotional issues surrounding a legal issue, including stress, confidence, and trust. TJ also considers the court system and how it affects society from either a therapeutic or nontherapeutic perspective. Often referred to as practicing law as a healing profession, TJ covers almost every practice area. Estate planning lawyers can help clients deal with the emotional issues of growing old, death, and disability. Employment lawyers can work with employers on relating well to employees. Trial lawyers can consider the emotional impacts of litigation.

Chapter 2 of *Non-Adversarial Justice,* by Michael King, Arie Freiberg, Becky Batagol, and Ross Hyams, further describes therapeutic jurisprudence and is included in the Appendix with the permission of the authors and publisher.

A CASE STUDY IN THERAPEUTIC JURISPRUDENCE

Lawyer Donna Boris says she practices law as a healing profession. In addition to her law degree, she has a degree in energetic healing and she blends her skills. As an employment lawyer, she often works with victims of workplace sexual harassment. She told me one story about a case that is a good example of the therapeutic use of the litigation system.

> *Donna's client "Mary" was a mid-level professional. When her boss began to make unwanted advances, she didn't know what to do. She was afraid that if she complained, she would face retaliation and her reputation in her industry would be harmed. She didn't know how to say no, but she didn't want to have to change careers. When she came to Donna to file the lawsuit, she feared facing the perpetrator in court.*
>
> *Donna was sensitive to the needs of her client and listened to her. Mary and Donna recognized that facing the perpetrator in court and telling her story would be scary but that it could be the breakthrough she needed to be empowered. Donna has often seen that standing up to the perpetrator, "speaking truth to power," can be transformative to some clients, and she was willing to help Mary with that challenge.*
>
> *Donna was surprised to find where the healing actually did occur. Mary attended the deposition of her boss. As Donna firmly questioned him, Mary saw a new role model of a woman who was able to be a strong, calm, and respectful professional. She told Donna that she had learned a new way to disagree with an authority figure from a place of confidence and power.*

Donna told me that she goes into every case knowing and trusting that healing can be possible. Seeing her role as both lawyer and healer opens up the possibility of being an agent of transformation with her clients and provides her with a more satisfying law practice. In an e-mail to me, Donna said this:

> *In one situation I was representing a plaintiff in a sexual harassment case. My client had suffered significant emotional distress, was being treated for depression and anxiety, and was unable to work. The first day of her deposition was extremely stressful. I perceived opposing counsel as being unnecessarily aggressive and insensitive in the manner in which he conducted the deposition.*
>
> *The second day of deposition I decided to focus my awareness on the lawyer's compassion. This was strictly a matter of intention and intuitive awareness since I had not seen any evidence of compassion on his part. However, I knew from healing school that when you focus your awareness on a point in someone's energy*

field, it causes that energy to open up. I wanted to open up his compassion and allow it to be expressed in the deposition. Another way to view this is that by focusing on his compassion, I created the space for it to be expressed. And, in fact, the second day of the deposition was much easier than the first. He still asked the questions he needed to, but the hard edge was gone, and it was much easier for my client to respond to the questions more completely. The previous day she had had a difficult time remembering and giving complete answers as she responded to the extremely aggressive manner of opposing counsel.

Few practitioners of therapeutic jurisprudence are also energy healers. Most are just lawyers who have decided to take an approach that considers the emotional, psychological, and nonlegal impact of the legal system on their clients and the other players in the legal system.

Law in the Public Interest

Bruce Winick

©Michael Matthews

Early in his law career, Bruce Winick was successful in two adjudications that would point him toward his life's work. At age 28, he successfully shut down the electric chair as an option for punishment in New York State, and he sued the Selective Service System (read: "draft board") and "changed that law." "It really gave me that sense of how we could accomplish so much as lawyers. And I realized I wasn't really going to do that at the law firm."

What evolved, in Winick's professional philosophy and in his mission as an educator at the University of Miami Law School, was "lawyering in the public interest, a lawyer in the interest of social change. . . . I've tried to model that behavior for my students," he said. "I think that so much of what we teach isn't what we tell them, it's what we show them. I'm very conscious of the fact that the kind of lawyer I am, and show myself to be, in the classroom, without beating them over the head, teaches them an important lesson of what lawyering is all about." Winick says, "The implicit message is, yes, you need to participate in your community, you need to take up good causes. Money isn't everything. It's about doing good works, it's about serving your client, it's about participating in the political process." Winick's philosophy/mission eventually crystallized into what is popularly known as "therapeutic jurisprudence."

"David Wexler is, of course, my therapeutic jurisprudence partner," Winick said. *"David was at Miami on a sabbatical semester from the University of Arizona. We met; we became friends; we went to lunch; we realized we had a common interest in mental health law. We became fast friends and, over the years, we began to see a certain common style in our scholarship."* Both were working in mental health law, and in legal articles each wrote *"the usual, crunch the cases, construe the statutes, make constitutional arguments"*—but both would include a section at the end in which *"we would criticize the law, as, ironically, being anti-therapeutic."*

There followed an effort by both to suggest constructive ways to change the process, in a point of law or in a case, *"to avoid that dilemma,"* which both realized could create dysfunctional behavior in clients or others in the system. *"At a certain point in the mid- to late-80s, we decided to call that approach 'therapeutic jurisprudence,'"* Winick said. *"We conspired on a book, written in 1991,* Essays on Therapeutic Jurisprudence. *It was a very simple notion: the law, whether we know it or not, has inevitable effects on people's emotional well-being. Let's understand law in that regard. Let's look at law in action, not just in the books. Let's understand law with an interdisciplinary perspective. We need to be anthropologists and psychologists and economists and understand all those dimensions of law. We can't just see law as a sort of cardboard cutout. It's not that. It's real people. It's how that law plays out in the lives of people."*

—Profile by Michael Grant based on interview at: http://www .cuttingedgelaw.com/video/bruce-winick-agent-social-change.

COLLABORATIVE LAW

COLLABORATIVE LAW is a voluntary, nonadversarial, problem-solving approach to resolving legal disputes. In collaborative law, the clients and their lawyers contractually agree to remove the threat of going to court through a participation agreement that sets out the structure of the process so everyone can focus on settlement. The clients and the lawyers are all working for the same goal: a fair resolution. If they are unable to come to an agreement, after a cooling-off period, the clients may retain new lawyers to serve as litigation counsel. The entire collaborative process is considered to be settlement negotiations and is not admissible in court.

Collaborative law, also called collaborative practice, has been practiced in divorce settings for more than 20 years and has quickly expanded to other family matters. It is being tested in probate, medical malpractice, employment, and several other civil contexts. Collaborative law is practiced in almost every state in the United States and in more than 20 countries. The International Academy of Collaborative Professionals (www.collaborativepractice.com) has approximately 4,000 members.

Collaborative Lawyers:

- Shift our perspective, increase our skills, make different use of old tools.
- Move from a view of conflict as a battle of wills to the creation of opportunities.

- Are less concerned with rights than discovering interests and fulfilling needs.
- Detach from the outcome, allowing our clients to choose unpredictable outcomes.
- Accept that the legal answer is only one possible answer—just because a judge is required by law to rule in a certain way, it does not control clients' decision making.
- Use their legal knowledge as a guide, not an absolute.
- Trust that clients know what is best for them in the long term.
- Guide clients from anger and disappointment to higher intentions and long-term views.
- Plan forward, not look backwards.
- Use community resources and focus on working together toward solutions.
- Rely on the team for answers. The lawyers don't have to know it all.
- Know that threatening to go to court is a violation of the principle that clients know what they want and need and have power to invent solutions that work.
- Do no harm.

The Collaborative Commitment

The *collaborative commitment,* a contractual pledge made between the clients and lawyers, is at the heart of the collaborative process. In the collaborative commitment, the lawyers agree that they will not go to court. If the clients are unable to resolve their differences through the collaborative process, the lawyers withdraw and the clients must obtain new representation. The lawyers also promise they will not use litigation tools or an adversarial posture with each other or the clients. Signing the agreement creates an environment of trust and safety for resolving conflict and requires the lawyers to call upon a different skill set based on cooperation, creativity, and mutual benefit. Without the threat of court, everyone is able to "think outside the box" and create solutions that are unique to their situation, not necessarily what a judge would do. The agreements are often far more creative and flexible than what a court could order, and agreements created in this manner are enduring and reflect the ongoing needs of the clients and their children.

Nonadversarial Advocates

In collaborative law, each party is represented by a specially trained lawyer whose job it is to facilitate a win–win settlement. More than 10,000 lawyers have been trained in collaborative law in the past decade. Collaborative lawyers can draft all consent orders, qualified domestic relations orders, separation agreements, deeds, etc.

In *The New Lawyer, How Settlement Is Transforming the Practice of Law* (Vancouver: UBC Press, 2008), Professor Julie Macfarlane describes the new approach to advocacy that is common to collaborative practice:

> *The new lawyer will conceive of her advocacy role more deeply and broadly than simply fighting on her client's behalf. This role comprehends both a different relationship with the client, closer to a working partnership, and a different orientation toward conflict. Conflict resolution advocacy means working with clients to anticipate, raise, strategize, and negotiate over conflict and, if possible, to implement jointly agreed outcomes.*

NEUTRAL EXPERTS AND INTERDISCIPLINARY TEAMS

Collaborative lawyers often work in interdisciplinary teams with financial professionals such as certified public accountants (CPAs), business valuators, and financial advisors; they also work with therapists and social workers, who serve as divorce coaches and child specialists. These interdisciplinary teams serve not only legal needs but also the clients' emotional and financial needs. The clients are also valuable members of the collaborative law team. While the lawyers may have the legal knowledge, the clients know the facts and circumstances and potentially the best possible outcome for everyone involved. The clients maintain control. They are the ones who decide the case.

✄ · ✄

[W]hat I and the other collaborative practitioners with whom I do the very deep work of CP [collaborative practice] know is that CP is itself a very robust process that requires the special skills of each member of the collaborative team; skills that are most often fundamentally different from those applied in an adversarial approach.

Indeed, the skill required to properly screen a case for CP is a very small subset of the skills and understanding required to engage effectively and fully in CP. It is imperative that we as collaborative practitioners truly understand and appreciate the paradigm shift of CP and have the concomitant skills required to build the strongest container possible in which to enact that process. It is in that context that collaborative practitioners are best able to screen cases for CP, because they understand what CP requires.

—Doris Tennant, Newton, MA

✄ · ✄

WHAT MAKES COLLABORATIVE LAW DIFFERENT?

- **Collaborative law requires a complete and honest exchange of information**. By agreeing to voluntarily provide all relevant information, clients avoid the time-intensive process of discovery. Clients are an integral part of the process of identifying and classifying property, and there the discovery process is informal with the clients providing the information voluntarily.

- **The collaborative law process is an interests-and-needs-based solution that takes into account the highest priorities of both parties**. In collaborative practice, an important part of the process is discussing the needs of all involved. Once the needs are identified and everyone is aware of them, everyone can work together to meet those needs. This approach is future-focused and avoids blaming anyone for what has happened in the past. The goal in collaborative law is that everyone's needs be addressed and included in the settlement.

- **Face-to-face meetings with the lawyers, clients, and sometimes other professionals occur at one meeting**. In collaborative law, the parties and their lawyers control their calendars. If clients need a break, the process can be stopped. If clients are in a hurry, appointments can be scheduled sooner. Generally collaborative law cases are resolved in weeks or months, not the months or years of litigated cases.

- **Resolution beyond legal matters**. In litigation, the win-at-all-costs approach aggravates feelings that are already hurt. Relationships that were strained break down completely. In custody cases, after waging war against each other, clients still have to figure out how to co-parent. In collaborative law, each client is able to talk and share. The old hurts are healed, or at least not made worse. After the case is over, clients are able to move forward in their relationship. It isn't unusual for a couple to finish their collaborative case and then go out to dinner.

A COLLABORATIVE CASE STUDY

When they decided to divorce and enter the collaborative process, Danielle and her husband John had been married 12 years and had no children. One of their mutual goals was to remain friends and continue to have healthy relationships with in-laws and mutual friends. Early in the marriage, John, an engineer who had worked for General Electric (GE) for ten years, had left his job to do other things. A few years into their marriage, he went back to GE and was allowed to "buy back" years of a defined benefit pension. So, for several years a portion of his marital paycheck went to GE to add to the value of a nonmarital asset (the benefit he accrued before marriage). Danielle, a graphic designer, switched to a career as a healer—sound healing, flower essences, and the like.

At first John did not even want his own lawyer. He hoped that he and Danielle could just work it out with the help of Theresa Kulat, Danielle's lawyer. Theresa said if it truly was as simple as they made it sound, there might be one or two meetings and they would be done. She referred John to another collaborative lawyer in her practice group. He agreed to represent John, and they entered the collaborative process. They all agreed to use a neutral financial specialist for cost-saving reasons.

In exploring the couple's finances, Jack, the financial specialist, found out about the nonmarital pension. John had not understood the distinction and had a hard time conceiving that his payments during the marriage were marital. One of the meetings got very heated because John just could not understand why as Danielle's lawyer, Theresa, kept asking questions. Jack stayed neutral. Brian, who was John's lawyer, supported John in providing full disclosure. Because it was a collaborative case, everyone on the team was always respectful. Theresa said, "No matter how John 'hit' me with words, I let it go but would not let go of the fact that we needed to know how much he had spent to restore this nonmarital asset." Danielle was shocked at what John had "hidden," although in his mind it was irrelevant.

All three professionals recommended that formal pension valuation be done, but the spouses agreed that they did not want to go down that road. So ultimately, Jack's rough estimates were accepted as the values for the total pension, the nonmarital portion and the marital contribution to the non-marital asset. Once John saw that Theresa was not attacking him or even insinuating that he did anything dishonest, he calmed down and they made progress. He came to see Theresa's questions as just legitimate inquiry. When everything was settled, they had the classic collaborative signing ceremony where everyone hugged at the end and there were smiles all around.

Danielle later wrote:

> In my recent collaborative divorce process, Theresa was instru-mental in bringing out truth on a level that was previously a challenge for my ex-husband and myself. Until we were in a collaborative meet-ing one day, I had not fully understood some of his behaviors and the consequences thereof. These behaviors I'm referring to are related to how he handles money.
>
> Although he had not actually lied to me, he had deceived me by omission of some facts in regard to investments and his pension plan. Due to Theresa's diligence and caring for me, as her client, she brought this all to the surface. Looking back now, I realize that at the time I was somewhat in shock and was probably misunderstood by others at

the meetings, as I was quiet much of the time. I am the type of person that often needs to digest information and then make decisions, not just jump right in. There were other instances of communication that were very effective as well. . . .

Theresa, and the collaborative process, pulled my relationship with my ex-husband to a place of more openness and communication that was beyond what we had experienced in years. Overall, her services and the collaborative process had an effect much like couples' counseling would have. Whenever more truth is brought to light, I believe healing will happen. Theresa definitely brought more truth to light for me/us.

Giving Away Collaboration

Stuart G. Webb

©Michael Matthews

Stuart G. (Stu) Webb, the "Godfather of Collaborative Law," seemed cut out to be a lawyer. He was a Navy veteran and a principal in his family's pharmacy business when the law called in the early 1960s. He graduated first in his class at the University of Iowa Law School and was editor-in-chief of the law review. Then he went to work. "I hated my litigation practice," he said. *He likened himself to an Old West gunslinger who stuck his hat on a stick through the open door of his office before entering to see if anyone would shoot at it. "I was ready to quit," Webb said. "Then I decided, if I'm willing to quit, maybe there's some way to do it outrageously, where I can do what I like to do, and not do what I don't like to do."*

What Webb liked to do was find settlement. What he didn't like to do was go to court. In the beginning, he found a like-minded lawyer, and they successfully settled "about a dozen" cases. Then came a tough case, contentious, like gunslinging, and Webb made a pivotal mistake. He didn't walk away. "We took it to trial, and it was horrible," he said. He lost his friend. But there was compensation: Webb had his "aha" moment.

"If you're a settlement lawyer, and it doesn't settle," he said, "you've got to get out of the case and turn it over to the trial lawyers." That's the British solicitor-barrister model, where "solicitors work up the cases, and the barristers try them. Aha, that's the way to do it! So on January 1,

1990, I declared myself a collaborative lawyer." He expressed his intentions to other lawyers and found interest. "The remarkable thing was, it was like a tuning fork," he said. "It vibrates, and another tuning fork vibrates with it when they reach the same frequency. By the end of the year, we had about nine people. That's when I got the idea of having potlucks. What is wonderful about a potluck is that the trial lawyer comes in with his casserole, and everyone says, 'Oh, I love that, can I have the recipe?' And it takes all the power out of him. It's just a wonderful thing to have happen, to see how that worked."

Soon, Webb was speaking to lawyers in California about collaborative law. "One of the great things about this movement, we just share everything, and that inspires other people to get involved." After that meeting, in Santa Cruz, California, a "collaborative board" was formed, to share information nationally with interested lawyers. A fee was considered, then abandoned. "When you've got a movement like this," Webb said, "you give it away, and it comes back to you exponentially."

The movement is now global. At a collaborative law conference in the spring of 2007, 16 countries were represented. "It's very gratifying," Webb said, "to see that something is making law better. The main thing that's different about collaborative law is that, in litigation, the responsibility and the focus are with the lawyer. With collaborative law, the focus is on the client."

—Profile by Michael Grant based on interview at http://www .cuttingedgelaw.com/video/video-stu-webb-godfather-collaborative-law.

MEDIATION

AT Dictionary.com, *mediation* is simply defined as the attempt to settle a dispute through a neutral party. That is a broad definition and covers a lot of ground—as does the field of mediation. Settlement is the goal of some mediation, and it is the mediator's job to broker the resolution. It is considered "mediation" when retired judges act as evaluators and convince litigants to agree to a settlement that has been developed by the mediator. The parties involved usually meet in separate rooms and never talk with each other. Success is defined by a written agreement of the issues. On the issue-settlement end of the spectrum, the threat of litigation is often used as a tool to pressure settlement.

The recognition of our unity is the healing of all our wounds. Yet how do we convert the consciousness of humanity to a perspective of spiritual oneness? And what would the world look like if we did?
—*Marianne Williamson*

How do we convert the consciousness of humanity to a perspective of spiritual oneness? Within the section, we share a profound vision: a dream of peace, an intention to make a difference in the world, and a desire to help others. The purpose of the Spirituality Section is to provide a professional community, which affirms this vision and supports members in bringing their highest vision in their practices, their careers and their lives. In this way, as each of us takes our work and our wisdom out into the world, we will collectively realize our deepest dreams.
—*The Association of Conflict Resolution Spirituality Section's website, http://www.mediate.com/acrspirituality/pg21.cfm.*

However, repairing the relationship can also be a primary goal of mediation, and the legal conflict is viewed as an underlying relational one. In this type of mediation, it is considered successful if the relationship is transformed; settlement of the issue is not so important. Emotions are brought to the table and expressed face to face, and in this way, healing of the relational rift begins.

There are many different models and applications of mediation that fall between impartial settlement and relational repair. All forms of mediation could be considered peaceful resolutions, and most can be approached with a transformational perspective. Some approaches lend themselves to a more transformative approach and some mediators take a more transformative perspective.

I join Susan Daicoff in considering that *transformative mediation* is a part of the movement toward a holistic, relational, and humanistic approach to law, and include some other styles of mediation as well.

TRANSFORMATIVE MEDIATION

The transformative mediation framework was first articulated by Robert A. Baruch Bush and Joseph P. Folger in *The Promise of Mediation: Responding to Conflict Through Empowerment and Recognition* (San Francisco: Jossey-Bass) in 1994. It has grown and is used in mediation, facilitation, and conflict management training all over the world.

The focus of transformative mediation is not only on resolution, but provides conscious emphasis on transforming the interaction from negative and destructive to positive and constructive. Practitioners use the complementary models of empowerment and recognition. In this model, the focus is on revealing and understanding the underlying dynamics of the conflict, to both resolve the presenting issue and prevent future similar ones.

The conflict is viewed in the context of human interaction rather than "violations of rights" or "conflicts of interest"—as part of the basic dynamic of human interaction in which people struggle to balance concern for self with connections to others. When the relationship is out of balance, there is a crisis and the human interaction becomes alienated and destructive. Conflict is seen as destabilizing to the parties' experience, increasing vulnerability. Negative attitudes create a vicious circle that intensifies each party's sense of weakness and self-absorption, and the interaction between the parties quickly degenerates and assumes a mutually destructive, alienating, and dehumanizing character.

The separation and lack of connection is seen as the most significant impact of conflict. The transformative framework for mediation seeks to help people regain their footing and shift back to a restored sense of strength or confidence in self (the empowerment shift) and openness or responsiveness to the other (the recognition shift). The transformation of the relationship dynamic is seen as more important than the presenting conflict. Success is measured not by settlement, but by party shifts toward strength, responsiveness, and constructive interaction. The parties can then choose to leave the mediation and work out the issues themselves, based on the new understanding and relationship.

THE UNDERSTANDING MODEL OF MEDIATION

Another model of mediation that falls in our spectrum is the Understanding Model pioneered by Gary Friedman and Jack Himmelstein. From their website, http://www.mediationinlaw.org:

> *A central challenge facing people in conflict is how they can together assume the responsibility for resolving their conflict. Taking on that challenge is important for individuals and organizations in conflict in part because the results reached by their working through the conflict are much more fulfilling and the path taken much more rewarding.*
>
> *But we are also motivated by the larger challenge facing humanity to learn ways to work together to resolve the deep conflicts we face in today's increasingly interconnected world. The aspiration to search those ways has motivated us to explore a different approach embodied in what we have come to term the Understanding-based approach to mediation.*
>
> *In this approach to resolving conflict, the mediator seeks to work directly and simultaneously together with the parties throughout the mediation in the effort to support their finding their resolution to their conflict. Stated most simply, we seek to support the parties in making knowing and informed choices together. We wish to do that in a way that is respectful of the parties and also fosters respect by them for themselves and for each other.*
>
> *In developing this approach, we do not feel so much that we are inventing something new, but rather uncovering what is innately there in the ways that many people in conflict have often dealt with one another and, more often, have wished to be able to do so. This is an essential point, because many today would say that parties to conflict lack the desire and the ability to go through conflict together, but for us it is that perception that frequently poses the greatest obstacle.*
>
> *We believe the impulse to work through conflict together is there and a natural part of the human condition. It may be nascent, buried, or blocked; and it certainly receives little support in our society. But it is very much there, waiting to be tapped and given room for expression. And the same is true for the capacity of those in conflict to work through their conflict together. It may be undeveloped, but it is often readily available to those who are motivated and given the support and structure that will allow it expression. This approach to mediation seeks to tap that impulse and give expression to that capacity.*

Expanding the Use of Mediation: James Melamed and Mediate.com

© Michael Matthews

James Melamed

The Internet was not invented by a mediation lawyer. To mediation lawyers like James Melamed, it just looked that way. He not only instantly recognized the Internet's power as a tool in mediation law, but acted on it.

When Melamed created the Mediation Center in Eugene, Oregon, in 1983, his business was bringing bodies together. Today, his business is bringing digital bytes together. And the benefit to mediation law has been great, including one memorable benefit Melamed identified in 2002. "It is impossible," he wrote, "to receive a bloody nose over the Internet."

In 1996, only a couple of years after the commercial emergence of the Internet, Melamed co-founded Resourceful Internet Solutions (RIS) and Mediate.com. "Adapting Internet technologies to mediation was not accidental," he said. "Increased use has been based upon the effectiveness, convenience, and affordability of various Internet strategies."

The speed, ease, and affordability of transferring volumes of information to a central place stood out in strong contrast to the effort required to bring people and files to that same central place, which routinely was somewhere inside a crowded city. This included not only case-specific information, but access to global mediation literature. Over time, the new technology naturally started to affect client expectations.

Early on in this work, Melamed could envision a day "when the context and medium for mediation discussions may in fact become primarily electronic, with face-to-face meetings being the augmentation, perhaps even the exception." Now in its 14th year, Mediate.com receives more than 14,000 visitors daily. In November 2009, the site's feature, "The Mediate.com Weekly," published its 300th issue. In that span, more than 1,000 authors have contributed mediation law articles to the Weekly, which is free to users. The site makes available, to mediators and the public, more than 5,000 articles and resources, organized into 25 categorical sections. Another feature, Mediation Today, chronicles "the ongoing and increasing use of mediation throughout the U.S. and around the world." The 2010 American Bar Association (ABA) Lawyer as Problem Solver Award was presented to Mediate.com as the institutional recipient.

Melamed received his degree in psychology from Stanford University, and his law degree from the University of Oregon. He was the first president and executive director of the Oregon Mediation Association (OMA) in 1985, and in 2003 received the OMA's Award for Excellence. He received the 2007 John Haynes Distinguished Mediator Award from the Association for Conflict Resolution.

Although the Internet is an astonishing tool in Melamed's work, mediation is still at the heart of that work. "Our continuing goal is to expand the use of mediation," he says. Melamed saw the election of Barack Obama as an endorsement of mediation's future. He called the Obama candidacy "mediative consciousness's coming-out party," something that "all mediators, whatever our political leanings, should take great pride in. This is an accomplishment that should not go unnoticed." What should also not go unnoticed, by the media or the public, was Obama's unprecedented use of the Internet as a central stage for that coming-out party, bringing together, as Melamed does, bytes instead of bodies. It worked for Obama as a bridge to the presidency; in his work, Melamed uses it as "a bridge between mediators and those who benefit from our services."

—Profile by Michael Grant based on interview of James Melamed at www.cuttingedgelaw.com.

COOPERATIVE LAW

*C*OOPERATIVE LAW focuses on settlement. Like collaborative practice, in cooperative law there is an agreement among the lawyers and clients for a peaceful settlement—however, it does not require the lawyers to withdraw if settlement cannot be reached. A leader in the development of cooperative law, the Wisconsin Cooperative Divorce website describes the principles of its agreement as follows:

> *Both parties and attorneys commit in good faith to do the following:*
> - *Cooperate by acting civilly at all times and by responding promptly to all reasonable requests for information from the other party.*
> - *Cooperate by fully disclosing all relevant financial information.*
> - *Cooperate by obtaining joint appraisals and/or other expert opinions before obtaining individual appraisals or expert opinions.*
> - *Cooperate by obtaining meaningful expert input (e.g., from a child specialist) before requesting a custody study or the appointment of a guardian ad litem.*
> - *Cooperate in good faith negotiation sessions, including 4-way sessions where appropriate, to reach fair compromises based on valid information.*
> - *Cooperate by conducting themselves at all times in a respectful, civil and professional manner.*

Cooperative lawyers report that they prefer this method because they fear that clients will be pressured toward settlement by the withdrawal of their lawyers in the event of litigation, as in the collaborative model.

Under this pressure, cooperative lawyers believe a client may accept a settlement that does not meet all of her or his needs. Some holistic lawyers offer either collaborative law or cooperative law and put the choice in their clients' hands.

"Cooperative practice" is a recent innovation using an agreement by the parties that structures a negotiation process to produce early and efficient settlements. In essence, Cooperative negotiation is a joint early case management process. It is similar to Collaborative practice but does not include the customary Collaborative practice provision limiting lawyers' representation to negotiation. . . .

Typically, Cooperative negotiation agreements involve a commitment to negotiate in good faith, provide relevant information, and use joint experts as appropriate. Cooperative processes have been used in divorce and employment cases and can be used in virtually any civil matter. For example, Garvey Schubert Barer, a Seattle-based law firm with four U.S. offices and one in China, uses a Cooperative process it calls "Win2"_that is, Win Squared_in employment cases (see www.gsblaw.com/practice/area .asp?areaID=131&groupID=53).

The Boston Law Collaborative, a Boston law firm focusing on ADR [alternative dispute resolution] practices, offers a Cooperative negotiation process in family, business, and employment cases (available at http:// www.bostonlawcollaborative.com in the Resources area, under "Forms, Statutes, Rules, and Other Material"). In addition, members of the Divorce Cooperation Institute, a Wisconsin family lawyers' professional group, use a Cooperative process in divorce cases. The bottom line is that the Cooperative process is highly adaptable, so businesses and their lawyers can readily modify the procedures for their cases. [See] http://cooperativedivorce.org.

—John Lande, http://law.missouri.edu/lande/publications/Lande%20
Cooperative%20Practice%20study%20Alternatives.pdf.

The following case study was offered by David Hoffman of the Boston Law Collaborative:

In this case, my client (Smith) and her husband (Jones) were divorcing after a 25-year marriage. They both wanted a collaborative process and seemed like exceptionally good candidates for one. They were involved in productive couples counseling to discuss how best to co-parent their younger child, and they intended to remain working together in a small business that they co-owned. They clearly respected each other and cared for each other a great deal, despite their decision to divorce, and they communicated effectively. They had considered carefully the advantages and disadvantages of a CL [Collaborative Law] participation agreement and decided on a CNA [Cooperative Negotiation Agreement] instead. The primary reason for their decision was that their funds were limited, and they feared having to hire new counsel. They also said they were very pleased with their choice of counsel and did not want to lose the opportunity to work with us. The five four-way meetings that were held in this case were among the most productive, collaborative, and deeply meaningful sessions I have had in 23 years of work in the area of family law. There were a few challenging issues, and one very challenging issue regarding the primary residence of their younger child (the older was in college). But the parties had enormous respect for each other, and the principles contained in their CNA supported their good intentions. At the final four-way meeting, my client asked if someone in my office could take a picture of the four of us, because she wanted it as memento of the good feelings that the process had engendered. (I have never, in the several hundred divorce cases I have been involved in, had such a request and I found it a rewarding reminder of the potential of cooperative negotiations.)

—Excerpted from: Cooperative Negotiation Agreements: Using Contracts to Make a Safe Place for a Difficult Conversation by David Hoffman. http://www.bostonlawcollaborative.com/

COURT INNOVATION AND PROBLEM-SOLVING COURTS

In our complex society, courts are increasingly being asked to address social problems that are not compatible with the traditional system of adversarial justice and punishment. Recurring societal problems—such as drug use, homelessness, domestic violence, child neglect and abuse, mental illness, and driving while intoxicated—come before courts every day. Traumatized veterans return from war zones and have trouble fitting into society. *Problem-solving courts* attempt to address the root causes of crime by addressing the recurring problems that lead to the criminal offense.

In 1989, the first drug court was started in Miami, Florida, and since then, thousands of problem-solving courts have sprung up across the United States and around the world. Problem-solving courts focus on treatment of the underlying issue rather than incarceration. For example, if someone writes bad checks to pay for drugs and is arrested, the drug court approach would be to create a structure of support to break the defendant's addiction to drugs. The defendant would likely be regularly drug-tested, be required to attend a program such as Narcotics Anonymous, be required to obtain housing and employment, and so on. The support structure might include drug treatment, social services, and a whole team of resource people. The defendant must comply with the case plan set out for him or her, often over a period of up to three years, or the case reverts to the punishment system.

Judges in problem-solving courts generally take a therapeutic jurisprudence approach, whereby they see each defendant as a person and recognize the role of the court as having an opportunity for effecting lasting therapeutic change. Many such judges become parental figures, meting out advice, enforcing consequences, and cheering for success. Proponents of problem-solving courts argue that there is a significant cost savings: providing the support for rehabilitation increases the probability that the defendant will become a productive, tax-paying citizen.

In 2007, the National Association of Criminal Defense Lawyers established a Task Force on Problem-Solving Courts to assess the extent to which these increasingly popular courts affect fundamental rights. Made up of seven experienced criminal defense lawyers from across the country, the Task Force was asked to conduct an extensive inquiry into problem-solving courts, to make findings regarding the practices in those courts, and to develop recommendations for ensuring that the courts meet constitutional standards of fairness and due process. Drawing upon the testimony of well over 100 witnesses at seven hearings, a comprehensive review of existing literature and studies, an Internet questionnaire of practitioners, and hours of discussion and debate, this report details the procedures utilized in problem-solving courts, highlights best practices, and makes recommendations for change. The report is available at the National Association of Criminal Defense Lawyers website at http://www.nacdl.org. Here is a summary of the report's recommendations:

- Treat substance abuse as a public health issue rather than a criminal justice one.
- Open admission criteria to all those who need, want, and request treatment.
- Enforce greater transparency in admission practices, and rely on expert assessments, not merely the judgment of prosecutors.
- Prohibit the requirement of guilty pleas as the price of admission.
- Urge greater involvement of the defense bar to create programs that preserve the rights of the accused.
- Consider the ethical obligations of defense lawyers to their clients, even if they choose court-directed treatment.
- Open a serious national discussion on decriminalizing low-level drug use.

Righting Wrongs

In his famous 1968 eulogy for his slain brother, Teddy Kennedy said Bobby was simply a good and decent man who "saw wrong and tried to right it." Teddy could have been speaking about three American judges who are, among others, at the heart of the mushrooming problem-solving movement in the nation's courtrooms. In their courtroom experiences, each saw wrong, and not only saw it, but invoked their judge's office to try to right it. The three judges represent hundreds of others and are profiled here as examples. They are:

1. *Retired Judge Peggy Hora, a California Superior Court judge for 21 years; now a worldwide teacher and advocate for therapeutic jurisprudence*
2. *Judge Tracy McCooey, a circuit court judge in Montgomery, Alabama, since 1998*
3. *Judge Steven Leifman, in the Miami Dade County Court System, and a special advisor on criminal justice and mental health to the Florida Supreme Court*

Peggy Hora

Peggy Hora

©Michael Matthews

Peggy Hora said, when she got started as a judge, that she did what she was told to do: criminal and civil cases, traffic cases, small claims. It wasn't long—only a year—before she began to sense something was wrong. "With criminal law," she said, "I sent them to jail. I'd say, don't drink; don't use other drugs. And then, they would. And I was shocked." She shrugged. "I had a civil background. What did I know about criminals? And they would come back into the system, getting into the same trouble."

After that first year, she said, she began to "ponder" her situation. "There is something different about these people that I'm not understanding," she reasoned, "and unless I'm going to engage in senseless acts for the next 20 years, I need to figure it out. So I took classes in chemical dependency. And I discovered: Ah! Addiction! No wonder they can't do it, because they can't not do it."

Hora decided that she had to do something better, do something different, in handling these criminal drug cases. "What we were doing was expensive, and it didn't work."

She learned about a new "drug treatment court" being established in Miami. "It was the first drug treatment court in the United States," she said. "I chaired the committee that set up the first one in California, which was the second one nationally, in 1992." She laughed. "They always call me a 'pioneer.' So, I have been in the problem-solving court business since the very beginning. It was the only thing that made sense."

So the "wrong" that Hora encountered was not particularly moral, or good versus evil. It was just a traditional way of doing things that no longer made sense. Hora became a "spinner," taking the raw cotton of law and creating unique new threads that she then wove into a new cloth of jurisprudence. She saw a new way of doing things that made the law less wrong and more right for all concerned: the offender, the victim, and the community.

The new problem-solving approach in the courtroom differed from the traditional approach by rooting up and confronting the issues underlying each case. "What is the behavior, what is the underlying issue, that is bringing this person back to court over and over again?" Hora asked. "Can we use the power of the court, and the power of a collaborative justice model, to help solve the problem? Let's get to the root of what is going on here."

As Hora and her associates in both the judicial system and the community moved forward with the work, she noticed things beginning to change. A new openness was developing; stakeholders began to talk about "alcoholism and drug issues" instead of "crimes" as a traditional basis for bringing offenders into court, and began to explore alternative processes involving better treatment and better understanding of treatment.

"We now know that 60 percent of people don't want nonviolent drug offenders to go to jail," Hora said. "They know that it is a waste of money. All of these things started coming together pretty much at the same time. The problem-solving movement is not quite 20 years old, which is a snap of the fingers when you are talking about a judicial system. We don't make changes quickly."

In 1990, the National Association of Drug Court Professionals was founded. "There were 100 of us at that very first meeting," Hora said. "There are now over 3,500 problem-solving courts in the United States, and the approach has spread to 20 countries. If you had sat me down in

1990 and said, this is the way things are going to be by 2009, I would have said, no way." Yet, there it is. Hora said problem-solving courts have expanded to include domestic violence courts, mental health courts, veteran's courts, homeless courts, unified family courts, and child abuse and neglect courts.

Tracy McCooey

©Michael Matthews

Tracy McCooey

Tracy McCooey, who was elected to a circuit court judgeship in 1998, was not long on the bench in Mont-gomery, Alabama, before she saw something wrong in her courtroom.

"Court was a very sterile environment," she said. And in this traditional, highly structured environ-ment, "we expected people to change in two minutes. And I always thought: How stupid is that? People fail to remember that we are dealing with human beings, and every human being is different. We know noth-ing about these people and their backgrounds, but we expect them to change in two minutes. And when they don't, we act like we're disappointed or upset. These are human beings and it takes a little bit of time to give them a reason to quit using drugs, to find out what is it that triggers them." The answers to these questions were of value not only to judges, lawyers, and others in the legal system, but to the other anonymous figures in the courtroom: the victims.

McCooey's solution to her problem was victim–offender conferences; she started them in 1999. "The district attorney said, 'What kind of cases are we going to do?' And I said, 'We're going to do every kind of case. I don't care if it's a murder or a theft; if a victim and a defendant want to sit down and meet together, we're going to do the case.'" McCooey smiled. "That almost sent her through the roof. She said, 'We're not doing serious cases,' like murder." My response: 'The great thing about being a judge is that I can do whatever I want in my courtroom. And we're going to do every kind of case that there is.' I was very serious. In fact the second case we did was a murder case."

It was a case, McCooey said, that very much brought her point home. There was a woman whose son had been murdered, gang-related, by four

defendants. The woman sat down with McCooey and one of the defendants in a victim–offender conference. Eventually the woman attended
the defendants' trials, and after the trials, she sought out Judge McCooey
and offered her thanks. "She said she couldn't have sat through the trials without that meeting," McCooey related. "She said she had a peace
within herself. And I thought: that's what it's all about. If you go home
tonight and someone has murdered your entire family, are you going to
have questions? Are there all kinds of things going through your mind?
Yes. And only the person who did that wrong can answer those questions.
As hard as that is for us to hear, it's very much needed for that victim."
"The worse the thing is that happens to you," McCooey reasoned, "the
more you hurt, the more you need to talk to that person. It's voluntary.
Not everyone wants to meet. But, do we systemically need to offer it to the
folks who need to talk? Yes. In 1999, victim–offender conferencing wasn't
really known, and it sounded voodoo, really out there. Now, thankfully,
restorative justice has become acceptable."

Steven Leifman

©Michael Matthews

Steven Leifman

Judge Steven Leifman, in Miami Dade County,
Florida, was likewise inspired by a unique case that
wound up changing both a life and the law. It was a
mental health case that came before Leifman when he
was "assigned to what is called the Jail Division," he
said. "There are three kinds of offenders in a jail division," Leifman said. "There are those that are too poor
to bond out; those that have serious charges pending
and are not allowed to bond out; and there are those
with mental illnesses that don't know how to get out."
He said that last category, when he took the bench, was
growing "really badly."

"I had this really horrible case that woke me up to
do something about it," he said. Before Leifman stood a "brilliant man,
[who had] gone to Harvard, had a late onset of schizophrenia; he was
recycling through the criminal justice system, picking up all these quality-
of-life offenses. And now he was homeless in Miami." Before a hearing,
the man's parents requested a meeting with Leifman. The parents were

distraught and basically "begging me to get help for their son." As Leif-
man started to stand and go into the courtroom, the mother said that
there was one more thing: her son was the former head of psychiatry at
Jackson Memorial Hospital. "It really took me aback," Leifman said. "I
went into the courtroom and called his case and he was in fact brilliant.
He knew so much more about mental illness and the law than I did.
He was really sharp—except he was homeless-looking, probably hadn't
bathed in months, and he was in jail."

Leifman said that, eventually, he asked the man a question: "I just
don't understand one question: I don't understand why a Harvard grad-
uate would be homeless, and in jail, if there weren't some other issues
that I really need to look into. The man got really upset, started to go into
crisis, violently shaking, whips back and starts pointing to the back of the
courtroom where his parents were standing. He said, 'Your honor, before
I go on, I'd like that couple removed.' I said, 'Well, aren't those your par-
ents?' He said, 'Oh no, my real parents died in the Holocaust and these
are impostors sent from the CIA.'"

"Now mom's crying and there's not a dry eye in the courtroom. I
immediately ordered a battery of psychiatric evaluations." When the
evaluations came back, they found that the man was incompetent to
stand trial. "This was great," Leifman said. "I'll release him, get him
treated, we'll all live happily ever after."

But there was a catch. Something was wrong. As Leifman was about
to order the man to involuntary hospitalization, a public defender at the
bench said, "With all due respect, you can't do that." She presented a state
Supreme Court decision, which said county court judges "have no legal
authority to involuntarily hospitalize anybody." Leifman was restricted
to simply giving the man a conditional release.

"We all agreed it was a horrendous decision, but it was very clear,"
Leifman said. "This was going on for years. And I'll tell you, none of us
become judges to become part of that kind of problem. It was a fascinating
opinion; at the end of it, it basically said 'we really don't like this opinion
either and we're strongly urging the Florida legislature to fix it.' That case
was in the late 1990s, and of course they still haven't touched it."

So Leifman had a problem to solve. "My goal was just to get this one
guy treatment," he said. How to do that? "One of the best things about
being a judge," he said, "is you have an opportunity to get involved in
these kinds of issues and make really positive change." He recalled, wryly,
a letter he had composed and sent some years earlier, as a public defender,

calling for a meeting to address the growing problem of mental health cases in the courts. The letter received no response. Now, as a judge, he was sending essentially the same letter again. He called a meeting.

"Everybody was there early," he laughed. "For two days, we had in the room all the traditional and nontraditional stakeholders—sheriffs, police chiefs, state attorneys, public defenders, emergency room people, provider types—and we figured out that there was a better way to deal with this." As a result of that meeting, he said, "we began to change the way we were dealing with people with mental illness in our community." They were no longer dumped back onto the street; they were diverted to a crisis stabilization unit. "We lowered misdemeanor recidivism from 70 percent to 20 percent within the mentally ill population," he said.

As the solution gathered steam, the state donated a building, and the county passed a $22 million bond issue "to renovate the building into a first-of-its-kind facility that will be a forensic diversion facility with all the services under one roof," Leifman said. "We can start to put people in recovery and keep them out of a system that they never should have gotten into. The Eleventh Judicial District Criminal Mental Health Project was designed and implemented to divert people with serious mental illnesses who commit minor, misdemeanor offenses away from the criminal justice system and into community-based care. It brings together the resources and services of health care providers, social service agencies, law enforcement personnel, and the courts."

"This is about justice," he said. "We want to do the just thing. There's a way to do it and protect the public safety at the same time. The traditional way is very expensive and it actually threatens public safety—we spend all this money on the deep end, basically stabilizing people so we can restore them to competency to try them, and then release them right back to the community without ever providing them access to appropriate services."

Leifman developed a specific insight into the value of the collaborative process in problem solving. "I think litigation sometimes has to be the last resort, not the first resort," he said. "If you order people to do things, and they don't really want to do it, they're never going to do it well, or right. But when you engage people, and you get them to collaborate on the issue, they become part of the solution. They are much more likely to do a good job."

Leifman, echoing and summarizing the convictions of Hora and McCooey, said, "There's a certain moral authority of the judge's office, that if we use it well, you really can bring people to the table." That judge's prerogative to take action is the philosophical theme of the stories of these three leaders in the problem-solving movement.

—Profile by Michael Grant, based on interviews on www .cuttingedgelaw.com.

COMMUNITY-ORIENTED LAWYERING

Community lawyering refers to the work of a public interest lawyer who works primarily at the intersection of law and organizing and who views her or his work as reflecting the needs and interests of a particular community. It has also been called "cause lawyering" and has been referred to as "integrative lawyering" in some academic writing. It is a values-based way that public lawyers such as prosecutors can be involved in shifting the legal profession, and it also offers opportunities for pro bono work.

In the 1980s, police departments began to experiment with proactive problem-solving partnerships with communities and prosecutors, and defense lawyers followed suit a few years later. In this community-oriented lawyering model, prosecutors began to evaluate cases differently. Their decisions began to be influenced by the potential to solve neighborhood problems. Working with city agencies, prosecutors became advocates for solving problems like trash-filled lots, nuisance properties, parks without lighting, neighborhood-wide drug problems, and so forth.

Roger Conner wrote one of the first articles on community lawyering in the *National Institute of Justice Journal* in January 2000. He noted:

The basic unit of work is not just crimes and cases but rather people and places. Beyond the individual drug sale, they look at the drug market.

The definition of success is not about winning the case or securing the benefit. The bottom line for the community lawyer is solving problems, increasing neighborhood safety, preventing crime, improving the quality of life, and fostering economic development.

The relationship to the community shifts in that the community is not a passive complainant but rather a potential partner. Lawyers are no longer controlled by the community but rather oriented to it, and the community becomes a participant in defining success.

Collaboration with other groups is the norm, not working alone. Meetings, public education, sharing information, and power become part of the job.

The tool kit for the community lawyer is large—civil remedies, new forms of action, new organizations (such as community courts), negotiation, and voluntary compliance [are] among . . . these tools.

The key question is "What's happening?" rather than "What happened?" One is trying to assign responsibility for the past while the other is future focused.

Community Lawyers: Broadening the Scope of the Job

In a 1994 interview in Ebony *magazine, Eric Holder was talking about his days as a Superior Court judge in the District of Columbia.*

"Perhaps that was the hardest part of being a judge in D.C.," he told the interviewer, "sentencing huge numbers of young black men to jail. In fact, it was one of the reasons why I wanted to be U.S. Attorney so I could try to turn that around and do things in the community that would prevent people from becoming involved in the criminal justice system and to harness that talent, that energy, in more positive ways."

Holder's response was to create a "community prosecution" pilot project in 1996, wherein he assigned prosecutors to develop crime-fighting strategies in partnership with the neighborhood and the police. Roger Conner of Vanderbilt University, writing in the January 2000 edition of the National Institute of Justice Journal, *called it a seminal step in what he called "community oriented lawyering," or, "a war for the neighborhood."*

"What I hope to do," said Holder of his 1996 project, "is broaden the scope of this job so that we try to take meaningful prevention activities that deal with the problems that breed crime. I think too often law enforcement people focus on the enforcement side and don't deal with the prevention side. And unless you do both, how are you ever going to ever really get a handle on the crime problem?"

By 2009, Holder was Attorney General of the United States, and community lawyering was a broad-based movement keyed on a shift from the enforcement side to the prevention side.

"The key question is different," Conner writes. "The lawyer in conventional practice asks, 'What happened?' Community oriented lawyers ask, 'What's happening?' In other words, the angle of vision is profoundly different. One is trying to assign responsibility for what has *happened, the other to reshape what* will *happen." Conner names David Dominguez, of the law faculty at Brigham Young University, as a leader in finding this new angle of vision, focused on what will happen.*

"Community lawyering teaches that there can be no justice for all until legal problem solving is a common civic duty shared by law school graduates and everyday Americans," Dominguez says. "But where is the opportunity? For the past 30 years I have taught law students and community members alike to pursue dispute resolution as 'Samaritan Justice.'"

Dominguez, who is working on a book about the subject, says Samaritan Justice "empowers everyone, from the poorest to the richest, from highly cultured to least sophisticated, to break the silence, cross the street to unfamiliar neighbors, and tap each other's problem-solving capabilities. Erstwhile strangers—even enemies—are trained to create new opportunities for handling conflict.

"My law school curriculum," Dominguez says, "recasts law students in a new attorney role, as a team player in the classroom and a community partner in the field. I teach them that the lawyer of the 21st century, as an indispensable member of a problem-solving ensemble, must assert legal training and expertise to draw public attention to the importance and urgency of the matter. At the same time, the attorney's method of resolving disputes must have as a key goal the strengthening of community ties among strangers and opponents, even among enemies."

At the heart of the matter, Dominguez says, is the "core civic mission set forth in the U.S. Constitution, to form 'a more perfect union.'" His goal, and the goal of his students, in law and in the community, is to "identify those ways that our legal system falls short" of that core mission.

—Profile by Michael Grant

PREVENTIVE LAW

Lawyers are typically regarded, and regard themselves, along only one dimension: the Fighter who advocates zealously toward vindicating the violated rights of a client. The aim of California Western School of Law, its Louis M. Brown Program in Preventive Law, and its McGill Center for Creative Problem Solving, is to explore and promote two other dimensions of lawyering: the Problem Solver and the Designer.

—Thomas D. Barton and James M. Cooper

Sometimes the best approach to a potential legal issue is to prevent it from ever happening at all. The *preventive law approach* is aimed at assessing risks before there is an issue and putting in safeguards to reduce the risk. Included in Susan Daicoff's comprehensive law vectors, preventive law is more than just getting legal advice before taking action; it is a way of approaching a matter from a preventive perspective, aiming not to put structures in place to help win lawsuits, but to keep them from happening altogether. Preventive law means that the lawyer anticipates the problem. In dealing with individual clients, the lawyer moves from reacting to events to becoming the shaper of environments. Here are some guidelines for addressing problems preventively:

1. Attempt to structure workplace, financial, family, or personal environments for clients that prevent problems from arising.
2. Where problems do arise, promote independent reflection by the problem holder on the meaning and implications of the problem.
3. Promote cooperation and communication among contending parties and with other lawyers.

—http://www.preventivelawyer.org/content/
pdfs/Multi_Dimensional_Lawyer.pdf

The solution could be to file a lawsuit, or it could be to apply for a government grant or build a fence.

—*Harold Brown*

CREATIVE PROBLEM SOLVING: MULTIDIMENSIONAL LAWYERING

The Center for Creative Problem Solving (CPS) at California Western School of Law (CWSL) is a leader in exploring application of *creative problem solving* to law. CPS defines problems so as to permit the broadest array of solutions. It is about breaking out of the normal ways of doing things and finding solutions that examine many points of view, at many levels: individual, institutional, societal, and international. The goals of creative problem solving include expanding resources and enhancing relationships.

This is an inherently interdisciplinary effort that envisions a more imaginative, more helpful lawyer who can prevent some problems from arising and who can often solve more peaceably and constructively those problems that cannot be avoided. Creative problem solving stresses flexibility of mind, active listening, the ability to frame problems in multiple ways, and choosing the best ways—among a broad range of skills and decisional procedures—of addressing any particular problem.

The Center for Creative Problem Solving develops curricula, research, and projects to educate students and lawyers in methods for preventing problems, where possible, and for creatively solving those problems that do exist. The Center focuses both on using the traditional analytical process more creatively and on using nontraditional problem solving processes drawn from business, psychology, economics, neuroscience, sociology, and indigenous communities (among others).

Thomas Barton, a professor at CPS at CWSL, recommends creative legal problem solving not only for the results it produces for the client, but also for the effect it has on the lawyer involved: lawyers enjoy doing creative work and resolving dilemmas. Barton says that there are two major steps involved: expanding the context of the problem so that all the dimensions are exposed and building a larger repertoire for resolution, which includes being open to whatever constitutes "success" in the client's mind.

The American Bar Association recognizes individuals and organizations that use their problem-solving skills to forge creative solutions with the Lawyer as Problem-Solver Award. According to its website:

> *Recipients will be acknowledged for their use or promotion of collaboration, negotiation, mediation, counseling, decision-making, and problem-solving skills to help parties resolve a problem in a creative and novel way. The lawyer as problem solver, in both orientation and skills, demonstrates:*
>
> * *the ability to analyze situations or to consider expert analysis from a multidisciplinary perspective, taking into account the broad array of client or party interests and the multitude of factors and circumstances that impact the "problem" presented;*
> * *the ability to translate positions into interests;*
> * *the ability to generate and assess—and to help the client or parties involved generate and assess—both conventional and novel options to address the problem; and*
> * *the ability to build consensus around an option which best addresses the goals and interests of a client or the involved participants.*

OTHER EMERGING MODELS AND ORIENTATIONS

T HE FOLLOWING approaches are emerging models that have potential for growth and align with the values and ideas discussed in
this book. They are not included in Susan Daicoff's models of comprehensive law, but they have caught my attention. The previous
approaches have thousands of followers who would usually be able to
tell us that they practice restorative justice or that they are collaborative lawyers. Some of these approaches may not even be recognized as
separate models—even by their practitioners. They may not have as
many followers. Some are just beginning to develop.

In addition to these, there are dozens of alternative dispute resolution (ADR) models that are emerging: the settlement counsel model,
early neutral evaluation, early case assessment, and others. There are
tools like public conversations, conversation cafés and world cafés that
offer opportunities for group resolution.

One of the great characteristics of this movement is that every
lawyer can create a model that fits his or her practice. When shared,
these new models can propagate. Many offspring can result, sharing
characteristics with their ancestors but having the uniqueness of their
creators.

Unbundled Lawyer as Peacemaker
by Forrest (Woody) Mosten[1]

Unbundling[2] is not a new concept. It is currently used in law offices worldwide.[3]

Essentially, unbundling is an agreement between the client and lawyer to limit the scope of services that the lawyer renders. Many of the consumer benefits of unbundling come from mediation to encourage the empowerment of the parties.

A working definition of unbundling is that the client is in charge of selecting one or several discrete lawyering tasks contained within the full service package.

There are numerous replicable models of lawyers successfully unbundling their services to increase legal access. Unbundling can be either vertical[4] or horizontal.[5] Vertical unbundling is breaking up the lawyer role

---

1. Excerpted from: *Lawyer as Peacemaker: Building a Successful Law Practice Without Ever Going to Court*; Published in FAMILY LAW QUARTERLY, Vol. 43, No. 3 (Fall 2009) p. 489–518. © 2009 by the American Bar Association. Reprinted here by permission of author.

2. Also known as limited scope representation, discrete task representation, and legal coaching

3. See Chart developed by the National Center for State Courts (www.ncsconline.org) describing the unbundling laws and rules state by state. See also sample court forms for limited representation developed by the California Judicial Council.

4. Some examples of vertical unbundling include:

Advice: If a client wants advice only, it can be purchased at an initial consultation or throughout the case as determined by the client with input from the lawyer. The lawyer and client collaborate in helping the client decide if and when further consultations may be needed.

Research: If a client wants legal research, a personal or telephonic unbundled service provides this legal information. Research may take as little as fifteen minutes or as much as ten hours. The client is in charge of determining the scope of the job and who will do the work: the lawyer, client, or a negotiated collaborative effort between the two.

Drafting: Lawyers ghostwrite letters and court pleadings for the client to transmit, or just review and comment on what the client has prepared.

Negotiation: Lawyers teach clients how to negotiate with opposing parties, court clerks, and governmental agencies.

Court appearances: If a client desires, an unbundled lawyer can convert to full representation for court appearances, hearings, and mediation. Discrete tasks are agreed on between the lawyer and client.

See F. S. Mosten, *Unbundling Legal Services ABA 2000 and FS Mosten Unbundling Legal Services to Help Divorcing Families* in KELLY BROWE OLSON AND NANCY VER STEEGH, INNOVATIONS IN FAMILY LAW PRACTICE, AFCC, 2008.

5. In horizontal unbundling, the lawyer may be engaged for the issue of spousal support only and the client will either represent himself and/or engage another representative

into a number of limited services, each service or a combination available for sale. Horizontal unbundling is the limitation of lawyer involvement to a single issue (spousal support) or combination of issues (child custody and property excluding retirement rights.)

Limitation of legal services based on informed consent and a written agreement is permitted in every state and in many Western countries.[6] Every consultation with a lawyer, therapist, or accountant that goes no further is an unbundled service: the professional has more services to offer and often either the client chooses or cannot afford the "full service package" offered by the professional. "Second opinions" are classic unbundled services: the professional limits his/her scope to review and comment on the work of another professional but does no more. Every time a lawyer writes a single letter instead of three possible letters or making several phone calls, the services are limited and unbundled. Collaborative law and limited scope representation of clients in mediation are also unbundled services as will be discussed later in this section.

If you offer unbundled services, you will be able to offer otherwise unrepresented parties your experience and skill level at a cost that they can better afford. You can be paid at your customary hourly rate, have fewer unpaid receivables, perform work that is within your competence, and give you a chance to help people who need it. Another benefit for you is that once unbundled clients try doing some of the work on their own and experience the challenges and frustrations of having do all their own work (including dealing with opposing counsel), these clients may convert to full service work and be ready to pay you the necessary retainer and additional fees. In short, unbundling prepares family law parties to be more informed and more appreciative consumers.

In addition to providing more legal access for the unrepresented public and more potential income for family lawyers, unbundling offers opportunity for peacemaking and constructive help to repair families in distress. One of the biggest deficiencies of self-representation is that pro se parties are deprived of the referrals to mental health professionals and

---

for all other issues. In the same way, a lawyer might represent a client in a hearing on single temporary child custody but the client will represent herself at subsequent hearings on child custody or at trial on all issues. Lawyer and client are in charge of determining the scope of representation and in unbundling friendly jurisdictions, the court and other party are required to honor that lawyer-client decision.

6. See Model Rule of Professional Responsibility 1.2 (c): "A lawyer may limit the scope and objectives of the representation if the limitation is reasonable under the circumstances and the client gives informed consent."

other community resources that family lawyers know about and make available to our clients.[7] If you offer unbundled services, you can provide a peacemaking perspective and encouragement in the following ways:

All-purpose Unbundled Counselor, Coach, and Advisor

The most frequent unbundled service is for clients to come in for an office consultation or schedule a phone conference to obtain advice and strategy. While many of these contacts will be to address a technical issue on the law or get your views on improving the client's position, you can use these opportunities to try to lessen overall conflict and recommend a different, more constructive perspective.

By asking questions, inquiring about possible professional referrals and looking for ways to diffuse the conflict, you may be bringing peace to the situation. Here are some possible peacemaking interventions:

- *Ask how the client, her children, and her spouse are doing. If appropriate, discuss a possible referral to family or individual therapist or other resource.*
- *If the parties are at loggerheads, ask the client how important is the issue at hand and whether it is possible just to "move-on" without expending more time or expense in trying to persuade or threaten the other side.*
- *Ask your client what he could do differently to improve the situation. At appropriate times, raise the possibility of having your client sincerely apologize for something to change the dynamics and feeling of the relationship.*

By asking questions, inquiring about possible professional referrals and looking for ways to diffuse the conflict, you may be bringing peace to the situation.

Ghostwriter for Letters, Contracts, and Court Documents

Whether you edit your unbundled client's draft or write a document for your client's signature, you have a peacemaking opportunity. Clearly, you can tone down any adversarial language or threats as well as eliminate any personal attacks. In addition, you can draft invitations to consensual

---

7. See findings in CONNIE BECK, BRUCE SALES, AND RICHARD K. HAHN, SELF-REPRESENTATION IN DIVORCE CASES, ABA 1993.

dispute resolution options, apologies, mutually beneficial solutions, and preventive planning that can help both parties. In those states that require ghostwriters to disclose their identity on court pleadings in order to be relieved from making a full appearance,[8] your peacemaking drafting will not only effectively support your clients' positions but also create a positive and resolution-focused impression for ghostwriting with judicial officers and other attorneys.[9]

Negotiation Planner and Simulation Role Player
Self represented parties need help in preparing for negotiations that range from a short telephone call to a full blown court mandatory settlement conference. You can be invaluable in helping your clients think through what they really need rather than what they have been demanding (interests rather than positions). You can help modify (lower) their expectations by helping them think about "what they can live with" rather than their legal entitlements or their moral/psychological justifications for retribution, reparations, or other pay-back for past wrongs committed by the other party. You can give a short primer on "win-win" strategies, how to frame an offer, how to focus on the problem, dig under stated positions to get to interests,[10] brainstorm options, and other negotiation basics. You might even give them a copy of Getting to Yes or other negotiation book or article.

If you role-play with your client, you can give your client the opportunity to "sit in the shoes" of their spouse: the first step to understanding and empathy.[11]

---

8. See Ghostwriting Rules for Florida, Colorado and other states, www.unbundledlaw .org.

9. Once filed with the court or submitted into evidence, pleadings and exhibits (often letters sent between parties) are part of the public record. Children of the parties, business associates, IRS, and the press have open access to these court files. A peacemaking approach to drafting such documents may have a long term effect on the personal and financial future of both parties.

10. "Interests motivate people; they are the silent movers behind the hubbub of positions. Your position is something you have decided on. Your interests are what caused you to so decide" (Fisher, Ury, and Patton, 1991, p. 41).

11. Consider using a video recorder so your client can replay this simulation at home. Another viable option is for your client to bring a friend or family member to provide honest feedback and suggestions to improve negotiation performance.

Shadow Court Coach

While some states have court rules and approved forms for limited scope court appearances,[12] the basic unbundled role is for the party to self represent in the courtroom with the unbundled lawyer helping in litigation preparation.[13]

In addition to recommending which court pleadings to prepare and help with drafting, some other tasks that you can perform as court coach are:

Prepare Documents and Visual Exhibits: *You can help your client organize and select documents, make sufficient copies for the court and opposing party, and provide summary of all exhibits to be presented.*

Practice Opening and Closing Statements: *You can help clients write outlines or actual narratives of their statements. You can help your client find reasonable approaches that will also not further escalate tensions and make it more possible for the family relationship to be repaired later.*

Direct and Cross-Examination: *In the same way that you highlight key points for opening and closing statements, you can prepare your client as a witness to present direct testimony and get ready for the other side's (or court's) cross examination.*

Representative of Parties in Mediation as Peacemaker

You may enjoy the satisfactions of a lawyer client relationship and do not have the interest or commitment to obtain the training to serve as an impartial neutral. You can still maintain your peacemaker card by representing individual clients during the mediation process in either a full service or unbundled role. The role of consulting lawyer in mediation is different from the traditional role of counsel in family law. Unlike the adversarial duties of the court advocate or negotiating counsel to maximize

---

12. See www.unbundledlaw.org.

13. Some unbundled lawyers accompany their clients to court and sit in the public gallery. (It has been sometimes suggested that like witness counsel, the coaches can sit at counsel table—most judicial officers and legal access scholars believe that this crosses the line.) As long as the court coach does not interfere with the court proceedings (hand signals or signs clearly are not permitted), if the client wishes to pay for you to come to court to critique the client's advocacy performance and consult during breaks, nothing seems to prevent this role as well. As a mediator and collaborative attorney, I have recommended that clients take a courthouse field trip and have sometimes been invited along.

financial results and attempt not to leave any "money on the table"[14], the consulting lawyer in mediation must delicately balance the optimum short term bottom dollar result against the successful completion of a fair and informed mediated agreement. Rather than engaging in "turf struggles" over such issues as where the mediation will take place or who the mediator will be, as a consulting attorney you may adopt an approach of "let it go"—actually deferring to the process requests of the other party in order to lower conflict and make sure the case gets into mediation. Just as importantly, you can display respect and support for your client's choices made during the negotiation that may differ significantly from what a court might order or what you might have tried to negotiate.

THE COACH APPROACH TO THE PRACTICE OF LAW

California lawyer Phil Daunt has created an approach that he calls the Coach Approach to the Practice of Law, in which the lawyer works collaboratively with clients to help them transform their legal problems into opportunities for personal growth and positive change. While the development of the approach is Daunt's, there are many lawyers who have been trained as coaches and use their coaching skills in their law practices. The lawyer-coach engages the client in conversations about choice; the client's own interpretations of events; the significance to the client of those events; and their legal problems in the context of their lives, goals, aspirations, and dreams.

According to Daunt's website, http://www.coachapproachlawyers.com, there are distinctions that are in the lawyer-coach's toolbox:

- Perception and reality, story and fact, and the consequences of confusing the one for the other.
- Emotions and feelings and the consequences of confusing the one for the other.

---

14. See Michael Becker, *Representing Parties in Private Divorce Mediation*, TRIAL MAG., Aug. 2001, at 60, "Clients now seek the services of lawyers who understand and support mediation, and who possess the skills and knowledge to work effectively as consulting counsel. Lawyers often play a proactive role in mediation. Stated broadly, the consulting counsel offers information, assistance, and advice to ensure that a party makes good decisions, based on a full understanding of the law and possible outcomes. Consulting counsel usually works with his or her client in between mediation meetings, and is most often not present at the actual mediation sessions. There are times when the presence of one or both attorneys is useful, especially at the end of the mediation, when agreements are being finalized or specific options evaluated."

- The "truth" and "beliefs," the difference between disempowering beliefs and empowering beliefs, and the consequences that arise from choosing one over the other.
- Affixing blame and accepting responsibility for a legal problem and the impact that choosing one response over the other has on a client's ability to move forward toward a workable solution to his or her legal problem.
- Sin and mistake (generating either guilt or reasoned regret) and the consequences of believing that a past act was one or the other.
- Thoughts that generate adrenaline/cortisol and those that generate endorphins and the impact on the client's health of the presence of one or the other substance in the client's body.
- Motivation and inspiration and the pressure or the vacuum that results from choosing one over the other.
- Illusionary force and true power of unattached intention and the consequences of choosing thoughts and actions that create one or the other.
- Acting from a domination paradigm and a partnership paradigm and the consequences of operating from one or the other.
- What cannot be changed and what can be changed and the implications of focusing on one or the other.

Learning to distinguish blame from responsibility, then to embrace responsibility, may enable clients to explore creative solutions to legal problems and focus their energy on what can be changed, not on what is beyond their control, eventually helping them to shift their lives to new levels of productivity and fulfillment.

CONFLICT COACH

Attorney, former social worker, coach, and mediator Cinnie Nobel of Cinergy Coaching (cinergycoaching.com) is a conflict coach. According to her site:

Conflict coaching is a one-on-one process for helping individuals improve their conflict understanding and skills, to manage conflict and disputes more effectively. This definition, and variations of it, are used to describe a technique with the fundamental objective of coaching people to better engage in their interpersonal conflicts in both their personal and professional lives.

Assisting individuals with their interpersonal conflicts is not a new concept. Indeed, one of the many roles of organizational ombudsmen is to assist staff members on a one-on-one basis. In various ways others, such as union representatives, counselors from employee assistance programs, managers, supervisors, and HR professionals, routinely assist individuals with conflict situations in the workplace. Similarly, therapists, psychologists and other human services professionals assist people with conflict in their personal and professional lives. The word "coaching" however, is being used by many professionals and practitioners in these various groups, although their practices may not necessarily fit within the definition of coaching according to one of the coaching field's main organizations, the International Coach Federation (www.coachfederation.org).

APPLICATIONS OF CONFLICT COACHING

Currently, conflict coaching as a distinct technique appears to be growing mostly in workplaces as an additional option for employees and tool for mediators, whether or not there is an Integrated (Informal) Conflict Management System. This technique may be used instead of, or in tandem with, mediation and other ADR processes. In addition to helping individuals improve their conflict management skills in any context, some other applications of conflict coaching include:

- as a pre-mediation or pre-other ADR process to help individuals anticipate and prepare for any challenges and to effectively participate in the process;
- to prepare clients to actively and effectively participate in collaborative law meetings;
- as a post-mediation or post-other ADR process to help individuals with the aftermath of any unresolved matters and ways to manage ongoing interactions;
- to help managers, supervisors and others focus on aspects of their conflict conduct requiring improvement;
- to help people enhance their negotiation skills;
- as an integral part of conflict management training, to provide individualized ongoing assistance with participants' specific challenges; and,
- to facilitate self-reflective practice of conflict management professionals and others who work in any capacity with people in conflict.

Conflict coaching has gained attention and respect in workplace settings. For example, the Transportation Security Administration (TSA), an agency of the U.S. Department of Homeland Security, initiated the development of an Integrated Conflict Management System in 2003, A Conflict Management Coaching Program was an integral component of the system.

SPIRITUAL LEGAL COUNSELING

In the course of a recent month, I came across several lawyers who talked to me about combining their legal expertise with spiritual counseling. This isn't a vector with an organization or collective website. I include it here because of the synchronicity of having met lawyers in Washington, California, North Carolina, and Massachusetts who all told me that they had the idea the same week, and then meeting several others since then. I think this is going to grow.

This new breed of *spiritual legal counselor* engages in deep spiritual work that informs their counseling of clients who are interested in more than a legal approach. The lawyer combines knowledge of the legal system with spiritual guidance. Andrew Weiss is one such example. From his website, http://www.justicespirit.com:

> *Andrew combines his years of experience as a practicing lawyer with his knowledge and understanding as a mindfulness practitioner and teacher to provide spiritual and emotional counseling to those going through legally-oriented problems. Too often the human side of events gets lost or even exacerbated when legal institutions get involved. Andrew takes up that human end of the equation, providing insight, direction, empowerment, and support.*

Legal Rebel Cheryl Conner (http://newprospectscollaborative.com/) also serves as a legal spiritual coach. A former federal prosecutor, economist, integrative educator and consultant, her work is deeply rooted in a fifteen-year apprenticeship with a Tibetan teacher. When her teacher was alive, he encouraged her to share insights gained from extensive retreat and practice in her professional life. As a clinical law professor, she cultivated reflective, humanistic and holistic perspectives, inspiring lawyers, law students, and judges to undertake personal transformation and explore alternative forms of law practice. She founded and ran Lawyers with a Holistic Perspective and was the first Contemplative Fellow in Law Teaching of the American Council of Learned Societies. Recently she hosted an inquiry with law students, envisioning a new legal system.

Since Cheryl lived in the wilderness in Lincoln, Vermont, for three years, she has been informed by earth energies and Native American sensibilities. She has traveled around the country, speaking and leading workshops and retreats, and now combines perspectives about individual transformation with a call for cross-sectoral systemic transformation arising from the collective consciousness.

CHAPTER THREE

MAKING THE TRANSITION

Are you curious about what it would be like to practice within this new paradigm? Do you wonder where to start?

The only place you can start is from where you are right now. If you are deeply engaged in a litigation practice in a big firm in the city and want to start a solo practice in a small town, your path will be different from the small-town practitioner who just wants to rearrange her practice to offer holistic choices to her clients. If you have a solid plan with goals and know that you're ready to make this transition, your path will be different than that of the lawyer who has a nagging feeling that something could be different, but isn't sure where to start. This section is an overview of the tools that can help you make the transition.

COACHING

The International Coaching Federation (ICF) defines coaching as partnering with clients in a thought-provoking and creative process that inspires them to maximize their personal and professional potential.

—www.coachfederation.org

Coaches help people improve their performances and enhance the quality of their lives. They are trained to listen, to observe and share their observations with clients. Coaches honor the clients as the experts in their lives and work and believe that every client is capable, creative, resourceful, and whole. Standing on this foundation, the coach's responsibility is to:

1. Align with and clarify what the client wants to accomplish.
2. Encourage client self-awareness and discovery.
3. Empower the client to generate solutions and strategies.
4. Hold the client responsible and accountable.

Professional coaches provide an ongoing partnership designed to help clients produce results in their personal and professional lives. When I was in the swirl of transforming my practice, I was lucky enough to find a coach who helped me set manageable goals and prioritize my to-do lists. With the help of Coach Brad Swift, I created my life purpose and organized my life and my practice around this purpose and my values. I found ways of earning money doing what I love. I chose clients whose work I enjoyed. Later, I trained and became a coach for others, and I've seen these lawyers blossom and prosper. If you take only one piece of advice in this book, choose to get a coach.

Choosing a Coach

Each coach has a different set of experiences and a different toolbox. Most coaches have the tools to get you where you want to go if you accept the coaching. With lawyers, that "if" is a big contingency.

Choose a coach whose intelligence you respect. Typically, we lawyers are smarter than the average bear, and you should make sure you find a coach who is just as smart as you are. I often recommend that lawyers choose coaches who are also lawyers. You will be challenged by your coach. If you are serious about creating results, you don't want someone who buys your excuses instead of gently confronting them. Among coaches, there are many tales of working with lawyers who attempted to run circles around their coaches.

Choose a coach you can trust. As you develop your plans, you'll be talking about the most intimate details of your life—exploring what has stopped you in the past and creating breakthroughs for the future. You want to be able to share those vulnerable parts of yourself and try out ideas in a safe place before you take them outside the coaching relationship.

Choose a coach you like. You're going to be spending some quality time with your coach. Why not make sure it is someone you enjoy being with?

Finding a Coach

There are many ways to find the right coach. There are enough coaches who are also lawyers that there are special sections of the major coaching organizations. A special interest group of lawyer-coaches meets by telephone on a monthly basis. Before trying a Google search, ask around to see if anyone you know already has a relationship with a coach. A call to your bar's Lawyer Assistance program is likely to result in some local referrals. The International Coach Federation (www.coachfederation.org) is a credentialing organization with a referral program.

Coach or Therapist?

For lawyers who are under tremendous stress, there is often the question of whether to seek a coach or a therapist. *Coaching* emphasizes action, accountability, and follow-through. It provides a structure for doing what you may already know how to do, but haven't been able to do on your own. Often, a natural outcome of good coaching is to help you feel better, but it is different than therapy.

Therapy focuses on resolving psychological and emotional difficulties from the past, which hamper emotional functioning in the present. Therapy helps you deal with present circumstances in more emotionally healthy ways; it treats dysfunctional behavior. However, therapy and coaching are not mutually exclusive—some of my coaching clients also work with therapists. It is a good idea for the coach and therapist to be in sync and not working at cross-purposes. Some coaches are also trained in therapy and, if you think you might require both coaching and therapy, you could seek someone with both skill sets and training.

You should find a therapist if:

- You have suicidal thoughts or thoughts about harming others.
- You have been diagnosed or believe you may have phobias, post-traumatic stress disorder (PTSD), eating disorders, addictions, or bipolar disorder.
- You are depressed or chronically feel hopeless. Symptoms of depression include sleep problems, appetite problems, concentration problems, self-esteem problems, and low mood.
- You are extraordinarily angry, confused, anxious, or desperate. Signs of anxiety include sweaty palms, racing heart, tightness in the chest, difficulty concentrating, etc.
- You are primarily focused on exploring and making sense of your past emotional experiences and are less willing, or ready, to look to the future.
- You don't feel you can cope with daily living.

MENTOR OR COACH?

I consider myself to be both a mentor and a coach. Sometimes I play one role and sometimes the other. I mentor many law students and lawyers. When it gets to the point of a regularly scheduled call, I switch to the paid coach role but combine that with my mentoring role.

Coaches sometimes do what mentors do, but more so. A coach may not even be in the same industry as the person being coached. He or she offers structure and accountability. Acting as a partner, a coach helps the coachee create goals and the detailed plans for how to reach those goals. The coach holds the coachee accountable for taking the steps they have co-created. Coaches are on the hook with you, sharing the commitment to the goal. With a coach, you can risk looking bad while you work through what stops you from succeeding. Coaches generally charge for their time, and you schedule time together on a regular basis. Therefore, there is more structure and often more results than with other kinds of helpers.

Mentors have already gotten somewhere you want to go or have reached a goal to which you aspire. They share their experience and advice, which the mentee can take or leave. Often, it is very good advice and experience. Mentors also offer contacts and may even introduce you to someone else who can help. You usually want to impress your mentor, and sharing your fears and mistakes may or may not be a good idea, depending on the mentor. Mentors are usually volunteers, and you work around their schedules.

Do you know what to do but still procrastinate? Consider consulting a coach to get yourself moving. Is money a concern? The more you pay that coach, the more motivated you will be to do what you say you will do. Are you disciplined and self-motivated but need to meet the right people? A mentor will provide that kind of guidance. Do you need someone who understands the ins and outs of your particular industry? If so, make sure you choose a mentor or a coach with mentoring ability and experience in that industry. For example, most lawyers find that they prefer to work with a coach or mentor who can understand the nuances of how ethical rules shape marketing choices.

MAKING A LIVING PRACTICING HOLISTIC LAW

Approximately a decade ago, I decided to focus totally on peacemaking and refuse any further litigation. While I was afraid that I would eat tuna casserole four times a week, with the support of my wife, I turned down large retainers and referred all potential court clients to competent litigators in my community. My practice is now divided roughly into two equal parts. I serve as a neutral mediator 50 percent of the time, and the other half is composed of four representative roles: client representative during mediations presided by other neutrals (often with a litigator co-counsel); collaborative lawyer; unbundled lawyer for self-represented parties; and transaction lawyer building relationship agreements such as premarital, post-marital, cohabitation, and other matters involving long range relationships such as business partnerships, probate disputes, and adoption and surrogacy agreements.

Rather than being a financial disaster, my decision to be a non-court family lawyer resulted in rapid growth of my practice beyond my most optimistic expectations. My gross receipts increased by over 33 percent during my first year of practice and uncollectable fees went down from 30 percent of gross billables to 2 percent.

The financial benefits, though important, pale in comparison to the joy and rejuvenation I feel towards practicing family law. Although I am over 60 years old, I get up in the morning ready to run to the office. I cannot imagine retiring from law practice. Mounting the one horse of "non-litigation," I have rediscovered that it is not only possible, but personally and professionally rewarding to serve as a family lawyer. What I do, day after day, is to work for peace for my clients and their families and I have become increasingly comfortable with my role as peacemaker.

Forrest (Woody) Mosten

We all know lawyers who are not making a substantial living in their traditional practice areas, especially in the recent economic downturn. And we all know others who are somehow able to maintain an abundant lifestyle no matter what they try. This movement is no different. I conducted a survey recently. Only 34 people participated, so it is by no means scientific. The anecdotal evidence was interesting. I asked them to report their income from litigation as compared to their income from a more peacemaking-oriented practice.

Current Income

More than $500,000 per year	0.0%
$250,000 to $500,000 per year	14.7
$200,000 to $249,000 per year	14.7
$150,000 to $199,000 per year	11.8
$100,000 to $149,000 per year	8.8
$50,000 to $99,000 per year	26.5
Less than $50,000 per year	23.5

Income Before Peacemaking Practice

More than $500,000 per year	0.0%
$250,000 to $500,000 per year	21.4
$200,000 to $249,000 per year	14.3
$150,000 to $199,000 per year	21.4
$100,000 to $149,000 per year	7.1
$50,000 to $99,000 per year	25.0
Less than $50,000 per year	10.7

In comments, some indicated that their income had actually gone up after they adopted the new type of practice:

- The change in income is largely due to the fact that, in litigation, I often don't charge for all the hours that I spend on a case, like having to review the case before a continued hearing and other trial preparation time. In mediation and collaborative cases, I bill for almost all the time I spend on the case.

- My income has actually grown somewhat since I began the shift, primarily because collaborative clients are happier clients and more willing to pay, whereas litigation clients, no matter how happy they may be with the result, tend to forget about their lawyer's bill when the case is over.
- I have not had a change in income, partly due to the limited number of collaborative cases I have handled. However, my quality of life has improved by taking on this type of work!
- I was better at putting transactions together than fighting in court, so that probably has put me into a practice type that I market better.
- I have a high percentage of satisfied clients paying their bills (low collectibles) and good referrals from previous clients, as well as low-to-no advertising costs.

Some reported transitional changes in income and unrelated issues that affected income:

- After I first made the switch, I had two lean years. Now my income is as high as it ever was.
- My annual income decreased considerably when I left the partnership in 1993. Starting in 2001, I followed the Barbara Brennan School of Healing in Florida for five years, [which] took more than 50 percent of my working hours. After graduation in 2006, my income did not increase. I could not find energy to continue my practice full time again. In 2007–2008 I took a sabbatical period and started thinking about how jurisprudence and conflict resolution should be shaped in a sustainable society. Since my return, I am changing my practice, and my work. At the moment, my turnover and income is extremely low. I write articles and expect that my new activities will generate a much better income within one year. In any event: I feel much happier the way I am working instead of practicing adversarial law.
- My income decreased due to the economic crisis and my own drive to have more time on my hands.
- I believe the recession and failing real estate market have contributed more to my loss of income than the change in my mission.

Or that their work habits changed and that affected their income:

- I work many fewer hours per week. I have a more balanced life that allows me to do many other things that interest me. My primary other source of income is my husband's earnings.
- I do less intentionally.

In my survey, I also asked for comments about quality of life.

- [The major change in] the quality of my life is the decrease in stress. When I don't have frequent court appearances and deadlines, my whole demeanor changes. I have more time for myself, and I'm much happier and relaxed.
- I am a lot happier and I live on less.
- I am more in charge of my schedule.
- [I have a] more positive quality of life as I work with both clients and colleagues with a different attitude. I also have enjoyed getting to know collaborative colleagues from many different communities. I do not wake up at night so often, worried about my cases.
- I love my practice, for the most part. I used to be a criminal defense attorney and now I get to work with families. Clearly, I like working with and helping folks through distressing times in their lives.

And finally, I invited the respondents to give advice to anyone considering making the change:

- I think the practice of law is changing, and it's better to be at the forefront than left behind. Most clients want a different approach, so it makes both business and quality-of-life sense.
- Collaborative professionals (especially lawyers) need advanced training and experience before they really have a clue what they are doing in a collaborative case. It is much harder than litigation. It requires far more thought and intellect.
- Be authentic and very present. Do not give up. Following your passion will reveal itself in the quality of your work and the abundance of your practice.
- I still welcome litigation if I like the client and feel it's the right thing to do, and that we are the right fit to work together. That doesn't mean I am glad that the client is in litigation, only that as long as litigation is around, I'll probably keep doing some contested divorces for the right clients.
- The important thing is to make a plan about transitioning, setting goals, and trying to meet them. Otherwise, it simply won't happen. Finally, and perhaps most importantly, turn down the cases you don't want by telling the litigation referral that you've changed your practice and appreciate their referral, and send it to another attorney who hopefully will reciprocate with a mediation or collaborative referral. It can be hard to turn down cases at first, but it's necessity to make a transition.

WON'T PEOPLE LAUGH AT ME AND CALL ME WEIRD OR FLAKY?

Have fun, be crazy, be weird. Go out and screw up! You're going to anyway, so you might as well enjoy the process.

—Anthony Robbins

The short answer is, yes; they probably will. But if you value your own happiness, you won't make your decisions based on whether someone else is going to laugh at you. If you're worried about it and feeling a lack of confidence, you may find that you are uncomfortable with some reactions from others because you're having those same doubts yourself. Address your doubts. Others will sense your confidence and take you seriously.

When I started practicing law as a peacemaker and healer, I ran into a lot of laughter. "Lawyers as healers?" nearly sent people into hysterical fits. However, clients remembered me and sent their friends. A 2003 article about me was still one of my top referral sources in 2008 when I closed my office. I haven't had a telephone book ad in several years, and clients are willing to work with me only by phone and Internet just so they can get my perspective. Ten years later, I'm writing a book for the American Bar Association (ABA) and was named one of the Legal Rebels (www.legalrebels.com) for being an innovator and changemaker in the profession. Ha, ha, indeed.

Of course, I am no different from anyone else, and my heart is filled with many fears. But despite everything, the fruits of my life speak for me, and if some day a tragedy happens, I know that I have not spent my life without taking risks.

—Paulo Coelho

REDESIGNING YOUR LAW PRACTICE

Every day you may make progress. Every step may be fruitful. Yet there will stretch out before you an ever-lengthening, ever-ascending, ever-improving path. You know you will never get to the end of the journey. But this, so far from discouraging, only adds to the joy and glory of the climb.

—*Sir Winston Churchill*

You can improve the quality of your life and practice, and begin the transition toward a more holistic workplace, by making simple changes and shifts at your office. This includes changing the physical space, your relationships with co-workers, and the systems in your office. We're going to explore some of those new ideas in this section.

THE PHYSICAL SPACE

Are you comfortable in your workspace? Is it a welcoming place for clients? Does your office express your unique personality? Would small changes make a big difference in the quality of your office life?

My work area had bulletin board space where I could post reminders and photographs. There was space for me to display personal items like vases made by my children. I could keep reference books at arm's length. It was usually a mess, but no one saw it except my co-workers. The public areas were clean and professional. It was the best of all worlds.

In the past few years I've been in some wonderful nontraditional law offices. Round conference tables, gurgling water fountains, workplace altars, espresso machines, and other unique expressions have found their way into law offices that still look professional and workable.

One coaching client of mine was inspired to have a feng shui consultant work with her on redesigning her corporate counsel office. After redesigning the office, she noticed that everyone wanted to come by and visit her. Meetings were being scheduled in her office. She was actually glad—she didn't want to leave her office either. She began to feel a sense of community with her co-workers, who stopped by more and more often.

Workplace Thinking Has Been Altared

By Pat McHenry Sullivan

In 1976, I accidentally discovered that many workers keep spiritual items in their desks. While seeking correction fluid at a temporary job, I found a book on Buddhism and a Bible. At another desk, an inspiring quote on beautiful paper fell out of an expense file. During hushed conversations, co-workers shared what they hid in their desks.

Today, spirit has come out of hiding places in desk drawers and onto the desk tops. Some workers select and use devotional items with such care that they create altars.

Altars are a natural response to the need for respectful reflection wherever we are—at home, in a temple, in the woods, at work. They can last many lifetimes or be temporary and spontaneous. "Stop here long enough to consider what matters," altars invite. "Reconnect here to the wonder of life. Gain strength and guidance."

Because of business practice and labor laws, workplace altars need to be discreet. The underground workplace of Patsy Attwood, a station agent for the San Francisco Bay Area Rapid Transit System, is an example. You could walk by and never notice how she has altered her space to integrate faith and work. Attwood's glass-walled booth is enlivened by plants and flowers. Whenever she enters her space, she blesses it. On her phone console, a prayer she wrote helps her live her values moment to moment.

Attwood's inner work helps her deal better with job stress, like an angry customer whose ticket wouldn't work. "When he approached me with an eat-you-up attitude, my stomach instantly jumped," she said, "like it does in an earthquake." As the man stepped closer, Attwood prayed, "Lord, help me." Inner turmoil turned to peace. She then dared to ask, "Why are you talking to me this way? I want to help you." Surprised, the customer relaxed, and she fixed his problem. Later, he sought her out. "I don't know what you did, but after I talked with you," he said, "my day was great."

"Whatever we put in our workspace can have a profound effect," says William S. Johnson, a Santa Fe businessman. He notes that many executives have "ego walls" filled with photos and trophies designed to impress people. Others use their space for enrichment. "Sometimes altar artifacts provide a nice icebreaker to initiate conversations between strangers." Johnson keeps a Bible at his desk and uses it often, but he has never seen a religious text on anyone else's desk. "I see more religious symbolism in New York City taxicabs than I ever see in corporate offices."

That, according to managers and labor lawyers, is fitting. If having spiritual items at work helps employees be less stressed and more productive, employers often say that's fine. [Note: You need to know your company policy on displaying religious items, and should check with your direct supervisor, before doing so.] Practices that interrupt business are never okay.

Most employees agree that their right to practice spirituality at work is balanced by other employees' rights to practice different values. An unspoken etiquette is evolving: in private space (desk drawer or a section of the desk that faces away from visitors), it's usually acceptable to place small symbols of a particular faith. In more public space, including office walls and desk sections that face visitors, employees need to be extra careful not to make others uncomfortable.

Many workplace altars begin instinctively. During a hard time, Brenda Fuller, a Washington, D.C., legal secretary, placed a prayer she loved by her telephone. Later she added a photo that makes her laugh and a quote by Goethe to go boldly toward her dreams. Tiny frames filled with prayers graced her computer monitor stand. People on the go also have altars. Inside his locker, a firefighter posts meaningful words and pictures. A meter maid keeps devotional materials in her truck. So does a carpenter, who also blesses his tools and each task.

While attending conferences and seminars in fluorescent-lit buildings, publicist Kathryn Hall builds a mini-altar of leaves, a bit of moss, or other natural items that draw her attention as she walks to the site. Each day the altar grows, often because fellow attendees add to it. Afterward, Hall returns each item to its setting with a prayer of gratitude.

The PBS documentary Jane Goodall: Reason for Hope *shows ecologist Goodall carrying four symbols of hope wherever she goes. A leaf from a tree that survived the atomic bomb in Nagasaki speaks to the restorative power of nature. Chunks from the Berlin wall and the South African prison where Nelson Mandela and his comrades were incarcerated call forth the power of the human spirit to overthrow injustice. A stuffed toy chimpanzee, touched by attendees at Goodall's workshops, spreads laughter and hope among people throughout the world.*

The documentary didn't use the word "altar," let alone "workplace altar." As Goodall spoke about each symbol, however, faces in her audiences glowed. There was reverence not for the items themselves, but for the spirit they evoked, and that's what altars everywhere are about.

—Originally published November 28, 1999, in "Vision and Values" columns for the joint publication of the *San Francisco Chronicle* and the *San Francisco Examiner.* Reprinted here with permission of the author, Pat McHenry Sullivan. Pat McHenry Sullivan is a spirit and work pioneer, www.spiritworkandmoney.com.

Want a Smoothly Operating Productive Law Office? Create a Collaborative Workplace.

By Dolly Garlo

Would you like an office environment where work seems to flow effortlessly without struggle, you produce extraordinary results with ease, and you leave at the end of the day exhilarated rather than exhausted? Think about that one day where everything worked: co-counsel provided excellent summaries of the applicable law before you needed them; your legal secretary efficiently combined it into one organized document; you found the file completely in order and could immediately put your fingers on exactly what you needed; you were able to focus on finalizing the document without interruption using a computer program that functioned flawlessly; the transmittal letter and exhibits were assembled, labeled, and the proper number of copies prepared; the printer produced the final document without jamming; the file clerk arrived at your door on time, got to the courthouse an hour before the filing deadline, and pulled into a parking space by the front door that someone just left with time on the meter. Call it synchronicity, synergy, flow, or magic, most lawyers have had at least one such experience. It is possible to employ some simple strategies to recreate such experiences consistently rather than randomly—okay, maybe except for the parking.

Lawyers get little to no training in running a business. Operating an effective law practice is not covered in the typical law school curriculum. How to develop a successful professional practice and handle the "business" of law is likewise not taught in most law firms. Formal mentoring in these subjects is often lacking since senior lawyers have little training beyond their own experience, perpetuating tradition rather than promoting business innovation. The art of advocacy taught in law school, adversarial in nature, is not conducive to the effective management of time, people, information, finances, and related day-to-day work systems. Alternative Dispute Resolution legal training provides some subject matter transferable to creating a successful office environment, with its focus on interests, values, and minimizing conflict, yet this practice is generally applied to resolving litigation and not to typical law firm work situations.

So how can you create a collaborative workplace where everyone joyfully contributes their best efforts to more easily and productively create the intended results? Volumes have been written on business management, which is too overwhelming to administer while trying to simply get the legal work done, anyway. However, consistent and uniform application of some simple concepts in the four areas of Team Alignment, Responsibility, Communication, *and* Operations *can promote an effective office environment without the related information overload. While simple, to work in practice there must be a commitment to consistency of application at all levels of the organization best started by the express agreement of each member to use them. They are* basic *performance standards applicable to* all, *a deviation from traditional top-down management style.*

The foundation for use of these concepts is the recognition that making a business operate optimally is difficult, if not impossible, for one person to do alone. Any lawyer just starting out in practice or leaving a firm to go solo can readily tell you how many hats there are to wear to get through a work day, a billing month, and simply produce the legal work, let alone deliver comprehensive legal services. A varied group, and not just attorneys, is needed to handle the business of law. In a large firm they may be organized on one campus and in a smaller operation they may be contracted, off-site or geographically dispersed. Even in this technological age an attorney produces very little legal work without the assistance and support of a number of other people. It is much easier and more effective if that group operates as a Team.

In building a team and working as one, the first requirement is to acknowledge the tremendous contribution of each person to the operation of the business—the ultimate delivery of and payment for excellent legal service. From that perspective, we must treat one another as equally important to the final outcome, no matter what role we play. The lawyer, although burdened with the ultimate responsibility for the outcome, is no more important than the firm's file clerk and office manager—if the work cannot be produced consistently, timely, with client satisfaction and regular collection of fees, the business is not running. Without the synergy[1] produced by that conscious focus, the group is simply a disorganized sum of various parts, rather than an exponentially high-performance team. Law firm culture is the glue that either holds the firm together or doesn't; and is directly and subtly shaped by the attitudes and actions of its licensed attorneys. That culture determines the commitment and level of involvement of all members, as well as the overall success of the firm, its management initiatives and its objectives. As keeper and steward of that culture, it is each attorney's responsibility to hold this focus and provide the example needed to maintain it.

Holding that focus requires a willingness to suspend an overactive belief in self-importance or superiority, and is aided by a commitment to collaboration. Collaboration involves an effort to work with another to find a solution that fully satisfies the concerns of both people. A high level of assertiveness demonstrates strong concern for self, and a high level of cooperation demonstrates strong concern for others. A high level of both must be present for collaboration. Thus, willingness to both speak up without fear and listen fully must be fostered among all individuals in the workplace, by encouraging those who generally speak to listen and those who generally listen to contribute. Collaboration is effective when there is an objective to learn, merge insights on a problem from people with different perspectives, to gain commitment by incorporating others' concerns, work through hard feelings, and correct or avoid interference with an interpersonal relationship.[2] These are standard operational goals of a personal service oriented workplace, dependent upon the actions of a variety of people. These goals can be easily thwarted if the competitive nature of law practice is also used as a management style.

---

1. Synergy is the "behavior of whole systems unpredicted by the behavior or integral characteristics of any parts of the system when the parts are considered only separately." R. Buckminster Fuller, *Critical Path* 251, St. Martin's Press (1981). "Bucky's" favorite example was chrome nickel steel, an alloy with ten times the tensile strength of its weakest component and six times the tensile strength of the strongest. Examples of synergy occur in all of nature, especially applicable to human systems.

2. K.W. Thomas & R.H. Kilmann, *Thomas-Kilmann Conflict Mode Instrument* (1974), available through Consulting Psychologists Press, Inc. at www.cpp-db.com (last visited on May 15, 2001).

Emphasizing collaboration also supports the notion of personal mastery by each member of the organization, characterized by several elements conducive to business and professional excellence: sense of purpose, an ability to work with change rather than resist it, commitment to continual learning and creativity, and deep connection to others and life itself. These elements of personal mastery are considered "a special level of proficiency in every aspect of life—personal and professional." Contrary to popular belief, supporting individuals' personal mastery has been shown to contribute to rather than undermine organizational success. Promoting the full development of each member of an organization supports his or her reciprocal commitment[3] to the organization.

That being said, a coordinated team can be established and maintained through three basic steps of Team Alignment.

First, secure the express willingness of all members *of the organization to support the organization's purpose, rules, policies, and goals, and to work together. Include, at a minimum, acknowledgments to refrain from abandoning a teammate in need and from letting personal issues stand in the way of the applicable task. Paradoxically, the latter is best secured by the organization's express willingness to acknowledge and support the personal lives and needs of its members. This is commonly known as creating a* win–win *environment.*

Second, it is important to engage in regular dialogue *with the entire team by way of regular meetings. Schedule meetings with reasonable frequency, perhaps every two weeks at first and then monthly after a routine is established; and for a fixed duration related to the size of the group and the agenda. Get the agreement of the group members as to the most convenient time. Utilize a planned agenda of work related topics to which all members can contribute, and at the beginning of each meeting, ask for a round-table contribution from each member.*

Finally, alignment requires a commitment to reach resolution *in conflict situations, which takes into account everyone's interests, rather than compromise: in which someone (who might be you) must give up something. This commitment to resolution takes time, energy, and creativity; and making the effort is worth the results.*

The second concept involves the demonstration of Responsibility. *Basic to this concept is for each person to acknowledge his or her own*

---

3. Peter M. Senge, The Fifth Discipline: The Art & Practice of the Learning Organization 311, Doubleday (1990). *See also id.* at pp. 139–173.

responsibility in every situation and avoid blaming others or attempts to justify a negative result.

One of the most important ways to demonstrate responsibility is by completing agreements, *in particular, time agreements. While attorneys are keen about this with courts and adversaries, the practice internally with co-workers and staff (and in personal relationships) often suffers.*

Make only agreements that you are willing and intend to keep. *Think about how often something you say may be counted on by someone else, and consciously avoid making comments inadvertently or in passing. Practice this by eliminating even the socially appropriate but insincere temptation to say "Let's have lunch" or "I'll get back with you on that" when you have no intention of doing so.*

Communicate any potential *broken agreement at the first appropriate opportunity with as much advance notice as possible. When it appears you are not going to have a report or research summary done when you thought you would, let the intended recipient know so they can stop anticipating it and re-adjust their schedule as well. This demonstrates you are a steward of your word.*

Similarly, clear up any broken *agreement at the first appropriate opportunity; don't avoid it or wait to see if you will be challenged. Acknowledge your responsibility with an apology.*

Clear Communication *is the third important concept.*

The foundation of good communication is active *listening. This includes acknowledging what another speaker communicates, such as by repeating or summarizing what was said; you also need to acknowledge within yourself that it's true for them and honor their perspective, whether or not you agree with it.*

After careful listening comes the art of speaking supportively. *This requires a willingness to* compassionately *tell the truth and to receive the same from others, without making judgments of "wrong" or "right," as well as to communicate concerns directly to the person involved rather than someone else. This contributes to resolution and prevents the potential harms of gossip and ineffective or possibly damaging triangulation.*

As with active listening, delivering spoken communications is more effective when you clarify your communication *through verification of the response. Communication is not the message you send, it is the response you get. Don't simply assume a message has been accurately sent or received; ask the listener to repeat his or her understanding. Then you can clarify further if there is misunderstanding or plain missed communication.*

Agree as a team that when you have a doubt about what's being communicated, you will examine your feelings and intuition, and include a focus on the emotional tone behind the words, *to confirm what you think you heard; particularly if you experience a sense of unease or upset. Communication is delivered with more than just words.*

Upsets are an opportunity to learn something important. If an upset lasts longer than 30 minutes, agree that each party will seek input from an objective *advisor and return to complete the communication later. Upsets in communication often result from the thoughts, feelings, past experiences, and sometimes personal baggage someone brings to the conversation, rather than from disagreement over the subject of the current conversation. Agree that each party will do an internal check to see what their part may be in creating or maintaining the upset, and then attempt resolution.*

In the busy world of the law office, it is also helpful whenever possible, to honor the importance of another's work and time by putting communications in writing, *unless it is something urgent where disrupting them may be necessary. Production by all members of the law office is hampered by disruptions caused by the need to shift focus from the work in front of them to an oral comment from someone passing by a workstation or doorway. This applies equally to attorneys and all legal support or administrative staff members. Such disruptions are costly to operations, not to mention disrespectful. Use of e-mail, electronic scheduling, voice mail, or even a good old memo pad can significantly improve everyone's productive time, benefiting the organization as a whole.*

If this level of honor and respect in communications exists between members of the organization regardless of hierarchy, it is amazing how much more forthcoming everyone will be with concerns, problem-solving ideas, and information necessary for the organization to grow and flourish. This prevents what is known as "mismanagement of agreement,"[4] a costly problem often more insidious and harmful than actual disagreement. Members of an organization will simply agree to things they really think are stupid or unworkable because they are afraid to tell the truth from their perspective about what may be a really bad outcome.

Aligned team members each committed to act from a high level of personal responsibility and engage in clear and respectful communications can much more effectively address Operations *in the law office. This is the fourth area of focus. Smooth operations result from a belief*

---

4. *See* Jerry Harvey, The Abilene Paradox and Other Meditations on Management, Jossey-Bass (1996).

and recognition that each person in the organization wants to do their best and be acknowledged for it,[5] a commitment to mutually create an environment conducive to that result, and a basic understanding of systems. Systems thinking *involves looking at wholes, interrelationships rather than linear cause and effect chains, moving pictures rather than snapshots in time concerning how things happen or get done. It involves seeing circles of influence and patterns that repeat themselves over time causing results that improve or deteriorate. Systems are the "what" and "how" of activities, dependent for consistency and effectiveness upon clearly defined, outlined (and communicated) processes, rather than a focus on "who" is doing them. In many cases problems arise from flaws in the system rather than from the failure of a single individual who is often doing their best to implement an unclear or inaccurate procedure or instruction for getting something done. They become a convenient target for blame without ever fixing the underlying problem, which allows the problem to recur. A focus on creating and maintaining effective office systems requires only a few key commitments.*

First, when problems arise look to the system for corrections. *Are the steps clearly designed to accomplish the desired outcome? See where the system may have failed and correct that. Avoid blaming the individuals involved allowing everyone to learn something from the situation to fine-tune the system, do things differently next time and prevent a recurrence.*

Encourage individuals involved with a problem to take their solutions *to the person who can do something about it. Similarly, be open to such proposed solutions when that person is you. Operations, and improvements to them, require course corrections—implemented without invalidating the people involved. Create an operational environment that does whatever it takes to support all team members and promote their best efforts.*

Focus on what works. Be positive. Ask "What's needed here?" not "What's wrong?"; "How can we do this differently?" rather

---

5. A survey of health care employees illustrates this important point. They ranked the following 10 job attributes as follows: 1. full appreciation of work done; 2. being included in on things; 3. understanding of personal problems; 4. job security; 5. good wages; 6. interesting work; 7. opportunity for promotion and growth; 8. organizational loyalty to workers; 9. good working conditions; 10. tactful discipline. This information was updated with 1985 and 1995 statistics, showing subtle changes in ranking relative to changes in the health care industry. "Job security" rose to number 3 and was very narrowly behind number 2, "being included in on things." "Full appreciation of work done" remained first. See CHARLES R. MCCONNELL, THE EFFECTIVE HEALTH CARE SUPERVISOR, 4th Ed., 1997.

than "Why isn't this working?"; "How can we?" rather than "Why don't you?" *Attempt to consciously use language conducive to generating creative ideas, rather than reiterating what has not been effective or emphasizing what went wrong. Law practice hones the art of uncovering potential problems. Effective office systems require a focus on the continual development of solutions. Focus on what outcome you want to create, rather than on the problems themselves.*

Finally, commit to optimize every event. *Be effective and efficient. Work to add value and seek improvement in the way things are done whenever possible. Seek out and acknowledge the contributions from everyone involved in a particular operation. Each person involved has a certain level of expertise to contribute from his or her particular perspective. Developing those contributions can save time and expense, improve results, streamline operations, and create a more enjoyable workplace.*

A true team orientation and conscious focus on respect, honesty, sincere accountability, appreciation, and a willingness to look at the interrelated nature of people and activities in operating a law practice may be a fundamental shift in the way we currently view the workplace and our relationships within it. That shift does not require an advanced business degree, but rather a commitment to strengthening individual characters, which in combination produces extraordinary results. A desire to achieve such results requires moving away from the "conventional view of leadership [that] emphasizes positional power and conspicuous accomplishment [and instead] creating a domain in which we continually learn and become more capable of participating in our unfolding future . . .[setting] the stage on which predictable miracles, synchronistic in nature, can— and do—occur." [6]

NEW OFFICE PRACTICES

If you are operating a nontraditional law practice, how do you communicate that fact to potential clients? The conversation begins when they make first contact. Your website is an opportunity to share the benefits of your new practice.

I soon learned that it was my task to discourage calls from people who were not my clients. There are many people who relish the opportunity to get a lawyer on the line and ask them questions with no intention of ever hiring

---

6. JOSEPH JAWORSKI, SYNCHRONICITY: THE INNER PATH OF LEADERSHIP 182, Berrett-Koehler Publishers (1996).

them. It wasn't a good use of my time. I used my outgoing telephone message as a tool for eliminating callers who were not my clients. My firm name (approved by the North Carolina bar) was "Healers of Conflicts Law and Conflict Resolution Center," so it shouldn't have come as a surprise for callers to hear a message saying we choose not to go to court and if they were looking for someone to represent them in court, please call someone else. Over several months, the message was refined to indicate that we were, indeed, a law office, just lawyers who chose to collaborate or mediate. Unsuitable clients rarely left a message so that those who did usually turned out to be good prospects. For me, new clients are about quality, not numbers. I'd rather turn away several people than spend time with consultation appointments that don't convert to real clients. Also, I find it harder to say no to clients who are sitting in my office than those who are calling on the phone.

When one of the lawyers in our office did talk with a potential new client, we probably spent a little more time on educating them about our services than if we had been an adversarial firm. We thought it was a better investment than actually making an appointment with someone who was not a good match for our services. Being helpful and referring them to someone else built goodwill and sometimes led to referrals from friends of those whose cases we were rejecting. In most cases, the screening process was focused on helping the client determine whether we had services that might be a match for them and ensuring that they would pay for the consultation. For example, if they were already embroiled in a trial, was it possible that both parties would be willing to suspend the litigation and attempt resolution?

Because most of my practice has been in collaborative law or mediation, we spent a lot of time explaining those practices and the differences between them and the traditional practice of law, until I managed to get a page on my website with that information. Then, I was able to give the link and encourage them to explore for themselves.

When I do make an appointment with a client, I send them an intake form by e-mail. The intake form includes information about the appointment, how to park, and so forth. I also attach any information about the practice that wasn't covered on the phone—and sometimes even if it was covered.

My intake form is another way that I alert clients to the idea that they are not going to a typical adversarial law office. I ask questions: What are you committed to? Who are the important people in your life? How do you handle stress? How do you wish for your life to look in five years? Following is an annotated version of the intake form used in my firm.

A HOLISTIC INTAKE APPROACH: ANNOTATED

Taken from Healers of Conflicts Law & Conflict Resolution Center
J. Kim Wright, JD, Managing Attorney

"Information for First Meeting" is sent to clients when they make their appointment, usually by e-mail. This creates a relationship and tone for our first meeting and helps clients understand what to expect. On the other side, we have a sense of what is important to our client before we actually hear the story or give any advice. Clients are encouraged to check out the website for more information about their particular type of issue. Some basic legal information is on the site so they can have some of their questions answered before they even arrive in the office.

Information for First Meeting

The first meeting is an opportunity for us to get to know each other and for you to determine how we may be of service to you. Most clients find that the first meeting offers more than just advice. It is a very valuable opportunity to get clear about their goals, the available approaches to resolving their problems and to choose the best course of action.

Please return the attached form to us ASAP, and no later than the day before your appointment, if possible. The form gives you the chance to tell us what you want us to know. Spending some time on the form will save time in the meeting and will allow us more time to address your questions rather than spending precious meeting time on getting foundational information.

You may return this to us by email to XXX@healersofconflicts.com

Fax to _____

Mail to _____

We intend that the appointment last about an hour; our hourly rate is $250. Occasionally, meetings extend beyond the one-hour time period. Additional time is charged at the regular hourly rate of $250. Please come prepared to pay for your first meeting with either a check or cash. If you are bringing cash, it is a good idea to plan for the possibility of a longer appointment rather than cutting your time short because you're not prepared with sufficient cash.

Parking information:

_____

_____

Today's Date: _____ Appointment Date & Time:_____

Name: _____

Occupation: _____

Home Address:_____ [ ] Preferred address

Place of employment: _____

Business Address:_____ [ ] Preferred address

Day Phone:_____

Evening Phone: _____ Fax Line: _____

Cell Phone:_____ E-Mail address: _____

Okay to leave messages everywhere?____ If not, specify:_____

Preferred means of communication: _____

Date of Birth:_____ Age _____

Names of important people in your life (spouse, partner, children, friends, etc.):

_____

_____

We confirm our understanding of the appointment date and time. If we haven't received the form within 24 hours of the appointment, we call to confirm the appointment. We have few no-shows.

We get the statistical information prior to the appointment so we don't spend our time on it during the appointment.

Emergency Contact:_____

How did you hear about our services? _____

Why did you choose our office (instead of some other law office)?

_____

_____

Often, they say that they prefer a peacemaking approach in this space.

Tell us briefly about the issue that brought you here. _____

_____

_____

_____

Are you here because you have an issue with another person(s)?
If yes, who is it?
Name: _____Relationship to you:_____
Address:_____

_____

Phone Numbers: Home:_____ Work: _____
Cell or other number: _____Email: _____
Does this person have an attorney? If yes, name of attorney:_____

What are your most significant commitments?

_____

_____

_____

_____

This is very important for understanding the client and keeping them in their own integrity.

What are your most cherished values?

_____

_____

_____

_____

Clients report this is a favorite question and the answer often tells a lot about them. Our conversations and plans often refer back to these answers.

How do you respond to stress?

_____

_____

_____

We can talk more about this one in our appointment and I'm alerted to what to expect.

What emotional and spiritual support structure do you have in your life (close friends, family, religious community, etc. that you can lean on when you're upset?)

_____

_____

_____

_____

This also helps me know who else will be giving them advice.

Where you are on a scale of 1-10 (10 is "excellent") in each of these areas:

Physical Health:

Financial Integrity:

Emotions:

Play and Relaxation:

Work Relationships:

Personal Relationships:

Productivity:

Spiritual Life:

This alerts me to pending emergencies so we can prevent them! If there is a physical problem or financial emergency, we can address those.

What challenges & opportunities are you facing right now?

_____

_____

_____

_____

_____

_____

_____

_____

_____

This gets the client looking at the separation from a different paradigm.

How do you want your life to look five years from now?

_____

_____

_____

_____

_____

_____

_____

_____

This is the first time I ask this question but we'll do much work on this as we build the new life. It gets the client focused on building a future rather than blaming his/her spouse for the past.

What is your goal for the conflicted relationship?

_____

_____

_____

_____

_____

_____

_____

_____

Most people say they want to retain a friendship. I can bring them back to this over the course of the case.

SCREENING CLIENTS FOR APPROPRIATENESS

Why is it that there are only a few articles about screening clients to see if they are appropriate for adversarial litigation but there are many articles about screening for other approaches? Do most lawyers ask if a client is appropriate for a knock-down, drag-out courtroom battle? Each of the vectors has different considerations for screening clients but there is some common ground.

- **Self-determination**. Each of the approaches we've discussed allows the client to self-determine as much as possible. Collaborative law clients choose from a menu of possible approaches. Restorative justice is voluntary. Problem-solving courts are opt-in programs. Lawyers explain the options and may make recommendations, but the final word is generally the client's. Proper education is important for informed consent by the client.
- **Appropriate for the lawyer (competence)**. Lawyers have an ethical obligation to only take on cases for which they are qualified and competent. Holistic models are no different.
- **Team support**. The vectors all have room for multidisciplinary team members who can support the clients and other professionals. Counselors, financial (and tax!) professionals, child psychologists, realtors, and almost any other expert you can imagine may be added to the team to make the attorney–client relationship work.

Problem-solving courts have interests beyond their clients. They are also concerned about public safety and scarce resources. Screening issues for a drug court might include:

- **Risk**. What is the risk that the person will commit other crimes while in the program? Offenders with a history of violent crimes are generally excluded.
- **Motivation**. What will keep the person in the program when he or she is challenged? Drop-outs are expensive.
- **Need**. Drug court helps people who are addicted. If the defendant is not addicted, the structure won't be helpful. Drug dealers without an addiction are unlikely to get value from the program.
- **Workability**. Is the person likely to be successful? Is she or he enthusiastic? Are the services she or he needs available? Is there a co-occurring mental illness that will challenge the workability?

BILLING PRACTICES

As pioneers and innovators in the legal profession, many of us have been experimenting with different billing practices. I've tried sliding scale and flat rates with varying results.

Has the Billable Hour Made Fools of Us?

By Irene Leonard

Is it time to consider the impact of the billable hour on the practice of law and make some changes? In my opinion, we need to find a more rewarding and fulfilling way to value legal services for the benefit of both lawyer and client alike. The required number of hours a lawyer must bill each year has gone up significantly in the past 30 years, and there are those who believe the impact of increasing billable hour demands has made us nothing more than piece workers—something has to give for lawyers.

The profession is well known for the amount of volunteer, pro bono, law and justice reform, and bar association activities in which lawyers engage. However, with the demands of the billable hour, lawyers have reduced time to devote to the altruistic aspects of practice. Time for office camaraderie with other lawyers and staff is also suffering. Senior lawyers are less able to spend time mentoring young lawyers. What kind of lawyers are we turning out as representatives of the profession when we don't have the time to give them the help they need? The seriousness of the impact of this change remains to be seen.

The legal profession is working hard at trying to increase respect for lawyers. These efforts include a significant amount of advertising to convince the public they should respect us. Perhaps we would be better served and more likely to turn public opinion around by considering what might be at the root of this lack of esteem.

I wonder if there is any correlation between our negative image and the increased demands placed on lawyers to focus on high billable hours. I also wonder how the pressures of the billable hour are impacting our ability to remain courteous and collegial when stressed, and to help those who need help just for the sake of helping. Elimination of discretionary time has taken its toll on our ability to be involved in our communities and, more importantly, our families. Where or how will this end?

How do you feel about how you charge for your services? Should the benefit of becoming more proficient/efficient in your work through the use of technology and other means be passed onto the client, or should you be able to earn more because you are now more expert (and faster) at delivery of services than before? Are hours spent really a true indication of value? What are we selling? Time or skill?

The 1960s were the start of the billable hour becoming the standard way in which lawyers charge for their legal services. The use of the billable hour was intended to address antitrust concerns regarding the use of bar fee schedules, to provide lawyers with a means to determine their productivity, and as a response to client requests for more detail regarding how they were charged.

Prior to the 1960s the use of the one-line letter "For Professional Services rendered—$1,000" was the norm. Clients enjoy the detail and the ease of being billed by the hour. However there is a significant inherent problem for clients—there is no incentive for lawyers to work smarter rather than longer. The more hours lawyers spend, the more they make. This concept causes clients to distrust and question our bills.

It is time to make some fundamental changes in how we value our services. Just because the billable hour is easy is not a good enough reason to continue with it now that we are seeing the negative consequences. We need to find alternatives for the billable hour, alternatives that will acknowledge the increased efficiency and improved technical methods lawyers now use to deliver legal services. This does not necessarily mean the end of billable hours, but that billable hours should not be the only means of valuing legal services. The ultimate goal should be that the client receives a fair bill and the lawyer has a fulfilling, more enjoyable practice.

In 2001 the American Bar Association commissioned a report to look at the challenge of considering value over hours when determining fair payment for services. The Commission on Billable Hours Report *was co-chaired by Jeffrey Liss, chief operating officer for Piper Rudnick LLP, and Anastasia Kelly, senior vice president and general counsel for Sears, Roebuck and Co. The report, which was a resource I used in writing this article, can be found at: www.abanet.org/careercounsel/billable.html.*

Current billing alternatives include:

- **Fixed or flat fees.** *Lawyer provides a specific service (e.g., estate plan) for a previously agreed upon price.*
- **Contingency fees**. *Lawyer is paid based a percentage of the recovery, settlement, or amount saved for the client.*

- **Retrospective based on value.** *The amount of the fee is based on the value the client stated up front, although the fee is determined by the lawyer at the end of the matter.*
- **Retainer.** *Client pays lawyer a certain set amount each month in return for which lawyer guarantees his or her availability for that period of time.*
- **Capped fees.** *Client pays lawyer up to a specified maximum amount, but no more.*
- **Blended hourly rates.** *All time is billed equally by the law firm regardless of who works on the matter.*
- **Volume discounts and discounted fees.** *Law firm reduces its hourly rates in return for client guaranteeing a certain volume of legal work.*

Many of these alternatives are based on some form of billing by the hour. As a profession of creative, resourceful problem solvers, I trust that we can find ways to change the direction in which we have been moving, from more and more billable hours per year and the potential erosion of the high quality of the practice of law, to another more life-enhancing, fulfilling way of valuing our services.

RELATIONSHIPS WITH "OPPOSING COUNSEL"

Part of the redesign of law practice is the redesign of how we relate to the lawyers who represent the other party in a conflict. In collaborative law, we sometimes call them our "collaborative counterparts," rather than "opposing counsel."

REDEFINE ZEALOUS ADVOCACY

Elsewhere I told the story of the adversarial lawyer who taught me to fire clients. Most local bars have a lawyer like him—one who sets emergency hearings interrupting our vacations, who plays all the dirty tricks he can think of. I've talked to lawyers like him who have told me that they thought they had to be that way to zealously advocate for their clients.

On my collaborative team, we talk about zealous advocacy from the perspective of the client's long-term best interests. If my client tells me that she wants to be able to co-parent with the father of her children, then working to a settlement that allows them to be friends is a top priority.

LITIGATE WITH DIGNITY

If you must go to court, treat the other side with dignity and respect. Nurture your relationships with other lawyers—you never know when you may see them again in a nonadversarial setting, and and it will be that much easier to negotiate if you're already both coming from a foundation of respect.

TAKE A LAWYER TO LUNCH

When Stu Webb was creating the first collaborative law practice group, he invited the family lawyers to potlucks. He knew it was hard to break bread one day and then be nasty in court against the same person on the next day. Invite other lawyers out to lunch. Share a cup of coffee.

CUT SOME SLACK

I was in a collaborative four-way recently when the client went ballistic at her lawyer. He had made some mistakes, missed a critical e-mail, and been out of communication for several days. As she read him the riot act, I was filled with compassion for his honest mistakes; but, at the same time, I saw him revert to his old adversarial reactivity. Stu Webb is fond of saying that the paradigm shift is not a one-time event. We all struggle with it on a daily basis. When we are most stressed, we are most likely to fall into those old patterns. Perhaps the adversarial jerk is just overwhelmed.

It won't always work. Some lawyers are wired for conflict and won't respond. They offer you the opportunity that I had when I decided to fire my clients and never practice against that lawyer again. Or you can take on the challenge of finding the way to connect and improve your relationship. One of my first adversaries, whose office was around the corner, became my friend when we realized that we both worked late. We often discussed cases at 11:00 p.m. That led to stopping over at each other's offices for a cup of coffee on some evenings. Soon, we were friends. We still represented our clients and we still went to court, but we no longer disliked each other—and I think my clients actually fared better in our negotiations. My coaching clients and mentees have learned that they feel better when they reach out, even if the other lawyer doesn't respond.

*I did my first trial this week (custody) but I never got to do any question-
ing of witnesses or introduction of evidence because we settled. It wasn't
an ordinary 11th-hour settlement though. . .*

*Our civil court judge has very little family law experience and was
assigned the trial because the family court judge who was supposed to
hear it was unavailable at the last minute. The other attorney is a family
law specialist known as a litigator who is aggressive and very good, with
25 years of experience. I represented Dad. Mom and maternal grandmother were both parties since Grandma was joined to the case several
years ago.*

*We started on Wednesday, but there were several preliminary mat-
ters to take care of in chambers—we all wanted the child re-interviewed
because it had been almost a year since anyone neutral had talked with
her—she's 13 years old. The judge declined our request and said he'd do
it only if it became absolutely necessary.*

*Then the mother's first witness had contacted her that she was ill
and couldn't come to court but would be willing to testify by telephone. I
objected. The judge said he'd rule the next morning.*

*Then there was the mother's second witness—the child's therapist
who had told us she'd be claiming privilege. So then the trial began. The
mother's attorney made her opening statement. I had not prepared one—
this case was difficult for me because I just felt so strongly that it should
not be going to trial and my brief was only 6 pages because I had little to
say in the way of spinning the facts to make Dad look better than Mom.
The opposing brief was 12 pages plus another 25 pages that included an
updated Income and Expense Declaration and an attachment. At first I
was a bit unnerved by it, but then I relaxed because trashing Mom was
not my game but defending Mom was the other attorney's whole case.
So . . . I took notes on the opening and responded to her points that tried
to attack Dad, pointed out the child's dilemma, and then gave the reason
my client felt that the child moving in with him was in the kid's best
interest.*

*Then the therapist took the stand and claimed privilege; the other
attorney made her argument why privilege didn't apply, and I argued in
favor of sustaining privilege. The judge breathed a sigh of relief as he took
note that it was noon and time for lunch.*

*When we came back, the judge asked the other attorney for an offer
of proof regarding the issue of privilege. She started rattling off a bunch
of stuff that her clients had told her, but then the judge pointed out that*

she had said that she intended to have the therapist testify as to Mom's progress and her parenting. She agreed and said a few more things about that.

Judge asked me for my comment, and I said I thought it was all irrelevant because we did not perceive Mom's parenting to be at issue. Well, I thought I'd have to scrape the other attorney off the floor. . .she now had no case to try.

We took a break and went back to chambers. The judge asked if we could settle. The other attorney said no, the parties were polarized and had been unable to talk to each other for a long time. After reviewing some alternative custody arrangements that were not acceptable to one side or the other, I suggested that we bring the parties, without Grandma, together to see if we could get them talking. The other attorney agreed. What happened next was amazing. . .

I treated it like a collaborative practice four-way. Mom was pretty over the top emotionally during that first meeting, but with some validation for her feelings, we were able to craft a potential resolution. The next day she came back transformed, and these two people who hadn't been speaking for years, except with hostility or through Grandma, had a rational dialogue, signed the stipulation, and, by the time it was over, were talking casually and laughing. We were all teary eyed. . .I had to tease the other attorney about going collaborative.

They agreed to allow their daughter to go to live with Dad for one school year beginning in the fall. Mom gets two weekends per month, most holidays and the bulk of the summer, with the daughter returning at the end of the school year, when Dad will get that same visitation schedule. After we had left the courtroom, Grandma came up to me, shook my hand, and thanked me most sincerely.

Post Script: Mom picked the daughter up at school and took her to a park near Grandma's to meet Dad. Then they told her together of their decision! I am hopeful that this was the beginning of a healing for this entire family. . .it was truly amazing.

One other interesting result of this is that the other attorney, who had originally told me she was not interested in CP [collaborative practice] and was not sure it works, says she wants to take a training session and explore it.

When I asked her how she felt about the four-way, she said it was more like therapy than practicing law. . .She also says she tends to take sides, which is why she isn't a good mediator . . . It's all in the training—learned skills (and unlearning some of the law school and adversarial system instilled attitude). When she said she likes going to court, I told her it isn't an either-or choice; it's another tool in the box.

Most important in this situation:

The attitude of the judge—*he was thoughtful, accommodating and flexible—he gave us trial time and the jury room to have our discussions.*

The ambiance of the courtroom itself. *The old courthouse is warm and inviting (architecture and the design of a space is really important) and his staff (deputy, clerk, and reporter) were warm, friendly, and welcoming. They helped us wherever they could, from the deputy offering us information about how the judge runs his courtroom, to the clerk making sure we all had water and there was a bowl of candy on her desk if we needed a sugar infusion. (The judge had peppermint patties in his chambers.)*

This was such a sharp contrast to the Family Court, which is cold and uninviting and there is nowhere to sit down and have the kind of interaction we had in that jury room. I think if the Family Court had been available to try the case, we may not have settled it.

—*This is an e-mail sent to Kim Wright by Jennie Winter. The author is a member of the California Bar and took this as her first case, pro bono, within a week of being sworn in.*

PRO BONO SERVICE: HEALTH BENEFITS OF ALTRUISM

One of the ways to change your legal practice is to offer pro bono services. Pro bono service offers the opportunity to express purposes and values that are related to service. Pro bono cases tend to call on more holistic skills and put you in touch with different members of the community. In some places, you can provide pro bono service in the area of collaborative law, restorative justice, or other approaches. For example, Memphis Legal Services offered lawyers a free collaborative law training in exchange for an agreement to handle two collaborative cases on a pro bono basis.

A 2009 *New York Times* article reported that giving and volunteering can actually be good antidotes for stress and depression ("In Month of Giving, a Healthy Reward," http://www.nytimes.com/2009/12/01/health/01well .html?_r=1):

> *An array of studies have documented this effect. In one, a 2002 Boston College study, researchers found that patients with chronic pain fared better when they counseled other pain patients, experiencing less depression, intense pain, and disability.*
>
> *Another study, at the Buck Institute for Age Research in Novato, Calif., also found a strong benefit to volunteerism, and after controlling for a number of variables, showed that elderly people who volunteered for more than four hours a week were 44 percent less likely to die during the study period.*
>
> *How giving can lead to mental and physical changes in health isn't entirely clear, although studies suggest that altruism may be an antidote to stress. A Miami study of patients with H.I.V. found that those with strong altruistic characteristics had lower levels of stress hormones.*
>
> *By contrast, being self-centered may be damaging to health. In one study of 150 heart patients, researchers found that people in the study who had more "self-references" (those who talked about themselves at length or used more first-person pronouns) had more severe heart disease and did worse on treadmill tests.*
>
> *. . . A 1988* Psychology Today *article dubbed the effect the "helper's high." Analyzing two separate surveys of a total of 3,200 women who regularly volunteered, the article described a physical response from volunteering, similar to the results of vigorous exercise or meditation. The strongest effect was seen when the act of altruism involved direct contact with other people.*

The Service Side of Holistic Law—Integrating Pro Bono as a Means Towards Great Well-Being as Lawyers

By Jennifer Foster

I found my path back to my heart and my true whole self as a lawyer primarily through service: service towards low-income clients and my fellow lawyers. Twelve years after law school, I was deeply unhappy, but had not yet given up, when I discovered the holistic law movement through the author of this book, my friend and mentor.

I started studying mediation and joined the International Alliance of Holistic Lawyers (IAHL). I was seeking some way to continue my profession and reclaim my soul, which was lost. I simply did not fit within the adversary system. Kim Wright and I then organized a dozen local lawyers in Asheville, North Carolina, who wanted to explore holistic practice and collaborative family law into a monthly lunch discussion group. We set out to offer a three-part Continuing Legal Education series: "Lawyers as Peacemakers"—"Peacemaking from the Bench," "Lawyers as Peacemakers," and "Finding Peace Within." When more than 70 people [more than 10 percent of the local bar] showed up for each event, we knew we were on to something.

Finally gathering the courage to follow my heart, I made the move into service in my profession, to pro bono management for the Mountain Area Volunteer Lawyer (MAVL) Program administered by the independent, community-based Pisgah Legal Services. From there I blossomed, for not only was I returning to my ethic of service for low-income clients that initially motivated my entry into law school, but I also saw a great opportunity.

Pisgah Legal Services had already been employing its version of holistic legal aid intake and representation for some time. Recognizing that a legal "Band-Aid" does virtually nothing to eliminate poverty and suffering, the attorneys at Pisgah adopted a culture asking more probing questions and seeking deeper solutions: "Why don't you have any income?" "Are you disabled?" "Are you safe and healthy in your home and family life?" "Can we refer you to any appropriate community agency for comprehensive help?" Capturing as many outcomes as possible for each family, sometimes opening several cases for each client, the advocates at Pisgah began to sense the possibility for transformation as we helped lift people up out of poverty slowly and/or relieve their suffering. Pisgah is now striving to train volunteer attorneys to be more comprehensive in their pro bono cases. After all, if a person is helped with one or two issues and not another critical issue, the work done might not be as effective, viewing the situation in a comprehensive manner.

Then I came along—self-proclaimed holistic law attorney turned pro bono manager. I saw the possibility for merging the concepts of holistic law and legal aid holistic intake into the realm of pro bono, thus motivating volunteer lawyers to seek lasting and even transformational results as part of their service ethic. This, I postulated, could lead to greater fulfillment in the practice of law.

Guess what? Both on both a personal level and through professional observation, I discovered that a freedom can come through pro bono. It is the freedom to discard the issue of fees and open your heart to your client. Often times, poverty law clients can be directly empowered by attorneys through mere empathetic listening and honest care and concern.

Issues of power and discrimination can be healed through legal action, and some clients (not all, obviously) can benefit from counseling regarding victimhood, apology and forgiveness.

The culture of the Asheville Bar was ripe for this approach. Turns out, I was not the only one in distress, as attorneys confided privately. At the same time, so many had a true heart and wanted to use their skills and position to help others. As we started to focus on pro bono as an opportunity for meaningful change, lawyers expressed how much they valued the experience and even found joy! While this had no doubt been going on for years within a bar rich in an ethic of service, for the first time an express link between our own well-being and our pro bono service formed. Not only has this brought lasting results for the clients, it broke the silence and denial regarding our own well-being.

In January of 2010, the local bar recognized my efforts and embarked on programming regarding combating stress and exploring "vicarious trauma" in attorneys. While not having yet reached the Holy Grail, the Asheville Bar is well on its way towards maintaining and restoring good health and happiness through our service.

CREATING A
COMMUNITY

T HE MOST successful transitions seem to include a strong community that comes together. In 2000, I offered a tele-class on
Transforming Practices, Steve Keeva's new book. The conference line
held only 30 people, and we filled up immediately. Among those callers was Maureen Holland, a lawyer from Memphis. Maureen asked
me to continue the conference calls, and I hosted a drop-in call at 4
p.m. on Thursday afternoons for several years. We talked about ways
of practicing law holistically and provided support for lawyers from
around the country.

In 2007, Maureen and a group of colleagues created a conference
on Lawyers as Peacemakers. With national leaders as speakers and
local leaders as organizers, they involved a broad spectrum of legal services, judges, big-firm lawyers, and solos. The Peacemaking organizers have become a national force. So far, they have sponsored events on
therapeutic jurisprudence, collaborative law, and restorative justice.
Legal Services' pro bono coordinator Linda Warren Seely obtained a
grant to fund training in collaborative law to train a pro bono team,
pioneering access to justice issues in the movement. The credibility of
the out-of-town experts allowed members to experiment with various
peacemaking approaches. The organizers became friends as well as a
support structure for each other.

The success of collaborative law can be attributed to the practice
group. Stu Webb wisely gathered his first team by having potlucks. In
a collaborative law practice group, the team members create protocols,

discuss best practices, and share food and drink on a regular basis. Problem-solving courts are based upon a community of supportive interdisciplinary professionals.

"Other people matter." Chris Peterson's three-word summary of the key findings of positive psychology. Seems simplistic and sugary at first, but the more I keep it in mind, the more places I find it applies and the more nuanced it becomes!

—*David Shearon*

GETTING STARTED

I F YOU'VE read this far and still don't know where to start, the strongest recommendation I can give you is to find someone to share the journey with you. Find a coach, a practice group, a buddy. Call them on the phone or have lunch. Join a website or Facebook community. Start talking to someone else about what you want to do, your dreams, your challenges. Get out of your head and into action.

Making your mark on the world is hard. If it were easy, everybody would do it. But it's not. It takes patience, it takes commitment, and it comes with plenty of failure along the way. The real test is not whether you avoid this failure, because you won't. It's whether you let it harden or shame you into inaction, or . . . whether you learn from it; whether you choose to persevere.

–President Barack Obama

Why doesn't insight always translate into action? It can, sometimes. But in my practice I see that action is often more likely to yield insight. The "just do it" mentality, when it comes to facing our fears and changing our behavior, can be powerful and effective. I think we need to break through the idea that the only path to action is motivation. Action often precedes motivation.

If many of us waited to feel inspired to exercise we might wait a lifetime. Once you actually exercise, you feel better and think "and why did I resist working out? I know I always feel better afterwards." So, here is the key. Our thoughts. With exercise, it may not be wanting to do it but telling yourself you will feel better afterwards. Don't confuse wanting to do something with being willing to do it.

Paula Bloom Psy.D.

From http://www.pbs.org/thisemotionallife/blogs/
just-do-it-insight-motivation-and-action

MULTI-
DIMENSIONAL
HOLISTIC
WELL-BEING

WE ALL know that we can't take care of anyone else if we're not taking care of ourselves, and many lawyers take only minimal care of themselves. Most of us still try to take care of others even when we're running on empty. That is one reason our profession often shows up on the most miserable lists—high rates of depression, suicide, and addiction. However, we also can't have a holistic practice without affecting our own lives, which means that the health you practice will seep into your entire life. Well-being is the foundation of a holistic law practice. The elements of an interrelated, intertwined, and interconnected balanced and whole life are many. In this chapter, we look at some of them that most affect lawyers.

⚘ · ⚘

Gretchen Duhaime shares a definition of wellness that includes the physical, inner, analytical, relational, external, higher, and reflective dimensions of well-being:

> The Physical dimension is the body itself. Nutritious food, adequate shelter, restful sleep, and regular exercise provide for self-preservation.
>
> The Inner dimension is comprised of the passions and emotions underlying our decisions. Whether we're conscious of it or not, the Inner aspect seeks self-gratification; it needs to pursue life with zest. When the Inner dimension is neglected, we can develop harmful coping strategies.
>
> The Analytical dimension is our inquisitive and rational mind, seeking self-definition. Curiosity sharpens the mind, and routine dulls it. If the Analytical is overpowering the other dimensions, we can rationalize actions that hurt ourselves and others.
>
> The Relational dimension is our capacity and desire for love. Self-acceptance is prerequisite to social enrichment and all types of love. An underdeveloped Relational aspect can result in poor communications and even dehumanizing others.
>
> The External dimension is how we fit into society. Through work, play, and creativity, the External aspect seeks self-expression and is fulfilled with expressing and receiving gratitude. An unbalanced External dimension confuses gratification with material wealth.
>
> The Higher dimension is our search for self-knowledge and meaning in life. When we ask the big questions, we exercise the Higher aspect of ourselves. Envisioning a satisfying future and

believing it will happen creates hope, which fuels the Higher dimension. Shattering ourselves by creating compartments for Work and Personal cripples our Higher self.

The Reflective dimension exercises self-reflection; it is our tool for understanding ourselves.

—Gretchen Duhaime has an attractive graphic on her website (www .practicingonpurpose.com) that would make a good display for your desk if this model works for you. Her article, "Practicing on Purpose in the Law Firm: Providing Productivity and Profitability with Personal Wellness and Professional Values" is in the Appendix.

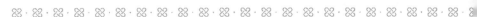

PHYSICAL
WELL-BEING

W<small>E ALL</small> know that we should take care of our physical bodies by maintaining a healthy diet and incorporating exercise into our routines. This is a major challenge for lawyers when we're working 80 hours a week and eating delivered food in front of our computers or picking up fast food on the way to court. We know what we're supposed to do to keep physically healthy, and we know we'll live longer and be happier, better lawyers if we do it. We just have to make time for it and stick to it—it's as simple as that. And as difficult.

I recently created relationships with *two* well-being coaches in an attempt to break my patterns and do what I already know I need to do. I do have some physical practices that are very supportive. For example, I almost always sleep until I wake up without an alarm clock. I listen to the rhythms of my body, which sometimes wants to go to bed at 10 p.m. and sometimes wants to stay up until 3 a.m. Sometimes I wake up at 6 a.m. Sometimes I sleep until 10. If I am on a tight schedule of appointments and haven't had enough sleep, I make sure to make up the "sleep debt" within a couple of days. I signed up for dance lessons and found a fun way to incorporate movement into my life. I joined Weight Watchers.

For most of my legal career, I have scheduled a weekly massage appointment on Friday afternoons. The massage allows me to leave the stress of the week behind and be present for my family on the weekends. Thanks to talented and skillful massage therapists, I also became interested in reiki and energy healing. I am convinced that there is more to our physical well-being than just our weight, blood pressure, or cholesterol numbers.

I'm also exploring the concept of *somatics*, which means "wholeness of the body." Our body is responsible for so much of our communication through our "body language." Only when we are present in our mind, body, and spirit do we have access to all of our resources. Our ability to move in the world, our feelings, sensations, intuition, and center, all depend on being present in our bodies. I am exploring the ways I hold my body, the size of my body, the location of the tension, and how all that has seemed separate from who I actually am. I've lived in my head for so long that I haven't paid much attention to the rest of me. As I age, this is becoming increasingly clear, and I am working on the integration of body, mind, and spirit, becoming whole.

Research shows that our bodies become physically shaped and conditioned over time based on our early beliefs, our identities, and our worldviews. And because our body minds are a bio-feedback system, our bodily shape then affects our thoughts, worldviews, and identities. Some examples of classic shapes are collapsed, aggressive, rigid, and avoiding.

At the physical level, our breath, energy, stress levels, neurological, and immune systems are compromised by restricted shapes. We react more easily to triggers, and we do not have all of our resources available, such as our intuition, our deep feeling state, clarity of mind, and our aliveness.

Most people are unaware that they have these conditioned tendencies. Their shape affects almost every aspect of their lives—their identities, thoughts and attitudes, perceptions, worldviews, relationships, responses, and ability to expand their capacities for leadership and success.

As we become aware of our "shape," we can consciously choose to present in a way that reflects what we want and intend in life, rather than our defenses and reactions. Think about the presence of those whom you trust, follow, connect with. Our body–mind connection is a powerful tool for change and growth. Becoming conscious and proactive in this area will change your life and your world.

—*Jane Faulkner (www.janefaulkner.net)*

EMOTIONAL WELL-BEING

The Illicit Relationship of Lawyers and Emotion

By Jill H. Breslau, JD, MA

When I mentioned the title of this article in an e-mail to another lawyer, she responded, "Hmmm. I missed that one in law school—and unwittingly took the practicum on 'Just the Facts, Ma'am.'"

Well, yes, me too.

The law is about Reason, not Emotion. If we had wanted to learn about emotion, we would have gone to graduate school to study psychology. Instead the goal was to learn to "think like a lawyer." During my years in law school, I wondered if I had, and if I had learned it well enough. When I did well in law school, I felt as if I had joined a very elite club, and too bad for all the people out there who failed to understand that logic and reason were the right way to go about decision-making. I took great pleasure in the intellectual dance that is legal analysis. More recently, I could still relate to the judge who told me, with considerable satisfaction, that he thinks in outline form.

However, it did prompt a wonderful image. I began thinking about the deadly iceberg encountered by the Titanic—icebergs,

137

of course, have the bulk of their structure under the water, 90 percent, I am told, invisible to the eye. The part of the iceberg under water is dark, unknown, secret, hidden. This seemed an apt metaphor for the relationship of the law to reason and emotion. The lawyer focuses on what is visible above the water line: the conscious, logical, rational, factual. Under the surface are our emotions, hidden, powerful, mysterious structures we ignore at our peril.

Lawyer Unhappiness

The statistics about unhappiness in the practice of law are not improving. Professor Susan Daicoff describes a "tripartite crisis" facing the legal profession:

1. *Low levels of job satisfaction and mental well-being among lawyers. Lawyers experience depression at least twice as frequently as it occurs in the general population (almost 18 percent of lawyers are depressed.) Lawyers also suffer higher than normal levels of anxiety, paranoia, obsessive-compulsiveness, insecurity, hostility, stress, anger, and marital dissatisfaction. And 18 percent of lawyers, again about twice the general population, are alcoholics.*
2. *A lack of professionalism on the part of both lawyers and judges, as demonstrated by frequent complaints of incivility and discourtesy, inappropriately aggressive litigation, and behavior verging on the unethical.*
3. *Low public opinion of lawyers and the legal profession.[1]*

Source of Suffering: No Feeling

I believe that these problems arise because the greatest strength of the legal system, its idealization of clear thinking, becomes a tragic flaw in legal practitioners. The Law, as an institution, as an educational system, and as a practice, values reason, logic, objectivity, and predictability above all other values. Fairness and justice in our legal system can only be attained by the careful application, in an adversarial process, of reason and objectivity. As one judge said to me, "Courts don't have feelings."

The Law rightly is concerned that decisions should have logical and rational bases, that to ensure predictability and conformity of outcomes,

---

1. Professor Daicoff's excellent book, *Lawyer, Know Thyself* (2004), explores personality characteristics of lawyers and their relationship to the tripartite crisis she documents.

decision-makers should be free of personal feelings. Similarly, a lawyer should be able to walk around a problem, to see not only the two obvious sides but the angles at which any interested party might approach the problem. Lawyers fear that emotion will cloud our objectivity or hook us into a position from which we can no longer grasp the big picture or move fluidly from the intellectual understanding of one position to another.

But we convince ourselves, as lawyers, to settle for using only part of our brains and for experiencing only part of our lives. Values that may be appropriate for an institution are not necessarily the values that work best for human beings. Despite contemporary references to the "legal industry," with connotations of cogs in a wheel, stages in an assembly line, or lawyers as mere technicians, lawyers are human beings. We are not suffering, as a profession, from our inability to think clearly or analyze properly, we are suffering because we have been trained to ignore our emotional dimension. We might like to feel happy, but we have been trained not to feel anything.

Brain Research

The research of Dr. Paul MacLean, an evolutionary neuroanatomist at the National Institutes of Health (NIH), has demonstrated that humans have a "triune," or three-in-one, brain. These three distinct sub-brains have cellular and functional differences, because they emerged from different ages in the evolutionary history of human beings. These brains communicate with each other, but sometimes they have very different interests, and sometimes their communication is imperfect.[2]

The brain stem or reptilian brain (sometimes called the "lizard brain"), resting above the spinal cord, manages our automatic functions like breath, heartbeat, the gag reflex—the vital control centers of the body. The startle reflex is in the reptilian brain. When we say a person is "brain-dead," it is the reptilian brain that is still functioning, keeping the breath flowing, the heart beating, salt and water balanced in the blood. The reptilian brain, however, lacks the capacity for anything resembling feelings. It allows for basic aggression, territorial defense, and

---

2. A wealth of material on the brain, especially the limbic system, can be found in *A General Theory of Love* (2000) by Thomas Lewis, M.D., and others. Much of the factual information about the brain which I have discussed in this article relies on the work of Dr. Lewis, including his book and a lecture which he gave at *Understanding Connection*, a conference held at the California Institute of Integral Studies on October 22, 2005.

mating behaviors, but reptiles have no emotional life. Many reptiles cannibalize their young, which is why baby reptiles are usually silent.

The part of the brain that we usually identify with is the neocortex, the rational brain. This part of the brain is the thinker, speaker, writer, planner, strategist. The neocortex gives us the capability for abstract thought, for imagining and planning a future. It is the seat of will, the determination to follow a particular course of action. Many people, not only lawyers, consider these the highest attributes of human nature.

The midbrain or limbic system (also called the mammalian brain and the emotional brain) is the part of the brain that forms attachment to others. Mammals nurture and protect their young, they sing or vocalize to their young, they love play, and they can dream. All mammals have limbic systems. That is one of the reasons that we feel so attached to our dogs and cats. They may have small neocortical brains in relation to ours, but they have limbic systems that allow them to read and respond to certain emotional states. They know when we have had a bad day, when we are angry or upset. Some dogs are so limbically attuned that they can detect the minute changes in the brains of people around them that are the precursors to seizures.

In the human brain, the limbic system curves above the brainstem and below the bulk of the neocortex. I was taught that the limbic system is responsible for the 6 F's: fight, flight, freeze, food, feelings, and . . . sex. By the way, fight or flight responses, according to current research, tend to be different in the male and female brains. Fight or flight appears to be a primarily male response to threat. Females, perhaps because of the presence of more oxytocin, the hormone relating to nurturance, are more inclined to a response called "tend and befriend" or "mend and attend." Females thus gather in groups for mutual protection and support.

The healthy limbic system, in an infant, learns love and joy, anger, fear, excitement, and disappointment from the infant's caregivers. We know that the neocortex learns by exposure to stimulating experiences, so we encourage parents to talk and read to their children, to play with them, to expose them to other children and to educational toys. The limbic system learns in an even more subtle way, by repeated exposure to emotions in a process called limbic resonance, an exquisite attunement to the inner states of other mammals. The limbic brain not only experiences the emotional states around it but adjusts to them; in effect, learning to match the limbic brains of others.

In experiments with rodents, those animals having their limbic systems excised treated their brothers and sisters like furniture, climbing over them, ignoring them, apparently not recognizing their own species. As humans have evolved, the limbic system has become the seat of conscience and of empathy; yet there are people, not unlike the experimental mice, who lack properly functioning limbic systems. Often they are labeled psychopaths or sociopaths; they have no experience of the humanity of another, nor do they have the sensitive mediator in the human brain that adds discernment and judgment to intellectual power and physical ability.

How to Deal with Emotions

Given the existing legal culture, even if we believe emotions have value, we might wonder where they fit and how to handle them. The nature of the limbic brain and its interaction with the neocortex and brainstem reveal the following facts about feelings:

1. *Emotions are not durable but evanescent, like musical notes that dissolve into silence. Our unconscious thinking about an event that triggered an emotion creates the impression of a lengthy emotion.*

2. *Because the limbic brain cannot distinguish between incoming sensory stimuli and imaginary events, emotionally charged events we think about or imagine have the same physiologic effect as those we actually experience.*

3. *What we resist, persists. When an emotion is acknowledged consciously, it can move through us without being recycled endlessly. If we experience intense emotion that we deny or suppress, we eventually may have to deal with somatic consequences.*

4. *When we move physically, emotion can flow more readily through us.*

5. *Emotions are cumulative; that is, if we have a couple of events that trigger frustration, and then we experience a small annoyance, our frustration about the third event is likely to be excessive because the neurological pathways for that feeling are already primed.*

6. *When we suppress one emotion, we suppress other emotions on that spectrum. Thus our decision not to feel sad inhibits our capacity for joy.*

7. *Emotion comes from our internal states, including our thoughts. It also comes from the internal states of those with whom*

we come in contact, since our brains are built for emotional resonance.

8. *Emotion arises, as well, from our own facial expressions, which can amplify and regulate what we are feeling. (If you want to feel empathy for someone, consciously mimic his expression.)[3]*

Lawyer Metaphors: All Reptilian

Not long ago, I created an informal survey and asked some lawyer friends what metaphors they most often heard used for lawyers. "Snake," "shark," and "bottom-feeder" were most frequently mentioned. I then checked Amazon.com for books about lawyers, finding 9,330 titles. When I narrowed my search to lawyers, nonfiction, the first title that appeared was Trapped in the Lawyer's Den with Bloodsuckers *by Thelma N. McCoy. These metaphors were particularly interesting to me because the creatures mentioned lack limbic systems; sharks, snakes, bottom-feeders, and bloodsuckers do not have emotional brains. If a lawyer is perceived in that way, we are talking about someone with instant reflexes and a narrowly focused instinct, without feelings or conscience, with only a reptilian brain. If that is the public perception of lawyers, no wonder we are unpopular.*

Sadly, the process of legal education and the practice of law, both explicitly and implicitly, foster this perception of lawyers. While bar associations initiate public relations campaigns to improve the public perception of lawyers, the legal system unintentionally conspires to perpetuate the behaviors that stamp a different perception indelibly in the minds of lay people. In ignoring emotional awareness, the system continues to attempt to persuade the public that we are good people while denying them the experience of connection with real human beings. Our clients may believe they only need our intellectual dexterity and our legal knowledge. But they actually want and deserve more: to have the feeling that we are really present to them, we are connecting with them, we are interested, we are not judging them, and that they are more than their cases.

The Law seems to offer an either–or choice: You can be objective (and be a good lawyer) or you can be emotional. I say we have to be both.

---

3. In a *New Yorker* article called "The Naked Face," (August 5, 2002), Malcolm Gladwell writes about a San Francisco psychologist, Paul Ekman, who studied facial expression and discovered that expressions mean the same thing everywhere in the world, that even when one assumes a social mask, a fleeting "micro-expression" can reveal his true feelings, and that just making expressions of anger and distress can make people feel terrible.

We must acknowledge the value of emotion; we need to learn to recognize our own feelings and those of others. We can integrate our thoughts and feelings, for greater personal and professional satisfaction and for the kind of connection with other people that acknowledges our mutual humanity.

Freedom from Fear

by Janet Smith Warfield

The new councilman (we'll call him John) strutted around City Hall, ordered the janitor and cleaning lady to work faster, and shouted down anyone who dared to express an opinion different from his own. Rumors circulated that he abused his wife. Some people said that she had been hospitalized.

I had been the contract attorney for the City's in rem tax sale foreclosures for years. As delinquent properties were foreclosed, resold, and returned to the tax rolls, the City's coffers increased tenfold over what the City paid me.

As obnoxious as John was, I tried to be polite. After all, he was one of the councilmen who would vote on my contract. However, I received neither politeness nor respect in return. "Why do you care?" he demanded when I suggested a change in the direction of a City street that would make traffic flow more smoothly. "It's none of your business."

During his campaign, John had asked me to place his campaign sign in the front yard of my home. I politely declined. I was a nonpartisan City contractor. I would not have placed any candidate's sign on my property. John took my "no" personally. As soon as he was elected, he began attacking both me and my contract.

He proclaimed that the City was paying me far too much money. John would show the City how to cut its budget. He pulled my contract off the Council Agenda three times, asserting he needed more information. The information had been previously supplied. He refused to return my phone calls. He demanded that I appear before Council to defend myself.

I was terrified. I knew how ugly this man could be and how he hated women. Women attorneys were even worse. I felt like an innocent victim being punished for a crime I did not commit.

Would I lose a contract that was a major source of income? Would I have to let my wonderful paralegals go because I could no longer pay their salaries? Would I lose my own home to foreclosure because I could no longer pay my mortgage? I had a son to support and my own bills to pay. Moreover, I was doing an excellent job in an area of law where few attorneys had my expertise. It was an area of law that John did not understand, nor did he understand the financial ramifications of his actions for the City. However, his ignorance and arrogance had become an unpleasant fact of my life.

Sleepless night after sleepless night, I tossed and turned. What would John do and say at the Council meeting? Would I appear incompetent? Would I make a fool of myself? Would the other Councilmen agree with John? What defenses could I make? How should I prepare? I trembled as my "what ifs" continued to torment me.

Fortunately, I had had several years in NarAnon, a support group for families and friends of addicts. The more I thought about John, the more I realized his behavior was addictive—bullying, lying, belligerent, angry, manipulative. NarAnon had taught me I couldn't fix the addict. I could only fix myself. I needed the help of a Power greater than myself. I had been taught to "let go and let God."

I didn't much like the word "God." It always made me think of an old man with a long white beard, sitting on a thundercloud with a lightning bolt in his hand, waiting to strike me dead if I didn't do some unclear thing he wanted me to do. I had always considered myself an intellectual agnostic. I liked the words "Power greater than myself" better than the word "God." At least, they were tolerable.

One morning, still trembling in terror, I sat myself down on my living room sofa, consciously brought my mind back to the present moment, and repeated over and over, "Let go and let God." Suddenly, my trembling stopped. Here I was, safe and sound in my own living room. I could manage this present moment. I suddenly knew that I could manage each and every "future present moment," one moment at a time. All I had to do was prepare thoroughly, "let go" and let a Power greater than myself support me.

On the day of the Council meeting, I sat in the front row with a big, fat file on my lap, glaring at John. He refused to look at me, his face muscles taut and his hands shaking. While he made a few half-hearted attempts at blustery remarks, the verbal gusts soon petered out as other

Councilmen jumped to my defense. John muttered under his breath, then reluctantly stopped talking altogether. When the vote was taken, my contract was unanimously renewed.

Awareness and Choice

Struggling with fear and terror is never fun, but the challenge strengthens us, develops our courage, and allows us to step into our unique, personal power. I have learned two important words over the years about releasing fear and stepping into my own power. Those words are awareness *and* choice.

Awareness has two aspects: awareness of my external world and awareness of my internal world. Awareness of my external world is easy. It is what I have been taught all my life. Awareness of my internal world is harder. It is much easier to blame someone or something "out there" than to look inside myself and take responsibility.

While being aware of my external world may be easy, there are consciousness tools that make it easier. While I am noticing my external world and making discernments about it, it is vital that I detach emotionally from other people's dramas. That includes the media, bullies, arrogant government officials, and "poor me" victims. It is also vital that I not judge people who are imprisoned by their own dramas. I am never right for others. I am always right for myself. I can never fix others. I can only fix myself. Fixing others is not my job. Fixing myself is. By fixing myself, I affect others in positive ways.

While being aware of my internal world may be harder, it is vital to transformation. Is my breath shallow? Is my heart pounding? Are my muscles tense? Am I trembling? While these may be things I don't like to look at, I can't release them if I don't notice they are there. Again, consciousness tools can help. Where is my mental focus? Is it in the future? Is it on what someone else may think, say or do?

If I'm feeling fear, I can be sure that I've allowed my mental focus to stray into the future or on to what someone else may do. By focusing on the future or on what someone else may do, I give my present personal power away. By bringing my mental focus back to the present moment and focusing on my own next action step, fear disappears. In order to figure out that next action step, I have to ask myself the right questions: What do I think? What do I feel? What do I need? How can I get what I need without hurting others? We always have choices. At minimum, in any given moment, we can choose to act or not act.

Here are consciousness choices I've found useful in releasing fear:

- *When my fear shows up, I welcome it into my life and give it a little love. It is a wonderful messenger, bringing me information I need to know. All I have to do is figure out the message.*
- *I get clear on what I want, right now in this moment. The present moment is always manageable.*
- *If I notice that my mental focus is in the future, I can keep it there in order to plan and organize, or, if I'm feeling fear, I can bring my mental focus back to the present moment.*
- *I ask myself, "What is my next step?"*
- *When I have time to think, my choices expand from two to three to ten. Which choice is best for both me and others? If the two seem to be in conflict, I figure out what choice is best for me and let the other person figure out what choice is best for him or her. This could include either working together or going separate ways. It could also include working together in some areas and not in others.*

When I have time to mastermind with others, my choices expand from 10 to 20 to 100 to infinity. No choice is right or wrong. Some simply lead to less painful and more joyful solutions than others.

♲

Transforming Anger

By Barbara Stahura

It's one of those stories that can help define a life, although the hero of this one says it was just part of a progression. S. Leonard Scheff had already been "messing around with Buddhism for years" when he handled quite a bit of legal work to help facilitate the Dalai Lama's visit to Tucson, Arizona, in 1993. So, he figures, he was probably already receptive to the message His Holiness presented. At the same time, though, getting that message to hit home took another, less kindly teacher.

A Tucson attorney who specializes in real estate law, Scheff received a special honor as a thank-you for all his help: a front-and-center seat during the Dalai Lama's four-day teaching. The problem was, he felt he couldn't miss a session or do something as ungracious as falling asleep because he didn't want to offend His Holiness (although Scheff suspected he probably wouldn't mind) or, worse, the people who had arranged for his seat. As the teaching went on, though, he found himself becoming even more uneasy with the lessons themselves, in which His Holiness frequently suggested that people would be much better off if they gave up their anger. This was much more serious than his fear of dozing off; this unease flowed from Scheff's deepest sense of self, from how he defined himself as a person and an attorney, and it gnawed at him. While he believed the Dalai Lama to be "a really nice man," he says, "if he thought I was going to give up anger, he was crazy."

The day after the last teaching session, the unsettling contradiction of the Dalai Lama's peaceful words and Scheff's own beliefs about anger had not yet dissipated. As he drove through Tucson, another car pulled a little too close to him, so Scheff honked his horn in warning. In return, from the other driver's rolled-down window came "the digital sign of disrespect held high in the air." Scheff's immediate reaction was a desire to ram the other car, or at least roll down his window and shout an insult. But something clicked in his consciousness before he did either: Maybe he should try putting into practice what the Dalai Lama had been trying to teach him. After all, His Holiness had certainly dealt with events much more anger-inducing than this one. So Scheff asked himself what had made him angry with this vehicular teacher. In an instant, he knew.

"I wanted respect from this total stranger," he explains. "It was me who gave this insult its meaning. And I started laughing at myself." Immediately, he realized how much better it felt to laugh than to be angry. "I was hooked," he says.

This was the beginning of a new definition of life for him, and he set about conscientiously applying within himself the Dalai Lama's teachings about anger. But he eventually realized there was a great need for these teachings within the legal community, so he expanded his individual work in order to help others in the same unsteady boat. He created a seminar titled "Transforming Anger," which he presents to lawyers, judges, and anyone else willing to listen.

A native of Texas, Scheff came to Tucson in 1949. He's resided there in the desert ever since, with the exception of time spent attending Boalt School of Law at Berkeley. He's not sure why he chose the law as a career, except to say "it seemed very clear that I was going to be a lawyer." His father was a real estate agent in Tucson and referred a lot of clients to him when he began his practice there. So he specialized in real estate law, which he still practices today, at age 73.

Until that insightful, laughing moment in his car in 1993, Scheff had somehow suspected that anger wasn't the best strategy to make his point or to get his clients what they asked him to get, but it was the only way he knew. "It was a source of distress, but I didn't know it," he says.

Tall and lanky, with thinning gray hair and a slight forward stoop, Scheff is unpretentious, wearing brown running shoes with light-colored laces to the office. He radiates a solid calmness, and it seems as if nothing could ruffle him. He's a great punster, too. For example, back in 1993 when he was dealing with the lawyer for His Holiness the Dalai Lama while working on the Tucson visit, he says he asked if the lawyer was the "Loop-holey-ness."

Once, he was addicted to anger, as are many attorneys. Maybe he even took pride in his aggressiveness, as men are encouraged to do, and he did believe that anger was a permanent part of his personality. But in that one instant in his car, he saw it didn't have to be. "We define ourselves as having a personality," he says, "so we create this fiction, which, by and large, is an impediment."

Why a fiction? Because our thoughts about how we are or how we think we need to act stem from our reactions to innumerable past experiences, which become physically patterned in our brains. These patterns then become an automatic function, a default, that reappear in the presence of the right stimulus. The problem is, the original stimulus could be 10 or 15 or 40 years old and totally inappropriate for the current situation. In Scheff's case, he had somehow picked up anger along the way and carried it so tightly that it became his default. It was like the tree growing by the seashore where the wind always blows, he says. The tree is bent over, and even if the wind stops, the tree remains bent.

Fortunately, the Dalai Lama taught Scheff that what is learned can be unlearned. Unlike trees, we humans can stand straight up if we choose. While anger is part of the standard package of human emotions, we always have a choice about what to do with it when it arises.

Before Scheff chose to look at his options, "I have the feeling that I did a lot of damage to my clients," he explains. "One thing I did notice was that I very seldom got referrals from other attorneys. Obviously, they thought I was a jerk. A smart jerk, but a jerk nonetheless. Anger has a lot of coattails," he continues, "and one of them is the need to reform people to make them behave right. I was always telling people how it should be."

Another one is that we can come to believe that acting out of anger defines us, much as we can believe the car we drive or the clothes we wear define us. Many people believe that acting in anger is automatic and that they have no control over it. People who are addicted to anger may welcome occasions to be angry, Scheff says, or even seek out those occasions.

He did, once upon a time. But he's profoundly changed. He understands that anger and aggression don't equal effectiveness in the courtroom, or anywhere else. In fact, an angry person, like the scorch-and-burn attorney, is much less likely to be effective. "When you're angry, your options narrow profoundly," he explains. "When you're angry, you either want revenge or to become a martyr. And so you don't examine options. You also close down the other person when you're angry."

Married for nearly 40 years, Scheff admits that his wife, Sue, almost left him because of his anger. "I wouldn't still be married if I hadn't made these changes in myself," he says. His legal practice has also benefited. He now receives many referrals both from a "devoted clientele" and colleagues who appreciate him.

Scheff tells a story from his practice to illustrate an option he chose when faced with an irate U.S. attorney from Cleveland, another anger junkie. This attorney called him one day about a case and, in the course of a 15-minute rant, insulted and threatened him numerous times. "He finally ran out of steam," says Scheff, "and then he said, 'What have you got to say for yourself?' I said, 'I'm very sorry you're distressed.' There was an incredibly long silence. He's been very nice to me ever since."

There is never anything we need to be angry about, says Scheff. Never. Not even in the case of the worst injustice. "You need to deal with the injustice, but if you're angry, you limit your choices," he says.

Again, he tells a story to illustrate. A man told Scheff about an incident he had witnessed in a parking lot. An elderly woman was slowly maneuvering her car into a parking space as an impatient, young male driver was trying to get by her, unsuccessfully. Once she had parked her car and gotten out, the young man jumped out of his vehicle and came over to her, screaming and venting his anger on the shocked woman. The poor woman was "shaking like a leaf," the man told Scheff. "I knew I should do something. I was so angry, all I could think of doing was slugging him." So Scheff asked the man to close his eyes and mentally take himself back to the scene. "But instead of focusing on him, focus on her," he suggested. In a minute, the man opened his eyes and said, "I just should have gone over and stood next to her."

Scheff's three-hour Transforming Anger workshop isn't some theo-retical, let's-just-love-everyone kind of event; neither do participants whack anything with plastic bats. Instead, at this time when they are not gripped by anger, they are asked to examine their long-held beliefs about it, think through their options, and investigate specific tools to deal with it.

Anger, he explains, is the result of an unmet demand. And we can choose how to respond, particularly when we understand the four hypoth-eses about anger, which form the basis of the workshop:

- *Anger is almost always a destructive emotion.*
- *The first person damaged by your anger is you.*
- *You can, if you choose, reduce the amount of anger in your life.*
- *As you reduce the amount of anger, your quality of life improves.*

Participants are not required or even asked to accept any of these hypoth-eses as true. Instead, Scheff asks them to experiment with them, using examples of anger from their own lives, to see if the process might be true for them. If so, he would like them to continue experimenting after the workshop.

The workshop has affected many people in positive ways, according to Scheff. Many people have told him later how he has changed their lives. But he's a little worried about that. "Nothing I bring to this work-shop isn't out there, available," he says, "and if people are living these painful, ineffective existences, and they can be changed in three hours, something is really, basically wrong." At the same time, he admits, "It's very gratifying, after years of being a hostile lawyer, to be a healer."

It's good to let go of anger. First of all, you feel better. "It's unpleas-ant to be angry," he says. "That doesn't need any proof, but it needs to be said out loud. And you have more choices. And the love that's out there comes in instead of being kept out."

On the other hand, hanging on to your anger is like this, he says: "You get up and get dressed, and you get your tie adjusted or your jewelry, and you're all ready to go. But just before you go, you pick up a huge pot-ted plant, and you carry it with you all day. And you wonder why you have trouble getting around and getting things done and getting through doors."

Scheff hopes he can make a contribution to society with his work-shops and by his own example, admitting that might sound "a little gran-diose. But there's a saying: 'To a carpenter with a hammer, all the world's a nail.' I see all the world's problems in terms of being angry."

That driver that flashed Scheff the finger back in 1993 should look out, though. Scheff would love to give him a hug in thanks for bestowing such a great gift on him.

—For more information about Leonard Scheff's Transforming Anger workshops, please go to www.transforminganger.com or see his book, *The Cow in the Parking Lot: A Guide for Transforming Anger for a Happier, More Effective Life* (Iuniverse, 2008).

The transformation of anger into positive emotions has a better chance of becoming a life-long practice—by only managing anger, the sources of anger will continue and you are always in the position of "restraining the beast." When anger is transformed, you learn that you can chose not to be angry, or if you are, you can transform that anger into compassion.

—Leonard Scheff

GOOD
RELATIONSHIPS

DO YOU get energy from your relationships, or do they exhaust you? It may depend on whether you are an introvert or extrovert. Extreme introverts are exhausted by almost all social interactions, while extreme extroverts are enlivened. However, whether you are an introvert or an extrovert, there are some people who require more of your energy than others.

As lawyers, we're trained to fight, and argument is the water many of us swim in. We joust with each other and joke sarcastically. We've learned to approach conflict without making it personal. Cross-examination is a handy skill in a courtroom but isn't as effective in encouraging your teenager to confide in you.

Considering the popularity of lawyer jokes, we might conclude that lawyers are not particularly skilled at personal relationships or that lawyers don't value interpersonal connection. Dr. Fiona Travis, married to a former prosecutor, is the author of *Should You Marry a Lawyer: A Couple's Guide to Balancing Work, Love & Ambition* (available at the bookstore at www.LawyerAvenue.com). Travis reports she has "found that lawyers do value their personal relationships but lack the skills needed to build intimacy. Lawyers listen to clients and go straight to solving the presenting problem. However, you may not be as good at listening to loved ones and providing emotional support because you are always problem solving."

How can we improve our relationships?

- Self-awareness is the beginning of successful relationships. Get to know and *like* yourself.
- Choose your relationships carefully. Don't confuse professional contacts with real friendships. If being with a particular person drains your energy, limit the time you spend with that person. Choose friends who share common interests outside of work, people in whom you can confide, open up, and let down your guard.
- On your way home from the office, practice shedding your lawyer persona. Imagine yourself taking off the coat of lawyering and leaving it at the office. Take a deep breath, and blow out your work and breathe in the next stage of your day with family or friends.
- Practice listening without interrupting.
- Ask before offering advice or solving problems. (After all, you're not billing for this time.) Respect the input of others.
- Give and receive emotional support. Admit that you don't always know the answers and that you sometimes need help. Be honest with yourself and others about your feelings. If necessary, seek the help of a therapist or relationship coach to help you become a better friend, spouse, or parent.
- Invite your family to point out when you are being argumentative, and don't argue when they do (if you start to argue, you're really just making their point for them!). This is probably the hardest item on the list and will require your complete commitment to improvement.

If the research in positive psychology has taught us anything, it is that a happy life and meaningful human relationships go hand-in-hand.

INTEGRATING MINDFULNESS AND CONTEMPLATIVE PRACTICES INTO YOUR LIFE

So what is mindfulness? It is the practice of concentrating our awareness on the present, of being fully alive in this very moment. Elements of mindfulness are found in many other programs. For example, Alcoholics Anonymous and Narcotics Anonymous encourage people to focus on the present by living one day at a time. Participants are also encouraged to be aware of situations that cause stress, fear, or suffering and may lead to ingesting intoxicants. In mindfulness of consumption, we are aware that what we take in may lead us to negative behavior, including our "ingestion" of situations that encourage use or abuse of intoxicants. Mindfulness compels us to consider the effect of everything we consume, including television programs, books, films, magazines, and conversations.

Without mindfulness, we are easily distracted by the incessant internal chatter of our minds, the barrage of shallow advertising, the seduction of consumption. Mindfulness allows us to be aware of these things, but not caught by them. It allows us to touch the miracle of life instead of thirsting for things we hope will bring us happiness.

In mindfulness we develop awareness of four principal elements: body, feelings, mind, and objects of mind (e.g., thoughts and perceptions).

—*Leslie Rawls, lawyer and Buddhist minister (http://www.cuttingedgelaw*
.com/content/mindfulness-practice-and-stress-reduction)

MINDFULNESS AND CONTEMPLATIVE PRACTICES

Mindfulness is the practice of cultivating nonjudgmental awareness of one's body functions, feelings, or consciousness. Any activity can be done with mindfulness—you could look at it from the perspective of paying close attention to what you're doing in the moment. It is a component of many religions and is practiced outside religious traditions. Contemplative practices include many activities to quiet the mind and help us develop the capacity to concentrate and pay attention. The Center for Contemplative Mind in Society has a marvelous graphic of a tree that illustrates dozens of contemplative practices. The branches symbolize a particular kind of practice—stillness (like sitting quietly, sitting meditation), movement (like yoga, tai chi, qi gong), relational (like dialog, deep listening), creativity (artistic practices), ritual (like Shabbat, altars), activist (volunteering, vigils), and generative (visualization, prayer). The graphic is at http://www.contemplativemind.org/practices/tree.html. For lawyers who are used to juggling a dozen tasks at once, the idea of being very present to one task can be a stretch.

Throughout the day, in pursuit of mindfulness I often stop for a moment and take a deep breath and bring my attention to my body. In my sister's house where I'm writing, there is a clock that isn't quite right—it usually surprises me when it chimes at five til the hour. I take that moment to pay attention to my breath, to check in with my attention. Doug Chermak sets a random chime that reminds him to be mindful. At my house in New Mexico, the arrival of a butterfly or hummingbird at my window was a reminder to stop and be grateful.

Other possibilities for integrating contemplative practices into your life: meditation groups, yoga classes, chi gong, tai chi, organized hikes—try to go to a regular class until you have developed the discipline, knowledge, and muscle to practice on your own.

Doug Chermak

© Doug Chermak

The Law Program at the Center for Contemplative Mind explores ways of helping lawyers, judges, law professors, and students reconnect with their deepest values and intentions, through meditation, yoga, and other contemplative and spiritual practices. The program has sponsored a series of insight meditation retreats for lawyers and law students, including instruction in contemplative practices and group discussions about combining these practices with a life in the law. The Law Program's coordinator is Douglas Chermak. His video interview is at http://www.cuttingedgelaw.com/video/doug-chermak-peaceful-environment.

MEDITATION

Meditation is the mental discipline of getting beyond the reflexive, "thinking" mind into a deeper state of relaxation, awareness and attention. Attention is paramount in the law: attention to details; to legal, ethical, and moral principles; and to clients, colleagues, judges, and juries. Meditation can help lawyers pay better attention, as well as deal better with stress, develop self-awareness and understanding of others, improve concentration and creativity, and perform better as lawyers and mediators.

Taking a moment to quiet the mind may seem a luxury in a busy schedule. Contrast this with what the Dalai Lama said when asked about his busy schedule and four hours of daily meditation: reportedly he replied that when he is very, very busy, he finds he sometimes needs to meditate for six hours each day to get it all done.

I, too, have discovered that the more intense my to-do list, the more contemplative time I need to maintain the focus and attention to get it all done. For me, that means that almost every day I spend time doing something my friend calls "beditation"—simply lying in bed, quieting my mind before I get up. On busy days, I may beditate for more than an hour in preparation for my day, then engage in other contemplative practices during the day. Sometimes I watch my breath or listen to a guided visualization. Rarely do I fall asleep, but I don't beat myself up if I do.

The following meditation comes from lawyer Leslie Rawls. Use it at stop-lights, as designed, or when you find yourself gripping the sides of your desk. Simple as it seems, a single deep breath can create miracles.

Stoplight Mindfulness

Are you gripping the wheel, figuring out how late you'll be, glancing at the cross light, wondering if you should have taken the other lane? Forget it. You have stopped. Be grateful to the stoplight for a brief pause. You have no choice but to sit still and breathe.

Let go of the steering wheel. Allow your gaze to relax. Pay attention to your in-breath and your out-breath. If you get three or four full breaths sitting at the light, you will feel relaxed and refreshed. If you don't quite get three breaths, you will look forward to the next stoplight for another chance. Here is a verse to help focus and relax at stoplights. (It's useful other times too.) You can use the longer version with a line for each in- or out-breath or the shorter form with just a word for each.

(Long version)

Breathing in, I know I am breathing in.
Breathing out, I know I am breathing out.
Breathing in, I calm my body and mind.
Breathing out, I smile.
Breathing in, I dwell in the Present Moment.
Breathing out, I know it is a Wonderful Moment.

(Short version)

In, Out.
Calm, Smile.
Present Moment, Wonderful Moment.

The smile is simply a half-smile to relax your face. The verses can be used anytime you want to bring your attention into the present.

The Path to Mindfulness

1. *Recognize where you are in relation to where you want to be.* Where do you focus your attention? Is it on the past, or maybe on worries about the future? As lawyers, we have been trained to imagine the possibilities and often the worst-case scenarios. Any time you think about the future, it is pure speculation. Why not recognize the possibilities instead of the pitfalls, and then spend your energy on manifesting what you want to happen?

2. *Ask yourself how you would need to be in order to live your dreams.* Now that you are focusing on what you want, imagine yourself manifesting the outcome you would like to achieve. How would you need to be in order to manifest that goal? Lawyers seem to constantly be playing catch up with their schedules, yet there are many things in the day that are under your control. You likely want more time to accomplish things and feel more in charge of your day. What feasible changes can help you make more time and feel more in control?

3. *Recognize the energy is within you.* If you have a vision of how you want to be, then some part of you must already have the energy it takes to be that way. If you didn't, you simply would not have that vision. By simply paying attention to and focusing on what you want, you already know what you need to do to have more control of your day. You just need to do it.

4. *Tap into that state of consciousness and focus on your dream.* Now that you know what you want, you know how you need to be in order to achieve it, and you know that the energy is within you, all you have to do is focus on that dream and allow it to manifest naturally. After all, focusing on what you do not want (your nightmares) has seemed to manifest just that so often, why not try focusing on what you do want for a change? Look at your schedule before you go home. Get up early, read the paper, and enjoy your coffee before heading straight to court. Block out time for writing your brief, and reschedule that client for the day after your brief is due.

5. *Let whatever happens be okay.* Finally, we will likely experience some disappointments even when we focus on what we want. It's important to remember that life is about the journey.

While focusing on our dreams, we can remain detached from the outcome, and appreciate the joy of living and learning along the way. No one is perfect, and no one gets what they want all of the time. Besides, if we did life would likely be rather boring. So let whatever happens be okay, get creative with your dreams, and enjoy the ride!

—Kali S. Tara

Happiness is when what you think, what you say, and what you do are in harmony.

—Mahatma Gandhi

Yoga and the Americans with Disabilities Act

By Melissa Cole Essig

Yoga, I have always thought, saved me from the law.

I became a lawyer, in the narrative I have set up of my life, because I was blind to my heart. It was the path my mind led me down, the safe, manageable world of knowledge and surface communication and clear organizing principles.

Sure, I told myself I went to law school to change the world. Certainly not because my parents were begging me to do it. But I also fully acknowledged, at the ripe old age of 24, that I would end up going to law school eventually, so why not do it while I was young?

I did, to my credit, fight the good fight. Much of my first year was spent in tears as I tussled over the meaning of justice with other students who were plainly in the game to make six figures a year. (We're talking the pre-dot-com 1990s, when you had to actually work your way up to a six-figure salary at a big law firm.) I sought refuge in the nascent

Columbia Journal of Gender and Law, *reasoning that an organization run on consensus must be a warm and welcoming haven, even if we were publishing articles about law by people who practiced and taught law. I jumped at the chance to work in the Fair Housing Clinic during my third year and ended up feeling alienated and discouraged at the thought that once someone needs to consult a lawyer, there's nothing much the lawyer can do to correct the harm she's already suffered.*

In other words, the law broke my heart over and over again.

But I didn't know how to do anything else. When I tried to think of something, I came up blank. I had, after all, spent three years of my life and a great deal of my parents' money getting a law degree. I couldn't imagine any other job for which I was fit. I knew from a mercifully brief but unfortunate college experience that I am not the least bit suited to waiting tables, which surely meant I couldn't take any chances on a creative-type lifestyle.

So I pursued the public interest dream. I graduated from law school jobless. I volunteered with some public interest organizations as I studied for the California Bar while living in my parents' home. ("You should reach for the stars," my mother would say, her eyes shining with passion, as we crossed paths in the kitchen. "Work for a law firm!" Plainly, her universe is a lot smaller than mine.) And I stumbled into a clerkship in [Washington,] DC, buying myself some time and some legal street cred.

Then the clerkship was over and I was back in the dispiriting search for public interest work. Even at the time, I knew my heart wasn't in it. But I couldn't see my way to anything else. And when time was running out on my gainful employment and one of my co-clerks told me the law firm in which he had spent a summer was looking for associates, I dumped my résumé in the mail and tried to forget about it.

In the interest of full disclosure, I did not work every weekend for the 22 months I lasted at the firm; in fact, I think I worked a grand total of three of them. I billed exactly as many hours as were expected of me, took my vacation and holidays, and was lucky enough to work with some good partners on some good issues. But I walked around much as I had in law school, with a big lump of tears crouching in my throat just underneath my smile. Because I just did not know the person in the suit (even if it was tangerine orange with a skirt that fell a good six inches above my knee).

The only way I knew how to get out was to go to graduate school; I know how to go to school, and I know it is a safe place, predictable, patterned. I was in the American Studies program, but I was teaching a writing course at—you guessed it—the law school. Before long my little brain started sussing out my options. Law school teaching: better salary than college teaching, shorter tenure track, less onerous requirements, lighter teaching loads . . .

Next thing I knew, I was an associate professor at St. Louis University Law School. And, for a brief year or so, I was pretty sure I was happy.

Then I discovered yoga. I discovered my heart. I learned how to follow it instead of my head. I began to see why, even when things were good, even when I was surrounded by friends, I was still deeply unhappy. I quit my job to write. I met my husband. I started a life with him in which the occasional legal project is nothing more than a means of contributing to the mortgage, certainly not a part of who I am or how I would define myself. And, of course, I discovered the joy of being a mother that led me to YogaMamaMe, my website about discovering who we are after we become—or don't become—mothers, with a lot of help from yoga principles.

Then I read an article about a piece of legislation passed by Congress. It reversed a truly evil Supreme Court decision that had gutted the Americans with Disabilities Act [ADA] and rendered hundreds of thousands of people with disabilities powerless to fight against discrimination. And as I read about it I started to cry.

The Heart of Law

The Supreme Court's decision—issued in 1999, just as the ADA was starting to have any real positive effect on the lives of people with disabilities—stated, to put it simply, that if you can mitigate your disability, you don't really have a disability.

In other words, say you have epilepsy. Because some people are scared of epilepsy, you have trouble keeping a job and, consequently, have no health insurance with which to buy medication that will control your seizures. Congress passes the ADA. Now, when you apply for a job, the employer can't say, "Epilepsy! What if you have a seizure and scare off all my customers? No way I'm hiring you!" That would be discrimination against a person with a disability.

So say the employer hires you. You get health insurance. You start taking medication that controls your seizures. You never have them anymore. You're living the American Dream. One day, you mention to your

*supervisor that you have epilepsy, controlled by medication. "Epilepsy!"
she cries. "What if you have a seizure and scare off all the customers? No
way you can keep working here! You're fired!"*

*According to the Supreme Court, that's not disability discrimination.
Really. You can look it up.* Sutton v. United Air Lines *(1999).*

*Well, it took Congress nine years, but they finally passed a bill telling
the Supreme Court what an incredibly stupid decision that was.*

*The reason I cried as I read about this isn't that I consider myself a
person with a disability. I cried because what happened is so unfair to
people who do. It's the same way I cry when I read about the Civil Rights
Movement or California recognizing—then not recognizing—gay and
lesbian marriages. It just speaks to my heart.*

*In this sense, I see—in a wobbly, uncertain, almost fearful way—
that the law does have heart in it. In yoga, the same principle that
informs civil rights law is called* ahimsa, *or nonharming. I've written
about it in the context of giving yourself a break, treating yourself well,
not giving in to the drive we all have to push ourselves too far and too
cruelly.*

*But ahimsa also means practicing nonharming toward others. It
becomes possible through its own practice—the more care you take not to
harm others through your words and actions, the easier it becomes. And
it automatically happens whenever you practice yoga. Because every time
you practice yoga—whether in an asana practice or by meditating or
simply by buying local, all-natural foods and humanely raised meats—
you open your heart. And when you open your heart, you share your own
peace with the world.*

*Just think what would happen if we all were trusting enough to open
our hearts and offer a prayer of peace to the world. Those politicians and
Supreme Court justices would have nothing on us.*

*Okay. So law and yoga are compatible, right? Isn't that what I'm
saying? That there is heart in the law, as long as you don't let all the
head-y stuff obscure it? That my life's path hasn't been one of correcting
35 years spent wandering alone in an intellectual vacuum? That it's all
of a piece, those utterly miserable three years at Columbia Law School
and these joyful times of expanding motherhood and family?*

*Actually, I'm not saying any of that. Because something in me resists
it, as if admitting it will spin me back into the awkward, fearful, uncertain person pretending to be—you know, fun and pretty and smart*

and. . . . I don't even know what it was I wanted to be back then. Maybe that's what scares me.

Honoring Your Past Instead of Running from It

We all have regrets. That six-year relationship we stuck with just to prove we could do it. That time we drank way too much at a party to impress a cute guy only to find when he finally did lean in for the kiss that closing our eyes gave us unbearable spins. The decision in tenth grade to take Spanish 3 instead of drama.

The trick is letting go of the regret. Which is, of course, not easy. I think about going to law school and I feel—literally, viscerally feel—what it was like to walk the halls: the sense of not moving fully; the out-of-body sensation of someone watching me act like an awkward version of me; the tense, edgy wariness of being prepared for an argument at any moment. Because, in my experience, lots of law students think confrontation is fun.

So those feelings overtake me and I just cannot embrace law school. I try to think about the good people I met. My clinic partner and our client, a beautiful black woman with an even more beautiful laugh whose landlord did things like leaving pictures of nooses on her door. My contracts professor who was also a jazz musician and had a worn old armchair in his office where I could sit any time I felt like I needed to belong. The friend with whom I sang Indigo Girls songs about changing the world before he dropped out at the end of our first year.

But all those thoughts end in sadness. I don't know any of those people any longer. I'd be hard pressed to name a single person from my law school days with whom I am in any sort of contact at all. Because, I suppose, I have run fast and far from the person I was toward the person my heart always knew was there.

So I'm not there yet—not to the place where I can honor my past rather than run from it. But—you know what I'm going to say—that's the beauty of yoga. It's about practice, not about being perfect. There is always somewhere to go, something to learn. There is always the possibility of forgiving yourself for not being there yet.

And there is always—always has been, always will be—a place in which I can, for those brief, tearful moments when I read that the law has done something good for people who deserve it, find the place in my heart that once called me to it.

Undoing the Eggshell Plaintiff Persona through Yoga

By Annabelle Berrios

Humpty Dumpty sat on a wall;
Humpty Dumpty had a great fall.

How many of us have felt like Humpty—fragile, imbalanced, triggered by a whisper, on the brink of falling? In a field of advocates, who advocates for the personal care of lawyers? Could the presence of a "reasonable care" standard enhance the quality of the legal representation we provide? After all, can an empty balloon bounce? Can an empty cup relieve thirst? Is it an efficient use of time and energy for one individual to try to take care of another when feeling depleted? Like the Enquirer *says: "Inquiring minds want to know."*

When I was a criminal law attorney working at New York Supreme Court, I had the privilege of teaching lunchtime yoga classes to a conference room full of lawyers. I say teaching because I was the one standing in the front of the room calling out movements. Yet, in truth, I was there to learn as much as I was there to share. Before me, in varying body sizes, shapes, races, and nationalities, my rainbow of neuroses was mirrored back to me. One woman smoothed out her shirt every time her body rose from a forward bend while another sneaked surreptitious peeks at the body next to hers. Nearly everyone's faces looked like they were in labor, and a few made fists with their hands during the final resting pose. Many reported skipping breaths until they heard me say "breathe." Mind you, this was gentle yoga. I saw this as a classic example of overzealous issue spotting. I was witnessing a cult to the words "should" and "right," rather than an attitude of curiosity and play. In my own experience, taking everything seriously meant I wasn't having any fun, which meant I was not relaxing enough if at all. When I did not relax enough, clarity eluded me—and in a busy workweek, the absence of clarity was a "luxury" I could not afford anymore.

Yoga is not just stretching and pretzeling; the degree to which any of that is involved is subject to individual needs. Yoga, like the law, provides a methodology for identifying what is going on, but in yoga, the focus is on one's body, breath, emotions, and mind. While the law focuses on problem spotting, however, yoga focuses on relief spotting. Unlike in law, in yoga there is no binding legal precedent setting a uniform standard to follow. A lawyer who practices yoga is practicing humility, in that feeling good is not a matter of doing, but undoing; it is not about fixing, it is about allowing. According to yogic philosophy, the wisdom of each individual body is complete and perfect; all there is to do is learn to listen. To me, this feels like such a relief, *which in turn leads me to relax, which in turn invites clarity, which in turn allows joy—and getting work done.*

The lawyers at New York Supreme Court showed me how it's done—they learned about letting go in their perfectly imperfect way, laughing all the way. Then one day after class, after someone asked for help with a legal issue, a woman jumped up and announced she had just finished an article on the very subject. This is yoga off the mat—collaboration, ease, meaningful connection. Yoga's motto could be summed up as: "Work smarter, not harder."

It is my experience that yoga is an effective tool of self-care. I challenge you not to take my word for it. Only experience disperses doubt, however reasonable. After all, there is no wiser teacher than the inner teacher.

CREATIVE EXPRESSION

The process of creating a life that works for you does not unfold logically. It proceeds in fits and starts, involves unlearning as much as learning, and requires you to push forward amidst ambiguity. You have to act before you're ready to act, consider that your true interests and preferences might surprise you, and defer evaluation until you have collected a lot of evidence. You have to get out into the world, seek out new experiences and connect with new people.

—*Michael Melcher*, The Creative Lawyer

Increase Your Creativity Through Rest and Play

By Harvey Hyman

Creativity is not just for artists. As a lawyer, creativity can be one of your greatest allies. Too often the lawyers on each side get stuck in a mental rut. They just repeat the same arguments over and over again, getting louder and more insistent each time, without moving the process of resolution forward. Then the light goes on. One of them gets a creative idea that enables him to see the situation and re-present it in a whole new way that opens up the mind of the other like a window. The case gets resolved.

If we could be more creative, more of the time, our work would be more inspired, effective and enjoyable.

Over-thinking dulls the brain and reduces creativity. Our brains were not designed to work without periods of rest. When you do little else but read, write, problem solve, multi-task, and yak on the phone, you're depriving your brain of the rest it needs to function best. Over-thinking occurs when we keep wrestling with how to solve a problem and we become progressively more agitated and confused. Lawyers who over-think are demonstrating a lack of trust in the power of their subconscious mind to help them come to good decisions.

Rest and play are two ways of accessing your subconscious mind. By rest, I don't necessarily mean taking a nap. Rest is broader than that and includes engaging in an activity that has nothing to do with the one that has stymied you. It's a way of taking your conscious mind off the problem. In play, you allow your imagination to take over and fiddle around with ideas, images, and impressions.

In Spontaneous Evolution: Our Positive Future, *Dr. Bruce Lipton distinguishes between the conscious mind (which operates by observation of and attention to an object) and the subconscious mind (which developed long before the conscious mind in evolution and can operate automatically). Our brain mass and our brain functions are heavily weighted in favor of the subconscious mind. Dr. Lipton calls the subconscious mind an astonishingly powerful information processor. While our prefrontal cortex (where consciousness is housed) can process 40 nerve impulses per second, the subconscious mind processes 40 million nerve impulses per second.*

The conscious mind is primarily concerned with analyzing the past (for what went right or wrong) and seeking to anticipate, predict, and control the future. The subconscious mind operates beneath our awareness in the present moment to take in real-time data; rapidly process it; and convert it into real time emotions, decisions, actions, and behaviors. While our conscious minds are moving back and forth from past to future, we are living our lives in the present. According to Dr. Lipton, the conscious mind contributes only 5 percent of our total cognitive activity, while the subconscious mind contributes the other 95 percent.

If you want to be more creative, you need to start using your subconscious powerhouse. A good example of the power of the subconscious comes from studies on consumer choice. We now live at a time when choice can be overwhelming—we have so many options when purchasing things, from meals to paint color to cars. We all know people who occupy different points on the spectrum of thinking through their choice before making a purchase. Some read every article ever written in magazines like Consumer Reports, *while others go from the gut and pick the first one they like. Whose decision is more accurate?*

Dr. Ap Dijksterhuis has tested the accuracy of consumer decision making with regard to considerations like product usefulness, quality, reliability, cost, and so on. He found that for simple purchases, like oven mitts, thinking it through helps, but for more complex purchases, like cars or apartments, too much thinking lowers accuracy, and it's better to use your subconscious mind.

In February 2006 Dijksterhuis and his colleagues published a paper about buying an apartment entitled "On Making the Right Choice: The Deliberation-without-Attention Effect" [Science, 311 (5763) 1005-1007]. Three groups of people were fed tons of information about apartments and asked to find the optimal one.

One group was given time to think before responding. A second group was asked to respond immediately with no time for conscious processing of data. A third group was immediately shifted to a different cognitive task, and then asked to respond. The group given some time to think did better than the group asked to answer right away. The group distracted from analyzing the data about apartments chose better than the other two groups. The conclusion was that we are more accurate in making complex choices when we are given time to process the data, but we do not dwell directly on it and instead allow our subconscious mind to go to work.

Based on anecdote, we know that highly creative people deliberately cultivate periods of mental quiet in which the steady chatter of the conscious, thinking mind gets switched off. Great leaders and teachers who practice daily meditation, such as the Dalai Lama, are able to use periods of mental quiet to dispel confusion, create mental clarity, and balance their mental energy. This enables them to develop the kind of piercing wisdom that reduces thorny, complicated issues about how to live into easily understandable, inherently compelling bits of sage advice.

Great scientists, mathematicians, and inventors have used periods of mental tranquility to allow their subconscious minds to solve problems that exceeded the powers of their conscious minds. There are many examples from the history of thought. While bathing, Archimedes discovered the correlation between the volume of an object and the amount of fluid it displaces. Newton identified the force of gravity while sitting under an apple tree when a falling apple conked him.

The German biochemist August Kekule labored unsuccessfully at his desk to figure out the chemical structure of the benzene molecule. He turned his chair toward the warming fireplace, dozed off, and had a dream about a snaking biting its own tail. He awoke to realize the structure of benzene was a ring. In September 1928 Alexander Fleming returned to his lab after a two-week vacation, feeling rested and alert. He noticed a culture dish overrun by staphylococci bacteria, except for one small spot. Because he had time to ponder the implications and was not feeling rushed, he ended up discovering penicillin and saved millions of lives.

Overloading one's mind with data or simultaneous tasks is harmful to creativity. In The Overflowing Brain, *Torkel Klingberg, PhD, says the basic design of the human brain hasn't changed in 40,000 years, and it wasn't designed to handle the massive amounts of data or the multi-tasking we ask our brains to handle today. Klingberg says evolution designed our brains to work well with a small group of people in a simpler environment with fewer tasks and fewer distractions, where less data went a longer way.*

Our two principal memory systems are working memory and long-term memory. Working memory (housed mainly in the frontal lobes) briefly holds bits of information in consciousness so that we can use that information to do cognitive work. Much of the data in working memory gets tossed out, because it's not important or not relevant to our cognitive goals. Some of the data in our working memory gets put into long-term storage in many different parts of the brain, which can be retrieved later when needed. The hippocampus in the inner temporal lobe is the brain organ that converts working memories to long-term memories. It malfunctions when stressed, and can be damaged by chronic stress, which elevates the blood level of the stress hormone cortisol.

Klingberg says there are several factors that contribute to people underperforming cognitively at work. First, human working memory can only hold seven bits of data at one time, so you are overloading it when you try to cram too much information into your brain. Second, asking your brain to perform two separate tasks simultaneously impairs your performance on each task, because the tasks are competing for the use of the same brain processing areas. Third, the ability to multi-task begins a long, slow decline at age 25. By age 55, many people multi-task at the level of a 12-year-old.

Klingberg is a professor of cognitive neuroscience. Edward M. Hallowell, MD, is a physician who spent 20 years teaching at Harvard

Medical School. He has written a book called Crazy Busy. *Hallowell says we are choking on data. We have way too much, yet we believe we always need more to make informed decisions. To solve human problems constructively we need less busy thinking—the kind crammed with data—and bolder, creative thinking that draws upon our inner resources.*

Klingberg and Hallowell agree that our modern addiction to speed in the realm of thinking and doing is harming our creativity. Klingberg says exceeding the limits of our brain won't bring success, yet we love to be stimulated and we insist on more information, more impressions, and more complexity delivered to us as fast as possible. Hallowell says we are at a cultural point in which people equate slow with boring and stupid, and fast with exciting and brilliant. We love entertainers and other people who generate thoughts with lightning speed—even if their thoughts are glib, shallow, and unwise. We hate hesitation, pauses, and uncertainty, yet the pause represents the space where old impressions can re-form through creativity into a new insight.

Hallowell reminds us that it was Albert Einstein who said, "Please explain the problem to me slowly, as I do not understand things quickly." Hallowell says it's the slow processor who looks at things carefully from many different angles, who comes up with profound and original views. You can't birth your best ideas when you're overwhelmed by data, demands, and deadlines. They clog the mind, which has to be at its most flexible to be most creative. People need to stop, fiddle around, and play with objects (including ideas) to get creative. They need respite to allow their subconscious, the great incubator of our creative ideas, to work.

Hallowell asks where do you do your best thinking, and suggests it's probably in the shower and not at work. Why? At work you're goal directed, expected to think fast on your feet, and consumed with "worry, blather, and clutter." Showers promote good thinking because they induce a state of comfort, calm, and relaxation. Showers activate all five senses. Unless you have a truly weird shower, there is no one telling you what to do, what to work on, or what to think about.

When you step into the shower, the mind stops gathering data and goes into a state of play. Hallowell says that play lies at the heart of creativity. Play lifts you out of the mundane. It activates and engages the imagination. Play goes off on tangents, knows no timetable, subverts the existing order, and transforms it through imagination.

In his book Play, *Stuart Brown, MD, says play enhances creativity because it erases self-imposed censorship of how we think, feel, move and behave. Play, not necessity, is the mother of invention. Brown says creative people know the rules of the game, but are open to improvisation and serendipity. They don't automatically reject new ideas that more straight-laced people would scoff at. Play promotes the mixing of fantasy and reality. It activates brain areas with different functions and integrates them in a synergistic way. To play, you have to be able to tolerate mistakes and take risks. You have to see the game element in all the activities of life and not be dead serious all the time.*

Brown notes in his book that play has benefits beyond innovation or creativity. Play can improve depression. Play can lift the lid off our true selves and put us back in touch with wonderful traits of character and ideas about what we really want to do in life that we've suppressed for years. Brown uses Al Gore as an example. It was only after he lost the presidential election that Gore decompressed, cut loose, and began to play. It was only then that he shed his stiff, clamped down way of living, felt fire in his belly, and stopped holding back. Brown says you can't help but see and be affected by the passion, emotion, and joy Gore brings to his work on global warming.

Brown advocates the use of play at work to reduce the constant sense of urgency and anxiety people feel, as well as to increase social cohesion. A very interesting study published in September 2009 showed that Oxford University rowers who trained together could tolerate twice as much pain as they could while training on their own. The authors concluded that synchronized activity as a group increases endorphin production, bonhomie and positive affect.

To support creativity it's a good idea to be well rested. Sleep physicians say we need at least eight hours of sleep per night and giving up just one hour per night (to watch dumb TV or do extra legal work at home) causes significant, measurable decline on cognitive tasks.

Conclusion

Lawyers often complain their jobs make them feel tense and don't afford them opportunities for creativity. The two conditions go together. If you found a way to be less tense you would be more creative, and if you were more creative you would be more playful and less tense. Tension and lack of creativity come from nonstop data gathering, goal-directed activities, multi-tasking, and rushing to beat deadlines. The billable hours system is slowly being reformed, and this opens up time for rest and play at work.

Each firm and each solo practitioner can decide what works for him or her. No one size fits all. Rest could include a nap, extended time for lunch, taking a walk, going to a museum, practicing yoga or meditation, or reading a book that has nothing to do with the law. Play could include group activities like sports, attending a sports event, laughter yoga, comedy improvisation, or art projects. The options are as unlimited as the characters, cultures, and preferences of the lawyers who make them. The important thing is to recognize the great value of rest and play in generating creativity at work.

ALIGNING WITH YOUR PURPOSE AND VALUES

I N MY most cynical times, I sometimes say that law school was a soul-ectomy. Our minds are well trained but to say that our emotions and matters of spirit are discouraged in our profession would be an understatement, at least in the law schools of the past. There is nothing wrong with thinking like a lawyer, which has many uses, but there is more to a human being than a mind. No one told us that after graduation we could return to those disowned parts of ourselves.

WHY ARE YOU HERE?

Several years ago, I found myself in the buffet line next to Dean David Hall, then of Northeastern Law School. David Hall is a very tall, quiet man who exudes spiritual peace. I thanked him for the work he was doing in the legal profession, on behalf of all of us who benefited from that work. Humbly, he dismissed my praise and said he was called to do it. "Yes, but you answered the call," I reminded him. So often, we hear the call and ignore it. It eats away at us. We know it is there. We feel it when we get up in the morning. We self-medicate to quiet it.

What does your heart yearn to do? What cause or action would fulfill the promises you made to yourself before cynicism and despair took over? What difference were you born to make?

> Purpose answers the question, "Why?" When I talk about life's purpose, I am talking about the why of your life. . . .Why are you here? Who are you meant to be? What are you meant to do?
> —Tim Kelley, in *True Purpose: 12 Strategies for Discovering the Difference You Are Meant to Make*

Answering those questions can be frightening. My own answer had me give up my home and office and become an itinerant person for the past 18 months. It had me spend every dollar I had and seek more to fulfill my mission. It gets me up in the morning, hungry for more opportunities to transform the legal profession, to tell the stories of others who are doing that work.

Answering that question can be freeing. I have never felt more alive. *This* is what I was born to do. *This* is the world I want for my children. I no longer have the burden of doing work that isn't fulfilling my deepest purpose. All my time, attention, and resources are aligned for one purpose. I *love* what I'm doing.

Over the past 18 months, we've done more than a hundred interviews, heard more than a hundred stories of people experiencing transformation and going against the mainstream because their hearts and minds called them to make a difference. My purpose is fulfilled in sharing the stories, in giving attention to the courageous and creative lawyers who stepped forward as pioneers in a movement that has the potential to save the world.

LISTEN TO THE "LITTLE VOICE"

In the chaos of our chattering minds, there is a quieter voice that helps us know who we really are. It is the voice that tells us what is right and what is wrong for us. It isn't the same voice that is clamoring about the to-do list. We can hear it when we are quiet enough or when it is so agitated with us that it shouts above the din.

There are so many other voices around us asking us to do X, Y, or Z. They all want us to play the role they want us to play. Sometimes those voices clamor for attention, too. My father always wanted to be a lawyer, so part of me went to law school to please him. Part of me wanted the intellectual exercise. And there may have been a part that was destiny. After law school, my little voice wouldn't "let" me practice law, even though it would have pleased my dad and certainly would have provided more intellectual stimulation and income than what I was doing. I didn't want to be one of those adversarial jerks. When I learned about holistic, peaceful approaches, the little voice leaped for joy! Finally—a way to honor the part of me that went to law school to make a difference!

Schizophrenic? It may seem so.

My little voice tells me when I am in alignment with my purpose and when something isn't quite right. It knows when I'm selling out and when I'm honoring my own values. My little voice guides me and helps me shape my life.

It wasn't always so. I've done my share of people-pleasing. I stayed in relationships where the little voice was screaming for me to get out. I've gone to meetings because I was expected to. At times, my little voice still negotiates with my sense of obligation. Seeing the results of ignoring it, I have learned to hear out the little voice and to honor its perspective, and I follow it most of the time.

I learned that my busyness and the chatter made it difficult to hear the little voice and that the more I listened, the better my life worked for me. Contemplative time offers an opportunity for listening. The stress of trying to please others dissolved when I began to please myself more and more. I love the life that I've created in partnership with my little voice.

✕ · ✕

The next morning, I went to a criminal courtroom to try to find my love for trial law. Instead, I saw the courtroom with new eyes. Rather than a forum for justice, I saw a giant hate party predicated on the illusion of separateness.

I watched the judge needlessly belittle the lawyer, the spectators. I watched the accused sitting in the box, cast in the role of the bad guy. Yet I didn't see a bad guy. I saw someone living out his karma, playing an essential part in this survivalist melodrama.

I tried to imagine how this scene would play out in a world not attached to narrow notions of right and wrong. Okay, maybe he did it, maybe he didn't, but what if we let go of our attachment to duality? How might we understand these events through a soulful lens? What decisions brought each player to this stage today? Is their role in this drama intrinsic to their true-path? Where would they be without each other?

Then I inquired into my own place in this melodrama. Why was I in this courtroom at this moment? I imagined myself in the role of the defense lawyer. No sweet stirrings. No spark in my body. Nothing. I certainly believed in the presumption of innocence that Eddie [my mentor] had fought so hard for, but I didn't seem to covet this game anymore. My soul gaze had shifted from the laws of the land to the laws of the universe: the presumption of Essence.

—From Soul Shaping: A Journey of Self-Creation *by Jeff Brown, published by North Atlantic Books, © 2009 by Jeff Brown. Reprinted by permission of the publisher.*

Life Purpose: Do We Create It or Discover It?

Ralph Redfox

Some people believe that we are born with a life purpose and it is our job to discover it. Others believe that we can create our own purpose. I think both positions have some validity. I first worked with my life purpose coach in the mid-1990s. At that point, I went through his process and created my life purpose as being a "catalyst for peace" and began my journey of bringing peace to the legal profession.

Over the years, I have questioned that particular expression of my purpose and have tried on different ways of saying it. I often believe that the words fail to convey everything I want to say, but I feel the whole purpose in my body. I can tell the difference between something that is aligned with my purpose and something that is not by checking my gut.

On our travels around the country in the summer of 2008, I had a purpose-related experience when we visited the Medicine Wheel, an ancient spiritual site in Wyoming. After a series of delays that proved opportune, we happened to arrive there when an elder, Ralph Redfox, the last survivor of a Cheyenne clan, was conducting a rare ceremony. I walked around the outside of the Medicine Wheel slowly as the elder conducted his ceremony and sent my good intentions toward them.

When the ceremony was over, we were asked if we wanted to be blessed. (His companions said he never had offered blessings to bystanders before, so this was extraordinary.) He blessed us and a few others at the Wheel; then we visited with the individuals involved in the ceremony. Our conversation focused on where we came from, and we discovered many commonalities among us: a member of the group had recently been in Asheville, our point of departure. The other members of the group represented other stops on our journey—Wisconsin, the Black Hills, Idaho, and Oregon. There was a feeling of serendipity and communing among us.

The Native American ceremony had included the traditional tying of prayer cloths or flags on trees and on the fence so that the prayers could be carried far in the wind. We were invited to choose a prayer cloth from the small grove where they'd tied their prayers at the end of the ceremony. I was immediately drawn to a particular red and yellow one, and I just knew it was mine. I had to climb through the trees, got hooked on some branches, and was stuck a couple of times—but there was never a question that that particular cloth was mine and I was going to have it. When I came back to the cluster of people near the elder, I asked whose prayers I had chosen. I was told that I had chosen the Doorkeeper's prayer cloth, and several of the ceremonialists told me that it meant that I too am a doorkeeper for new thoughts.

When I went to meet the elder's apprentice, the Doorkeeper whose prayers I had chosen, I introduced myself by name. He looked deeply into me and told me that they had known my name for a long time. This man who had never met me and knew nothing about my life or purpose told me that I have much work to do in bringing peace to all two-leggeds and sharing new thought with all.

"Catalyst for peace" no longer has the juice for me that "bringing peace to the two-leggeds and sharing new thought with all" has. As I write this book, I experience the fulfillment of expressing that purpose.

VALUES

Coaches and motivational speakers sometimes talk a great deal about your "values" as if they are some magic pill that you can take and transform your life just by identifying them. Like "purpose," values are personal and intrinsic to everyone, and you probably know whether you're living true to your values or not without making a long list of them. However, at times, I've found it helpful to go through the exercise of creating a list of my values and posting them on the wall as a reminder to me. I recall once sitting at my desk working into the night on a client matter and looking up and seeing my list of values. Near the top was "time with family." I took a deep breath and looked at the pile of work, made a quick list of urgent items to handle the next day, and drove home. My values won that night, and so did my family. If my list of values had said something like "having all my work done on time" or "bill as many hours as possible this week," I would have happily stayed late and lived true to my values.

Even the people closest to us may have very different values than ours. Where do our values come from? Are they inherent or a result of our environment? This is the age-old question of nature versus nurture: Are we born with our values, or do they develop as we grow?

Not surprisingly, I tend to come out on the side that both are correct. There are some essential values that define us, and we come into the world knowing those. There are some that are shaped and morph according to our environment and circumstances. It is not a problem when our values change at different times in our lives and under different circumstances. For instance, I don't see it as a problem that family is not on the top of my list anymore. There was a time and place for that. I still love my family and I still value them, but everyone is grown and it is no longer necessary for me to organize my life around them.

In law school, many of us were shaped in subtle ways—and some were shaped in ways that were not so subtle. Law school typically values analytical reasoning, order, and predictability. Compassion, empathy, and flexibility are not valued nearly as much. After three years spent swimming in law school values, a lot of people find themselves questioning the values that used to be most important to them. Add to that that most law students are in their early 20s. They haven't had the chance to establish their own values yet.

You don't have to accept the premise that making seven figures each year, or being a partner in a big firm, or even a small firm, is the only way to be happy and helpful in your practice. Don't get trapped into unconsciously accepting that notion. First and foremost, you decide what will make you happy. Go ahead. Think about it. Why did you decide to go to law school in the first place? Why did you choose your current job? What were your hopes when you began your professional journey? What did you want to achieve? Do you still want those same dreams, or do you have new ones? Write them down. Reconnect with the desires that drove you to become a lawyer. Look for the spark within you."

—*Kevin Houchin, in* Fuel the Spark: 5 Guiding
Values for Success in Law & Life

The values listed in the accompanying table are by no means all the values that someone could have. Some of the words are actually considered synonyms, but they feel a little different to me. You will undoubtedly think of something that I haven't included here, or you may express your values in different language. It is important to choose the words that resonate with you. Perhaps this list will help you in identifying your own values in your own words.

I suggest that you go through the whole list and circle every value that you think fits you. Of that list, choose the top ten. This may require you to combine some similar ideas. For example, you may value artistic expression and beauty for similar reasons and choose to combine them into one value called beautiful art.

Now the hard part: Reduce your top ten down to three to five values that are the ones you want to focus upon. With more than three to five, you won't remember them all and be able to constantly hold them up in your life. If you must name more, just choose three for focus now and rotate them in a few months. Right now, my focused values are "clear, authentic communication," "transformation," and "adventure." "Consciousness" and "commitment" are also important to me, and I may make them my focus in the near future. A new value that has never made my top ten is starting to have some attraction, too: stability and rootedness.

Accomplishment	Accountability	Accuracy
Achievement	Acknowledgment	Advancement and promotion
Adventure	Affection	All for one and one for all
Appreciation	Artistic expression	Authenticity
Autonomy	Beauty	Being around people who share your values
Calm, quietude, peace	Certainty	Challenge
Challenging problems	Change and variety	Cleanliness, orderliness
Client satisfaction	Close relationships	Closure
Collaboration	Comfort	Commitment
Communication	Community	Competence
Competition	Concern for others	Connection
Consciousness	Contemplative time	Content over form
Continuous improvement	Cooperation	Coordination
Creating closure of past	Creating new futures	Creativity
Decisiveness	Delight	Democracy
Discipline	Discovery	Diversity
Ease	Ecological sustainability	Economic security
Effectiveness	Efficiency	Equality
Ethical practice	Excellence	Excitement
Fairness	Faith	Faithfulness

Fame	Family	Family time
Fast living	Flair	Flexibility
Focused attention	Freedom	Friendship
Fun	Future planning	Global view
Goodwill	Goodness	Gratitude
Growth	Hard work	Harmony
Having a family	Healing	Helping other people
Helping society	Honesty	Honor
Human rights	Improvement	Independence
Individuality	Influencing others	Inner peace and harmony
Innovation	Integrity	Intellect
Intellectual stimulation	Intensity	Interconnectedness
Involvement	Joy	Justice
Knowledge	Leadership	Love
Loyalty	Maximum utilization (of time, resources)	Meaning
Meaningful work	Merit	Money
Nature	Openness	Order (tranquility, stability, conformity)
Particular location	Patriotism	Peace, nonviolence
Perfection	Personal development	Personal growth
Personal responsibility	Physical challenge	Physical exercise
Play and recreation	Pleasure	Power and authority
Practicality	Preservation	Privacy
Progress	Prosperity, wealth	Public service
Punctuality	Purity	Quality of work
Quality relationships	Quality service	Recognition (respect from others, status)
Reflection	Relationships	Reliability
Religion	Reputation	Resourcefulness
Respect for others	Responsibility and accountability	Responsiveness
Resting body and mind	Results oriented	Rule of law
Safety	Satisfying others	Security
Self-awareness	Self-care	Self-reliance

Self-respect	Serenity	Service (to others, society)
Simplicity	Skill	Solving problems
Sophistication	Speed, quick work	Spiritual expression
Stability	Standardization	Status
Sustainability	Strength	Supervising others
Synchronicity, serendipity	Systemization	Teamwork
Timeliness	Timely completion of work	Tolerance
Tradition	Tranquility	Transformation
Travel and new experiences	Trust	Truth
Understanding	Unity	Variety
Wealth	Wisdom	Work under pressure
Work with others	Working alone	

A Values-Guided Practice

Since graduating from Georgetown University Law Center in 1999, I have frequently found myself wondering whether I made the right decision to go to law school. I loved law school so much that it was a total shock to my system to leave the nurturing environment of idealism and enter the world of practice in a big law firm.

I knew I had gone to law school to make a difference in people's lives, to be a shining light in the world and empower people around me. Being a big-firm lawyer seemed to have no relationship whatsoever to that ideal. Because I didn't have a clear handle on my values, I struggled internally.

I spent a lot of time thinking there must be something wrong with me because I couldn't appreciate the amazing job I had, at one of the most prestigious law firms in the country, making six figures per year, serving the most successful people in the world (including Warren Buffett). How could I not be happy? Thousands, if not hundreds of thousands, of law students would kill for the opportunity, and I was seemingly taking it for granted.

Because I didn't have a clear handle on my own values, I convinced myself that there was something wrong with me. It took several years of deep, internal, personal work to begin to discover my values and step into my own truth. Ultimately, that work led me out of the big law firm into starting my own firm, where I would be able to do things my way. And that led me to revolutionize the broken business model that leaves so many of us and our clients wishing there was something more.

As I left the big law firm, I hired a coach to help me make the transition, and I remember when I began to tell him some of my radical ideas about how I wanted to run my own law firm. He told me that I would fail if I tried those things. He told me my best bet was to continue working with him and get my law firm set up the way all the other successful lawyers he coached had set up their businesses.

Fortunately, by then, I knew enough about my own values to be able to say, "No way, you're wrong. You might have been doing this a lot longer than me, but I'm not going to keep doing things the same old way they've always been done," and fire him.

Time and again as I was building my law firm under this model I call the Personal Family Lawyer® way, I heard from naysayers who thought what I was doing was impossible. Fortunately, I was living by the guiding values I had discovered over several years, and that allowed me to stay on my course. Now I'm blessed to understand why I went to law school in the first place.

I did not go to law school to help rich people save more taxes; to bill my time in six-minute increments; or to prepare form documents for people that they would sign, take home, and never look at again. I went to law school to make a huge difference in the world, to empower people to understand more of who they are and think bigger about that than they ever thought possible, and to shine the light of truth and awareness.

Ten years ago, I couldn't understand how that fit into being a lawyer. Today, I do.

To learn these lessons, I had to work with several coaches, make a huge number of errors, and experience a lot of struggle. But it was all worth it: Today I have a life and a business that is in alignment with who I am, making a tremendous difference in the world and providing a great lifestyle for my family.

—Alexis Martin Neely, from the foreword to Fuel the Spark *by Kevin Houchin, used here by permission of both Alexis Martin Neely and Kevin Houchin.*

SETTING GOALS

ONCE YOU'VE identified your purpose and values, what do you do? One possibility is to set some specific goals for expressing them. They don't have to be specific or measurable results, but you can keep score if you want to. (Those of us who value competition often want to keep score so we can win.)

Your goals do have to be meaningful and inspiring for you; if a goal doesn't pull you forward, it is probably not a goal that has meaning for you. Having a challenging goal may seem daunting because you have no idea how you're going to pull it off, but it shouldn't be something that you think of as a burden or obligation. Goals should energize you. They're *your* goals and you get to design them.

As you read through this book and think about how you'd like to be living, goals will occur to you. Write them down. Create a list. See if they stay with you over time. We all know how it is to go to a seminar or read a book and come away with ideas we would like to pursue. Usually, they fade with time; however, some of them do seem to revisit us time and again, and these are goals you should pursue. I always wanted to travel, but my life circumstances weren't lined up until my children were grown and gone. When the time came, I was ready. What are the goals you've always wanted to aim for?

PAY ATTENTION TO SYNCHRONICITY

For some readers, this will likely be way too out there. I share it here briefly as one of the building blocks of my particular practice because of a book by lawyer and leadership expert Joseph Jaworksi. His book, *Synchronicity*, was one of the books that launched my own journey.

> Arthur Koestler, paraphrasing Jung, defines "synchronicity" as "the seemingly accidental meeting of two unrelated causal chains in a coincidental event which appears both highly improbable and highly significant." The people who come to you are the very people you need in relation to your commitment. Doors open, a sense of flow develops, and you find you are acting in a coherent field of people who may not even be aware of one another. You are not acting individually any longer, but out of the unfolding generative order. This is the unbroken wholeness of the implicate order out of which seemingly discrete events take place. At this point your life becomes a series of predictable miracles.
>
> —*Joseph Jaworski, in* Synchronicity: The Inner Path of Leadership

I measure my alignment with my purpose and values by noticing synchronicities. If I'm on the right path, what I need seems to show up; people I wanted to talk to call me and tell me the very piece of information I need. When I was writing this book, the logical part of me thought I should stop reading my e-mail and answering my phone. After all, those would be distractions, right? Instead, I listened to the intuitive part, which encouraged me to stay in communication. I was in North Carolina working on the book one afternoon and the phone rang; it was Michael, my business partner, calling from New Mexico. He had just had an insight he wanted to share about how easy it is to focus on what we don't have and how we miss the abundance in our lives. It wasn't the first time we'd had that conversation, but he happened to call at the moment that I needed that reminder; it was the next paragraph of the chapter I was working on. The next day, my friend Sherry called to tell me that she and her business partner needed help on their operating agreement. Our conversation was a ride through the application of many of the ideas in this book and became an example of how business law can apply these ideas. Day after day, the right e-mail came into my box. The right posting was on my Facebook. This book is much richer and more interesting with those contributions.

It works like that a lot for me. I straddle the balance of following a path that I think is open and waiting for me, and creating my own path. I sometimes say that my life is a co-creation of *me* and *spirit*. If I'm on the path I'm meant to be on, life partners with me, opens the doors, and gives me what I need.

Until one is committed, there is hesitancy, the chance to draw back—concerning all acts of initiative (and creation), there is one elementary truth, the ignorance of which kills countless ideas and splendid plans: that the moment one definitely commits oneself, then Providence moves too. All sorts of things occur to help that would never otherwise have occurred. A whole stream of events issues from the decision, raising in one's favor all manner of unforeseen incidents and meetings and material assistance, which no man could have dreamed would have come his way.

    Whatever you can do, or dream you can do, begin it. Boldness has genius, power, and magic in it. Begin it now.

—*W. H. Murray, in* The Scottish Himalaya Expedition

GETTING IT ALL DONE: TAKING CONTROL OF YOUR SCHEDULE

Sometimes practicing law feels like being in the middle of a tornado—the wind catches us and takes over our lives. Every client has an emergency. We feel pulled in 100 different directions. Our to-do list stretches out the door and down the street—if we've had time to make a to-do list. If not, piles of paper loom from the desk, threatening malpractice if we don't dig through them and see what's there. Our e-mail inboxes are backed up. Everyone expects an answer to their question within 15 minutes, and if they don't get one, they send a text to see if we're paying attention. Nothing gets done without a deadline, and we try for extensions at every opportunity. Pink message slips rain on us, and all of them are marked "urgent." We know we've missed our son's last three ballgames and that we really need to make it home on time today. But there's a board meeting for the non-profit and we're going over the new by-laws. Thinking about a vacation is out of the question with so much backlog (the last "vacation" was actually a work-related conference).

Then some woo-woo business consultant starts talking about meditation and yoga and how exercise makes a difference with stress. Our malpractice carrier reminds us that most grievances stem from neglecting our clients, and calling them back promptly is most important. We've heard of other options for practicing law and we think it might be fun to try them, but it's a joke to think that we could add anything new to our plates when we can't keep up as it is.

We could laugh if we weren't about to cry. We know we can't find time to have a real lunch on most days, so we don't really know how we could possibly fit in another thing. If we sat quietly for 20 minutes, we'd fall asleep. We have to work long hours and we still don't get all the work done. And we have to get the work done to earn the money we need to maintain our lifestyle and take care of our families. We don't even have time to even think about what is important to us; we're too busy providing for everyone else.

Sound like a familiar swirl? Is your life out of control? How do you regain control and design your life and your law practice in a way that reflects what *you* think is important? How do you stop the tornado from spinning so you can get off, plant your feet on solid ground, and establish something according to your needs and within your control?

First, you need to realize and accept that you will *never* get it all done. You will probably die with a to-do list. Having realized that, you can make a conscious choice to do the things that you most want to do and to not do the things that you don't want to do. Of course, sometimes we have to do our taxes and there are holidays to spend with people we might not want to hang out with on a normal day. But those "have-to" events are exceptions, not the rule. Or they could be if you took control of your life and schedule.

When I was still litigating, there was a lawyer in our bar who epitomized the nasty adversarial litigator. If he heard I was going to take Friday off, he'd set an emergency hearing—or at least make sure that I was afraid he might. Five of my contentious cases had him on the other side, and they were the biggest thorns in my side.

One day, my adversarial colleague told me that his client was angry about how our hearing had ended (in my client's favor) and her family was on the street waiting for me, probably armed. He suggested that I find a way to go out the back door, even though he said that I deserved whatever I got if I went out the front door. Yes, that is right. This officer of the court thought that my getting shot on the street would be deserved.

A few days later, I was driving to a massage appointment and saw the other lawyer in my rearview mirror. He appeared to be following me, so I made an unexpected turn into a parking lot and he drove on. The next morning I called a litigation-loving friend of mine and asked if he wanted five new cases. We talked about how to transfer the clients smoothly, and then I called the clients and explained that I thought this other lawyer was going to be much more successful at the cutthroat litigation that was required in their cases.

I closed five files that day. It was a very, very good day. A part of me worried that I would starve without that income, but new clients came in the door. I became famous in my town for not taking cases with that other lawyer, and a few of my colleagues followed suit. None of us starved, but our quality of life improved dramatically.

You don't have to fire five clients; you can start much smaller. Say no to a client who is considering hiring you to do something you don't want to do. Make a to-do list and leave work early. Recommend mediation instead of litigation to a client you think is a good candidate for that option. Post your values and goals on the wall where you can see them every day, and make one decision based on your values that furthers your goals each day for a week. If you like that and it feels right, do it again the next week.

The Mindfulness Memo: The Motion for Extension of Thyme

By Scott Rogers

Question Presented
Whether mindfulness practices can help provide greater clarity of mind, focus, and ease in dealing with procrastination and time deadlines.

Answer
Thoughts like "I don't have enough time," or "I'll never get this done in time" have both a factual quality and a "fear-based" quality. While it can sometimes be the case that poor planning or circumstances result in a genuine rush, more often than not, the perception of "not enough time" is a conditioned thought that arises and, when believed, creates a "false" sense of crisis that undermines performance. The Motion for an Extension of Thyme is one method of effectively dealing with the source of procrastination and worry, bringing about a more effective use of time—and, often, more time.

Discussion
A popular court filing is the motion for an extension of time. It probably comes as no surprise to you that the procrastination that many lawyers experience continues unabated and perhaps even intensifies throughout their careers. And so, a subset of all "Motions for an Extension of Time"— couched in terms of the need to review recently discovered documents, or

owing to a family illness, or some such—are in actuality a pretext for what is more properly termed the "Motion to Excuse My Poor Planning and Procrastination."

In this month's Mindfulness Memo, we'll explore a simple mindfulness exercise that can begin to shift this habit, that is, to catch the procrastinating mind in the act and do something different, which can help break the habit and start the process of generating a different—and more productive—response to stressful situations.

In practice, the road to a motion for extension of time begins with the best of intentions. You've received opposing counsel's motion for summary judgment and have 45 days to respond. You place it on your calendar and tell yourself that you will begin to work on it promptly to avoid a last-minute rush. The thought itself feels good.

But, you find it challenging to focus on a far-away deadline. You'll work on it tomorrow, you tell yourself. Then, as the deadline draws near, a subtle anxiety creeps in each time thoughts turn to the assignment, and you find yourself distracting yourself with other discretionary work and unnecessary chitchat. Projects pile up, and you begin to generate excuses. You're pleased at how reasonable they sound.

At this point you start calling in favors from, of all people, opposing counsel, who is likely to agree to your extension or some variation of it. After all, once you file your response, the clock starts ticking down for the deadline to file a reply. Even if the motion is opposed, you will likely marshal your powers of persuasion and find a way to convince the judge that the demands of your busy practice and the needs of your client counsel in favor of a short extension in the interests of justice.

Immediately upon realizing that, one way or another, your deadline has been extended, a wave of relief washes over you. It's like forgetting to do your homework and then learning that school was canceled due to the weather. It's an old, familiar, comforting feeling. But here's the rub: Because the relief you experience is so pleasant, your procrastinating and counterproductive habits are reinforced. And so the cycle is primed to repeat itself again and again.

The good news is that research in neuroscience is finding that the brain changes in response to experience. Repeat unproductive habits and you build and strengthen their neural pathways. But, introduce something different, especially at the moment you start down the old familiar route, and different pathways will be forged. As you do this more and more, the old roads wash away and the new ones are paved.

Here is an exercise that you may find helpful when you're sitting at your desk, intent on working, and your mind begins to wander. Rather than allow yourself to get pulled off track where you'll eventually be wishing you had more time, and may begin to feel overly stressed, give yourself an Extension of Thyme.

On your next visit to the grocery store, visit the produce section and buy a pack of fresh thyme, or a thyme plant. Keep a sprig, or an extension, nearby. You can use one as a bookmark in a case book. You can leave some on your desk or in your car. Each time you begin to feel your mind pulling you in another direction, reach out and pick up the thyme. Look at it and notice the intricate detail. Then close your eyes, bring it to your nose, and smell its pungent aroma. Allow this moment to cue awareness of your breathing, slowly inhaling and exhaling. Sink into this sensory experience. As you do, the chatter in your mind will begin to subside. After a few breaths, open your eyes and, with awareness that you've got "thyme on your hands," smile. Everything will be okay.

This simple sensory exercise can help tone down subtle agitation and clear your mind. Over time you may find you are more productive and less likely to become sidetracked or distracted when you set your mind to a specific task or project. This practice will pay big dividends both professionally and personally throughout your life.

—This article is reprinted with permission from The Mindful Lawyer website, found at www.themindfullawyer.com. Copyright 2003–2009. Institute for Mindfulness Studies, Inc. All rights reserved.

Get More Done by Doing Less

By Debra Bruce

For fast-acting relief—slow down.

—Lily Tomlin

Life is full of paradox. If you feel harried and stressed at work every day, if you are always putting out fires, the counterintuitive best thing to do is stop everything else you are doing and read this article. Three steps will revolutionize your practice. I know you are in a hurry, so here they are:

- *Create blocks of quiet time.*
- *Prioritize your work each morning.*
- *Stop multi-tasking.*

Some of you are rolling your eyes and muttering disgustedly, "Get real!" or "Give me something I can use." You may be the ones who will have the most difficulty implementing this advice. You will also be the ones who will benefit most from it.

Creating Blocks of Quiet Time

This one step makes the single biggest difference *in the efficiency of the lawyers I coach. In our accelerated world of cell phones, e-mail and Black-Berries, clients' expectations of immediate response have increased, and with it the number of daily interruptions. Yet lawyering still requires a lot of heavy-duty brainwork with full concentration. Stopping the onslaught for even just one hour a day can work miracles.*

That requires discipline—of yourself, your staff, and your clients. Your clients are actually the easiest to train. They can't see you, and they already expect you to be unavailable when you are on the phone, in a meeting with another client, or in court. Their anxiety at not reaching you can usually be soothed if they receive a specific hour when you will return their call. Provide your "gatekeepers" with suggested scripts for handling incoming calls. They can say something like, "He's behind closed doors now, Ms. Smith, but I know he will want to talk to you. Can he call you at this number around 11 a.m.? Is there something I might be able to help you with right now?" If you normally answer your own phone, change your voicemail daily to indicate the hour when you will next return calls, and provide another contact person's number for urgent matters. Make sure that contact is scheduled to be available during your quiet time.

Lawyers and staff in your office must be retrained—it's likely you have trained them that it is OK to interrupt you at their convenience. Keep a tally to identify the most frequent offenders and the subject matters they bring to you. You may need to grant more authority to a submanager or give some additional training to remove yourself as a bottleneck in their workflow. Ask them to accumulate their questions until a scheduled time. If you schedule your uninterrupted block at the same time each day, they will be able to schedule their needs for you more efficiently and adjust their expectations more readily.

Some of the lawyers I work with have found it easier to actually leave the office for an hour each day. When they began to experience the benefits of the uninterrupted time, however, it strengthened their resolve to protect their time in the office.

Prioritizing Your Work

Many busy lawyers allow emails, phone calls and the priorities of other people to determine which projects they work on each day. Then they stay late or take work home because they are stressing over "not getting any-thing done today."

Avoid those pitfalls by taking the time to make a running written list of everything you need to do. That will free up the RAM in your brain normally used to run the reminder loop all day. You'll think more clearly and be more effective. Each morning before you begin work, review and update your list and identify the three most important items. Yes, there may be 57 items on the list, but you know you won't get them all done today; so first keep the focus on the three most important ones. When you complete them, you can return to your list. If those are all you manage to accomplish today due to genuinely important and urgent matters that crop up, you'll have the peace of knowing that you accomplished what was most important.

Implementing this time management tip provides the second-highest improvement in productivity for my clients. It's not new or revolution-ary, but do you actually do it now? Some lawyers feel they must review their morning e-mail before updating their list, in order to incorporate new matters coming in; that's fine, but you can't let someone else's haste determine your priorities.

Stop Multi-tasking

I gasped when my coach requested that I stop multi-tasking for a week. My deadlines and stress level had crept up on me again. The stress had gotten so uncomfortable that I was willing to try anything that didn't add another to-do to my long list. I found the shift challenging at first—as I drove to the office, I grabbed the cell phone to return a call, then realized that would be multi-tasking. I turned off the phone and even turned off the radio. That was hard. To keep from reverting to multi-tasking, I had to focus more intently on whatever I was doing. I started seeing things I had never noticed before.

As I gave myself permission to do just one thing at a time, I began to relax. The phantom sense of helicopter blades whirring in my head faded away. I let go of trying to accomplish a hundred things today because I had committed to doing one thing at a time. Knowing I could do only one thing, I paused and chose each next task deliberately. That night after dinner I almost enjoyed doing dishes, as I focused on why the job needed to be done and how I could do it efficiently.

Over the next few days, as I continued the experiment, I had the mystical sense of time expanding to permit me to accomplish what really needed to be done. At the end of the experiment, I had managed to meet all my deadlines as they arose. More importantly, however, I had regained my serenity.

As I reflected on my experience with some measure of awe, I realized that I had unknowingly engaged in what Buddhists call mindfulness practice. Through that practice, I had experienced some of what author Eckhart Tolle calls "the power of now." I have shared my experience with others, and several have tried creating a "multi-task free" zone themselves. They, too, report increased peace of mind.

I haven't completely given up multi-tasking, but I do direct more effort to fully focusing on what I am doing in the moment. If I feel myself building up stress, I go back to doing one thing at a time. Try it. You may be surprised.

Attention is such a critical capability of human beings that philosophers have reminded us that we are our attention. What I pay attention to is who I am. If I pay attention to the stress and the strain of law school, I will be creating a mind that gives birth to a stressed and strained person. If I pay attention to my advancement and growth in legal expertise, and to the goal of being a lawyer, I can become a satisfied lawyer.

Paying attention is not easy and most people don't do it very often. In order to pay attention, a person has to have thoughts instead of the thoughts having him or her. As most of us drift through each day, our thoughts are automatic and impulsive. Paying attention is a learned skill, one that takes practice. It requires a necessary ability to step back mentally and observe what your mind is doing, to observe as an "impartial spectator" your thoughts and feelings and preferences and moods.

—Stephanie West Allen and Jeffrey M. Schwartz, "Law Students: Create A Well-rounded Life," The Complete Lawyer, *Volume 3, Issue 3, 2007*

THE ADVANCED COURSE FOR GETTING CONTROL OF YOUR SCHEDULE

Once you've gained some control of your life, it is time that your daily schedule should begin to reflect that control. This won't work unless you've built some muscle into keeping your word to yourself and those close to you. If you can't be reliable to make it home for dinner one day a week, how can you plan a week of activities?

The following exercises are designed to create new habits. I used to follow these all the time but have loosened my structures as they've become second nature. When I'm particularly pressed for time, I still lean on these practices to get it all done. Try this for one month. If it works, keep it. If not, you'll at least have a much clearer idea of how you spend your time.

1. Write your life's purpose at the top of the page.
2. Write your top three to five values under your purpose.
3. Now we're going to make some lists. On a week-by-week period, make:
   - The list of appointments you have with other people.
   - The list of deadlines and things that must be done this week.
   - The list of tasks that you need to do to take care of yourself and those close to you. (These include cooking, eating, sleeping, laundry, recreation, exercise, and downtime.)
   - The list of tasks that someone with your purpose and values would do this week.
4. On each list, put the estimate of how long it will take to do each task. Be realistic, and don't forget travel time. It is probably a good idea to double most estimates.
5. Now get your calendar—paper or electronic. We're going to begin to fill it in. In this order:
   - Put the appointments on your calendar.
   - Schedule the work with deadlines by making an appointment for yourself to do the work.
   - Schedule a block of time each day (or a morning block and an afternoon block) for returning calls, handling emergencies, and answering e-mail. Be realistic about this—make sure you schedule a big block if these activities usually fill your days.
   - Schedule your life tasks: reading your daughter a story, eating, cooking, cleaning, sleeping, recreation, exercise, banking, family functions. If you're using an electronic calendar, use the repeat function as appropriate.

- Schedule time to work on your to-do list. First, just work on the to-do list itself: Get clear about what there is to do and then schedule it for future weeks, before it reaches the urgent deadline stage. To give yourself an incentive to finish the work, schedule a time for the client to come in and go over it a few days after you schedule time to do it. If this requires you to clean your desk, that needs to go on the schedule, too. Notice that you are creating priorities for future weeks. If the appointment isn't a priority, don't make it.
- Make appointments on your calendar to handle "normal" daily work—that which needs to be done but isn't urgent.
- Schedule significant future projects. For example, if it is February, schedule doing your taxes.
- Now, look at the remaining time on your calendar. If your schedule is already full, look at what you can postpone from your appointments and deadlines, or what you might be able to delegate. Make room for the purpose and values activities. If you absolutely cannot move another thing, go into next week's calendar and block out two or three hours for your purpose and values list.
- If there are any substantial time blocks left, schedule half of them as down time and half as time for handling unexpected events and tasks. If you've gotten to this point and have no time for downtime, schedule a full day off next week or as soon as your deadlines and urgent items allow. (I've learned that I either schedule time to unwind or my body will take it by getting sick.)

6. Watch your own patterns about when you are most productive and schedule work for those times. I rarely do any focused work before 2 p.m. so I schedule routine tasks for the mornings and focus on my writing in the afternoons and evenings. Some menial tasks can be done safely, and without sacrificing attention, while multi-tasking (like catching up on your e-mail while doing laundry) while others (client appointments) require your full attention. Notice that you are usually underestimating how much time minutiae takes.

This may seem like a lot of detail. The truth is that you're either already doing all those tasks or avoiding some of the ones that feel less important—and it's your family that tends to suffer, right along with your health. If you're overwhelmed with too much to do, it's time to make some decisions about how you are spending your time. Being conscious about choosing a busy schedule is one thing. Falling into an unorganized busy schedule because you haven't planned anything else is another.

With this system, when someone asks you to do something on Thursday night, you can honestly say you can't because you have another commitment—even if that commitment is a night in front of the boob tube or a walk in the woods alone to replenish yourself. Start controlling your schedule, and you'll start controlling your life.

CONSCIOUS IMBALANCE

There are times when lawyers have to work long hours. Maybe you have a trial or a big deadline. Maybe you are leading a continuing education program. When we work long hours, we choose to postpone other important tasks. Sometimes that just happens. Texas holistic lawyer John McShane talks about times of "conscious imbalance." He suggests that we create what Michael calls a "psychological belay" for later. Like many of Michael's stories, a belay is a lesson he learned from survival in the wilderness. In mountain-climbing, a belay is a rope that is hooked to your climbing partner who is taking up the slack as you climb. If you fall, you won't fall far, so it provides security along with a safer climb. A psychological belay is the metaphorical equivalent. When we're working long hours and postponing other tasks, we need to find a way to promise ourselves that we will cut ourselves some slack later. Schedule catch-up time after the push and then have a vacation. Schedule some time to spend with family. Balance the time of intense work with some time of intense relaxation. For instance, when this book is finished, I'm headed to Key West for the winter. I will continue to work there, but I'll have lots of time to walk on the beach and watch the starry skies at night. It is part of negotiating with that little voice that is trying to take care of me. I've let her know that I heard her and I'm taking care of her, just not right this moment.

"NOT FOR MY HAND TO DO"

Isn't it great to be needed and talented in solving problems for others? Everyone wants advice from a lawyer. There are always external demands on our energies. There is a phrase that has helped me with this lesson, too. When a problem presents itself and I see that it is "not for my hand to do," I pass it on to someone else.

I believe that the lowest form of giving is the kind of giving that is begrudging, reluctant, and obligatory. Neither the giver nor the receiver is energized by such a gift, be it money or time. The difference between service and sacrifice is that service honors the giver and receiver. Sacrifice takes something away from the giver and therefore doesn't serve either giver or receiver. I like to think that there is always someone who could joyfully provide what I might begrudgingly do from a sense of obligation

A few months ago, I was asked to teach Business Law at my alma mater during the following semester, January through May. I loved teaching Business Law in the past, but I had already scheduled a trip for April. The department chair suggested that I could teach a term class instead of a semester course so as not to interfere with my trip. With that handled, I agreed.

Shortly after I hung up, my little voice began to scream at me. Several other opportunities for spring term showed up in my inbox. I knew that teaching the course was not for my hand to do, but I had already given my word that I would do it. I lost several hours' sleep that night as I tossed and turned and worried about what to do. Then I had a brilliant idea. My friend, Tom, might want to teach the class! Tom has an MBA as well as a law degree, and he is all about sustainability and entrepreneurship, cornerstones of the business department at the college. I realized that he was much better suited to it than I was. When I spoke with him the next morning, he said that he would love to do it. By noon, Tom had a job and I was off the hook. Everyone is much happier.

SELF-AWARENESS

According to an article in the February 2007, edition of Business Review: *When 75 members of Stanford Graduate School of Business' Advisory Council were asked to recommend the most important capability for leaders to develop, their answer was nearly unanimous: self-awareness.*
—Bill George, Peter Sims, Andrew N. McLean, and Diana Mayer, "Discovering Your Authentic Leadership" [Harvard Business Review, February 2007: 129–138]

Recently I was at a program at the National Association of Women Judges, and one of the leaders said that self-awareness was the most important skill that a judge could have. There were nods around the room. I wondered how we actually gain self-awareness. In my survey of other practitioners, they listed many of the same pursuits that I've followed, specifically:

- Reading
- Emotional intelligence/social intelligence/spiritual intelligence
- Enneagram/Myers Briggs
- Landmark/Mankind Project/Human Potential Movement
- Spiritual/contemplative practices/shamanism
- Travel/moving
- Empathy/compassion/open heart
- Coaching and coach training
- Conferences such as the International Alliance of Holistic Lawyers or the International Academy of Collaborative Professionals

The Enneagram: One Tool for Self-Awareness

By Moira McCaskill

The enneagram is one powerful tool for transformation. Identifying our enneagram type can be the first step on the inner journey home. Despite the depth, length, and individual nature of the inner journey, it is not without maps. The enneagram tells us that there are nine personality types and nine paths—and it certainly helps to know which one you are on.

Awareness of Personality

First, the enneagram requires us to identify our own type. No test will tell us our type, although it may narrow the options and point us in a direction. Some people recognize their type quickly and others take time to decide. Either way, self-awareness is required so that the transformational process is engaged.

Simply knowing our type, and how it differs from others, brings better understanding of self and better relationships. The enneagram is well worth knowing for this alone. However, this is just the beginning because what really happens is we take the first step on the path that is appropriate for our type.

Personal Growth

Once we identify our type, we are able to understand our personality structure with more objectivity and insight than ever before. We become aware of our habits of mind, typical behaviors, and attitudes. We learn that the gifts and challenges of our type follow a described pattern. The illumination of our personality structure is incredibly helpful for personal growth. The enneagram is full of information for each type that tells us how we grow and practices that support our growth.

The overarching development here is an expanding sense of awareness and conscious choice. We become less compulsive in our personalities, more flexible in our attitudes and behaviors. We increase in freedom and range. For example, an aware and developed Eight (the strong dominant type) will be able to feel weak and vulnerable and ask for support consciously when, in the past, feelings of vulnerability might have triggered aggression. This is why we say the enneagram does not put you into a box; it shows the way out of the box.

Transformation

Witnessing our personality in action, we begin to see "it" as not our true self. We see ourselves "doing" our personality, and even when we can't change or feel free in the moment, we experience a distance from our ego machinations. We develop what is known as the "inner observer," and some part of us is detached.

This is the beginning of the transformation from personality to essence—our true selves which are more vast and free and healthy than we could imagine. Now the path becomes spiritual and overlaps with other paths and practices. Although we may all end up in a similar experience of transformation and there are many ways to get there, what the enneagram so beautifully provides is a map and a shortcut based on personality type.

Resources

See www.enneagraminstitute.com for online tests by Don Riso and Russ Hudson and www.enneagram.com for typing tools by Helen Palmer. Both are leading enneagram teachers and authors. Many other enneagram websites and enneagram books are available; my personal favorite is The Wisdom of the Enneagram *by Riso and Hudson.*

DEALING WITH THE STRESS OF OTHER PEOPLE'S PROBLEMS

Iɴ Nᴏᴠᴇᴍʙᴇʀ of 2006, I drove a friend from North Carolina to Idaho to start her new life. As I drove cross-country, I received a call from a documentary producer. I'd been working with A&E and several co-producers on screening cases for a restorative justice series. The producer had a possible screening in Oregon and wanted to know if I could conduct an interview. Because my youngest daughter lives in Portland, I was thrilled for an excuse to extend my trip for business reasons.

The producer told me the tragic story. A young mother of four children had been using methamphetamine and caught the house on fire. Her four children, all under five years old, were killed in the fire. I was asked to meet with the father of the children and his family to screen them for a possible face-to-face meeting, where the mother could apologize and they could get their questions answered.

When I tell this story, I always want to stop and issue a warning: Viewer discretion advised. It is not a pretty story, even in the filtered and toned-down version. There are facts that I've never shared with anyone else because they are the stuff that nightmares are made of. Even writing this, I find myself revisiting some of the discomfort.

I met with the father, his father, and his sister in an office I borrowed from attorney-mediator Jim O'Connor in Portland. I taped the interview but have never brought myself to listen to the tapes or write the story beyond the minimal report I wrote for the producers. I have changed a few identifying details to protect confidentiality.

I walked into the appointment expecting to hear a story about a poor mother whose addiction cost her a high price: the loss of her children. As a mother, I imagined that was the worst thing that could ever happen to anyone. Instead, I heard a horrific story of a vengeful mother in the midst of divorce who may have intentionally set the fire, tied her children to their beds, and barricaded the doors before sitting on the porch and smoking a cigarette until a neighbor saw smoke. I heard how the father had been so devastated that his life seemed to have stopped that day, and so deep was his grief, he was still on disability several years later. (This case was being considered for victim–offender dialogue after all the appeals were complete.)

For five hours, I sat with the family and heard their pain. When the three were finished, they called the grandmother and had me talk to her on the phone and hear her story. Hour after hour, I listened to the grisly details of the fire and the conclusions that were made from the evidence. I saw pictures of the cherubic baby, the toddlers' smiling faces, and their graves. I heard about the fire chief who retired after that fire, the police chief who died of a heart attack, the despair and suicide of a lawyer in the case, and the judge's concern and apology to the jury for what they'd had to go through. It seemed that everyone who was close to the case was affected.

I was able to be completely present with the family during the meeting. I let them talk, asking only occasional questions for clarification and understanding. I urged them to talk about their feelings and not just the facts. They told me that no one had ever heard their whole story before, and they were transformed by our meeting. We talked about how hard it was to live in the world as a normal person after such a tragedy, how petty the concerns of their neighbors seemed, how isolated they'd become because former friends avoided them so as not to have to confront the pain, how the loss had changed them at some fundamental level. It was as though they had emptied their bucket of pain when they told the story. I was completely professional and compassionate and appropriate, and I had a straight conversation with the father about his not being emotionally ready to do the work of having a dialogue with the offender and suggesting that one of his parents might be a better choice.

At the end of our meeting, the family drove me to the light rail station and I got on the train to my friend's home. We hugged and they thanked me from the bottoms of their hearts. I told them what a privilege it was to have spent that time with them and waved good-bye. Moments later, the full weight of their experience fell on me. I felt like I'd been hit by a truck. Tears streamed down my face as I rode the 45 minutes home, and then I felt numb. I was barely able to engage in conversation that evening. I was in a fog. The next day, when I went to visit my daughter, I felt clumsy. Light conversation was impossible. I wasn't happy to see my daughter—I couldn't feel anything. To be more accurate, in one way it felt like I had no skin and everything could get in, but in another way, I couldn't feel anything at all. My emotional circuits were blown. For weeks, I cried at the drop of a hat. For months, I was overly sensitive to violence and medical procedures in media. I started watching only the family stations to escape the violence. Commercials for *Law and Order* grated on my nerves, and I cringed when the news came on. At one point, I was not even able to watch a rerun of *The Waltons* because it included a scene with an accident where someone was harmed.

As lawyers, we deal with a lot of trauma, and many of our clients come to us experiencing their own traumas or secondary traumas. Day after day, we stand with our clients as they face the most stressful life events. Even if we don't have cases that involve life and death, our jobs often require us to be in the middle of human drama. Being accused of a crime raises fears of loss of liberty. A custody battle may be the most traumatic event that some people ever experience. Even the more benign-looking events (like signing a will or closing a real estate transaction) can actually represent dramatic and life-changing events to our clients. Creating a business partnership isn't just about filing some papers. What is everyday business for us is a significant occurrence in the life of a client.

Vicarious Trauma

Vicarious trauma (VT) refers to the experience of a helping professional personally developing and reporting their own trauma symptoms as a result of responding to victims of trauma. VT is a very personal response to the work such helping professionals do. VT is sometimes used interchangeably with terms such as compassion fatigue, secondary trauma, or insidious trauma. This phenomenon is most often related to the experience of being exposed to stories of cruel and inhumane acts perpetrated by and toward people in our society.... The symptoms of VT parallel those of post-traumatic stress disorder (PTSD) and can be similarly clustered into the areas of re-experiencing, avoidance and numbing, and persistent arousal....The fundamental difference between VT and PTSD relates to the nature of the stressor. . . .[One researcher] distinguishes between these as primary (e.g., experiencing a serious threat to self or sudden destruction of one's environs) versus secondary stressors (e.g., experiencing serious threat to a traumatized person or sudden destruction of a traumatized person's environs). Empathy has been identified as one of the mechanisms of transfer between primary and secondary trauma. Thus, the empathy that is so critical to working with traumatized people also increases the likelihood of vicarious traumatization.

—*From Peter G. Jaffe, Claire V. Crooks, Billie Lee Dunford-Jackson, and Judge Michael Town, "Vicarious Trauma in Judges: The Personal Challenge of Dispensing Justice,"* Juvenile and Family Court Journal, *Fall 2003.*

Avoiding and Addressing Vicarious Trauma

I'm not a psychologist or an expert on vicarious trauma in the usual sense. I learned about it the way we lawyers learn most things. When the issue arose, I read a lot and I applied what I read to my experience. Besides the previous story, I have had many opportunities to experience vicarious trauma in my life—and to share my knowledge of it with others. One of my clients was murdered by her husband in front of their three children. Another, a divorce client in a contentious case and an emergency room doctor, calmly confessed that he was signing everything over to his wife because he was planning to commit suicide. We spent more than two hours objectively discussing the pros and cons, including the impact on his children. He was disconnected from his feelings, even his love for his children. His emotional circuits had overloaded long ago, and he was running on autopilot with no hope of anything better. When we realized that his despair stemmed from inhumanities he'd seen in the emergency room, I took the opportunity to explain vicarious trauma to him and to share my own experiences. He made no commitment to abandon his suicide plan, but he seemed more in touch with himself when he left my office. By the time he was out the door, I called one of the therapists on our collaborative law team and had my own support session! Later, the collaborative professionals talked it over, and we decided that we should not continue with the case in the collaborative process. The client became angry—*very angry*! An emotion got through the numbness. It is one of the few times that I thought family litigation was better than resolution. (Three years later, he is still alive.)

Because of my holistic approach, I also started paying attention to my own emotions and talking to people about their experiences. My house-mate was left alone at home one night and the dog barked at a noise outside. She flashed back to a time when she was working on a death penalty appeal, recalling the grisly murder and fearing for her life.

Vicarious trauma is very real, and it can have a significant and lasting effect on us. Even though I was not the victim of the fire, I had many of the behaviors that actual victims have. I wanted to tell the story with great detail. I didn't want to say the most horrific details—they seemed unbearable—so I focused on the mundane. Somehow the details allowed me to feel a little detached—as if it were a story, not something that really happened. My feelings were a confused mixture of numb and overly sensitive. I've noticed that the more that I participate in this profession and the more conflict and troubles I see, the less interested I am in engaging in arguments I view as petty. Cocktail party conversation was never pleasant for me, but I now pretty much insist on having conversations of more depth. I think I'm more serious than I used to be, and sometimes I wish I were not.

Avoiding vicarious trauma requires good boundaries. Empathy is obviously an important aspect of lawyering, but you have to find a way of separating yourself and not internalizing your client's terrible experiences. Be careful about how many cases you accept—particularly if they are difficult and painful cases—and find other activities that help you de-stress. Everyone's boundaries are different, so you'll need to find a way to separate that works for you. Meditation before leaving the office? Reading a happy story in bed every night? If you find that nothing is helping and you're reliving someone else's trauma, consider talking it over with a therapist.

Compassion Fatigue

Our profession allows us to help people in their worst moments. Unfortunately, those worst moments can accumulate over time and lead to compassion fatigue, similar to vicarious trauma but less about a traumatic event and more about the constant exposure to the troubles of others. Not long ago, a judge confessed to me that he never saw "normal" cases in his court any more. With all the non-adversarial options, reasonable people rarely appeared before him. The litigants appearing before him were the worst of the worst cases. He was exhausted and looking forward to retirement.

Compassion fatigue in judges is the result of vicariously becoming worn down and emotionally weary from hearing about and dealing with situations where people have been physically and emotionally injured, hospitalized, and all too often killed. These are litigants who suffer "on our watch," so to speak. These cases have a way of creeping into our lives, and that is only natural if the judge cares about and is engaged in his or her work. In thinking about the subject, I have come to understand that these cases affect us in many ways. For me, the volume and nature of the cases can sometimes be overwhelming. Indeed, even one case can be devastating, and most of my colleagues can recall a profoundly tragic individual case even though it occurred years ago.

The symptoms of compassion fatigue in judges are fairly predictable. Some judges reported internalized symptoms, including sleeplessness, eating disturbances, increased anxiety, depression, and hypervigilance. Others reported external symptoms, including becoming increasingly angry, irritable, and intolerant of others. Some judges reported increased fearfulness and security consciousness, the inability to make prompt decisions (procrastination), and increased difficulty focusing or concentrating. Some judges felt quite ambivalent and, therefore, anxious about critical decisions that were close calls. While most people experience one or more of these emotions or behaviors at some point in their lives, the frequency and acuity of the symptoms seem to elevate when we are responsible for the lives of others. Of great interest to me was our finding that compassion fatigue seems to peak at the seven-year mark during the judge's tenure. Efforts to address this well before the seven-year mark are obviously in order.

—*Judge Michael Town*

Obviously, compassion fatigue is also a major concern for lawyers, and something that is important to both recognize and treat.

MANAGING VICARIOUS TRAUMA AND COMPASSION FATIGUE

All of the self-care suggestions are helpful for managing your vicarious trauma and compassion fatigue. When you have challenging cases, you need more self-care. The following paragraphs offer some specific suggestions.

Observe the good in the world. Be grateful. When we're constantly dealing with problems, we can begin to believe that nothing is good. But the world really does have butterflies and hummingbirds. There are good people down at the soup kitchen feeding their neighbors. Take a step back and identify the goodness in your life. Celebrate your intelligence. Find the parts of your life that are working.

Realize that your emotions may be raw, and give yourself some extra pampering, whatever that means to you. It may be a walk around the park, a camping weekend, a bubble bath, time to play with your kids, or a shopping spree. Whatever recharges your emotional battery, do more of it. Take extra contemplative time. For every hour you are sitting with highly emotional people, take an hour to recover and replenish.

Schedule yourself for a massage or energy clearing. When I started practicing law, I noticed that by Friday, I wanted to go out after work and split a pitcher of margaritas with a co-worker. As time went on, I noticed that I was ready on Thursday afternoon. When I noticed myself wanting a pitcher on a Tuesday afternoon, I knew I needed some other option for stress relief. I scheduled a massage that Friday and for every Friday for the next four years of practice. Margaritas once again became a celebratory drink, not a tonic for stress.

Spend time with trusted friends and share what has been going on with you. Consider a support group or therapy, especially if you're working with clients whose traumas are similar to your own past traumas. Therapists who deal with the traumas of others often have peer support groups because they recognize the need to find an outlet to support them. Consider starting a support group for lawyers in your community or contact your local lawyer assistance program and ask they do.

Before you meet with a client, take a few moments to shield yourself energetically. Envision that you are surrounding yourself with golden light and that no negative energy can penetrate it.

Acknowledge the deep emotional impact of the trauma, but don't wallow. Let the emotion flow through you; feel it, then let it go. Eckart Tolle teaches about stepping outside of the body and witnessing the pain come in and then depart.

Remind yourself that you were not the victim. It is not your situation. You can be compassionate, but you do not have to carry the pain for your client. It is your job to support and hold space, not take the emotion away.

A number of factors connected with resiliency and recovery in the face of and following a traumatic event have been identified via research in the area. These factors are:

- The ability to cope with stress effectively and in a healthy manner (not avoiding)
- Being resourceful and having good problem-solving skills
- Being more likely to seek help
- Holding the belief that there is something you can do to manage your feelings and cope

Having social support available to you
Being connected with others, such as family or friends
Self-disclosure of the trauma to loved ones
Spirituality
Having an identity as a survivor as opposed to a victim
Helping others
Finding positive meaning in the trauma

All of these characteristics distinguished those who were able to recover from a traumatic experience from those who may have developed PTSD [post-traumatic stress disorder] or other problems.

—http://ptsd.about.com/od/causesanddevelopment/a/resiliency.htm

EXPANDING THE LAWYER'S TOOLBOX: SKILLS THAT WORK IN ANY PRACTICE

THERE PROBABLY isn't a skill that you could put in your legal toolbox that wouldn't be useful in this multidisciplinary, holistic practice of law. In the past 10 years, I've attended dozens of conferences on all the topics I've written about, and some skills show up at just about every one of them. Some are specific to certain approaches. This chapter looks at those tools that can be applied effectively across all the holistic vectors.

Like so much of this book, some of these ideas could easily have been put in other sections. For example: Working with victims could have been in the chapter on restorative justice, but it's broad enough to be its own skill. Feel free to apply any of these tools in all parts of your life.

CELEBRATING STRENGTHS

WHILE WE can always strive to be better, healthier, and happier, don't forget to celebrate what we already have going for us. In social work, psychology, and social change theory, there is a movement towards focusing on strengths, and proponents make a convincing argument for focusing on our strengths.

1. Every individual, group, family, and community has strengths.

The Strengths Perspective focuses essentially on identifying, mobilizing, and respecting the resources, assets, wisdom, and knowledge that every person, family, group, or community has, as well as their potential for transforming their experiences and lives.

2. Trauma and abuse, illness and struggle, may be injurious but they may also be sources of challenge and opportunity.

To say that negative experiences can bring opportunities to an individual, family, or community does not mean that we do not acknowledge their scars and pain. The Strengths Perspective acknowledges that frequently people who are facing adversity are resilient and resourceful and we should explore and learn from their strategies to overcome adversity.

3. Assume that you do not know the upper limits of the capacity to grow and change. Take individual, group, and community aspirations seriously.

People frequently are bound by an assessment, diagnosis, or profile that has become a verdict or a sentence in their lives. By holding high expectations of clients and keeping an alliance with their hopes, values, aspirations, and visions, we make an obvious deal with their promise and possibility.

4. We best serve clients by collaborating with them.

When we approach clients as helpers or collaborators (having specialized education, tools, and experience to offer, but open to the wisdom, knowledge, and experience that clients bring with them), we work with clients rather than on their cases. In the Strengths Perspective, clients' voices are heard and valued at all levels of intervention, including micro, mezzo, and macro levels, such as in practice with individuals, families, and groups, with communities, and in policy advocacy.

5. Every environment is full of resources.

Every environment is full of individuals, families, informal groups, associations, and institutions willing to help others. When given the opportunity, they contribute with all kinds of assets and resources that others profoundly need, such as knowledge, company, special talents, time, place, and the like. There are resources, partnerships, and strengths available in the community that are ready to be used while we engage in policy advocacy and social action in pursuit of social justice and structural transformation.

6. Caring, caretaking, and context.

Human well-being is essentially related to caring. We should facilitate and assist families, groups, and communities to care for their members. The Strengths Perspective focuses, in a sense, also in caretaking, since this is related to hope; "hope realized through the strengthened sinew of social relationships in family, neighborhood, community, culture, and country." (p. 20).

References

Saleebey, D. (Ed.). (2006). The Strengths Perspective in social work practice. *(4th ed.). Boston: Pearson Education, Inc.*

> *Central to Strengths Based Case Management is the belief that clients are most successful when they identify and use their strengths, abilities, and assets.*
>
> —The Strengths Model: Case Management with
> People with Psychiatric Disabilities *by Charles A. Rapp
> and Rick J. Goscha. Oxford Press, New York, 2006.*

THINKING LIKE A LAWYER

As lawyers, we have in common that we are intelligent and that we have been trained to think like lawyers.

I suspect it is impossible to graduate from law school without encountering the phrase "thinking like a lawyer." If it does not pop up during an introductory orientation lecture, it surely emerges during a legal skills course or perhaps highlighted and underlined somewhere in a previously owned casebook. While a search for the phrase in the legal literature will generate over 1,000 hits, maybe its most memorable use occurs in *The Paper Chase*, when Professor Kingsfield contrasts this notion of clear and coherent mental analysis with the "minds full of mush" that students show up with. Far less frequently, if ever, heard by law students or discussed in the pages of law reviews or mythologized in fictional law school pop culture is the phrase "thinking like a professional."

—Joshua Perry (*http://www.cuttingedgelaw.com/content/
thinking-professional*)

Professor Perry goes on to recommend many of the more holistic ideas that this book espouses in his expanded view of "thinking like a professional."

The skill of thinking like a lawyer is one of the important tools in the lawyer's toolbox, just not the only one. In law school, we learned to find and identify the important and relevant information in complex situations. We applied what we learned, and we somehow acquired the ability to do this all quickly. Previously, I'd avoided math and sciences and considered them hopeless pursuits. I "knew" I couldn't learn them, so I didn't try. I recall that shortly after graduating from law school and passing my first two bar exams, I was faced with a problem that required me to explore physics. Instead of running away in fear, I just buckled down and began to read, realizing that I knew how to learn anything. I surprise myself with how fast I can actually become conversant on almost any topic—and learning fast is a trait of all good lawyers.

We also learned to construct a cogent, rational argument. We learned to inquire deeply and not just blindly accept a proposition. We learned to consider the other side of any issue so thoroughly we could argue either side of a question. And we learned to set aside our emotions—but we didn't always learn when that was appropriate and when it was not. Incorporating your emotions back into your life and practice will make you a happier, healthier person. In turn, it's likely that you will have happier, healthier clients.

> *Too often we underestimate the power of a touch, a smile, a kind word, a listening ear, an honest compliment, or the smallest act of caring, all of which have the potential to turn a life around.*
>
> —Leo Buscaglia

HEALING

Healing is a spontaneous event that comes about through a kind of grace. It can happen anytime, and in any place. It may or may not happen in the context of a healing session. It may come about simply with a smile from a stranger, the breeze blowing through the trees, the song of a bird—some reminder of our connectedness and wholeness—the beauty of Life just as it is at this moment for us.

Healing can happen on many different levels. Sometimes our healing is not what we expect. We need to be open to the gifts which life is always ready to give us. It may be that a physical problem heals, but it may also stay awhile to teach us something. Sometimes a health challenge is a doorway to a deeper healing, a cry from deep within for attention to some part of us that has been unloved and feels separated from the Whole.

Regardless of whether our focus in healing is on the physical, mental, emotional or spiritual level, all levels are invariably touched by the process, and none can be separated out from the rest.

—Mary Maddux (www.heartofhealing.net)

When I talk about law as a healing profession, I am talking about the power of lawyers to facilitate deep healing of their clients' conflicts. We don't have to go back to school to become therapists or energy healers. We don't necessarily have to *do* anything to be healers if we are *being* the space for our clients to find their own healing.

A healer is a different role than that of advocate or problem-solver or adviser or warrior. Those are all certainly useful roles for lawyers at the right times, but healers do something different. They "hold space"—that is, they provide a metaphorical container for well-being and resolution for the person who comes to the healer for help. That container must be clear of the healer's issues. We do that by becoming self-aware so that we can separate our own issues from our clients' issues. With self-awareness, we are able to put our own issues aside and provide a clearing for nonjudgmental communication with our client. No particular training is required to be a lawyer-healer, but many lawyers have found that they are better equipped for "being the space" for healing when they've done their own healing work, when they have a practice of mindfulness, or when they have specific training in a healing art.

Healer Archetype (Wounded Healer, Intuitive Healer, Caregiver, Nurse, Therapist, Analyst, Counselor)

The Healer archetype manifests as a passion to serve others in the form of repairing the body, mind, and spirit. It expresses itself through channels other than those classically associated with the healing of illnesses, and so you need to look beyond the obvious definition of what you "do." You can be strongly guided by this archetype in any occupation or role in life. Some people, by their very nature and personality, are able to inspire others to release their painful histories or make changes in their lives that redirect the course of their future. Essential characteristics include an inherent strength and the ability to assist people in transforming their pain into a healing process, as well as having the "wiring" required to channel the energy needed to generate physical or emotional changes in another person.

—Carolyn Myss (www.myss.com)

COMMUNICATION AND CONFLICT RESOLUTION SKILLS

LISTENING

We must be silent before we can listen. We must listen before we can learn. We must learn before we can prepare. We must prepare before we can serve. We must serve before we can lead.
—William Arthur Ward

In law school we learn to listen for the purpose of critically evaluating what the speaker says so that we can quickly make a decision about the best course of action. We learn to take feelings out of the decision process, and focus on facts, legal principles, and logic. We develop the ability to think on our feet and make quick responses as we face grilling by professors in class or make arguments in moot court competitions. Then as lawyers we interrupt to clarify and focus on facts, disregarding feelings, which we deem irrelevant. We try to control the situation by doing more talking than listening, and what listening we do has a decidedly adversarial or challenging bent.

That approach may serve us well in the courtroom, but it causes problems when we need to build rapport and trust with clients. Effective listening builds rapport because it communicates our interest and concern, and helps us reach beneath our clients' words to learn what is really troubling them. Listening also alerts us to potential new developments in the client's business and additional opportunities to serve the client. In short, listening is an important marketing tool!

A large northeastern law firm decided to study their most effective rainmakers to see what they did differently from other seasoned lawyers in the firm. They discovered that the major rainmakers provided more than legal services to their clients. They became trusted advisors. As a result, executives turned to them again and again as a resource, regardless of their area of specialty or expertise, even to discuss nonlegal matters. Those rainmakers were able to strengthen their relationship with the client, and at the same time cross-sell additional services of the firm.

—Debra Bruce, from Listening Means Business

> . . . when you accept as a simple fact
> That I do feel what I feel, no matter how irrational,
> Then I can quit trying to convince you and can get about the business of
>   understanding what is behind that irrational feeling. . . .
> And when that's clear,
> The answers are obvious
> And I don't need advice.
>
> *—From the poem "Listening" by Ralph Roughton, MD*

BASICS OF GOOD LISTENING AND RELATING TO PEOPLE

Listening is a much broader skill than just hearing—it is an active and conscious act. To listen well requires attention, often on many dimensions at once. In the early 1980s, Howard Gardner developed the theory of "multiple intelligence." He and Daniel Goleman are popular authors of several books on multiple intelligences (including emotional intelligence, social intelligence, and ecological intelligence). Through their work, it has become widely accepted that we can improve our ability to relate to people.

Goleman distinguishes between people who listen with full emotional presence and those who do not. Those who do not listen with full presence are not really responding to what other people are saying or feeling. They say what they want to say, regardless of what the other person might have been trying to express. He distinguishes this as the difference between "talking at" a person rather than "listening to" a person. He even includes asking questions to solicit more information within the "talking at" category.

Goleman talks about a "two-way listening [that] makes a dialogue reciprocal, with each person adjusting what they say in keeping with how the other responds and feels." Pursuing a reciprocal dialogue leads to a higher likelihood of helping clients, customers, employees, and/or co-workers feel heard and understood, leading to strong relationships and teams. It seems some people are born with the knack for attunement, but everyone can cultivate the skills. *Self-awareness* is a foundation of emotional intelligence, and *empathy* is a foundation for social intelligence. Empathy allows you to read what others are feeling. If you're unable to read others' emotions—people with personality disorders and autism have difficulty doing this—you're more likely to offend, alienate, and even enrage others.

Beyond empathy is *attunement*, which is described by Daniel Goleman in his best-seller, *Social Intelligence*, as "attention that goes beyond momentary empathy to a full, sustained presence that facilitates rapport. We offer a person our total attention and listen fully. We seek to understand the other person rather than just making our own point."

HOW TO LISTEN

The first rule of listening is to be present. That means you are actually there with the client, not multi-tasking on your computer or BlackBerry. You allow the client to share. You pay attention. You get the big picture. You show some compassion. Presence also requires that you are listening to what the speaker is actually saying, not what you think he or she is about to say or where you predict he or she is going. You cannot be fully present to another person's words if your attention is focused on what you are going to say in response.

Know yourself. Be aware of your own listening style and clear judgments. Each of us has our own preconceived notions and judgments. We listen through filters and we often revert to a certain default style of listening. The more we take responsibility to become aware of our own filters, the better able we are to put these filters aside and truly listen to our clients. If you are filtering the communication through your own reactions to the speaker, then you are not listening to the fullest potential.

Listen to what they say and what they don't say. Sometimes what is not said is much more important than what is said. Is the client upset? Angry? Hurt? What is the emotion behind the words? What details are they leaving out? Is the client embarrassed to tell part of the story? What is the commitment behind the story? Has some standard been violated? Does the client feel betrayed?

In law school, we were taught that emotions and values weren't important and that we were to look past them. To our clients, they are often the most important issues. It is helpful to understand the neuroscience of emotion. Simply put, the higher the emotion, the less access the client has to the parts of the brain that allow creative thinking. High emotions = Fewer choices. I often sketch the following graph for clients to help them understand the need to address the emotional issues before we can move forward with solutions.

THE EMOTIONAL TRIANGLE

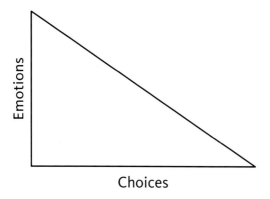

Second: Learn to listen to your own intuition. Everyone has intuition. Most lawyers have a story about how they had "gut" reactions to something that happened in a case, and the instinctual reaction pointed them in the right direction. In truth, the question is not whether you have any intuition, but whether you have chosen to develop your intuition and integrate it into your professional and personal life. Integrating this intuition into the way that you listen makes for better and more satisfying relationships with clients as well as spouses, partners, family, and so forth. For many of us, it is sometimes challenging to be able to tell the difference between our intuition and our judgments and opinions. When you have a hunch, check it out with your client by asking curious, but delicate, questions.

Why Lawyers Can't Hear

By Carl Michael Rossi

"My lawyer doesn't listen to me!" "She doesn't care!" "He isn't interested in me, he just keeps telling me what to do!"

I hope you've never heard these comments directed to you, but the odds are you have, even if you are a very good attorney. No client complaint is more common. Not even billing complaints.

How can that possibly be? You sat patiently as your clients went on about all the circumstances around the issue. Every chance you got, you focused your clients on the issue at hand and had them provide the details that you need to solve the problem they brought to you. And you've told them what they need to do to solve the problem. So what are they upset about? You did everything law school taught you to do—recognize and analyze the pertinent legal issues, elicit relevant facts, and come up with a strategy to solve the problem. Unfortunately, that is what your client is upset about.

Robert Bolton, in his book People Skills, *describes 12 common roadblocks to communications. These are activities by the "listener" that almost guarantee that the "speaker" will form a belief that she or he is not being heard. In short, the speaker ends up believing that listener doesn't care about them.*

Look at just two of these roadblocks:

1. *Excessive questioning. Questions that ask for what's important to your checklist send a direct message that you are more interested in your checklist than in what's important to your client.*
2. *Giving advice. Telling your client what she or he must do sends the message that they are inferior and incapable of running their own life.*

It may sound as though what lawyers do for a living—define the elements of the case in the client's situation and tell them how to change that situation—is the very thing that annoys clients most. Well, yes and no. You know that your clients are people, not case summaries in a tort law textbook. You do care about them. But how can you communicate to them that you both care and can get the job done?

It is possible to do both. As attorneys we have developed particular skills; issue recognition, relevant fact determination and problem solving are valuable, particularly to a client in trouble. We are also always working to develop additional skills, and effective listening skills can be learned.

Effective listening involves accepting the agenda as established by the speaker, and an appreciation that whatever is said is important to the speaker. Rebecca Z. Shafir, in The Zen of Listening, *describes this as getting into the speaker's "movie." Once you have accepted that you genuinely do care about your client, you can learn the skills that communicate that concern to your client.*

Once your client experiences your genuine concern, she or he will find it much easier to focus on the details you need to assess the case. They are less likely to call you to find out if you are working on their case. You will receive many fewer complaints, and many more referrals. You clients will want to entrust you with their problems.

Learning the skills that communicate your genuine concern for your clients is a great way to both increase your business and make it less stressful.

—Carl Michael Rossi, M.A., J.D., L.P.C. from the International Alliance of Holistic Lawyers' Website at www.iahl.org.

. . . full presence does not demand that much from us. "A five-minute conversation can be a perfectly meaningful human moment," an article in the Harvard Business Review *notes. "To make it work, you have to set aside what you are doing, put down the memo you were reading, disengage from your laptop, abandon your daydream, and focus on the person you're with." . . . Intentionally paying more attention to someone may be the best way to encourage emergence of rapport. Listening carefully, with undivided attention, orients our neural circuits for connectivity, putting us on the same wavelength. That maximizes the likelihood that the other essential ingredients for rapport—synchrony and positive feelings—might bloom.*

—Daniel Goleman, from Social Intelligence

SPEAKING

In working with clients, we can connect with and honor them by listening well, but eventually we do need to speak with them; after all, they are paying for our counsel. A good way to handle this is to spend a few minutes connecting and listening carefully, and only then move onto the business at hand and get the information you need. At particularly emotional moments, stop and return to listening, and eventually you will create a back-and-forth dialog.

Ask curious questions. Using your good listening skills, help the client tell you what you need to know to get the full picture. Ask about what the client isn't saying as well as what he is saying. Check out your assumptions. Don't assume that tears are sadness—tears can represent other deep emotion.

Acknowledge the content of what you have heard. Practice active listening— repeat back what the client says. This can feel awkward at first, but it is an amazing tool; as you repeat it back, the client knows you have heard the communication and is empowered to move on to the next concept.

Acknowledge the emotions behind what you have heard. Often, clients come to us when they are angry. They may also feel embarrassed, betrayed, helpless, upset, sad, or any other emotion. Reflecting back the emotion you hear has multiple purposes. First, it helps to clarify, for the attorney as well as the client, what emotions are attached to the client's story. Second, knowing the emotions are there can help identify what the client really wants in crafting a solution. Because the client is acknowledged, she/he is better able to feel compassion from the attorney, for him/herself, and anyone else involved in the dispute.

Reflective listening recognizes that there are two parts in spoken messages: the content of the message (the information) and the feeling underlying the message (the emotion). Often, the feeling part of the message remains unspoken. People don't always say how they feel about an issue, or they may be uncomfortable discussing their emotions, but there is usually a strong emotional component to events surrounding conflicts. Feelings can be discerned from the subtext—both from *what* is said as well as *how* it is said. Subtext includes cues from body language (open or closed, tense or relaxed, etc.), tone of voice, and facial expression. A reflective listening response identifies out loud the content of the speaker's message and the possible feeling underlying the message. This can be done in summary form, without repeating verbatim what was heard. Even if you're not correct, the client knows you're trying to understand.

> For example if a person says, "I am so sick and tired of always finishing Jesse's work. I've got my own things to do without having to do everyone else's job!"
>
> A reflective listening response might be: "Sounds like you're really worried about Jesse's work not getting finished?"

Acknowledge the unfulfilled expectations you have heard. The client may be complaining about something, but behind every complaint is an unfulfilled expectation. Discerning what the unfulfilled expectation is can help the client better see what is possible or not possible in crafting a solution to the dispute, as well as help them define the solution they want. At some point, the person may be able to take responsibility for expectations that they created, as opposed to those that were created by promises made by someone else.

Let the client know you care. Often, we lawyers jump right to the legal issues and tell our clients what the law will or won't do. Our clients are upset because in the heat of their conflict it can be impossible for them to differentiate among legal, financial, and emotional issues; if you just treat the legal issue, they won't feel satisfied. We should first acknowledge the client's frustration, and then help them sort out the issues.

For example, the other day a lawyer told me that a woman had called her about a broken relationship. The couple had been living together for eight years, and she always expected they would eventually get married. Now, the man had left her. She wanted legal recourse. The lawyer told her, correctly, that she did not live in a common law marriage state and that the expectation of being married someday was not actionable. The woman hung up on the lawyer, then called back to say that she didn't appreciate the lawyer's attitude. "I called a human being," she said, "and I expected to get a human response." In informing the client about her legal rights, the lawyer had overlooked the pain of the breakup. This scenario might have gone differently if the lawyer had said, "This must be terrible for you, to live with someone for eight years, expecting to get married, loving him, counting on a future together, only to have it end so abruptly. I wish I could help. It may not be fair and you may be justifiably upset, but the law doesn't provide any remedy for this sort of situation."

Help the client identify his or her values. Sometimes it isn't about the money involved at all (or not exactly about the money). As you have helped the client to sort out what is really going on and what they really want, you have begun a conversation about what is really important to the client. And once you've identified the client's values, you can use them to craft the most satisfactory solution to the conflict.

The principle of compassion lies at the heart of all religious, ethical, and spiritual traditions, calling us always to treat all others as we wish to be treated ourselves. Compassion impels us to work tirelessly to alleviate the suffering of our fellow creatures, to dethrone ourselves from the center of our world and put another there, and to honor the inviolable sanctity of every single human being, treating everybody, without exception, with absolute justice, equity and respect.

It is also necessary in both public and private life to refrain consistently and empathically from inflicting pain. To act or speak violently out of spite, chauvinism, or self-interest, to impoverish, exploit or deny basic rights to anybody, and to incite hatred by denigrating others—even our enemies—is a denial of our common humanity. (We acknowledge that we have failed to live compassionately and that some have even increased the sum of human misery in the name of religion.)

We therefore call upon all men and women to restore compassion to the centre of morality and religion; to return to the ancient principle that any interpretation of scripture that breeds violence, hatred or disdain is illegitimate; to ensure that youth are given accurate and respectful information about other traditions, religions, and cultures; to encourage a positive appreciation of cultural and religious diversity; to cultivate an informed empathy with the suffering of all human beings, even those regarded as enemies.

We urgently need to make compassion a clear, luminous, and dynamic force in our polarized world. Rooted in a principled determination to transcend selfishness, compassion can break down political, dogmatic, ideological, and religious boundaries. Born of our deep interdependence, compassion is essential to human relationships and to a fulfilled humanity. It is the path to enlightenment, and indispensible to the creation of a just economy and a peaceful global community.

—Charter for Compassion (http://charterforcompassion.org/)

COUNSELING AND COACHING

At some point, the client has been heard and you have all the information you need. It is time to respond and consider a plan.

Lay out the options—all of them. It is the client's issue, the client's risk, and the client's money. The client should decide how to proceed. The lawyer should be sure the client knows what the options are; discuss the financial, time, and emotional costs of each option, and discuss whether the client can live with the results of any decision. In so doing, the lawyer should let the client know that "doing nothing" is also an option . . . an option often overlooked by a client who feels very wronged.

Check in with the client periodically. It is always the client's prerogative to change his or her mind. It isn't unusual for a client to decide that a particular path isn't worth the trouble. The client's initial anger may dissipate. Circumstances and priorities may change. Sometimes, all they need is to talk through the issue with a good listener to feel as though it's resolved.

Support the client in following through. Sometimes the right thing to do isn't the easiest thing to do. Your client has other pressures; the family members who are saying it should be handled a different way, the financial and time constraints. Let your client know that you are there for him. And be there.

Help the client reframe. Reframing is another communication tool that focuses on creating a different context that assumes a positive intention or outcome—deciding to see the good behind an action instead of the inconvenient outcome. For example, if you were a diabetic and your sister baked a cake for you, you could complain that she knows you shouldn't be eating sweets and she never supports your well-being. Reframing with positive intention, you could decide to interpret the same action as your sister reaching out and baking a cake to make people happy in your honor.

Make proper referrals for nonlegal problems. Your client may need other professional advice or support. Make sure you maintain a list of competent counselors, financial advisors, spiritual advisors, and anyone else your clients may need. Once you have helped the client sort the legal issues from the other issues, it isn't difficult to have the conversation that a particular issue is beyond the scope of legal representation and might be better handled by another professional. In some situations, you may want to use neutral experts or work on an interdisciplinary team so that all the client's needs are being met, just not by you.

POWERFUL NONDEFENSIVE COMMUNICATION

Powerful nondefensive communication (PNDC; see more at http://www.pndc .com) has become a very popular model in collaborative law, mediation, and other dispute resolution approaches. Sharon Ellison is a speaker and trainer who teaches this model of communication; she is also the author of *Taking the War Out of Our Words* (Deadwood, OR: Wyatt-MacKenzie Publishing, 2009). PNDC starts with the premise that our current language is defensive. We are afraid to appear weak or vulnerable, and our communication reflects that. This defensiveness inhibits our ability to understand and learn and actually creates and accelerates conflicts. Defensive strategies, often unconscious, fall into three categories: surrender, withdrawal, and counterattack. Each of the strategies has a protection mode and a retaliation mode.

People generally have a particular default strategy. For example, in the "war model," communication tools such as questions, statements, and predictions are misused in defensive ways so that they convey an attitude of interrogation, setting up power struggles and manipulation. (Our families may respond to this by asking us to stop cross-examining them!) The powerful nondefensive communication model redefines these communication tools so that questions can be used in ways that are genuinely curious, open, neutral, innocent, and inviting. Questions become a tool for gathering accurate information and to stimulate sincere, honest communication. Statements are better used to provide others with information about our interpretations and reactions. And predictions help to create security and expectations. The PNDC model allows one person to change the nature of the communication, even if the other person doesn't cooperate.

Nonviolent Communication

Nonviolent communication (NVC; http://www.cnvc.org), also known as "compassionate communication," is another model of slowing down and more consciously communicating. It is a way of relating to ourselves and others in the present moment, free of past reactions. NVC helps people learn to identify and verbalize their own needs, to understand the needs of others, and to stay connected to what is important to them.

⊗ · ⊗

NVC guides us in reframing how we express ourselves and hear others. Instead of being habitual, automatic reactions, our words become conscious responses based firmly on an awareness of what we are perceiving, feeling, and wanting. We are led to express ourselves with honesty and clarity, while simultaneously paying others a respectful and empathic attention. In any exchange, we come to hear our own deeper needs and those of others. NVC trains us to observe carefully, and to be able to specify behaviors and conditions that are affecting us. We learn to identify and clearly articulate what we concretely want in a given situation. The form is simple, yet powerfully transformative.

As NVC replaces our old patterns of defending, withdrawing, or attacking in the face of judgment and criticism, we come to perceive ourselves and others, as well as our intentions and relationships, in a new light. Resistance, defensiveness, and violent reactions are minimized. When we focus on clarifying what is being observed, felt, and needed rather than on diagnosing and judging, we discover the depth of our own compassion. Through its emphasis on deep listening—to ourselves as well as others—NVC fosters respect, attentiveness, and empathy, and engenders a mutual desire to give from the heart.

—*Marshall Rosenberg, PhD, in* Nonviolent Communication: A Language of Compassion

⊗ · ⊗

The NVC process contains four parts:

The concrete actions we are observing that are affecting our well-being:
When you told me that you would do the dishes and I saw that you hadn't,
How we are feeling in relation to what we are observing:
I felt disappointed and angry,
The needs, values, desires, etc., that are creating our feelings:
because I value cleanliness.
The concrete actions we request in order to enrich our lives:
Would you be willing to do the dishes now?

Each of us is responsible for meeting our own needs and communicating requests designed to get those needs met without any expectation that the other person must be the one to meet them. The use of NVC slows down the communication and requires participants to be very methodical and conscious, thus helping to diffuse strong emotions.

STORYTELLING

Stories are powerful tools for communication and are often used in legal settings. Our clients need to tell their stories and lawyers often retell those stories in a legal context. Legal documents reflect stories. A trial is a stylized story. Stories are a fundamental element of the circle process. Narrative conflict resolution is a movement within the mediation field.

Our stories provide a context for our lives. How we put them together, the facts that we consider relevant, and the culture within which they occur all weave together. Telling personal stories helps us understand each other from a more intimate perspective. Positions can be argued with, but our personal experience is ours to share and cannot be contested. However, when stories do change, realities change. Sometimes telling the story is enough to shift the reality of the teller. Sometimes witnessing the story shifts the reality of the listener.

Story, as a pattern, is a powerful way of organizing and sharing individual experience and exploring and co-creating shared realities. It forms one of the underlying structures of reality, comprehensible and responsive to those who possess what we call narrative intelligence. Our psyches and cultures are filled with narrative fields of influence, or story fields, that shape the awareness and behavior of the individuals and collectives associated with them.

Story-reality is the reality that we see when we recognize that every person, every being, every thing has a story and contains stories—and, in fact, is a story—and that all of these stories interconnect, that we are, in fact, surrounded by stories, embedded in stories and made of stories. When poet Muriel Rukeyser tells us "the universe is made of stories, not atoms," she's describing story-reality. Ultimately, story-reality includes any and all actual events and realities, but experienced as stories, not as the more usual patterns—objects-and-actions; matter, energy, space, time; patterns of probability; etc. Story-reality is made up of lived stories.

—Co-Intelligence Institute (http://www.co-intelligence.org/
I-powerofstory.html)

Creating an Atmosphere of Wisdom

By Diane Wyzga

Being *homo narans*: a storyteller
The Inuit word for "storyteller" translates as: "person who creates the atmosphere where wisdom reveals itself."

In 1994 I found a book of best-loved stories told at the 20th Jonesborough, Tennessee, story festival. I read a story. I said, "I can do this!" At the time I had no clue how I would use storytelling; I only knew I was a storyteller.

Storytelling is a natural, instinctual process. We are wired to grasp narrative. We believe what we understand. We understand stories that mimic our life experiences, our world views. We intuitively use narrative to explain and define universal concepts and unique experiences. From birth on, stories engage our imagination, focus our attention on behaviors, help us understand those behaviors, and make sense of our world experiences.

Stories build bridges; connect the Us with the Them; demonstrate that there is really no "Other" except the one we create; are inclusive and not exclusive. They are natural aids to problem-solving. They build models for understanding, empathy, and communication because we are using a universally understood, recognized, and natural vehicle.

I joined organizations and traveled to conferences, workshops, and festivals. I learned stories and found venues to tell them. I taught college-level storytelling. Two of my students were long-time practicing lawyers who came to enhance their advocacy and presentation skills. I became a trial consultant focused on storytelling.

Imagination

"Imagination is more important than knowledge."

—Albert Einstein

Storytelling thrives on imagination. Images touch the heart and become sensations; sensations trigger memories; memories create meaning; and meaning leads to listener action. For centuries people told each other stories to convey information, record events, settle disputes, teach the young ones, explain events, heal, and so on. (Doesn't this sound like much of the work of lawyers?) As such they had to rely on imagination to create the virtual reality of the world in which the story took place. Einstein was right.

Universality

A story is heard individually and collectively. The more clearly we comprehend the universal story that embodies universal truths, the better able we are to see and hear and tell the story of our own life and, in turn, the lives of others. If you were to ask each person what story they heard, they would tell you a version of the story that was parallel to their particular world view. Yet, when you were done polling all the listeners you would discover a universal story that all the listeners could agree upon. And, profoundly, their universally accepted story would be grounded in values that acted as a moral underpinning to what they heard.

Joseph Campbell delved into the stories that have been told over millennia. He is especially well known for deciphering the "Hero's Journey" story construct. Generally, the Hero's Journey is made up of seven elements:

- *the hero is living a life and then*
- *encounters some upset*
- *that turns his life upside down, forcing him to go on a journey*
- *to figure out how to right his life, and along the way he meets allies*
- *and enemies*
- *who show him the way to the "truth" he needs to discover;*
- *when he has discovered the truth, he must return to his community to share his particular truth so the entire community is improved.*

Listening the Story Out of Our Clients

Stories are personal. A lawyer has the opportunity to hold the space for the safe telling of the client's story. People want and need to speak their story and their truth. When we tell a story to a therapist, a lawyer, a spouse, or a friend, we are telling our story. Our responsibility as lawyers is to first listen the story out of the client and only then tell it accurately so that we help lift the burden of carrying the untold story. Clients look to the lawyer to hear it, understand it, and retell it accurately. In this role the lawyer becomes a counselor, coach, and mid-wife.

The role of counselor in this setting is a three-fold process: listening the story out of the client/teller, hearing that story accurately, and then retelling it truthfully to someone who needs to act on the story. That process takes the exquisite ear of listening.

When we speak to each other we are looking for answers to the three universal questions: (1) Can I trust you? (2) Are you committed to me in this process? (3) And do you appreciate me for me not just the skills I have? This is no more true than in the attorney-client relationship.

The lawyer must do an archeological dig on herself and come to terms with her own stories; only then can she listen the stories out of others. It takes courage and willingness to examine what you are hearing with a critical—not criticizing—ear and then discover how to tell that story using language and images with power, passion, and precision.

Telling the Client's Story

The stranger who tells our stories when we cannot speak not only awakens our spirits and hearts but also shows our humanity—which others want to forget—and in doing so becomes family.
> —Proverb of Mende, a people of Sierra Leone

There is no greater burden than carrying an untold story.
> —Zora Neale Hurston

All trial lawyers want to know: How do I persuade, educate, inform, inspire, motivate, and ultimately lead a juror to action? The answer is in front of you: tell the story. One over-arching task of a lawyer is to speak for those who cannot. Even when the client loses the case, I believe that the saving grace is this: the lawyer has given the client the opportunity to tell her story and be heard.

Legal stories, like fairy tales, myths, and legends, create images, sensations, and memories that compel the listener to act. Law school discourages imagination. The skillful trial lawyer needs to overcome law school's linear analytical training that says he who dies with the most facts, wins.

In front of a jury, the better story wins. Each side has basically the same set of facts to work with. The difference is in how the story is told. The 'better story' is the one that is compelling and persuasive because it is emotionally meaningful. Facts do not engage. Facts cannot engage. The better story is grounded in values to which the listener can relate. The story that is emotionally meaningful to the listener will be persuasive and compelling. It will make sense to them. They will relate to it as being consistent with their story, their world view, and their experience of world order. The listeners to the legal story are seeking their universal experience in the story of the client. When they hear that story, the attorney and decision-maker become one, working in concert in a cooperative enterprise considering options, possibilities, and outcomes.

Support your listeners with a heartfelt story artfully told and they will support you. The personal, emotional, and conflicting aspects of the case create different stories from the same set of facts. Context gives the facts meaning and relationship to the decision-maker's world view.

Stories Provide Space for Healing
How do lawyers use stories as tools for healing rather than winning? Another way of asking this question is, "Who am I as a human being? And how do I practice my humanity in the legal profession?"

I have worked for the past few years with a Canadian lawyer who has been helping members of the First Nations tribes recall and recount their stories of abuse to perhaps claim some form of restitution from the Canadian government. These residential school abuses are horrific. Imagine what it took to return to those times, to revisit the abuses, to tell those shameful and secret stories to a lawyer.

Again, this is an opportunity to make use of the world of stories. There are myths and legends and tales that mimic a current event or situation. Using a story as a symbol, the client/teller can relate the story of the abuse as if he were a character in the story. And because our stories and movies follow the Hero's Journey format, the teller can begin the healing process in the careful hands of the listening lawyer. Now the lawyer fits her role as a true counselor-at-law.

We are lonesome animals. We spend all our life trying to be less lonesome. One of our ancient methods is to tell a story begging the Listener to say—and to feel—"Yes! that is the way it is, or at least that is the way I feel it. You are not as alone as you thought."

—John Steinbeck

Resources

The Hero's Journey. Joseph Campbell. New World Library. 1990

The Power of Personal Storytelling. Jack Maguire. Jeremy P. Tarcher/Putnam. 1998

The Healing Heart—Communities. Edited by Allison M. Cox and David H. Albert. New Society Publishers. 2003

The Healing Heart—Families. Edited by Allison M. Cox and David H. Albert. 2003

Inviting the Wolf In: Thinking About Difficult Stories. Loren Niemi and Elizabeth Ellis. August House. 2001

POWERFUL QUESTIONS

If I had an hour to solve a problem and my life depended on the solution, I would spend the first 55 minutes determining the proper question to ask, for once I know the proper question, I could solve the problem in less than five minutes.

–Albert Einstein

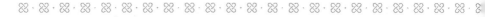

If asking good questions is so critical, why don't most of us spend more of our time and energy on discovering and framing them? One reason may be that much of Western culture, and North American society in particular, focuses on having the "right answer" rather than discovering the "right question." Our educational system focuses more on memorization and rote answers than on the art of seeking new possibilities.

We are rarely asked to discover compelling questions, nor are we taught why we should ask such questions in the first place. Quizzes, examinations, and aptitude tests all reinforce the value of correct answers. Is it any wonder that most of us are uncomfortable with not knowing?

The aversion in our culture to asking creative questions is linked to an emphasis on finding quick fixes and an attachment to black/white, either/or thinking. In addition, the rapid pace of our lives and work doesn't often provide us with opportunities to participate in reflective conversations in which we can explore catalytic questions and innovative possibilities before reaching key decisions. These factors, coupled with a prevailing belief that "real work" consists primarily of detailed analysis, immediate decisions, and decisive action, contradict the perspective that effective "knowledge work" consists of asking profound questions and hosting wide-ranging strategic conversations on issues of substance.

—From Eric E. Vogt, Juanita Brown, and David Isaacs, "The Art of Powerful Questions, Catalyzing Insight, Innovation, and Action" (http://www .theworldcafe.com/articles/aopq.pdf)

A few years ago, I was one of the facilitators for a community conference on sacred activism. The subject of the conference was a community inquiry about how to come together and make a difference. Our facilitation team spent weeks working on the questions for the inquiry part of the weekend. It gave me a new appreciation for the power of a question, and I later wrote a book of questions with some colleagues. As we tried on various inquiries, I found myself being transformed by the opportunities for reflection. You can't argue with a question—a question is rarely right or wrong, it just is—but you can express an opinion. Questions open us up to opportunities to learn together.

That is one of the reasons I am so intrigued by the practice of appreciative inquiry. Appreciative inquiry arose in the field of organizational development and focuses not on problem solving, but on what is possible. It opens the conversation.

Appreciative Inquiry: It's Not Easy, But It Is Simple

By Kathleen Clark

We all know attorneys who do outstanding trial work but can't keep associates. Some attorneys weave a tight and eloquent argument but can't settle a case. There are also attorneys who are only interested in winning, no matter what the cost to those involved. Many of them would benefit greatly from an understanding of a process called Appreciative Inquiry. Appreciative inquiry is the brainchild of Dr. David Cooperrider, Professor of Organizational Behavior at Case Western Reserve University's Weatherhead School of Management and co-founder of Appreciative Inquiry Consulting.

Appreciative inquiry focuses on possibilities, not problems. That sounds easy, but it requires an important shift from our usual, problem-centered approach to bringing about change. Appreciative Inquiry helps us discover what works, so that we can do more of it. It is inquiry based on positive questions. In appreciative inquiry, a clear, concise topic is chosen, positive questions are developed, and the consultant (or whoever is asking the questions) sits down with the client and asks the questions. Stories start to develop; patterns begin to emerge. Individuals recall and tap into positive achievements and stories that strengthen and inspire. The process, which is more fully described below, doesn't ignore problems—it just approaches them from the other side, the other side being what is working rather than what is not working. It can be used informally, such as in a conversation, or in a formal context, such as at a strategic planning conference or retreat. It can be used with two people or two thousand.

AI builds on several assumptions, including:

1. *In every society, organization, or group, something works.*
2. *What we focus on becomes our reality.*
3. *The act of asking questions of an organization or group influences the group in some way.*
4. *What we want already exists in ourselves, our firms, our organizations, and our communities.*

The first step in the process is choosing a topic. This is crucial because AI builds out from the topic choice. Change starts to happen with the first questions we ask. Because change begins to take place at the same time as inquiry, we want our inquiry to focus on what is working so that we can build on that. The topic should be one in which the team, group, or person is really interested and wants to learn more. The topic should be stated with positive wording, i.e., "What is the most satisfying . . . etc." It should (and will) generate possibilities.

Start with the topic that is most relevant or urgent to the organization—growth, client services, marketing, diversity, etc. If this seems too daunting, start with a small topic or a small group, even one person. Inquire about what has worked best for that person in her or his career, what work she or he is most proud of, or something similar. Once we learn how to do this, we can share the concepts of AI and our success stories with our firms, clients, and communities.

Let's look at some examples of questions aimed at bringing change around specific issues.

Attorney/Employee Satisfaction

- *What drew you to this firm?*
- *What situations or circumstances created your loyalty to this firm?*

- *Describe a situation in which you felt that you received exceptional mentoring.*
- *How are you best mentored?*
- *Describe your most meaningful experience of pro bono work.*
- *What is the most meaningful feedback you've received as an attorney?*
- *What do you most value about yourself? Your work? Your firm? Your profession?*
- *How do you stay energized and inspired?*

Satisfaction in the Legal Arena

- *What contribution have you made to the legal profession?*
- *What contribution have you made to your organization or community?*
- *Describe a situation in which you were able to work collaboratively with opposing counsel.*
- *Describe a situation in which you used new ideas to come to a resolution of an issue or case.*
- *Describe your part in a successful conclusion to a client case/matter that you were handling. Describe an organization that you've worked in that fosters continuous learning. How has the organization done that?*

Organizational Culture

- *Describe one or two situations in which you've observed the values of your organization in action.*
- *Describe one or two situations in which you felt most valued by this organization.*

Diversity/Sexual Harassment Training

- *Describe the best on-the-job experience you've had working on a project with someone of the opposite sex.*
- *How did the relationship get started?*
- *How did you build trust with this person?*
- *How did you deal with conflict?*
- *How did you develop mutual respect?*
- *Describe something meaningful that you learned from working on a diverse team.*

Whichever topic you choose, whatever groups or individuals you talk with, look for patterns in their responses. Pay attention to the attitudes of the responders, both at the time they respond and at later times. Take a step back; take some time to absorb the responses. Notice the changes that start to take place, the shift in thinking based on the inquiry and the responses, the conversation. The changes are likely to be subtle at first, so keep paying attention. This will allow you not only to see and experience the changes, but to more easily move into the next steps in the process.

If you want to create change, appreciative inquiry is a great way to begin. It is an affirmative approach to human and organizational development, and it tells you exactly what people like about their lives and careers so that you can help them create more of it. Appreciative inquiry springs from possibilities and from hope. Again, it works with 2 people or with 2,000. If structured correctly, all involved have the opportunity to co-create change and transform their organization. Everyone gets to be heard! It brings out the best in us.

Skeptical? Suspend judgment; experiment with appreciative inquiry yourself at home with your family (children!), with your clients, in your community, or in your workplace. Keep in mind the words of Gandhi, an attorney himself: "Be the change you want to see in the world." Remember—even the most innocent affirmative question evokes change. Often, the change is not what we expected, but welcome, just the same. For instance, asking the marketing questions above may not bring forth a new marketing plan but, instead, may bring a rededication to the core values of the organization or individual.

The use of affirmative language changes the way we think; changing the way we think will change the way we work. The shift in thinking begins with you, the questioner. You need to move beyond the ineffective problem-solving approach; you need to focus on what works, so you can do more of it. The problems won't disappear (wouldn't that be nice!), but they will be smaller as what works gets larger and greater in stature.

Bibliography/Resources

Cooperrider, David L., Sorensen, Peter F., Jr., Whitney, Diana, Yaeger, Therese F., editors. (2000). Appreciative Inquiry: Rethinking Human Organization Toward a Positive Theory of Change. *Stipes Publishing, LLC.*

Cooperrider, David L., Whitney, Diana. (1999). Appreciative Inquiry. *Berrett-Koehler Communications, Inc., 1999.*

Hammond, Sue Annis. The Thin Book of Appreciative Inquiry, 2nd edition. *Thin Book Publishing Company.*
Whitney, Diana, Cooperrider, David, Trosten-Bloom, Amanda, Kaplin, Brian S. (2002). Encyclopedia of Positive Questions: Using Appreciative Inquiry to Bring Out the Best in Your Organization, *Vol One. Lake Shore Communications.*

UNDERSTANDING CONFLICT DYNAMICS

When I tell non-lawyers that law school doesn't require courses in conflict resolution, they're perplexed. Isn't our business about conflict? Shouldn't all lawyers understand the dynamics of conflict?

Many lawyers get their first formal education about the dynamics of conflict from mediation training. However, conflict is a natural part of life, and we encounter and resolve differences constantly. Two plants compete for a few square inches of soil. Two managers have different goals for the company. We both want to sit in that chair. Two friends have very different political views. Two parents love each other—and they don't see eye-to-eye about money management or what's best for their children.

The Thomas-Kilmann Conflict Mode Assessment (TKI) is wonderful, inexpensive, and easy to administer tool for learning about conflict. I've used it for my own personal growth, exploring how I use the various styles in different situations, and have used it as a tool for clients. I have led trainings on the TKI for a wide range of audiences and always learn something new each time. For more about it and to purchase it, go to http://www.kilmann.com/conflict .html.

Briefly, the TKI identifies five responses to conflict. Each of us tends to have a default style of responding to conflict, our knee-jerk approach. The approaches are measured by assertiveness and cooperation. We learn our response from our culture, our environment, and our personalities. No particular approach is the "right" way to respond. Each is appropriate in some situations. Different roles and relationships trigger different responses.

The Conflict Avoider is both unassertive and uncooperative—the individual does not immediately pursue his own concerns or those of the other person. He does not address the conflict and side-steps, postpones, or delays. A conflict avoider may simply withdraw from a threatening situation.

Uses for the Avoidance Style

- When an issue is trivial, of only passing importance, or when other more important issues are pressing.
- When you perceive no chance of satisfying your concerns; e.g., when you have low power or you are frustrated by something that would be very difficult to change (national policies, Supreme Court rulings, etc.).
- When the potential damage of confronting a conflict outweighs the benefits of its resolution; the "pick your battles" option.
- To let people cool down, to reduce tensions to a productive level, and to regain perspective and composure.
- When gathering more information outweighs the advantages of an immediate decision.
- When others can resolve the conflict more effectively.
- When the issue seems tangential or symptomatic of another more basic issue.

Example: If I am walking down a dark alley and someone is coming toward me in a menacing way, I may cross the street to avoid a confrontation.

The Accommodating Style is unassertive and cooperative. When accommodating, an individual neglects her own concerns to satisfy the concerns of the other person. An accommodator is self-sacrificing and may show selfless generosity or charity, obeying another person's orders when she would prefer not to, or yielding to the other's point of view.

Uses for the Accommodating Style

- When you realize that you are wrong—to allow a better position to be heard, to learn from others, and to show that you are reasonable.
- When the issue is much more important to the other person than to yourself—to satisfy the needs of others and as a goodwill gesture to help maintain a cooperative relationship.
- To build up social credits for later issues that are more important to you.
- When continued competition would only damage your cause—when you are outmatched and losing.
- When preserving harmony and avoiding disruption are especially important.
- To aid in the managerial development of subordinates by allowing them to experiment and learn from their own mistakes.

Example: When my 70 year old mother asks if we can go out for a steak dinner, we go to a steakhouse even though I don't eat beef.

The Competing Style is assertive and uncooperative—a competing individual pursues his or her own concerns at the other person's expense. This is a power-oriented mode, in which one uses whatever power seems appropriate to win one's own position: one's ability to argue, one's rank, economic sanctions. Competing might mean "standing up for your rights," defending a position that you believe is correct, or simply trying to win.

Uses for the Competing Style

- When quick, decisive action is vital—e.g., emergencies.
- On important issues where unpopular courses of action need implementing—e.g., cost cutting, enforcing unpopular rules, discipline.
- On issues vital to group or organizational welfare when you know you're right.
- To protect yourself against people who take advantage of noncompetitive behavior.

Example: If a factory is dumping toxic waste in the stream above my house, I want to stop it immediately. We can talk about how to meet its needs later!

The Compromising Style is intermediate in both assertiveness and cooperativeness. The objective is to find some expedient, mutually acceptable solution that partially satisfies both parties. Compromising gives up more than competing but less than accommodating. Likewise, it addresses an issue more directly than avoiding, but doesn't explore it in as much depth as collaborating. Compromising might mean splitting the difference, exchanging concessions, or seeking a quick middle-ground position.

Uses for the Compromising Style

- When goals are moderately important, but not worth the effort or potential disruption of more assertive modes.
- When two opponents with equal power are strongly committed to mutually exclusive goals, as in labor-management bargaining.
- To achieve temporary settlements to complex issues.
- To arrive at expedient solutions under time pressure.
- As a backup mode when collaboration or competition fails to be successful.

Example: The used car is priced at $10,000. I wanted to spend no more than $8,000. We meet in the middle and settle on $9,000.

Collaborating is both assertive and cooperative—the opposite of avoiding. Sometimes referred to as the "Problem-Solving" style, collaborating involves an attempt to work with the other person to find some solution that fully satisfies the concerns of both persons. It means digging into an issue to identify the underlying concerns of the two individuals and to find an alternative that meets both sets of concerns. Collaborating between two persons might take the form of exploring a disagreement to learn from each other's insights, concluding to resolve some condition that would otherwise have them competing for resources, or confronting and trying to find a creative solution to an interpersonal problem.

Uses for the Collaborating Style

- To find an integrative solution when both sets of concerns are too important to be compromised.
- When your objective is learning, testing your own assumptions, and understanding the views of others.
- To merge insights from people with different perspectives on a problem.
- To gain commitment by incorporating other's concerns into a consensual decision.
- To work through hard feelings that have been interfering with an interpersonal relationship.

Example: My divorce client is in need of cash. The only significant marital asset is the family home, and her husband wants to remain in the home to provide stability for their children. Using the collaborative style, we will examine all the needs and possible solutions to find a creative solution that serves everyone.

The styles are mostly unconscious and bringing them into consciousness offers opportunities to experiment with different responses. For example, if you identify that your client's default style is that of Compromiser, you know that he has already "come to the middle" before even arriving at the table. If your opposing counsel is a Competitor, knowing that the most effective strategy is to stand firm without escalating the conflict may open up new opportunities.

HONORING CONFLICT

Many lawyers have begun to explore conflict from the perspective that every conflict is an opportunity for transformation, not only for the clients but the legal professionals in the case as well. Inquiring with a client about where they might learn and grow from the conflict can bring new insights into the conflict and open doors for creative and unconventional solutions.

INTERCULTURAL COMPETENCE

Many of our conflicts arise from cultural, racial, gender, regional, and other differences. A few years ago, I moved back to North Carolina with a Northern housemate. As I heard him directing the movers to put this there and that over there, I was mortified by how offensive he was behaving. He was pointing and ordering the men around in a way that would have been very polite in Northern culture. In our indirect, Southern culture, he couldn't have been ruder. He didn't even offer the guys a cup of coffee when they drove up. He wasn't asking them for their ideas of how to do the job but was telling them exactly what he wanted.

I can chuckle now as I look back at the situation. As an international studies major and lifelong student of diversity, I always considered myself to be culturally sensitive but this woke me up to more nuances than I knew. Do what you can to expand your cultural awareness. Travel. Expand your social circles. Don't just notice differences. Talk about them and explore together.

HARMONIZING POLARITIES

By design, litigation polarizes adversaries. Differences are highlighted and similarities are ignored. Conflict resolution aims to focus on the similarities and build bridges between the parties. Some conflicts are easily resolved when interests are shared. The peel of the orange and the juice of the orange conundrum can be resolved pretty quickly when each sees that both needs can be met. What about the more challenging conflicts? How do we build a bridge between the right-to-life and the pro-choice camps? How can we bridge the American political divide that seems to grow wider each day?

This book isn't going to answer those questions, but there are people who are asking those questions and who are engaged in deep discussions about them. In the meantime, there are other conflicts that might serve as practice to reaching a both/and solution. Sometimes inquiring into the paradox of seemingly opposite ideas will actually spur our creative thinking and provide new possibilities. Most either/or situations aren't quite so opposite. Rarely are there only two options for any problem.

Causes of Polarization

Polarization is caused by a number of related psychological, sociological, and political processes. It is closely tied up with escalation in a bidirectional relationship. In other words, escalation causes polarization and vice versa.

Escalation → Polarization → Escalation

As conflict escalates, the emergence of enemy images and stereotypes damages the relationship between adversaries. Important lines of communication and interaction that are normal to peaceful relationships are cut off, and trust diminishes. As parties begin to attribute their grievances to the other side, they often reduce the number of nonconflictual relations and interactions that they have with that party. Adversaries tend to become increasingly isolated from each other, and any intergroup communication is channeled through more antagonistic lenses. Because parties have fewer ties to individuals from the other group, they may feel freer to employ more severe actions against that group. . . . Group isolation and polarization is further aggravated by the tendency of partisans to try to win bystanders to their side, forcing people to take sides. As more people are drawn into the conflict, that conflict intensifies.

Conversely, escalation seems to increase polarization. Formerly neutral parties are pulled to one side or the other, and fewer community members can retain their moderate positions. In part, this is because those involved in the conflict demand that neutral nonparticipants decide whether they are "with us or against us." Those who would normally urge moderation and attempt to mediate the conflict are recruited by participants in the controversy, and forced to take sides. It is difficult for community members to remain neutral when people are fighting, damaging each other's property, and injuring each other. In such situations, there is a tendency to cast blame and to side with one party or the other.

Radical positions are further reinforced by group homogeneity and cohesiveness. Kriesberg notes that adversaries with little internal diversity are more prone to escalation. . . . They are more prone to polarization as well. This is because homogeneity makes it less likely that a group will consider alternatives to the severe tactics being advocated or employed by extremists. As parties assume more radical positions, group members tend to reinforce each other's negative stereotypes and enemy images. Any moderate positions go unheard or their proponents ostracized—or worse— as they are seen as traitors to the cause. As this process continues, parties are often further segregated, and their relationship with outsiders becomes increasingly hostile and competitive.

—Maiese, Michelle and Tova Norlen. "Polarization." Beyond Intractability. *Eds. Guy Burgess and Heidi Burgess. Conflict Research Consortium, University of Colorado, Boulder. Posted: October 2003. www.beyondintractability.org/essay/polarization*

Harmonizing Polarities

By Theresa Beran Kulat

Spiritual teachings applied to the practice of law can lead to a more joy-filled and manageable life. This article takes a fresh look at "opposites." By altering our perspective of things that seem to be "at odds" we can harmonize them and achieve more satisfactory outcomes for ourselves and our clients.

Regardless of age, position, or other outer conditions, when a person notices a struggle between "opposites" they have the opportunity to harmonize polarities. Our interior space relaxes when we accept that the two poles arise out of the larger essence. Think of a magnet. Think of our planet. North differs from south, but one is not "right" while the other is "wrong." Their existence is relational. However, when our planet was created, both poles emerged simultaneously. Further, this polar nature gave way to the spin and spiral dynamic that is life.

One depiction of this dance of polarities is the Chinese symbol of yin and yang. It symbolizes complementary relationship. We breathe in. We breathe out. The sun rises and an active day unfolds. The sun goes down and into darkness; we naturally rest. Yang is "masculine." It represents "doing." Yin is "feminine." It represents "being." The yin-yang symbol depicts wholeness with both polarities in balance. Within yin (black) is the seed of yang (the white dot). Within yang (white) is the seed of yin (the black dot).

The mythology of the Western world portrays this dynamic using the visual imagery and language of astrology. A circle has 360 degrees. In astrology, the circle is divided into 12 sections that alternate between masculine and feminine. The system places 12 archetypes around the circle in a particular order that represents how energy evolves. Moving beyond a mechanistic view of life, where astrology predicts future, the quantum worldview can use the language of astrology to describe patterns of energy and relationships within the field. The rich imagery of the mythology can be used to help us navigate the real-world decisions and challenges we all face. Looking at life symbolically, we can identify trends and come up with strategies for improvement.

One set of archetypes that I use to describe my work in the "legal field" is the "warrior" and the "peacemaker," two poles of the same energy. Aries, the first sign of the Zodiac, represents initiation and the urge to be born and survive. It opposes Libra, the sign associated with partnership and "open enemies" that represents being in relationship. Aries is ruled by the planet Mars, associated with the god of War. Libra is ruled by Venus, the goddess of beauty and love. Every chart, whether it has been drawn for a person, for a moment in time, or for a country, has these two archetypes in it, and the two archetypes are opposite each other. They are two poles of the same essence. At the center of a chart is the fulcrum point where these two archetypes meet. Imagine the infinity sign. On one side is the warrior; the other the peacemaker.

Every archetype has functional or healthy expression and dysfunctional or unhealthy expression. The true peacemaker listens to all voices at the table and facilitates communication until resolution emerges that meets the most essential needs of all the interested parties. The warrior defends and protects that which rightfully should be defended and protected. So, as yin contains the seed of yang, the peacemaker must honor the true warrior's assessment of what is to be defended/protected. Likewise as yang contains yin, the true warrior values peace and keeps that value in core during the discernment process. Unhealthy warrior energy picks a fight when boredom sets in. By excessive violence, the bullying dominates without regard to the destruction left in the wake. The dysfunctional peacemaker turns away from injustice in the name of keeping the peace. Over time, the unsettled "peace" degrades to tyranny and cannot be sustained. The oppressed erupts and retaliates. This false peace breeds violence.

We can apply archetypal imagery to explain how collaborative practice works. In its most functional expression, both collaborative lawyers and all of the allied professionals embody both archetypes. They model and teach the functional expression of the two archetypes to harmonize and transmute the experience of the couple moving through the divorce experience. The lawyer-coach for the "victim" encourages and models the expression of healthy boundaries. That client can take responsibility for his or her role in creating the problem and generate solutions to reclaim personal power. The other attorney-coach may work with the "domina-tor" client to develop active listening skills and learn to empathize.

The ability of the professionals to stay at the fulcrum and to allow the dance of the functional expression of these archetypes will determine the effectiveness of the collaboration. The professionals "hold core" for the people in the room during a difficult conversation. Connecting with the fulcrum of the polarity allows the professionals to easily move to the place (a warrior stance or a peacemaking motion) that will restore balance. Sometimes that means speaking up to reframe a position. It might mean silence so that the next voice can be heard clearly. The center of a circle is equidistant from all points around the periphery. The fulcrum represents the detached observer that respects both poles of the essence and can access behavior appropriate to the situation.

To harmonize means to allow each polarity its own expression. They are different. We don't try to make someone something that they are not. However, a person's "vibration" can be tuned such that it does not destroy or drown out all of the other voices. A well-functioning collaborative team is not a chorus of people all singing the same words and notes of music. Each has a rhythm and a tone that is unique yet allows for the other voices to be heard.

So, at the end of a successful collaboration, agreements are in place that will keep the peace and the parties have learned new skills. Then, should either true warrior conclude that the boundaries have slipped or new ones need to be drawn, they will be able to use diplomacy and nego-tiate a new peace. The professionals have supported the clients to achieve results that don't make it into the case law report. The results are in the hearts of the participants and in the lives of children who can love both parents. It is practical work with a spiritual essence.

INTEREST-BASED PROBLEM-SOLVING

First reported in *Getting to Yes: Negotiating Agreement Without Giving In*, by Roger Fisher and William Ury (New York: Houghton Mifflin, 1991), the interest-based problem solving model emphasizes understanding each party's needs and values rather than focusing on the positions of the parties or possible solutions. Distinguishing between interests and positions is important to the development of workable resolutions. A position is a demand or counterdemand: A parent who says "I must have the house for the children" is stating a position, and the only response is to agree or disagree. Interests are the underlying needs that make the positions desirable. "It is important for Johnny to have the stability of staying in the same school and living in the same neighborhood while we are in such transition." Giving Johnny stability can be addressed in many ways, including giving the house to the custodial parent.

Understanding why an issue is important allows the development of a workable solution. When all parties value and respect each other's interests, there is a better chance of developing a variety of solutions. Interests help to identify what part of the solution is important to each party.

There is a classic story to illustrate interest-based problem-solving:

> Billy and Bobby are arguing in the kitchen when Mom comes in. "I have to have this orange!" each exclaims to Mom. There is only one orange, and Mom offers to cut it in half [the default positional bargaining compromise]. They each scream in protest.
> "I must have the WHOLE orange!" says Billy.
> "No, I must have the whole orange!" cries Bobby.
> Mom is perplexed. "Billy, Why do you need the orange?" she asks.
> "Because I must have the peel of one whole orange to make Grandma's birthday cake."
> "And why do you need the whole orange, Bobby?" she asks.
> "Because I must have the juice of one whole orange for my cold."

When each interest was known, the answer was simple. One orange was enough for both of them to meet their needs.

CREATIVE PROBLEM-SOLVING

Creativity has been attributed to divine intervention, biological and cognitive processes, the social environment, and innate personality traits. It's been associated with genius, mental illness, and humor. Some claim that creativity is a trait we are born with, while others say it can be taught. Although popularly associated with arts, it is also an essential part of the problem-solving process in law and other professions. It's particularly important in a holistic practice, where the solution to a legal problem could be something totally new. The following are some creative problem-solving exercises that I have used in my work to break out of traditional, in-the-box legal thinking.

THE SIX THINKING HATS

Edward De Bono wrote a book called *The Six Thinking Hats* that offers a model for examining possible solutions. The six hats model is an example of *parallel thinking*, a term De Bono coined in the 1960s. Parallel thinking is cooperative thinking. In the six hats model, each person in the conversation looks at a problem from the same position at the same time. For example, when it is time for "black hat" thinking, everyone looks at the problem from a critical perspective, even those who might have been arguing on behalf of a solution being considered. "Red hat" thinking would find everyone considering the emotional implications of a particular plan. When several people look at a problem from many positions, all the ideas are discussed in an organized manner. The proponents of an idea are forced to discuss the negative aspects and vice versa. When all the ideas are on the table and fully explored, the solutions evolve organically.

ARTISTIC EXPRESSION

If creativity is like building a muscle, then exercising that muscle will strengthen the creative process for problem solving. Pursue writing, drawing, painting, song writing, or another creative pursuit that uses different parts of your brain than your logic and analysis center. You will find that you can solve problems better.

COLLAGING

For the trickiest problems, you may want to find ways to access subconscious motivations and assumptions. Grab a stack of magazines and tear out pictures that seem related to the problem you're working on. Arrange them into a collage and glue them on. Then look to see what the collage says to you. Is it dark and ominous? Does it have a theme you hadn't seen before? What do the graphics communicate that you hadn't consciously realized?

APPRECIATIVE INQUIRY

Appreciative inquiry can be used to indirectly address a problem by looking at the positive aspects; see more on AI on pages 238–242.

PHYSICAL ACTIVITY

There are many anecdotes about problems that have been solved during a walk or run around the block. Whether it is because another area of the brain has been stimulated or because the subconscious has had time to work on the problem, it is good for the body and for problem solving to take a break and get some physical activity.

BACK TO THE FUTURE

This is a useful tool when you have a goal in mind but don't know how to get there:

1. Create a clear experience of what accomplishing your goal will look like. Envision yourself with the goal accomplished. What will it look like? Sound like? Feel like? How will you know you've reached your goal?
2. Now, what did you do just before the goal was accomplished?
3. What did you do before that? How did you get the resources? What allowed you to reach your goal?
4. Work your way back from the future to the present, listing the steps of what you did just before the next step until you've reached your current situation.
5. Reverse the process to create your action plan.

BRAINSTORMING

In 1939, Alex Osborn developed brainstorming as a method for creative problem solving. Osborn was a partner in an advertising agency and was frustrated by his employees' inability to develop creative ideas for ad campaigns and products when working on their own. In response to this problem, Osborn began hosting groupthink sessions and noticed that the quality and quantity of ideas produced was much greater than those produced by individual employees. Osborn subsequently published a book, *Applied Imagination* (Scribner; 1953), that systematized his creative problem-solving methods.

You know what brainstorming is: a problem-solving method in which a group tries to find a solution for a specific problem by creating a list of ideas spontaneously contributed by its members. It is designed to create a list of many ideas of solutions that are not restricted by social inhibitions. Judgment is suspended initially to encourage the creative process, so there are no bad ideas; silly ideas are even encouraged as a way of opening up the creative energy. Just as going to the gym works out your muscles, brainstorming works out your brain. Practicing brainstorming strengthens your creativity in all areas of your client relationships and your life.

HOW TO BRAINSTORM WITH A GROUP

Schedule a meeting of at least one hour for the group, and make sure brainstorming is on the agenda so that participants can be formulating ideas in advance, even if not consciously. It is often useful to set a time period for the idea-generation stage of the brainstorming; for example, "We're going to brainstorm about this issue for 15 minutes; then we'll spend the next 45 minutes evaluating our ideas."

Make sure that everyone understands the problem or issue. Define the topic. The better defined and more clearly the problem is stated, the better the session tends to be. "We are going to brainstorm how Mary can meet her cash flow needs while she is in her nursing program."

When the meeting begins, write the initial topic where everyone can see it: on a flipboard or whiteboard. Choose a method for capturing ideas. You can choose a scribe (or more than one) to write down all the ideas on the common flipchart. The advantage to this method is that everyone hears and sees every idea. The disadvantage is how long it takes to write each idea and that other ideas may be lost in the process.

Another option is that each person writes ideas on sticky notes during the idea-generation stage. Then, the ideas are shared and placed on the flipchart, bulletin board, or whiteboard. During the evaluation stage, they can be arranged according to topic. The advantage to this method is that it is likely to produce more ideas as each person writes ideas for the full 15 minutes. Everyone gets to participate fully. However, it may not produce the energy and excitement that is created by shouting out the ideas and building on each other's suggestions.

Choose someone to be in charge of facilitating and making sure the rules are followed. (It is best not to choose the scribe as facilitator.)

Review the ground rules:

- Suspend judgment.
- All ideas are as valid. The aim is to produce a lot of ideas to be evaluated later. We're not looking for your best ideas but for quantity. Silly and radical ideas are welcome; they may have a nugget of gold within them! Don't censor any of your ideas; keep the meeting flow going. If you have an idea and don't say it, you're stopping your own flow. Share it!
- Listen to ideas of others. Try to piggyback on them to other ideas.
- Discuss the ideas or ask questions later. Stay with the flow of ideas.
- After the ideas have been generated, it is time to evaluate them. Ideas that are identical can be combined, all others should be kept. Go through the ideas and discuss their viability. Is there value in the more radical ideas? Some ideas may have generated a need for more information. It is useful to get a consensus of which ideas should be looked at further.

BRAINSTORMING ALONE

Sometimes you may wish to brainstorm alone. Perhaps you are alone in your office working on a problem. Perhaps you don't have anyone else to brainstorm with. Perhaps you're more of an introvert and want to prepare for a brainstorming session prior to the group work. There are several ways you can brainstorm alone:

- Get a legal pad and just write down ideas, quickly, without judgment.
- Write many ideas on sticky notes and then arrange them in order of which ideas are related to each other.
- You may also want to obtain a piece of thinking software that will help you look at your problem in different ways. I like www.inspiration.com, which has a free trial.

CEREMONY

Throughout human history, people have used ceremony as an important way of marking milestones and transitions. In North American culture, we have graduations; weddings; birthday parties, baptisms, quincianos, and bar mitzvahs; retirement roasts and funerals.

In North Carolina, it is now possible to get a divorce without ever having walked into a courthouse. We consider this no-fault approach to be progress. In some ways it is. However, we no longer have hearings that mark that final divorce. There is no ceremonial completion. There is a piece of paper that comes in the mail. The emotional completion, the finality of the event is not officially marked. Family and friends often don't know what to think, whether to offer condolences or congratulations.

In my law practice, I have found many ways of bringing ceremony into legal transitions. In our collaborative four-ways in Asheville, we always bring food to share. A shaman client of mine cleared the room with sage prior to each meeting. Houston holistic lawyer Fran Brochstein says she often prays with her clients, first asking them about their faith traditions. Eileen Dunn (warmlyeileen@yahoo.com) is an expert in ceremonial transitions. She is developing a product line of music, aromatherapy, readings, and journal exercises for processing the emotional issues of transitions. Seattle area attorney Stefani Quane (see her profile in the "Holistic Law" section) integrates ceremony into her law practice.

Adoptions can include birthday parties. In my social service adoptions, we invited everyone from the case management team, plus new family members. I bought a balloon that said "It's a boy!" We ate cake. The social workers said that it was an important milestone for them, too. (And for some reason, I had more social service adoptions than any other lawyer in town.) I suggest that my divorce clients find their own ways of having ceremony. Some faith traditions actually do have Uncoupling Ceremonies that allow friends and family to share the end of a relationship, just as most shared the wedding. The couple can acknowledge that the form of their relationship has changed while honoring what came before.

It isn't about proselytizing but rather about understanding the client's belief system and supporting them in honoring their transitions. It is another way to connect as human beings, to honor our spiritual lives. It is an opportunity to connect to something bigger than the individual, gaining strength and being the space for peace.

TEAMWORK

No one can whistle a symphony. It takes a whole orchestra to play it.

—H. E. Luccock

Working with a team is common in the holistic law paradigm. Collaborative practitioners work in interdisciplinary teams; problem-solving courts, restorative justice, and other approaches involve the collaboration of other professionals who share a goal. Teamwork provides the wonderful opportunity of bringing together people who have different perspectives, skills, and ideas. Teamwork also provides the challenge of bringing together people who have different perspectives, skills, and ideas. It gives us the opportunity to walk our talk and practice all our conflict resolution skills with each other.

DYNAMICS OF VICTIMS AND OFFENDERS

In organizing this book, this section got moved around a lot. Some of it started in the restorative justice explanation, but I was concerned that readers who were not interested in restorative justice might skip that section. True, we more often talk about victims and offenders in criminal law. But what divorcing couple doesn't have situations in which one spouse feels victimized? Isn't it "offensive" when you are the "victim" of a breach of contract? Offenders often feel like victims and victims become offenders. They are two sides of the same coin, intertwined by the harm that occurred between them.

Once Upon a Conflict: The Journey from Confrontation to Collaboration

By Gary Harper

What's Your Story?
In conflict, everyone has a story—or at least their side of the story. To better understand these stories, try prefacing them with the words "Once upon a time." Fairy tales feature three main

types of characters: the victim (often represented as a damsel in distress or an innocent youth); the villain (a witch, giant, or dragon); and the hero (the white knight or young prince). We encounter these same character types on the front page of our newspapers, in our favorite television shows, and on movie screens everywhere.

The Drama Triangle

Not surprisingly, we relate to these larger-than-life characters in our conflicts. Most often we see ourselves as the victim—innocent and powerless. Sometimes we play the hero and risk the danger of conflict to right a wrong and see justice done. Occasionally we may slip into the role of the villain, attacking the other person with anger or sarcasm. Each role limits our understanding of conflict; together they form a "drama triangle" that traps us in confrontation. This explains why people in conflict refer to feeling "stuck." Once we become aware of this pattern and our role in it, we can choose more constructive approaches. Instead of labeling the other person as a villainous adversary, we can acknowledge that they feel victimized and can seek to work with them as partners against the problem. In doing so, we shift from confrontation to collaboration.

Roles We Play

Innocent victim

In conflict, we experience being attacked, judged, or threatened in some way; victimized. In victim role we are convinced of our innocence and wallow in a sense of powerlessness. We might withdraw—the "flight" part of "fight or flight"—or even freeze like a deer caught in the headlights. Other times we wait for something to change or for someone to rescue us. (Remember Rapunzel, trapped in her tower.) Although some of us suffer in silence, most of us freely share our frustration, often attributing the conflict entirely to the personality deficiencies of the other person.

Noble hero

Sometimes we react by shifting to hero mode: we protect ourselves, stand up for our cause, and seek to even the score with our adversary. The hero ventures forth to do what must be done—justice will be its own reward. This role embodies courage, selflessness, and nobility. It represents the part of us that will step forward and risk taking a stand, despite our discomfort or fear.

There is a darker side to the hero role, however, when righteousness becomes self-righteousness. In the pursuit of justice, the hero slays or captures the villain. When we agree that the hero's cause is just, we condone and even applaud these aggressive behaviors. We justify our own aggressive, hurtful behavior by telling ourselves "they had it coming."

Based on actions alone, a hero is simply a self-righteous villain. In a different context, Robin Hood would have done five to ten years of hard time for extortion and armed robbery. Instead, his actions are not only excused but revered in legend because of his noble cause and earlier mistreatment by the evil sheriff. Similarly, Jack (of "Jack and the Beanstalk" fame) made his reputation through trespass and burglary, though these acts are seen as heroic because the giant was mean. You get the drift.

Evil villain
The size of the villain determines the size of the hero. "Without Goliath, David is just some punk, throwing rocks."—Billy Crystal, My Giant

Villains manipulate, control, or deprive the victim for their own ends. This role represents the part of us that can be mean-spirited and vindictive (what Star Wars *calls the "dark side" of the Force). This dark side is selfish, controlling, and fearful. The villain has no concern for the others and uses threats, aggression, and deprivation as tactics to control the situation. And when we experience someone controlling us, we quickly cast them as the villain in our conflict story.*

In fact, the behaviors of the villain are similar to those of the hero, distinguished only by how we judge them. Internationally, acts of violence we condemn as terrorism are seen as the selfless deeds of freedom fighters by other ideologies. Looking strictly at behavior in conflict, a villain is simply a misunderstood hero. Even people who act inappropriately or antisocially have their story, in which they see themselves as victims and in which they justify their actions as "evening the score." One person's justice is another's revenge.

Stuck on the Drama Triangle
These roles are interdependent. A victim requires a persecutor; a hero needs a cause. Neither can exist without a villain. And when we treat someone like a villain, they in turn feel victimized by us—and see us as the villain. Behaviors they consider self-defense, we experience as attacks

and further evidence that we cannot trust or work with them. And the walls of judgment and justification thicken on both sides.

The drama triangle and its roles inevitably produce a win-lose approach to conflict. One person wins; the other must lose. No one likes to lose, and we will battle ferociously to avoid defeat. Even if one person loses the battle, the war is seldom over. The loser continues to seek justice and retribution. The cycle of revenge persists and traps both people in a downward spiral.

Casting New Roles

How do we escape the drama triangle? Firstly, we can accept the role we have played in the conflict. Secondly, we can acknowledge that our adversary has, in their eyes, an equally valid perspective. And thirdly, we can strive for resolution instead of victory and seek possibilities that allow both sides to get what they need. Let's start with the role of victim.

From Passive Victim to Assertion

To set aside the role of victim is easier said than done. We can begin by taking responsibility for our feelings and reactions in conflict, not to deny or devalue our feelings or needs, but to accept them as our own. After all, whose problem is it if you go home frustrated with your boss at the end of a workday? Who "owns" the problem? (Hint: Your boss may be sleeping like a baby as you lie awake endlessly replaying the events of the day.)

Assertiveness is based on this principle. Consider the difference between the statements "You never make time for my issues at meetings" (victim) and "I'm frustrated that we didn't discuss the budget during the meeting" (accountable). The first statement is loaded with judgment, casts the other person as the villain, and blames them for how we feel. The latter discloses our experience, takes responsibility for feelings, and identifies the problem at hand.

Similarly, we can ask directly for what we need instead of complaining to others about our plight. This is uncomfortable, yet empowering. It's uncomfortable because we can no longer blame others and refuse to change; it's empowering because we become an active participant in shaping our life. To reap the rewards of assertiveness, we must risk the discomfort of confronting a person or problem.

In conflict, each person feels hit first.

From Hero to Problem-Solver

The role of hero can be as unproductive as that of victim. This self-righteous mindset condones our attack on the villain as justice. Attack is met with counterattack; the conflict persists and usually escalates. Our ego fuels the need to be right, and we become attached to a specific outcome. At this point, the conflict becomes a power struggle.

We can address and resolve conflict much more productively if we let go of the need to be "right" and focus instead on ways to get our needs met. This uncovers possibilities we might otherwise ignore. The energy devoted to a win-lose power struggle can instead be applied to problem solving (often referred to as "separating the people from the problem").

This in no way advocates accommodating or avoiding an issue just to keep the peace. We need to exhibit a hero's courage in different ways: to raise an issue directly and respectfully; to enter the uncomfortable place we experience as conflict and to stay there to see it through; to listen to viewpoints with which we may disagree; to forgo the pleasure of righteous indignation in favor of curiosity. In many ways, the hero's battle is internal.

From Controlling Villain to Collaborator

There is a fine line between the roles of hero and villain, and in conflict we can easily and unconsciously slip into the role of villain. When we attack another person (even in self-defense) and attempt to hurt them in some way, we have become the villain. Fueled by anger or frustration, we may come out with statements such as "I don't care what you think" and "To hell with you." We may even "lose it" and exhibit the very behaviors (threatening, interrupting, swearing) we find so objectionable in others. This victimizes the other person anew and perpetuates the attack-defend cycle.

Although others may see us as a villain, we can change their perception if we are willing to relinquish our need to control. When we surrender our need for control, we make room for fresh and creative possibilities to resolve our conflicts and even redefine our relationships. At the same time, we have to give up our need to be right. (I never said it would be easy.)

From Adversaries to Partners

When we live on the drama triangle, we see the other person as our adversary—the villain. If only they would change, we reason, things would be fine. They stand between us and happiness. Ironically, they are usually thinking the same thing about us. To resolve conflict, we need to relinquish our roles as victim, villain, and hero and work with the other person to solve the problem. If we need a villain, let it be the problem, not the person. The diagram below symbolizes this shift—from the drama triangle to the circle of resolution.

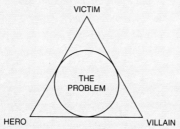

Interestingly, the circle and triangle intersect not at the three cor-
ners of the triangle, but in the middle on each side. Similarly, we must
meet the other person in the middle. This doesn't mean "splitting the
difference." It means letting go of our roles, retelling our story without
judgment or blame, and listening to their story with curiosity. Such communication opens the doorway of understanding through which we can
exit the drama triangle and enter into the circle of resolution.

Applications

*The concept of the drama triangle serves me as a mediator, as a trainer,
and in my own conflicts. As a mediator, it helps me make sense of wildly
divergent perspectives by remembering that each person genuinely sees
themselves as the victim in the situation. Identifying the moment when
each person began to see the other as the villain (the point of wounding)
allows me to focus discussion on the root conflict. We can examine the
intent of each party and the impact of their actions on the other, and
clarify the assumptions that fuel ongoing conflict.*

*As a trainer, I find that workshop participants intuitively identify
with the drama triangle and its roles. I often ask people to share a conflict
story with a partner, who in turn tells the story from the "villain's" perspective. This simple exercise produces many "ah-ha" moments as people
broaden their view of the conflict and begin (however reluctantly) to
entertain the notion that theirs is not the only perspective on the situation. This fosters the curiosity necessary for collaboration.*

*And finally, this concept helps me stay conscious in my own conflicts
by recognizing when I feel like a victim. Instead of railing against the
other person as the villain, I'm able to identify when I felt "the knife go
in" and respond assertively instead of aggressively. I am also more likely to
remain curious about the other person's perspective, knowing that they see
themselves as a victim (or hero).*

The simple concept of the drama triangle fosters a basic awareness of the dynamics of conflict. This awareness allows us to choose responses that move us beyond the drama triangle of confrontation and uncover the new possibilities that flow from collaboration.

WORKING WITH OFFENDERS

"Offenders," "perpetrators," "defendants," "law-breakers," "criminals". . . there are a lot of terms we could use for the people who break the social contract or cause another harm. I will use the term "offender" as the label for such folks, although in practice I prefer to use the name of the person. Any label has the effect of objectifying and dehumanizing someone who is already feeling separate from others.

Take a moment and remember a time when you said or did something you later regretted. Perhaps you lost your temper or maybe you were stopped while speeding. Or maybe you had a more serious brush with the law. How did you feel? What did you need? Were you afraid of what might happen to you as a result of your transgression? Were you ashamed, embarrassed? Was your opinion of yourself affected? Do you want to be remembered, defined, and known for your bad behavior?

We human beings can generally justify our behaviors even if we think we're doing something wrong. We all want to see ourselves as the hero in our own story, and offenders are no different than the rest of us—they often react with justification. In their stories about themselves, they are justified in their behaviors. Their value systems may be different than ours. Some have had violent upbringings where their black-and-white realities gave them the choice of being the perpetrator of violence or the victim of it. Some may justify their behaviors by blaming drugs or alcohol. They may believe they deserve a break because of X, Y, or Z. It seems a strange phenomenon that getting caught can sometimes generate the same reactions as victimization, as though the one catching us and exposing our offense is to blame for its happening.

The adversarial legal system encourages offenders to avoid responsibility. It becomes the lawyer's job to "get me off," and the court system becomes the enemy. Telling the story is the last thing that most lawyers want their clients to do, yet telling the story and making amends may be the very act that is required for the healing of all concerned. Restorative justice and similar approaches also hold offenders accountable by facilitating and enforcing reparative agreements, including restitution.

Accepting punishment under criminal laws is passive and requires no responsibility or affirmative acts from the offender. It often supports the reaction of victimization for the offender—the system becomes the persecutor in the drama. But offenders who face their victims and make agreements are much more likely to follow through on their restitution agreements. Most studies show they are also less likely to re-offend.

What offenders need to heal:

- *To express their remorse, sorrow, and regret for the harm done and offer apologies.*
- *To have someone accept their remorse as genuine.*
- *To tell their story without justification or excuse.*
- *To gain insight into effects of offending.*
- *To have someone understand and acknowledge their victimization—offenders have almost always been victims in the past.*
- *Opportunities to make things right.*
- *Meaningful accountability.*
- *Reintegration into community.*
- *Acknowledgment of their humanity and goodness.*
- *To have someone listen and to allow them to hear their own justifications.*
- *Help making wise choices and validating their wise choices.*

One of the most powerful victim–offender dialogues I ever witnessed was actually in a divorce case. My client, the wife, had an affair and ended the marriage. The husband was devastated. Emotions were sky high. Our efforts to bring settlement and closure kept failing, and we thought that we were going to have to end the collaborative process. Then, with the help and support of her divorce coach, my client issued the most thorough, dramatic, and heartfelt apology I have ever witnessed. She took full responsibility for her actions and acknowledged the pain she had caused. She listed her every transgression (the impact the affair had on her and her husband, the pain caused to their son and their community of friends, etc.). She told him that she had justified her behavior by telling herself that his behavior was emotionally abusive and that even if it were true, she could have taken a different path and that she was responsible for her actions, not him. She went on and on, letting him know that he had been fully heard and she knew she was responsible for his pain and the end of their marriage. Both of them cried. The case settled.

WORKING WITH VICTIMS

I use the word "victim," even though it is controversial. Besides the issue of labeling human beings, many prefer the term "survivor." Being a victim is different than having victim mentality. Sometimes bad things happen to good people who are otherwise powerful in their lives. We can't control the behaviors of others; we can only control our own response to what happens to us.

Although many laws about the rights and roles of victims are on the books, in most places victims remain witnesses for the government. They often feel that the system further victimizes them. In many interviews, victims have said that they felt more victimized by the system than by the original incident. Understanding victims may help prevent that reaction.

Have you ever been the victim of a crime? We all have had experiences of being wronged by someone else. A crime is particularly upsetting—a crisis that comes upon the victim suddenly, arbitrarily, and unpredictably. The normal reaction is shock, disbelief, denial, and emotional turmoil (anger, fear, frustration, self-blame, guilt, grief, confusion). The victim may feel isolated, less connected to others. He or she may lose interest in everyday activities, experience sleep disturbances, or have bad dreams. Hypervigilance and jumpiness are common, as are other intensified stress reactions. Some victims may have survivor's guilt. They may avoid activities that might remind them of the traumatic event. A victim may reexperience the traumatic event in many ways, and the repercussions can last for a long time.

Victims often have trouble with memory or concentration. They may seem overly emotional or numb and depressed. They want to tell their stories, often over and over and over and over. Repetitious storytelling is a symptom of victimization, but so is being completely shut down. Past victim experiences may be triggered and the reaction may be out of proportion to the current situation. Often victims strike out, becoming the persecutor because the pain of victimization is unbearable and they need to regain a sense of control in their lives.

Victims may feel ashamed of how out of proportion their reactions are, especially if the harm is viewed as minor by others. If someone breaks into your home and doesn't take anything or takes something of little value, it may be a small transgression in someone else's eyes. The victim's harm is to her or his sense of safety and well-being. Security and predictability are destroyed. It may just be a lost stereo to the police, but it is much more to the elderly woman who lives alone and fears the thief will return while she is there.

What victims need to heal:
- *Repair and redress.*
- *To tell the story of the impact and for someone to listen to it, especially the one who caused it.*
- *To restore a sense of control.*
- *Decision making about how the matter will be handled by the system.*
- *Education and facts.*
- *Realistic expectations.*

When working with a victim, be sure not to revictimize. You can say:
- *You're safe now.*
- *I am glad you are talking with me now.*
- *I am sorry it happened.*
- *It wasn't your fault.*
- *Your reaction isn't uncommon to such a terrible thing.*
- *It must have been really upsetting to see (hear, feel, etc.) that.*
- *I can't imagine how terrible you are feeling.*
- *You are not going crazy.*
- *Things may never be the same but they can get better.*

Don't say:
- *I understand.*
- *I am glad you can share those feelings.*
- *You are lucky that you weren't killed, it wasn't worse . . . (victims don't feel lucky!)*
- *It will take some time, but you'll get over it.*
- *I can imagine how you feel.*
- *Don't worry. It will be all right.*
- *Calm down and relax.*
- *Try to be strong for your children.*

It is important to create a safe environment for victims who are feeling especially vulnerable. If you're having a meeting that may include other people, explain who the others are. Sometimes allowing a friend or family member to attend a meeting with the victim will help him or her feel calmer and safer.

Also, it's important to spend some time processing your own feelings. It will help you deal with others' strong feelings. If you are not comfortable being with strong feelings, bring in a team member who is. Suppressing the feelings isn't going to help anyone's healing process. The goal is *not* to hurry them through their pain or even to make them feel better. It may be a side effect of the work you're doing, but allowing the victim to process at his or her own rate is respectful. In particular, if you are working with the victim and the offender, be very clear with the victim about when the offender will and won't be present.

APOLOGY

When we were children, our parents taught us we should always apologize when we hurt someone. In the legal profession, the prevailing wisdom has been to tell clients to admit nothing and to never apologize. While lawyers have meant well proceeding in this fashion and have thought they were saving their clients from liability, recent research has shown that lawyers may have been on the wrong track.

A lawyer friend of mine, Sharif, spent Thanksgiving Day of 2004 in the hospital. He went there for emergency surgery to remove his appendix. A few hours after the surgery, Sharif found himself in a pool of blood. Nurses tried to be super-professional in the midst of the emergency, but Sharif said he could tell they were in a panic, and he thought he was going to die. The quick diagnosis was internal bleeding (although Sharif said it looked very external to him!). He was taken back into surgery and the two little holes from the laparoscopic surgery became a five-inch incision. A few days later, Dr. A., the first surgeon, sat down to talk with Sharif. Dr. A. told Sharif that he was sorry for what had happened, that he thought maybe he had failed to close a blood vessel properly, that his colleague Dr. B, who performed the second surgery, may have acted hastily in such an invasive procedure, that the second surgery might not have been necessary at all and even if it had been, the laparoscopic punctures might have been the better access to repair the bleeding. In addition to his explanation and apology, he told Sharif that the hospital was going to forgive the bill for the extra surgery and extra recovery days.

Sharif told me that as the doctor talked, at first, he was seeing dollar signs and he was drafting the malpractice claim in his head. He was incredulous that the doctor was admitting his mistakes, and long-forgotten rules of evidence about admissions of a party opponent began to emerge from remote memory. But as the conversation continued, he found himself listening from a place of compassion, impressed by the doctor's candor, and recalling that he'd made mistakes in his life. By the end of the conversation, anger and thoughts of suing had disappeared.

Sharif's story isn't unique. Doctors around the country are discovering that leveling with their patients and apologizing are effective tools for lowering their malpractice claims. An Associated Press (AP) story reported that since 2002, hospitals in the University of Michigan Health System have been encouraging doctors to apologize for mistakes. Their annual attorney fees have since dropped by two-thirds, from $3 million to $1 million, and malpractice lawsuits and notices of intent to sue have fallen by half, from 262 filed in 2001 to about 130 per year.

Jonathan Cohen, a law professor at the University of Florida Levin School of Law, was an early researcher in the apology trend. In a 2000 presentation, I heard him speak about the Veterans Affairs hospital in Lexington, Kentucky. Cohen said that the VA hospital adopted the policy of apologizing in 1987 after some big malpractice cases. They went from being one of the highest net-legal-cost hospitals to among the lowest net-legal-cost hospitals in the VA system.

Heath care providers who apologize to patients or their relatives for things that go wrong are not just doing the right thing; it also makes sense business-wise. Kathryn Johnson, RN, Director of Risk Management at the University of North Carolina Healthcare System, writes in *Essentials of Physician Practice Management* that studies show litigation by patients was reduced when providers were forthcoming about mistakes they'd made and took responsibility for them. This was especially true of smaller mistakes, perhaps not surprisingly. Patients who are communicated with honestly and in an ongoing manner feel their providers are acting in good faith and are more forgiving of their providers' human errors, and ultimately less likely to want to punish them with lawsuits. Hospitals across the country are adopting similar policies.

Apology isn't just for medical malpractice. In 2002, the *National Law Journal* reported that Toro Co., the lawnmower company, had adopted a revolutionary policy. When an accident was reported to the company, a nonlawyer "product integrity specialist" contacted the injured party, expressed the company's condolences, and initiated an investigation to discover the cause of the accident. An engineer went with the product integrity specialist to look at the equipment that caused the injury, and, where appropriate, the company took steps to improve the equipment to prevent future injuries. In two-thirds of the cases, the product integrity specialist was able to resolve the matter without legal intervention. If not, the company offered to mediate, and almost all cases were resolved in mediation. According to the article, Toro reported that between 1992 and 2000, with more than 900 product liability claims referred to the program, legal costs per claim (lawyers' fees and litigation expenses) were reduced by 78 percent, from an average of $47,252 to $10,420. The average resolution amount for the period was reduced by 70 percent, from $68,368 for settlements and verdicts to $20,248.

In 2000, California passed a law barring the introduction of apologetic expressions of sympathy ("I'm sorry that you are hurt") but not fault-admitting apologies ("I'm sorry that I injured you") after accidents as proof of fault. Other states have adopted apology legislation, including bills that would exclude fault-admitting apologies from evidence.

Beyond the financial savings, there are other benefits to this new approach to apology. In the AP article, one man said that an apology might not have stopped him from suing over the misdiagnosis of a brain aneurysm that he contends left his wife severely disabled. But he said it might have saved his relationship with the doctor, who was once a close friend.

According to Aaron Lazare, author of *On Apology*, apologizing can be motivated by strong internal feelings such as empathy for another or the distress of guilt and shame. In such cases, the person issuing the apology seeks to restore and maintain his own self-esteem. Other motivating factors are external: wanting to affect another person's perception. In such cases, a person apologizes due to fear of abandonment, stigmatization, damage to reputation, retaliation, or punishment. People who don't apologize often say they don't do so because they fear the reactions of the people to whom they apologize, such as losing the relationship, humiliation, or punishment, or they are embarrassed and ashamed of the image they would have of themselves as weak, incompetent, or in the wrong.

Lazare points out the healing benefit of the apology to both parties: the harmed and the one causing the harm. The apology fulfills several possible psychological needs for the offended party, among them restoration of self-respect and dignity, a sense of connection and shared values with the other person, a sense of safety in the relationship, assurance that the offense was not his or her fault, and sometimes the sense that the offender is suffering from the harm. While it appears that the apology is for the person who was injured, the results for the person issuing the apology may be more dramatic. The apology often restores the person's self-esteem and dignity, allows him or her the opportunity to make reparations and reconnects him or her with the other person. And, as our mothers always said, and as Dr. Steve Kraman, former chief of staff of the VA Hospital in Kentucky pointed out, apologizing is "the right thing to do."

EFFECTIVE APOLOGIES

There is a lot more to an apology than the words "I'm sorry." I remember many times when I told my children to apologize for some offense they'd caused. My son would look at his brother and say, "I'm sorry I hit you," but clearly, I knew he was thinking, "but I'd do it again in a heartbeat."

There are no magic *words* for an apology, but there may be a magical way of *being* sincerely remorseful. A sincere, remorseful apology can be as short as a quick, verbal "I'm sorry," or it could be an elaborate written public apology. However, no amount of eloquence will replace sincerity.

A proper apology should always include the following:

A detailed account of the situation.

What did you do? This makes sure that you both know what actions you are talking about.

Example: *On November 5, I failed to stop at a red light and I hit your car.*

Acknowledgment of the harm, not only physical but emotional if possible.

I understand that your car was damaged and you experienced quite a jolt as a result of the impact. I believe you were also very frightened because you had your child in the car and you were concerned that he might be injured as well.

Accepting responsibility for the situation without making any excuses or justifications, even if it was not intentional.

It was completely my fault. I was driving too fast and I was on my cell phone and not paying attention.

A statement of regret and request for forgiveness.

I am so sorry. I hope you can forgive me someday.

A promise that it won't happen again.

I want you to know that I now have a policy of no cell phones while driving so that this will never happen again. I really learned my lesson.

A form of restitution whenever possible.

I would like to write a check to cover the damages to your car and your medical bills and those of your child.

FORGIVENESS

We must never lose sight of the curative power of forgiveness. Some bereaved may undertake a wrongful death case hoping to find closure at the end, but the results can disappoint on several levels. A defense verdict or an award [that] the client views as inadequate may reawaken earlier angers and sorrows. Even a fully "victorious" trial outcome may leave the bereaved feeling empty. I commend to you some of the more recent articles on the power of forgiveness—not as a biblical or religious concept but as a vehicle for recognizing that human beings can elevate themselves above anger and vengeance. Through forgiveness we acknowledge the human frailty, failings, weaknesses, and vulnerabilities of others—and in the process may see some reflections of ourselves.

—Robert Hall and Mila Tecala, Grief and Loss: Identifying and Proving Damages in Wrongful Death Cases, *Trial Guides, LLC (January 2010).*

The Top Ten Misconceptions about Forgiveness

1. *Withholding forgiveness hurts the other person.*
   The truth is: *Withholding forgiveness hurts yourself.*

2. *Forgiveness is a passive endeavor.*
   The truth is: *Forgiveness is a very active endeavor, where you can ultimately reach out in love and compassion to the other person.*

3. *Forgiveness lets people off the hook, so they aren't accountable to their actions.*
   The truth is: *Forgiveness and accountability are not the same topic. You can have both. Forgive another by offering empathy and unity; yet still uphold the process of accountability within the social structure.*

4. *Forgiving someone tells that person that whatever he or she did was acceptable with you.*
   The truth is: *Accepting their actions and accepting their true nature underneath it all are two very different things. You can make that clear.*

5. *Forgiveness is for the other person.*
   The truth is: *Forgiving another is an act we do for ourselves, to free ourselves from the pain or bitterness.*

6. *When you are forgiving, you are "pardoning" someone's bad behavior.*
   The truth is: *There is no "pardoning," just a clearer perception on who that other person truly is, and what they can still provide to your life, to a community and to a society.*

7. *Forgiveness is done by saying the words, "I forgive you."*
   The truth is: *Forgiveness resides not only in words but also in thought, feeling, and action.*

8. *Forgiving another person doesn't do any good really.*
   The truth is: *It not only uplifts you and that person in ways unseen, but it brings that much more light to a world in need.*

9. *Forgiveness is only for religious people.*
   The truth is: *It's for all of us walking the planet.*

10. *It's too hard to forgive.*
    The truth is: *It can be hard, but not too hard, not when you have the right support and perspective.*

—*Azim Khamisa (AzimKhamisa.com)*

I have learned a lot about forgiveness from my friend, Aba Gayle, whose 19-year-old daughter, Catherine Blount, was murdered in 1980. Aba Gayle tells me that she spent eight years as an angry, vengeful person. She planned to attend the execution of her daughter's killer. Later, she took a meditation class and began to seek healing through her church and by reading spiritual books. In 1988, she was in a study group for "A Course in Miracles," and when she saw a video of a Jew forgiving the Holocaust, she began to see the healing possibility of forgiveness. Aba Gayle was moved to write a letter to the man who killed Catherine, forgiving him. She was surprised to receive a letter back with an invitation to visit the man who had killed her daughter, and she went to see him.

On the website she created to share about her story (www.catherineblount fnd.org), Aba Gayle shares this:

When I arrived, in the visiting room for death row inmates I looked around with surprise. I did not see a single monster in that room. It was filled with ordinary looking men. (Perhaps neater and quieter than outside.) They were sitting with their grandmothers, or wives, or ministers, and/or their children. Everywhere I looked, I saw the face of God.

When Douglas came in, he said, "Gayle, you do me the greatest honor by paying me this visit." We talked together for over three hours. I cried and he cried. We cried together. He is a big, tall, very strong man, and he wasn't the least bit embarrassed to sit there, surrounded by other inmates, and openly weep. We talked about Catherine. We talked about Douglas' mother and her death. We talked about his losses. I realized the night Catherine lost her life, Douglas also lost his future.

When I left San Quentin that day, after only one visit, I knew that I would never stop spreading the word that these men were human beings and not monsters. I knew that I would be a political and social advocate on their behalf. And, I knew that if the state of California ever executes Douglas Mickey, they would be killing my friend.

Forgiveness is letting go of resentment and thoughts of revenge; it brings a kind of peace that can help your client go on with life. It is not a good idea to ask a victim to forgive before he or she is ready, and an apology from the offender does not obligate the victim to forgive.

The following is reprinted from a newsletter issued by the World Forgiveness Initiative in April 2005 (www.worldforgivenessinitiative.org; from an article by Eileen Epperson; see also http://www.cuttingedgelaw.com/content/forgiveness-case-mistaken-identity):

> Blaming others gives them control over us, not only when the awful deed was done, but also in all our future interactions—with anyone. Blaming others for the way we feel means we have to wait for them to change before we can heal. When we blame others, we effectively chain ourselves to them and give them all our power.
>
> The incredible absurdity of all this is that the people we blame usually don't even know we are still angry and hurt; they wouldn't care if they did know; they are also being controlled by whoever they have chained themselves to, and so on. So when we start blaming (I include complaining), how can we get out of it and stop the rage? Simply forgive. Forgiveness breaks the chains and lets us see the utter folly of the blame game. Forgiveness gives us the power to be honest and to say what needs to be said, straight and clear. Forgiveness fills us with incredible joy and happiness.
>
> "Let me be very clear. I am NOT talking about stuffing your feelings, repressing your rage, and telling someone, 'It's okay.' Forgiving is something you do for yourself, an act of self-love, not something to do to be a nice person. When we forgive, we are really saying, 'I am reclaiming from you the power to control who I am, how I think and feel, and how I behave from now on.'"

RADICAL FORGIVENESS

Author Colin Tipping distinguishes between "ordinary" and "radical" forgiveness. In Tipping's book, *Radical Forgiveness, Making Room for the Miracle* (Quest Publishing & Distribution; 2d (March 24, 2002) he considers *ordinary forgiveness* to be letting bygones be bygones—letting go of the past and still holding onto the idea that something bad or wrong happened. It often seems like a difficult task, and it usually takes time before feeling the forgiveness. Tipping suggests that at the soul level, those perceived as enemies are giving us an opportunity to heal and to grow.

Radical forgiveness focuses on the spiritual meaning in any situation, postulating that life is divinely guided and unfolding for each of us exactly how it needs to unfold for our highest good. If we are able to surrender to the flow of life, it is possible to learn that, ultimately, there is nothing to forgive. Proponents say that this approach allows the person to stop being a victim and find peace, even in the most unpleasant of situations.

GRIEF

Many of our clients are dealing with issues related to a loss. It may be the loss of a loved one, the loss of a dream, or the loss of liberty.

Elizabeth Kubler-Ross first identified five stages of grief in patients who were dying. Others have expanded her work to identify seven stages among the living who have experienced or are experiencing a loss:

1. **Shock and denial.** The first reaction is generally one of disbelief, numbness, and denial. Shock is a person's way of protecting her- or himself from overwhelming emotions. It resembles blowing a fuse due to an overload of electricity.
2. **Pain and guilt.** When the numbness wears off, there is often nearly unbearable pain. There may be a sense of guilt over what you did or did not do.
3. **Anger and bargaining.** The blame and unfairness is the next stage. You may lash out with misplaced rage and resentment. At this stage, there is often bargaining with a Higher Power: If you will only stop this loss, I will live a better life . . .
4. **"Depression," reflection, loneliness.** The true magnitude of the loss is realized. Feelings of emptiness and despair set in. It is an important time for grieving that must be processed.
5. **The upward turn.** Depression lifts as you start to adjust to the loss.
6. **Reconstruction and working through.** You deal with the practical and financial issues and begin to reconstruct life. You become more functional.
7. **Acceptance and hope.** You start planning for the future and recovering from the pain. Eventually, you are able to find joy in life, even if you are still sad about the loss. A sense of peace and acceptance may come over you.

The stages aren't necessarily linear, and one stage may last a few moments while another takes years. Each person grieves in his or her own way and in his or her own time.

Personal injury lawyer Robert Hall posted on the therapeutic jurisprudence list about his upcoming book *Grief and Loss: A Guide for Attorneys and Therapists*, co-written with Mila Tecala, a grief therapist. In the book, they make the following ten suggestions for lawyers undertaking representation of the bereaved:

1. Grief tends to be categorized by mental health professionals as either "normal" or "complicated." "Normal" is an unfortunate characterization. To the bereaved there is nothing normal about what they are experiencing.

2. The attorney needs to be aware of the signs and symptoms of complicated bereavement because it may be accompanied by clinical depression, be disabling, and interfere with family relationships. Referral to a qualified mental health professional is critical.

3. In that regard, a death in the family is a death of that family as then constituted, and the grief of each family member will interact with the grief of the others, frequently in ways that generate conflict. One family member's grief may be so overwhelming that they are unaware of or unable to accommodate the grief of others.

4. Grief has no timetable, is not "cured" because it is not a disease, changes over time, but not necessarily for the better, and is so encumbered by myths and folklore that it is frequently misunderstood.

5. The manner and cause of death (which bring these clients to our office) weigh heavily on the client's grief. Sudden, unexpected, frequently traumatic and preventable deaths stand apart from other deaths.

6. Death is always contextual. What else was going on in the family's life when death ensued? A man came to see me recently. He had just retired after 40 years as a doctor, he and his wife had separated, and shortly thereafter his only son was killed in an accident.

7. The legal system may generate additional pain. Rules of evidence may seem arcane and unsympathetic. Standards for proving fault may interpose obstacles or appear to be "stacked" against recovery. In many ways the system may fail to meet the bereaved's expectations.

8. The attorney must resist the temptation to self-promote, point out the big verdicts obtained, or reduce discussion of the claim to one dimension—money. The client is there to right a wrong or make the world safer so this doesn't happen again. While money damages may be the endpoint, it is rarely what brings them to our office unless as a symbol of the magnitude of their loss.

9. The attorney must avoid the customary bromides: "I know what you must be going through!" No, you don't. Don't go there. "God needed

her home with him!"—How could God be so cruel, etc. Our role is to be a patient, compassionate listener. We will bring comfort by our caring manner, not the fire of our rhetoric.

10. Finally, the attorney must remain acutely aware that pursuit of a wrongful death claim on behalf of a family may be contraindicated for reasons unrelated to the legal merits. A young man died because his driver was intoxicated. The driver was his brother. The decedent was the "good son," his brother the "bad son," and the parents were very angry. They wanted to sue him. We declined the case.

—Robert Hall and Mila Tecala, Grief and Loss: Identifying and Proving Damages in Wrongful Death Cases, *Trial Guides, LLC (January 2010).*

DRAFTING AGREEMENTS TO CREATE SUSTAINABLE RELATIONSHIPS

There are two emerging trends that align with the values of the relationship-focused movement in law: "results-focused" contracts that create and celebrate relationships and "plain language."

What if our contracts were ways of saying, "I commit to your success. You can count on me. And I trust you to be committed to my success"? What if they were personally meaningful because we created them? Contracts can set the tone for future mutual beneficial and supportive relationships. We are used to seeing a contract used primarily as a tool for protection—addressing what would happen if the other person couldn't fulfill his or her agreement. Now, consider the possibility that you could draft with the additional intention of providing how you would make things right if you were not able to fulfill your part of agreement.

Clients often come to us and ask us for a contract, an operating agreement, corporate by-laws, or some other document. They expect that we'll have something in our form bank that is one-size-fits-all and that we can just whip it out and give it to them without a lot of work. To their detriment, some lawyers do exactly that. With the ready availability of forms on the Internet, we lawyers now have an opportunity to distinguish ourselves by expanding our role in drafting meaningful contracts that create relationships, clarify expectations, establish the foundation of integrity in the contractual relationship, and prevent future litigation.

The time to create enduring contracts is at the beginning, while everyone gets along and the future is rosy. This is the time to lay the groundwork for avoidance or resolution of future conflicts—not from the usual perspective of predicting everything that might go wrong, but rather by predetermining how to resolve the issues that will invariably come up. There are several tools I've used in my drafting in the last ten years:

A State of Grace Document

The breakup of intimate relationships—business or personal—can be very adversarial and expensive. At such times, we wonder where that rational, reasonable, responsible human being we once knew has gone. The adversarial court system is a system designed to blame and accuse the other person. Maureen McCarthy is a business consultant. Several years ago, Maureen and her best friend went into business with each other. They loved and respected each other, so they "knew" that they could work out any difference that arose. As almost any lawyer would predict, eventually they reached a point of conflict. The business dissolved and the friendship ended. The state of grace that existed at the beginning of their relationship was ruined. From that experience, Maureen created her own tool for relationships, which she called the State of Grace Document, SOGD for short.

1. The Story of Us
Share what draws you to these people and this situation.

2. Interaction Styles and Warning Signs
The "blueprint of me," how I work best, what I look like on a good day/bad day, and what I might need that I couldn't ask for in the moment.

3. Expectations
Core values and non-negotiables, the structure you need to create and sustain this relationship.

4. Questions to Return to Peace

A tool to return to peace if the need arises, makes the difficult times shorter and easier.

5. Short and Long-Term Timeframes

How long you're willing to go before you make peace. An agreement of no outright harm, a willingness to keep an open window if the unimaginable happens.

We all have days when we screw up, which is exactly why we created the State of Grace Document. It's a tool used to shorten the frequency and intensity of the difficult times. Creating a Document with others, as well as a Document with yourself—addressing the relationship you have with that voice in your head that can spiral you down—enables you to build trust and resilience both internally and collectively.

—http://www.stateofgracedocument.com/whatisit.html

A few years ago, I tried out the SOGD in my business law class. At the beginning of the semester, we created a contract for how we wanted to be together for the semester. With a small class of only five students, it was important to me that everyone show up for our 8 a.m. class and that everyone participate. We talked about how each of us might sabotage our success. My concern about myself had to do with it being a morning class in winter and having a drive through the mountain roads. Knowing how busy I was, I also worried about not being properly prepared to teach the class. We worked out a plan that empowered all of us and included being able to ask, "Are you stressed out? Can we do something to help you be more fully prepared and present for class?" Students took on projects to teach various sections of the class. We invited guest speakers and created take-home tests. When we reached the season of midterms, we talked openly about the challenges of getting to class on time after late hours. Based on our conversations, we knew how to support each other—one student loved chocolate and when he was having a hard time, we shared a box of truffles. On the rare occasion when I was running late due to weather, I called a designated student, who would let everyone else know. At the end of the semester, the evaluations unanimously praised the relationships created in the class. Three members of the class declared as Business majors, and two have told me they plan to apply to law school.

AGREEMENTS FOR RESULTS

In addition to the State of Grace documents, I have integrated Stewart Levine's work on Agreements for Results. Below, Stewart summarizes his work.

Stop Negotiating Agreements for Protection, and Start Creating Agreements for Results

By Stewart Levine, Esq.

Every year in law schools across the country, each new generation of future lawyers learns to reproduce the mistrust that is the great tragedy of our individualistic and isolating society by learning that the purpose of legal agreements, or contracts, is to protect you from the Other, that stranger at arm's length who is out to exploit you for his or her own self-interest. Stewart Levine begins from the exact opposite premise—that the purpose of agreement is to build a bridge to the Other and to realize your common aspiration for connection. Writ large, this idea would revolutionize the study and practice of law and help to realize our spiritual nature as social beings in pursuit of mutual affirmation.

—Peter Gabel

The word agreements *conjures thoughts of long legal documents, lots of "what ifs" and how to protect against something you don't want to happen. Most people are concerned about protection. They do not want to get hurt. We would all be better off if, when beginning a new endeavor, we shifted our focus away from the calamities we want to avoid and instead worked on envisioning the results we want to produce. The essence of "Agreement for Results" is that we get into conflict because we never learned how to craft explicit agreements creating a meeting of mind and heart with people we want to collaborate with. The best way to prevent conflict, and have more productive and satisfying relationships, is to have "Agreements for Results" on the front end.*

The following Ten Essential Elements make up the template of essential items to be discussed if you want to create a vision and a map to getting the results you want. I have compared the mindset of an "Agreements for Results" perspective, with the traditional "Agreements for Protection" mental model. Notice the difference. Which one is more effective?

The Ten Essential Elements of Agreements for Results

1. **Intent and vision**. Create and define the "Big Picture" of what you want. The clearer and more specific the desired outcomes, the more likely you will succeed as visualized.

2. **Roles**. Define the duties, responsibilities, and commitment of everyone you need to achieve the desired results.

3. **Promises**. *Define action steps in terms of promises. Specific commitments tell you whether the actions will get you to the desired results, and everyone will know when and if the actions are missing.*

4. **Time/value**. *All promises have deadlines. The period during which the agreement will be effective is also defined. Is the exchange fair and does it provide enough incentive?*

5. **Measurements of satisfaction**. *The evidence that you achieved your objectives must be clear, direct, and measurable to eliminate conflict about whether you accomplished the purpose you defined when you began.*

6. **Concerns and fears**. *Unspoken difficulties need to be expressed and the fear behind them addressed. This deepens understanding of what you are taking on, and the partnership you are creating.*

7. **Renegotiation**. *No matter how optimistic and clear the agreement was initially, it will become necessary to renegotiate promises and conditions of satisfaction because things change. The agreement should take this inevitability into account. The quality of working relationships is more important than anything.*

8. **Consequences**. *Know the consequences for breaking promises, and what will be lost if the project is not completed.*

9. **Conflict resolution**. *Another inevitability is that conflicts and disagreements will arise. Agree to an "attitude of resolution," and an agreed resolution process.*

10. **Agreement?** *Should there even be one? When you have reflected on items 1 through 9, ask whether you "trust" moving forward. Do not move into action unless and until you can say yes and commit to embrace the future as an opportunity to be enjoyed.*

The model draws out both the vision and the road map to it. It provides a path to what you want to accomplish. Making an agreement with your client is an excellent way of framing the relationship!

Results Documents Versus Protection Documents

1. ***Intent and vision***

   Results: *Focus on what you want to happen.*
   Protection: *Focus on all the "what ifs" that could go wrong.*

   What we really want in any collaborative context is everyone focusing on desired results—the best possible vision of the future.

That will greatly improve the chances of what we want actually happening.

2. **Roles**

Results: *Making sure someone has responsibility for all critical tasks.*

Protection: *Narrowly defining responsibility to limit accountability and liability.*

We want to make sure we have what we need to get the job done without anything slipping through the cracks. We want clarity about who can be counted on for what, and do not want to hear someone saying, "that's not my job!" In the old context, people liked to hide. They did not like to take the responsibility for making something happen because if something went wrong, they were responsible. By changing the focus of the agreement from protection to results, hopefully the fear of making mistakes is no longer as powerful a driver it once was. We have all learned that the need for innovation requires experimentation. We know that mistakes cannot be "punished" if we want to encourage continued risking, the heart of entrepreneurship.

3. **Promises**

Results: *Contribution—committing to wholeheartedly doing your part required for success, not out of coercion, but from belief in the project's mission.*

Protection: *Doing the least; hiding behind qualifying words that cloud and condition what you are promising.*

This is the point where we define who specifically will be doing what. Consider this a project management plan. This is also a checkpoint—if everyone delivers what he or she promises, will you produce the desired results?

4. **Time and value**

Results: *Clear time commitments and satisfaction with the value given and received.*

Protection: *The most for the least.*

This section should be dedicated to clearly stated deadlines and duration of the agreement, "by when"s, and for how long the promises will be kept. Everyone must be satisfied that what they will get from the project is worth what they are putting in. If someone is undercompensated, she or he will be resentful. Resentful

*participants do not produce results that are beyond expectation,
but people committed to a vision do.*

5. **Measurements of satisfaction**
Results: *Goals that inspire and state clearly and measurably what
is expected.*
Protection: *Qualifiers to argue from and use as excuses.*
*What are the objective measures that will tell you whether
you accomplished what you set out to do? What will satisfy all
involved parties?*

6. **Concerns and fears**
Results: *Compassion for any anxiety-producing concerns and
risks that a partner sees and feels.*
Protection: *An edge to take strategic advantage of when you are
inside their head, in a position to play "games."*
*You address concerns and fears to make everyone as comfort-
able as possible about moving forward. Doing this is a way of
responding to "internal chatter" that might inhibit full participation. It solidifies partnership by addressing what is lingering
in people's minds. It enables people to clearly identify risks and
to choose to move forward anyway. In the traditional protection
model, can you imagine one party admitting his or her fears about
the business venture and partnership?*

7. **Renegotiation**
Results: *How can we make this work as unanticipated changes
take place?*
Protection: *How can changes be used to my advantage?*
*Putting a plan in place to solve a mutual problem to get
desired results, even though things happened that no one antici-
pated (which is one thing you can be sure of), is always a good
idea. Everyone has agreed to certain steps if a crisis arises, and
knows what to do.*

8. **Consequences**
Results: *What reminds everyone of the significance of promises
and failure?*
Protection: *What would be a good punishment?*
*Consequences are put in place not as punishment, but to
remind us of the loss of an unrealized vision and the sanctity of*

our promises. More important is what is lost if the vision is not realized.

9. Conflict resolution
Results: *What will get us back on track quickly?*
Protection: *How can the resolution process be used for leverage or advantage?*

It is very important to understand the cost of remaining in conflict; this should not be about gaining the advantage, but about minimizing and then righting the harm to the partnership.

10. Agreement?
Results: *Do I trust enough to be in an open, ongoing collaboration?*
Protection: *Can I get out without getting hurt? Is there an opportunity for a windfall?*

Has the process produced enough trust so you can say "Let's do it; I'm comfortable moving forward with you, and sense we'll be able to work things out as we go forward"? Has the deep dialogue exchanged between the parties produced a relationship based on covenant—a heartfelt connection and commitment to people and results, a meeting of mind and heart?

Agreements are a fundamental life skill we never learned when we were young. The ability to reach suitable agreements is the primary building block for all kinds of collaborations, and working with others is the only way results, productivity, and satisfying relationships happen. Try having a dialogue that incorporates the elements outlined here at the beginning of your next project. I guarantee that from then on you will become an advocate for "Agreements for Results" in all your endeavors.

—Adapted from Stewart Levine, The Book of Agreement: 10 Essential Elements for Getting the Results You Want *(San Francisco: Berrett-Koehler, 2002.)*

Plain Language Drafting

The plain language movement (or plain English) is an international movement toward writing documents that are free of unnecessary legal jargon and easier for readers to comprehend. Plain language has the goal of being understood by the widest possible audience. It encourages writers to prepare well-written, clear, simple, well-organized documents that meet the needs of the audience.

Rather than jargon like "the party of the first part," a plain language document actually refers to people by their names or by simple identifiers that are understandable to the reader.

Plain language drafting seeks to limit legalese and repetition of synonyms. Rather than prohibiting someone to "cut, mutilate, slash, tear up, or shred," a plain language document might say "don't destroy this." According to a leading proponent of plain legal language, Cheryl Stephens, "Legalese is a block to communication with clients; it has made lawyers the butt of jokes for centuries."

In 2008, the U.S. government passed a plain language law, the Plain Language in Government Communications Act of 2008, that requires agencies to rely on the Federal Plain Language Guidelines or the Securities and Exchange Commission's Plain English Handbook.

Plain language in legal writing is language that is professional and clear. It uses common words, like those we use in everyday conversation.

According to the Center for Plain Language (http://www.centerfor-plainlanguage.org):

> *Plain language is reader-focused writing. When you write in plain language, you create material (for print or online) that works well for the people who use that material. The definition of "plain" depends on the audience. What is plain language for one audience may not be plain language for another audience. Our measure of plain language is behavioral: Can the people who are the audience for the material quickly and easily find what they need, understand what they find, and act appropriately on that understanding?*
>
> *Plain language is more than just short words and short sentences—although those are often two very important guidelines for plain language. When you create material in plain language, you also organize it logically for the audience. You consider how well the layout of your pages or screens works for the audience.*

Traditional legal language is isolating—it isolates lawyers from the public and isolates the public from their rights and obligations. Plain language provides equitable access to the law. Traditional legal writing is depersonalizing, while the "voice" of the law in plain language is humanized. Its meaning is not obscured, it is more persuasive, and the parties can extend trust more readily.

When intimidating legal language is not imposed on people and their legal relationships, then people can be more genuine with one another. Clarity and shared meaning encourages dialogue.

Lawyers who see their role as servants to clients and society, and not to the bottom line, take easily to using plain language. Yet the evidence exists that plain language communication contributes to efficiency, effectiveness, and business improvements that also positively affect the bottom line. Firms that endorse and provide plain language benefit from improved client relationships and better reputation. Some even incorporate the benefits of plain language in their marketing campaigns and firm branding.

Empathy for readers and a belief in the human right to information form the ethical core of plain language. Access to justice requires accepting the public's right to understand. Several organizations are working to promote plain language in law and government. The oldest is Clarity (http://www.clarity-international.net/index.htm), a worldwide group of lawyers and interested laypeople. Its aim is the use of good, clear language by the legal profession through:

- *Avoiding archaic, obscure, and over-elaborate language in legal work.*
- *Drafting legal documents in language that is both certain in meaning and easily understandable.*
- *Exchanging ideas and precedents, not to be followed slavishly but to give guidance in producing good written and spoken legal language.*
- *Exerting a firm, responsible influence on the style of legal language, with the hope of achieving a change in fashion.*
- *Publishing a journal,* Clarity.
- *Sponsoring international conferences on plain language.*

The Washington, DC-based Center for Plain Language (http://www.centerforplainlanguage.org/) actively lobbies government for plain language laws. The Center's activities support four primary goals:

1. *Advocate for people to use, learn, and teach plain language in government, business, nonprofits, and universities.*
2. *Give people information and tools they need to achieve their plain language goals.*

> 3. *Do and share research that identifies best practices for using, learning, and teaching plain language.*
> 4. *Coordinate activities, such as our annual symposium, that help people know more about and use plain language.*
>
> *The Plain Language Association International (http://plainlanguagenetwork.org) has advocated for plain language since 1993.*
>
> *–Cheryl Stephens, author of* Plain Language Legal Writing *(PlainLanguageWizardry.Com)*

HUMANIZING LETTER-WRITING

We lawyers write a lot of letters and many of them are form letters. In a recent blog post, Marquette Law professor Andrea Schneider shared her reaction to such a form letter from the lawyer handling her grandmother's estate:

> As readers of this blog know, I lost my grandmother last fall. It was sad, but not tragic. After all, she was 99 and lived a long productive happy life. Last week, I (and my siblings) received a very formal letter from a lawyer with an enclosure—under Pennsylvania law, where my grandmother lived, beneficiaries of her estate are required to receive notice of her death. So, the lawyer duly enclosed the official Pennsylvania state language letting me know of my rights (to contest probate, etc.). The cover letter was equally formulaic,
>
> > Ladies & Gentlemen:
> > You will find enclosed with regard to the trust . . . the notice required under Pennsylvania Uniform Trust Act of your grandmother's death on November 3rd, 2009.
> > Thank you for your attention to this matter.

Here's the thing—this lawyer was at my wedding, invited to my son's Bar Mitzvah, and has known me since I was 10. I get the same cover letter as someone he has never met—really? And, even if we didn't know each other, the letter should be better. How about this as the letter:

> Dear Andrea,
> I am enclosing the official PA state notice that is required under law. Of course, you already know of your grandmother's death but we have to send this out. Please call me if you have any questions. In the meantime, hope all is well with you and, again, so sorry for your loss. May her memory continue to be a blessing to you.

That doesn't take much energy to produce and is only slightly longer time than the cut & paste job I am no doubt billed for in 6 minute increments. Why don't lawyers do this? Why can't we remember that we are human, our clients are human, and we might even be friends.

And, by the way, this letter ensures that our professional relationship will end when my grandmother's estate is closed.

HUMANIZING
LEGAL EDUCATION

The law student is becoming more argumentative over the least little thing, almost seeming to look for a chance to argue; they have become a little haughty, assuming an air of superiority; they seem older, as if they are trying to affect a range of experience beyond their years; or they are simply not as much fun as they used to be.. . .The simple fact is that there appears to be something about law school that disconnects people from the life they had before.

— Benjamin Sells, The Soul of the Law
(Rockport, MA: Element, 1994)

For many lawyers, the memory of law school is not a pleasant one. We endured it while we were there and we escaped. Others flourished in law school. What makes the difference? The very reasons that we either ran screaming away from law school or thoroughly enjoyed it are fertile ground for new ideas about humanizing the law. Many of the models in this book are based in law schools. And a new movement dedicated to humanizing law school is growing among law professors, deans, and clinical instructors.

Daisy Floyd, Dean of Mercer Law School, found that law students seem to be going through a grief process. She and her students have noticed that all of the stages of grief, ending with resignation, are expressed in law school. Perhaps, says Steve Keeva in *Transforming Practices*, this is a result of loss of self and what is important to the individual. In the quest for "thinking like a lawyer," students lose the ideals that called them to law school in the first place.

Research has documented the deleterious effects of law school on students' well-being and on their values. A study completed by psychologists Ken Sheldon and Larry Krieger tracks and correlates changes in well-being, values, and motivation among students from orientation through the third year of law school. The findings suggest that new law students are quite well adjusted and service oriented but that their well-being drops dramatically and their values shift toward less adaptive, "extrinsic" pursuits during law school.

The following interviews with law professors who are pioneers in humanizing legal education are available on the CuttingEdgeLaw site.

- Bruce Winick: An Agent of Social Change
- Professor Josh Rosenberg: Interpersonal Dynamics
- Professor Rhonda Magee: Challenging Norms and Doctrines
- Cindy Adcock, Director of Experiential Learning, Charlotte Law
- Tim Floyd: Director of Law and Public Service, Mercer Law School
- Professor Len Riskin, University of Florida: Mindfulness and ADR
- Dean Daisy Floyd, Pioneer in Humanizing Legal Education
- Larry Krieger: Humanizing Legal Education
- Professor Susan Daicoff: Comprehensive Law and Lawyer Personality
- Stella Rabaut: 21st-Century Lawyer
- Erica Ariel Fox, Lecturer at Harvard Law School

Other legal education resources can be found at: http://www .cuttingedgelaw.com/page/humanizing-legal-education.

These days, you can find many excellent courses on nonadversarial practice in law schools, particularly in the areas of restorative justice, therapeutic jurisprudence, and collaborative law. Law schools are also developing more balanced and healthy approaches to legal education. In my research for this book, I gathered enough information about innovations in legal education that I could begin a separate book. Following are just three of the many wonderful examples.

***

Washburn Law School has made some nice humanizing inroads. All of their entering students experience the following in their first semester of law school:

- They are placed in structured study groups, led by upper-division students, in which the focus is on collaboration and peer support.
- They complete what they call "the retirement-party exercise" in which they describe, in writing, what they hope people will be saying about them when they retire. They place the description in a self-addressed envelope, which is mailed to them when they graduate.
- They keep a reflection journal, in which they respond to prompts that engage them in reflection on their initial experiences in law school.
- They have a small section class in which they take a practice midterm and a real midterm.
- In all their other classes, they at least have a practice midterm option.
- Professor Michael Hunter Schwartz is innovative in his first-year contracts class, although he points out that he has only half the entering students in his class. In describing the classes, he writes:

  1. Every class session includes at least two small group or pairing experiences.
  2. I have lunch once per semester with all of my students in their small groups.
  3. I memorize my students' names before the first day of class.
  4. I ask each student to complete a card in which they explain why they are in law school and tell me one thing they want me to know about themselves, and, in class, throughout the semester, I refer, without mentioning any person by name, to what they wrote.
  5. I give two essay quizzes, an essay midterm, and weekly optional multiple-choice quizzes so students have a sense of how they are doing and what they need to do to improve.
  6. I encourage students to bring their significant others to class and promise them, on any day they bring a significant other, that I will call on them and make them look brilliant.
  7. When students express frustration with a rule of law, I congratulate them and encourage them to harness their passion to change the law.
  8. Rather than trying to catch my students making errors, I generally try to cause my students to develop good insights and then reinforce them for doing so.
  9. I do an annual kinesthetic lawyering skills exercise in which I ask all the students to stand up and tell them I will be reading a list of the skills identified in the attached survey of Arizona lawyers. I ask them to sit down when I list a skill they already had when they

came to law school. My goal is to help them see that lawyering success isn't all just about applying rules and applying and distinguishing cases.

***

In an e-mail from Julie K. Sandine, Assistant Dean for Student Affairs at Vanderbilt Law, I learned of some programs her law school offers its students. I wanted to tell you about them, so asked permission to post her e-mail; she graciously consented. Sandine writes:

> We've just concluded our fourth year of providing Supportive Practices, a noncredit offering for 1L [first-year law] students that teaches mindfulness meditation, Qi gong, cognitive strategies, and other techniques that can help reduce stress and enhance concentration, as well as one's overall sense of well-being. We meet once a week for an hour during the first ten weeks of class.
>
> We have also provided a Professionalism in Practice noncredit offering (previously entitled "Ethics and Professionalism") for the past four years, which is held once a week for an hour during the first ten weeks of class. In a small group setting, students are asked to read about and discuss relevant issues of ethics, professionalism, and one's role/identity in the legal profession, as well as engage in self-reflection and submit weekly journal entries.
>
> When I taught Professional Responsibility [PR] last year, I also required that students submit weekly journal reflections as a part of their final grade. I feel self-reflection is an important part of the process of forming one's professional identity (but not something people do regularly or even feel very comfortable doing) and so sought to encourage students to get into the habit of engaging in this process. I also started each class session with the day's reading from "The Reflective Counselor" in an effort to make students aware of the importance of quiet reflection, purposeful thought, and becoming more mindful of the many components of one's life, personally and professionally. I will be teaching PR again in the spring semester and plan to again incorporate contemplative practices to some degree.
>
> Interestingly, Vanderbilt University has a Contemplative Pedagogy group (of which I am a part), which meets regularly and shares ideas for including a contemplative practice in the classroom setting. One of our legal clinic faculty has also joined the group.

***

Appalachian School of Law (ASL) has a Lawyer as Problem Solver (LAPS) Certificate Program. ASL's founders created the first and, so far, only law school established with an alternative dispute resolution (ADR) focus. In 1996, when it began developing the law school, ASL's original Steering Committee envisioned a graduate who would emphasize problem-solving skills and adhere to high professional ethics. The curriculum offers students a unique opportunity to become leaders in the field of ADR.

Only nine law schools, including ASL, require all their students to take an ADR survey class. The curriculum reflects the realities of lawyering in an era of the so-called "Vanishing Trial." Research shows that ASL students who take only the required survey course likely have more training in ADR than most practicing lawyers.

ASL's Lawyer as Problem Solver certificate program focuses on the role of the modern attorney in facilitating strategic problem solving for clients both inside and outside of the courtroom. The program seeks to provide students with the skills they need to effectively serve their clients, including skills in oral and written communication; interviewing and counseling; negotiation; mediation; arbitration; transactional drafting; estate planning; and pre-trial, trial, and appellate practice. In 2008, 18 students earned the LAPS certificate, representing 20 percent of the graduating class. ASL expects 24 students or 25 percent of the graduating class to earn the certificate in 2009.

PUTTING OUR SKILLS TO WORK IN THE WORLD

LAWYERS ARE LEADERS, AND PEOPLE ARE FOLLOWING. WHERE ARE YOU GOING?

In this essay, I argue that graduates of law schools should aspire not just to be wise counselors but wise leaders; not just to dispense "practical wisdom" but to be "practical visionaries;" not just to have positions where they advise, but where they decide. Put another way, I wish to redefine (or at least to reemphasize) the concept of "lawyer" to include "lawyer as leader." The profession and the law schools should more candidly recognize the importance of leadership and should more directly prepare and inspire young lawyers to seek roles of ultimate responsibility and accountability than they do today.

Why do I advance this thesis? First, our society is suffering from a leadership deficit in public, private, and nonprofit spheres.

The core competencies of law are as good a foundation for broad leadership as other training. Second, the legal profession, by many accounts, is suffering from a crisis of morale, from a disconnect between personal values and professional life. Providing leadership can affirm—and test—our vision and core values. Third, other professional schools—business and public policy—have as their explicit mission the training of leaders for the public, private, and nonprofit sectors. The graduates of our law schools are at least as talented as those who enter other professional and graduate schools. And law schools should have a similar vision to enhance the careers of their outstanding students, thus serving society and addressing the values crisis that affects portions of the profession.

> —Ben W. Heineman, Jr., "Lawyers as Leaders," Yale Journal,
> the Yale Law Journal, Pocket Part 116: 266, 2007

⊠ · ⊠

***

⊠ · ⊠

... in its essence, leadership is about learning how to shape the future. Leadership exists when people are no longer victims of circumstances but participate in creating new circumstances. ...

The new leadership must be grounded in fundamentally new understandings of how the world works. The sixteenth-century Newtonian mechanical view of the universe, which still guides our thinking, has become increasingly dysfunctional to these times of interdependence and change. The critical shifts required to guarantee a healthy world for our children and our children's children will not be achieved by doing more of the same. "The world we have created is a product of our way of thinking," said Einstein. Nothing will change in the future without fundamentally new ways of thinking. This is the real work of leadership. And this book is a good place to begin the world.

> —Peter Senge in Synchronicity by Joseph Jaworski

⊠ · ⊠

***

A friend of mine with interests in both conflict resolution and environmental issues grew up with the goal of "saving the world." After law school, she told me that she was torn about where to put her energies. Would the world be destroyed first by conflict or by environmental disaster?

Sharif Abdullah, J.D.: Transforming the World

Sharif Abdullah

©Michael Matthews

Sharif Abdullah began his pursuit of social and spiritual change in Camden, New Jersey, when he was only a teenager. Sharif says of it, "Camden was a toxic relationship." Welfare, poverty, casual violence, and public housing were all realities in his early years. In spite of this, or perhaps in reaction to this, in his teens Sharif became a founder of the Black People's Unity Movement (BPUM), an organization that created a sewing factory, two day care centers, affordable housing, and a supermarket, among other things.

Sharif earned his B.A. in Psychology from Clark University in Massachusetts, and went on to earn his Juris Doctor degree from Boston University. After practicing public interest law for six years in Charlotte, North Carolina, Sharif lost faith in the adversarial process. Instead, he turned to social change based on the theories of inclusivity.

"We stand on the brink of one of the most profound cultural and spiritual shifts in human history. All around the world, people by the millions are actively catalyzing positive change, meeting the challenges of our times with creativity, joy and a deep spiritual reverence. They are acting like their lives have meaning in the world. These turbulent times are calling forth authentic leaders adept at surfing through chaos who are creating a world beyond war and beyond fear: a world that works for all. We encourage all people to walk this path." (Sharif Abdullah from www .commonway.org)

Sharif has found his purpose and lives aligned with it. "My life purpose is to serve as a catalyst for inclusive social, cultural and spiritual transformation. Spirituality for me is an unrelenting commitment to honor the Divine within each of us. I cannot do that if I am at war with others, or at war with myself. I am committed to ending the war. I am committed to creating a world that works for all."

One of his projects to change mindsets is called the Commons Café. The Commons Café requires a face-to-face dialogue where people from entirely different racial, economic, and ethnic backgrounds are gathered together to have conversations. People who would not normally come into contact with one another are placed at tables of six to ten people and are given note cards with questions to guide the conversations. The goal is to change pre-conceptions of those different from ourselves and to realize that our stereotypes are not always true empowerment.

In another project, he routinely traveled to war zones in Sri Lanka as he worked with Sarvodaya, an organization seeking a shift in consciousness that would create peace.

The author of Creating a World That Works for All (Berrett-Kohler, 1999) and the Power of One, (New Catalyst Books, 2007). Sharif recently published a new book, SEVEN SEEDS for a New Society, available as an ebook at www.commonway.org, with this description:

SEVEN SEEDS for a New Society offers a new way to approach our inner lives, our society and our spirituality. This book provides tools to help us move from a society based on fear, lack, violence and greed, to a society based on love, compassion and relationships with all beings.

Our present society, the dominant paradigm, is toxic and terminal. That's the bad news.

The good news: We stand on the brink of the next evolutionary leap for humankind, a leap that will transform all human societies!

At times inspiring, challenging and controversial, social-spiritual activist Sharif Abdullah articulates for us the need to transform our toxic "operating system" (how people interact in the world) to one based on love, compassion and relationship. Sharif challenges us to apply our spiritual and moral values in the world, in a practical, realistic way that can save humanity, all beings, and the Earth.

Sharif has been recognized with many awards for his consciousness-raising, peacemaking work. He is the recipient of the 2006 "Humanitarian Service Award" from the Unity and Diversity Council and the 2007 "Hero of Humanity Award" from the Art of Living Foundation, as well as the "Martin Luther King Lifetime Achievement Award" from the World Arts Foundation. Sarvodaya Shramadana in Sri Lanka also gave him the Universal Friend Award in 2006. He is recognized as a "Luminary" by the Institute of Noetic Sciences.

The world is facing a lot of problems these days. Many of them seem critical to the survival of the species or at least to the quality of life, peace, and security of our world. We need our best and brightest minds and most passionate hearts to be engaged in solutions, in finding common ground, in healing polarization, in addressing the critical problems of the day with reason and compassion.

Ours is probably the most powerful profession. Lawyers occupy a large percentage of the leadership positions in the world. About half of all the members of Congress have law degrees, and we all know that lawyers hold many other political offices—from local city councils to many seats in executive and judicial branches of all levels of government. Lawyers are on boards of directors of corporations, both for-profit and not-for-profit. In crises, lawyers are the ones who are called upon for advice. We are the protectors of human rights, the defenders of the Constitution. We are in positions to make a big difference— or should get ourselves there soon!

In the past couple of years, our lawyer brothers and sisters have been called upon to take to the streets in countries around the globe, to put their lives on the line to stand for the rule of law and civilized conflict resolution. How many of us can watch that without feeling the stir of peace and justice? And our revolution doesn't have to happen on the streets; it is a peaceful revolution, and it has the power to create a world that works for everyone.

In our first interview with Susan Daicoff, she talked about feeling like part of a whole body and mused that perhaps she was the little finger on the right hand. As long as she did her little finger work, the rest of the body would be able to do its work and everything would get done.

What is *your* part of transforming the world? If litigation is what makes your soul sing, do it where you will make the most difference. Fight the bad guys, whoever they are in your value system. If you prefer to make peace, do that, too. Do what is true to your heart. But *do* something that matters to you and to the planet. It doesn't have to be huge. It might just be reaching out a hand to someone in your own neighborhood, sharing yourself, being true to your own values. You don't have to move or quit your job. But, if that is what your heart calls you to do, don't be afraid to do it.

Change is urgent.

It is time to wake up! This is why we were born. This is why you went to law school. The world needs saving—and you're the one!

Be the change you want to see.

—M. Gandhi

AFTERWORD

It is a wonderful gift and honor to be chosen to write a book like this. The stories I've shared, the people I've highlighted, and the approaches and models I've outlined are part of a wonderful movement that inspires me every day. And movements do move.

In the few weeks that I was writing this, lawyer President Barack Obama won the Nobel Peace Prize for diplomacy and problem solving. Elinor Ostrom won the Nobel Prize for Economics for cooperation and collaboration. I received dozens of interesting and relevant articles and tools, many of which I have been able to incorporate into this book. This conversation is ongoing. Stop by CuttingEdgeLaw.com and participate. Help us move it forward.

POSITIVE PSYCHOLOGY: FIVE PATHS TO POSITIVITY

David N. Shearon, JD, MAPP,
Executive Director of the
Tennessee Commission on
Continuing Legal Education
and Specialization, and of the
Tennessee Lawyers' Fund for
Client Protection

SLEEP

CAN YOU remember the last time you woke up after a really good night's sleep? Remember how you felt? Now, how often do you get that feeling?

It is astonishingly easy in a world of electric lights and seductive, low-energy entertainment through television to end up going to bed on a regular basis too late to get sufficient rest. If you frequently are awoken from a heavy sleep by your alarm, feel tired and unready to start the day, and find yourself sleepy during the day, your first step toward more positivity could be increased time spent sleeping.

Marie-Josee Salvas, an international well-being consultant, suggests that those running short on sleep first rethink the importance of this topic. She notes research that chronic sleep deprivation impacts mental abilities, immune system functioning, and moodiness. We lose our capacities for self-regulation, with consequences ranging from overeating to binge drinking to yelling at the kids. She suggests:

- Regularity in sleep hours.
- Cut back on caffeine after noon.
- Preparing for sleep in a dark room (including lowered lights and no TV for a period prior to going to bed).
- Focusing on your comfort.
- Adjust your work to fit your patterns of alertness as much as possible.

EXERCISE

THIS IS not about training for a marathon. But the evidence in favor of regular, moderate exercise as a boost to well-being is overwhelming. For most of us, 30 minutes of moderate exercise three to five times per week is sufficient. Walking is good. Or many other exercises. Some such as Tai Chi or Yoga may also produce beneficial effects through mindfulness. But get moving. Get some small action going. Even if it's just two minutes of walking in place for every half-hour of TV. Start! Then increase incrementally until you reach a level where the benefits on your energy and emotional well-being seem to have leveled off.

THREE GOOD
THINGS

A LARGE-SCALE, random-assignment, placebo-controlled test of various activities included the practice of writing each evening about three good things that happened that day. After describing the event (who, what, when, and where), reflect, in writing, on those three things. Why did they happen? What was your contribution? What do they mean? The overwhelming majority of participants in the study registered increases in happiness that were sustained over six months. The participants who began the study as severely depressed also showed decreases in levels of depression equivalent to what could be expected from taking chemical anti-depressants, and these gains were also sustained over six months of follow-up.

USE YOUR
STRENGTHS IN
A NEW WAY

THIS IS another exercise from the large-scale, random-assignment, placebo-controlled test mentioned above. Select one of your Signature Strengths, plan a new way to use it in the coming week, then implement your plan. For example:

- One woman's highest signature strength is love of learning. She chose to check out and read a book on obedience training for dogs, something she wanted to do with her family's new puppy.
- Someone with a signature strength of kindness decided to do secret acts of kindness for co-workers.
- Another person's top strength is appreciation of beauty and excellence. She decided to visit a local art museum she had been meaning to see.
- Someone else focused on a signature strength of playfulness/humor. He chose to write a silly limerick that captured a key point for each of his classes that week.

CHALLENGE PESSIMISTIC THOUGHTS

L AWYERS, ESPECIALLY, tend to be pessimists. One way this comes out is in a tendency to have certain types of negative thoughts in the face of any adversity, big or small, personal or professional. These thoughts explain the adversity. They assign causes, and the causes are usually:

- Permanent—the cause will affect other events far into the future.
- Pervasive—the cause will affect many areas of life.
- Unchangeable—we cannot change the cause so there's no hope; we're helpless.

As you might imagine, it's tough to bounce back from events caused by permanent, pervasive, and unchangeable causes. These thoughts are about "always, everything, beyond my control!" One great way of being supremely pessimistic is to make the cause something about one's innate qualities or character. "I'm stupid!" is hard to overcome if one sees stupidity as an unchangeable quality. The same is true for "I'm not good at relationships," or "I don't have what it takes!"

Optimistic folks, on the other hand, tend to see causes that are temporary, specific, and changeable. So, a bad event is isolated in time and from other areas of our lives. When a bad outcome in a court case is due to weaknesses in that case, then there are no ramifications for the future and no reflection on their character. It's easy to bounce back. After all, it's over and done with and the next case is likely to be better!

To learn whether you have a pessimistic thinking style (and lawyers often do!), carry some note cards around with you for a week. When you hit any kind of adversity, big or small, as soon as possible write it down. Describe the event: who, what, when, where. Then try to write down as exactly as possible the thoughts that went through your mind in the heat of the moment. No cleaning up the language, rationalizing, or organizing. Try to record them exactly as they went through your mind. Also, note your energy right after the event. Did it drop? Did you find it hard to go on? Or were you still as energized as before and able to keep moving forward?

Then, each evening, pull out your note cards. First, look for patterns. Do you tend to find permanent, pervasive, and unchangeable causes? If so, carefully scrutinize each situation as if the thoughts that went through your mind were just some other lawyer's arguments. What did that lawyer miss? What evidence points to temporary, specific, and changeable causes? Assemble a persuasive case for the temporary, specific, and changeable causes. Then note how you feel. If you had initially thought of such temporary, specific, and changeable causes, would it have been easier to keep going? Would you have felt more energy and fewer or milder negative emotions?

Over time, you will begin to be able to challenge causal thoughts that are too permanent, too pervasive, and too unchangeable in the heat of the moment as they enter your mind. This can help you perform (and feel) in a more optimistic and hopeful manner. You can then cut back on the daily use of the note cards, but it would be good to recheck yourself by returning to the note-taking routine every so often.

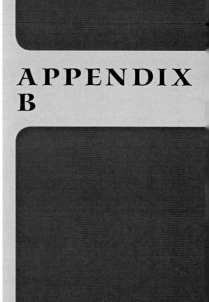

ARE COURT-ROOMS BATTLE-GROUNDS FOR LOSERS? NON-ADVERSARIAL APPROACHES TO RESOLUTION WITHOUT LITIGATION

Susan Daicoff

WHAT WE are doing in our legal system is not working. Clients are unhappy with their lawyers, the system, and the results. Lawyers are extraordinarily unhappy or even impaired. Nonlegal dispute resolution mechanisms in society have failed and society is depending on litigative processes to resolve conflict. As a result, society in general is suffering from the effects of law's overly adversarial, other-blaming, position-taking, and hostile approach to conflict resolution.

Perhaps in response to these developments, a number of alternative approaches to law practice are emerging to replace the old, outmoded monolithic system. Since about 1990, a number of seemingly unrelated developments, or "vectors," have appeared, all focused on reaching results for clients that optimize the clients' goals, satisfaction, emotional and relational health, and overall well-being. As these vectors became known, their similarities became evident and they began to coalesce into a larger movement across the country. This movement has been called "the comprehensive law movement," for lack of a better term, although names such as transformative law, integrative law, and law as a healing profession are also sometimes used. While this movement is not explicitly nonadversarial, its focus is on resolving legal matters in a way that leaves the parties in better or no worse shape, overall, than they were at the outset. It delights in creative, win–win solutions. It tries to preserve important interpersonal relationships. And it guards the parties' emotional wellbeing and functioning. As a result, it often encourages nonlitigative resolution.

For example, attorney Arnie Herz represented a large, imposing, ex-football player, "John" in a dispute he had with the new owners of the company he had just sold, after 15 years of successful solo ownership. John was furious with the new owners' treatment of him as an employee, post-sale, and with their mismanagement of the company. Unfortunately, he had signed a noncompete agreement as part of the sale, so he felt bound to stay working for the new owners, despite his frustration. Determined to sue the new owners for mistreatment and mismanagement, he approached Arnie. Arnie assessed that the lawsuit could be successful, but would cost well over $100,000 in fees and costs to litigate. John had the money and was ready to "write a check" for the $100,000, but Arnie decided to slow him down just a bit. The lawyer asked, "If you could have anything you wanted in your life, what would you want your life to look like six months from now?" John said more than anything he wanted to be free of the new owners and wanted to make more money, and thought he could make a lot more money if he were free of them, but he didn't want to let them "off the hook." Frustrated that this lawyer wasn't aggressive enough and was trying to talk him out of suing, he commented, "You are too nice. I need a tough litigator." and then packed up and started to walk out of Arnie's office. Assessing the situation, Arnie responded, "I know you think you are so tough and I am not but the truth is that in all my years I think you may be the weakest person I have ever known. You've set out a vision of where you'd like your life to be, which was to be free of these people. You didn't mention that you wanted to punish them, teach them a lesson, spend $100,000 of your own money and five years of your life. What you said was that you wanted to be free of them to be able to make a lot more money on your own. What I see is that you don't have the strength to hold on to your own vision and deal more effectively with your own anger. And I'll bet you have been doing this all your life." At first, John flushed red with anger. But something in what Arnie said rang true. He sat down and began talking and listening to Arnie. And together, they agreed on a plan of action that involved a more collaborative, nonlitigative approach to resolving the matter.

John was freed from his noncompete clause three weeks later. The new owners teetered on the edge of bankruptcy for years, so, as Arnie had predicted, even if he had sued them, he wouldn't have been able to collect anything. Free of the new owners, John was able to make a lot more money. Financially, the plan was a huge success. Personally, John later said that the process of resolving this legal matter allowed him to learn how his anger had been controlling his life, affecting his relationship with his wife and his kids, and blocking him from his full potential.

Arnie's approach to representing John is one illustration of how a "comprehensive lawyer" might conduct his or her law practice. Arnie went beyond the law to ask about this client's deepest needs, goals, and desires and then used that information to create, with the client, the best strategy for proceeding. Admittedly, this lawyer took a major risk early in the lawyer–client relationship and not all comprehensive lawyers would be comfortable doing what Arnie did. Using excellent interpersonal skills, though, Arnie assessed that John was a no-nonsense person who would only respond to "hearing it straight," which he did. Litigation in this case would have only wasted time and money and fueled the client's excessive anger. The process and outcome were not only financially successful, but personally and emotionally beneficial for John.

This illustration is only one example, though. The comprehensive law movement has at least nine converging vectors: collaborative law, creative problem solving, holistic justice, preventive law, the problem-solving court movement, procedural justice, restorative justice, therapeutic jurisprudence, and transformative mediation. Like the members of a family, the vectors all have things in common and yet are individually different from each other. All of the "vectors" intersect in two places, though. First, they seek to optimize the well-being of the people involved in the legal matter, whether by maximizing their emotional health, the health of their personal relationships, their moral development, or their integration into society. Second, they encourage the lawyer and client to focus on more than simply the client's legal rights and duties (or the economic bottom line). This is a "rights plus" approach, which considers things like the client's wishes, goals, desires, needs, resources, emotions, relationships, values, morals, and beliefs. In achieving these two goals, the vectors of the comprehensive law movement are often (but not always) non-adversarial, nonlitigative, noncompetitive, and collaborative. They are almost always creative, interdisciplinary, and extraordinarily satisfying to both the lawyers and clients involved.

Collaborative law is a nonlitigative, collaborative process employed mainly in divorce law, where the spouses and their respective attorneys resolve the issues outside of court in a four-party process. No litigation is usually instituted until settlement is reached. The attorneys are contractually forbidden from representing their clients in court should the agreement process break down. Basically, it puts the divorcing spouses with their respective attorneys into a collaborative, four-way series of discussions designed to resolve the issues without litigation. Because the attorneys must withdraw if the process breaks down, the attorneys' financial interests are the same as the clients'—to reach settlement. This contrasts with the usual process, where the lawyers "win" whether the clients settle or not, since they simply litigate if negotiations break down. There is a strong psychological component to the lawyer–client relationship in that emotions, needs, transference, etc., are openly acknowledged and dealt with in order to maximize results of the four-way conferences. Although currently being used only in the domestic area, collaborative law could be appropriate for other areas, such as employment law. Leading trainers include practicing attorneys Pauline Tesler (Bay Area, California) (website: http://www.divorcenet.com/ca/tesler.html) and Stuart Webb (Minnesota) (website: http://www.divorcenet.com/mn/webb.html). See also collaborativelaw.org.

Restorative justice refers to a movement employed most often with juvenile offenders in the United States, although it is more widely used in Australia, Canada, and the United Kingdom, in which criminal justice and criminal sentencing are done by the community, victim, and offender in a collaborative process. It may be as simple as post-sentencing victim–offender mediation or as complicated as sentencing that is done in a community conference with all parties present. It emphasizes relationships between the offender, victim, and community instead of a top-down, hierarchical system of imposing punishment. The website for The Center for Restorative Justice & Peacemaking at the University of Minnesota School of Social Work explains that "[t]hrough restorative justice, victims, communities, and offenders are placed in active roles to work together to . . . Empower victims in their search for closure; Impress upon offenders the real human impact of their behavior; Promote restitution to victims and communities. Dialogue and negotiation are central to restorative justice, and problem solving for the future is seen as more important than simply establishing blame for past behavior. Balance is sought between the legitimate needs of the victim, the community, and the offender that enhances community protection, competency development in the offender, and direct accountability of the offender to the victim and victimized community." One of its leaders is Mark Umbreit, a social work professor at the University of Minnesota (see http://ssw.che.umn.edu/rjp/).

Procedural justice refers to Tom Tyler's research finding that, in judicial processes, litigants' satisfaction depends less on the actual outcome (e.g., winning versus losing), and more on (1) being treated with respect and dignity, (2) being heard and having an opportunity to speak and participate, and (3) how trustworthy the authorities appear and behave. It is being used to reengineer dispute resolution processes (litigative and nonlitigative) to incorporate these three important features.

Transformative mediation is a newer form of alternative dispute resolution set forth in Bush and Folger's 1994 book, *The Promise of Mediation*. TM views conflict as a destabilizing "crisis in human interaction" rather than a violation of rights or conflict of individual interests. Its three-person mediations seek to restore balance between self and other, transform conflict into a positive, constructive process, and encourage parties to do two things: (1) regain their sense of strength and self-confidence (the "empowerment" shift) and (2) expand their responsiveness to each other (the "recognition" shift, much like empathy). By focusing on these goals, the parties are moved toward increased personal development and enhanced personal and interpersonal skills. Baruch Bush is a law professor at Hofstra University School of Law, and Joseph Folger is a communications professor at Temple University. The Institute for the Study of Conflict Transformation, Inc. is found at http://www.transformativemediation.org/.

Therapeutic jurisprudence is one of the most well-known vectors, with the broadest applications. Since around 1990, it has focused on the therapeutic or countertherapeutic consequences of the law and legal procedures on the individuals involved, including the clients, their families, friends, lawyers, judges, and community. It attempts to reform law and legal processes in order to promote the psychological well-being of the people they affect. Its website explains that TJ "concentrates on the law's impact on emotional life and psychological well-being. It is a perspective that regards the law (rules of law, legal procedures, and roles of legal actors) itself as a social force that can produce therapeutic or anti-therapeutic consequences. It does not suggest that therapeutic concerns are more important than other consequences or factors, but it does suggest that the law's role as a potential therapeutic agent should be recognized." TJ has been applied to almost every area of law, including mental health law, family law, employment law, health law, elder law, appellate practice, criminal law, criminal sentencing, litigation, and estate planning. It has been applied to police work and become very popular with judges. Its founders are David B. Wexler, Professor of Law at University of Arizona and University of Puerto Rico and Bruce Winick, Professor of Law at University of Miami. Its website is http://www.therapeuticjurisprudence.org, and it has a listserv and an extensive bibliography.

The **problem-solving court movement** resulted from judges' enthusiastic application of TJ to the adjudication process. Frustrated with recidivism and repeat performances, judges developed specialized, multidisciplinary "problem-solving" courts focused on resolving the interpersonal issues underlying the legal problems instead of punishing defendants or assigning fault. They take a long-term, relational, interdisciplinary, healing approach to judging. In the criminal setting, judges create collaborative and ongoing relationships with offenders and help professionals . . . supervise the offenders' rehabilitation efforts. Examples are drug treatment courts, mental health courts, domestic violence courts, and unified family courts. Drug treatment courts are reporting impressive drops in recidivism as a result of their changed focus and approach. The nonadversarial nature of these courts is consistent with the approach to civil matters taken by vectors like collaborative law and transformative mediation.

Preventive law has been around for many years. Like preventive medicine, it explicitly seeks to intervene in legal matters before disputes arise and advocates proactive intervention to head off litigation and other conflicts. It emphasizes the lawyer–client relationship, relationships in general, and planning. In recent years, its lawyering techniques were integrated with TJ concepts in order to describe "how to" practice TJ-oriented law, thus resulting in therapeutically oriented preventive law. Its founder was the late Louis Brown and it is associated with Professor and Dean Emeritus Edward Dauer at the University of Denver College of Law. California Western School of Law houses the National Center for Preventive Law, and it has its own textbook, reporter, and website: http://www.preventivelawyer.org/main/default.asp.

Holistic justice is a grassroots movement in which practicing lawyers "acknowledge the need for a humane legal process with the highest level of satisfaction for all participants; honor and respect the dignity and integrity of each individual; promote peaceful advocacy and holistic legal principles; value responsibility, connection, and inclusion; encourage compassion, reconciliation, forgiveness, and healing; practice deep listening; understand and recognize the importance of voice; contribute to peace building at all levels of society; recognize the opportunity in conflict; draw upon ancient intuitive wisdom of diverse cultures and traditions; and [the movement encourages the lawyer to] enjoy the practice of law" (from its website: http://iahl.org/). It is explicitly interdisciplinary, allows the lawyer to incorporate his or her own morals and values into client representation, and seeks to "do the right thing" for the lawyer, clients, and others involved. Like holistic medicine, it takes a broader view of legal problems and possible solutions. It is associated with the International Alliance of Holistic Lawyers, whose founder is practicing lawyer William Van Zyverden in Vermont.

Creative problem solving is a broad approach to lawyering that is explicitly humanistic, interdisciplinary, creative, and preventive. Its website explains that "clients and society are increasingly asking lawyers to approach problems [not always as fighters, but] more creatively." CPS seeks to prevent legal problems if possible and creatively solve those that exist. It "focuses both on using the traditional analytical process more creatively and on using nontraditional problem solving processes, drawn from business, psychology, economics, neuroscience, and sociology." CPS is associated with the McGill Center for Creative Problem Solving at California Western School of Law (website: go to http://www.cwsl.edu/main/home.asp and then select Creative Problem Solving), which sponsors a number of law school courses on CPS, national and international projects, and periodic conferences. The merging of the vectors is clear in CPS's use of preventive law and transformative mediation.

POTENTIAL
RELATED VECTORS

A NUMBER of other "movements" in the law have been suggested as part of the comprehensive law movement. These are law and spirituality; mindfulness meditation; the humanizing legal education movement; the religious lawyering movement (interjecting religious values into law practice); the movement to resurrect secular humanist values in law; the politics of meaning; the efforts of the Contemplative Mind & Society Institute, including the Yale Law School meditation project sponsored by the Fetzer Institute; and affective lawyering and rebellious lawyering, both important in the domestic violence context.

APPLYING THE VECTORS

SOME OF the vectors are more practical, concrete, and tangible, while others are more broad and theoretical and serve as "lenses" through which the more concrete vectors can be evaluated. For example, if dispute resolution is a collection of dispute resolution alternatives to litigation, including arbitration, mediation, private judges, and negotiation, then collaborative law, restorative justice, and transformative mediation should be part of this collection. These vectors, together with preventive law, give us new processes and techniques to add to our toolkits.

The other vectors, such as TJ, procedural justice, holistic justice, and CPS, are ways that a lawyer might look at a particular legal problem to evaluate which process will work best. For example, each of the legal processes can be viewed from a TJ (is this process therapeutic or not? how could it be made so?), holistic (how does this process take into account the healing of the client and lawyer?), procedural justice (how will this process affect the participants psychologically?), or CPS (does this process allow for the broadest, most creative approach to solving the problem?) perspective. A related lens might be religious lawyering (is this process consistent with the lawyer's and client's religious beliefs?).

COLLABORATIVE VERSUS ADVERSARIAL PRACTICES

A MASS of questions usually floods the minds of practicing lawyers who encounter a vector of the movement for the first time: Isn't this just rolling over and playing dead? Isn't this asking lawyers to be psychologists? Isn't this paternalistic and meddling in clients' affairs? Isn't this going to make me a whole lot less money? Will I be seen as less competent? Will I lose clients if I practice law this way? What if the client wants a pit bull attorney? Many of these questions are pointed at the wrong thing.

The comprehensive law movement is not about being exclusively collaborative, nonadversarial, "nice," or touchy feely. It is not about backing down and being a pushover. It is about having a few more tools in one's toolkit beyond the solitary "hammer" of litigation that we learned in law school and maybe the screwdriver of mediation we picked up in law practice. Even those whose toolkit already includes more than just a hammer (such as mediation and other forms of alternative dispute resolution) can benefit from learning to properly apply the comprehensive law movement's wide variety of conflict resolution processes and approaches to legal matters. We do need to know when to use what tool, however.

- We do not become psychologists; we become skilled questioners and good listeners, and we have a better idea when to refer clients to, and how to collaborate with, psychologists.
- We don't tell clients what they should or shouldn't do, how they feel, or how they should feel; we elicit from them their big picture, deep, long-term goals using excellent communication skills, and then we work within the lawyer–client team to develop ways to achieve those goals.
- We don't always suggest collaborative dispute resolution processes because, for some clients, hardball litigation is either the most therapeutic strategy or the only way for them to achieve their truest personal and legal goals.
- We need to be able to threaten (and provide) pit bull representation, often, in order to bring a recalcitrant opponent to the table. We need to be proficient at traditional approaches in order to successfully practice comprehensive ones.
- We need to be sure that we do not suggest a collaborative approach to a legal matter because we ourselves are inherently uncomfortable with confrontation or conflict.
- The lawyers who are proficient in this way of practicing law report no loss of income and a great increase in their own and their clients' satisfaction with their work. If, however, the lawyer stubbornly refuses to listen to and dialogue with his or her clients and routinely persuades his or her clients to abandon litigation and utilize cooperative dispute resolution processes, then yes, that lawyer is likely to lose credibility, clients, and income. That lawyer has indeed become paternalistic and rigid. He or she has perverted and collapsed the comprehensive law movement into a one-size-fits-all nonadversarial collaboration, which won't work.
- The client has the final say as to which approach to pursue, in resolving his or her legal matter. However, with comprehensive lawyering, the client will make this decision with full knowledge of all of the consequences of potential legal actions, including the emotional, developmental, relational, moral, and spiritual (if applicable) effects, as well as the legal and economic results.

Lawyers who were trained to practice law in the traditional manner may require a bit of new training in order to feel proficient in practicing the comprehensive law approaches. Trainings are regularly available in collaborative law, restorative justice, and transformative mediation through their individual websites. Conferences on therapeutic jurisprudence, preventive law, holistic justice, and creative problem solving are typically available annually.

Renaissance Lawyer Society networks lawyers and provides information about trainings and coaching in the general comprehensive law movement (http://www.renaissancelawyer.com/).

The comprehensive law movement may be part of the answer to the malaise infecting the legal profession and, some say, to the ills affecting society as a whole. If the growth of its "vectors" since 1990 is any indication, its approach is well overdue and sorely needed. At its best, the comprehensive law movement offers approaches to resolving conflicts and legal matters that help, not harm, people, relationships, and society. At the least, it offers us as lawyers more tools for our toolkit. Either way, our toolkits appear to be expanding; I invite you to add to yours.

Source: © Susan Daicoff, 2003. This article was first published in *GPSolo* in November 2003, by the American Bar Association as "Resolution Without Litigation." It was republished in its entirety with minor revisions in 2006 as "The Comprehensive Law Movement: An Emerging Approach to Legal Problems" in the book series *Scandinavian Studies in Law*, Volume 49, *A Proactive Approach*, Law Libraries (Peter Wahlgren, Ed.), and a large portion was republished in 2005 in a continuing legal education publication published in Vancouver, British Columbia. Also, some of ideas in this article were previously introduced in "Afterword: The Role of Therapeutic Jurisprudence Within the Comprehensive Law Movement," to the 2000 book *Practicing Therapeutic Jurisprudence* by Dennis Stolle, David Wexler, and Bruce Winick, Eds. (Durham, NC: Carolina Academic Press, 2000) and were later incorporated into "Law as a Healing Profession: The Comprehensive Law Movement," *Pepperdine Journal of Dispute Resolution* (2006). The article was previously available in draft form on Susan Daicoff's website from 1999. As it was originally published by the American Bar Association, it is here reprinted with express permission thereof.

APPENDIX C

THERAPEUTIC JURISPRUDENCE

Dr. Michael S. King

Therapeutic jurisprudence is an interdisciplinary study of the law's effect on physical and psychological wellbeing (Slobogin, 1995; Wexler and Winick, 1996b, p xvii). It proposes law reform directed, where appropriate, at minimizing negative effects and promoting positive effects on wellbeing. It is said to have "the advantage of expanding our horizons and has the potential of allowing the law to develop as psychology develops" (Wexler, 1991a, p 14). From its intellectual roots in the field of mental health law in the United States in the late 1980s (Wexler, 1991a, p 9), it has become today what one South Pacific commentator has described as "a baobab of ever-widening intellectual endeavors" (Oluwu, 2006).[1] It has generated significant scholarship in terms of articles, special issues of academic and professional journals, monographs and books. Progress since the 1980s has been swift: a LexisNexis search for articles in law journals using the search term "therapeutic jurisprudence" resulted in a total of 1320 hits as at January 2009.

However, therapeutic jurisprudence is not simply a field of intellectual discourse; it has significant practical implications in the daily work of the judiciary, lawyers, legal educators and behavioral science professionals involved in the work of the legal system. It has also entered the lexicon of government policy and has begun to generate change in courts, judging and legal practice in a growing number of jurisdictions. In addition, therapeutic jurisprudence has begun to be referred to in the reasons for decisions of courts and tribunals (for example, *Lee v State Parole Authority of NSW* [2006] NSWSC 1225 at [69]; *Re Peter Crook and Secretary, Department of Families, Community Services and Indigenous Affairs* [2007] AATA 1253 at [23]). Although it was formulated in the United States, it has been readily adapted to legal systems around the world, including those of Australia, Canada and New Zealand.

---

1. A comprehensive bibliography of publications on therapeutic jurisprudence is maintained by the International Network on Therapeutic Jurisprudence: <www.law.arizona.edu/depts/upr-intj>. For therapeutic jurisprudence in Australasia, see the Australasian Therapeutic Jurisprudence Clearinghouse via a link at <www.aija.org.au>.

THE DEVELOPMENT OF THERAPEUTIC JURISPRUDENCE

THERAPEUTIC JURISPRUDENCE developed out of work in mental health law conducted by David Wexler and Bruce Winick, law professors in the United States. They noted that the law, like psychiatry, was concerned with ordering human behavior (Winick, 1997). Yet they observed that the operation of mental health law often seemed to produce anti-therapeutic consequences, and legal actors did not always understand the implications of mental health findings. They began to consider the therapeutic and anti-therapeutic effects of the law in practice. In the late 1980s they began to use the term "therapeutic jurisprudence".

From an early stage, Wexler and Winick thought that other areas of substantive and procedural law may have therapeutic implications. In their early book on the subject, *Essays in Therapeutic Jurisprudence*, they noted that "Obviously . . . therapeutic jurisprudence will also have applications in forensic psychiatry generally, in health law, in a variety of allied legal fields (criminal law, juvenile law, family law), and probably across the entire legal spectrum" (Wexler and Winick, 1991, p x). Indeed, although the bulk of the articles in that volume concerned mental health law, there are also articles on criminal law, torts and legal education.

337

Following the publication of articles on mental health applications of therapeutic jurisprudence in the early 1990s, the field of therapeutic jurisprudence scholarship developed rapidly. Wexler and Winick (1996b, p xviii) noted in their introduction to a collection of therapeutic jurisprudence articles that over seventy scholars had written on the topic. That volume includes articles on diverse areas including correctional law, criminal law and procedure, family and juvenile law, sexual orientation law, mental health law, evidence, personal injury and tort law, the legal profession, labor arbitration law, contract and commercial law. It also includes commentary on therapeutic jurisprudence, its practical and theoretical implications and its relationship to other areas of scholarship within jurisprudence. The vast majority of scholars at this stage were American but Canadian and British scholars were also involved.

From the mid 1990s in particular, scholars also explored the relationship of therapeutic jurisprudence to other developing areas within the legal system and society, including restorative justice, preventive law, holistic approaches to law, mediation, problem-solving courts and creative problem solving (for example, Stolle, Wexler and Winick, 2000; Daicoff, 2000; Braithwaite, 2002; King, 2002).

Although the concept of therapeutic jurisprudence originated in the academy, practicing legal and health professionals soon undertook their own explorations. Judges began to explore how its principles could be applied in their court work. A major development was Hora, Schma and Rosenthal's (1999) article that asserted that therapeutic jurisprudence was the underlying philosophy behind the drug courts that had emerged at about the same time as, but independently from, therapeutic jurisprudence. This theoretical and practical connection between the courts and therapeutic jurisprudence has promoted increased interest within the judiciary, legal profession, court administrators, policy makers and academics wherever drug courts or other problem-solving courts have been established or considered around the world. Further, professional judicial organizations in the United States, Canada and Australia are increasingly recognizing its significance for judging, including it as a topic at conferences, in judicial education curricula and in professional publications.

In 2000, *Practicing Therapeutic Jurisprudence*, edited by Stolle, Wexler and Winick was published, containing articles describing an integration of preventive law and therapeutic jurisprudence approaches and explaining how they could be applied in the daily work of practicing lawyers in civil, criminal and family law contexts.

The current decade has seen the further expansion of therapeutic jurisprudence scholarship. Although most of it has been based in the United States, there is an increasing international contribution, primarily from Australia,

Canada and New Zealand. Some British scholarship has continued. The contribution of continental European scholars has begun, but the influence of therapeutic jurisprudence in continental legal systems is in its early stages (Van Manen, 2000-2001; Diesen, 2007).

The development of therapeutic jurisprudence has been accelerated by the conduct of conferences around the world, including three international conferences held in Winchester (United Kingdom), Cincinnati (United States) and Perth (Australia). Such conferences have often been followed by special issues of law journals on therapeutic jurisprudence or the publication of a monograph. This trend is in line with the prediction by Winick and Wexler that the development of therapeutic jurisprudence would be promoted through work conducted internationally (Wexler and Winick, 1991b, pp 317-320).

In recent years, there has been an impressive number of special issues of journals in various disciplines devoted to diverse applications of therapeutic jurisprudence, including magistrates' courts, problem-solving courts, the situation of children, nursing, clinical legal education and skills training, and to therapeutic approaches to conflict resolution in health care settings.[2]

The development of therapeutic jurisprudence has included the exploration by members of the judiciary, lawyers and academics of its application in differing legal systems and cultural contexts. Indigenous approaches to therapeutic jurisprudence have been considered (for example, Zion, 2002). Pakistan and some African nations are countries where such exploration has begun.[3] Although this work is promising, exploration of the relevance of therapeutic jurisprudence to legal systems not based on the common law and to non-Western cultures is in its very early stages.

The trend of therapeutic jurisprudence scholarship during this decade has been to build on research and the investigation of topics introduced in its first decade. The conceptual framework of therapeutic jurisprudence has been explored further. The application of therapeutic jurisprudence has expanded into diverse areas of the law. For example, recent work has:

---

2. These special issues or sections of issues of journals on therapeutic jurisprudence are: 1 *ELaw, Murdoch University Electronic Journal of Law, Special Series*: <https://elaw .murdoch.edu.au/special_series.html>; (2003) 30 *Fordham Urban Law Journal* 797; (2002) 71 *University of Cincinnati Law Review* 13; (2002) 8 *Journal of Nursing Law* 1; (2005) 17(3) *St Thomas Law Review*; (2005) 21 (4) *Georgia State University Law Review*.

3. Some of this work is included in Reinhardt and Cannon (2007). See also King (2006b).

- compared therapeutic jurisprudence principles to transformational leadership theory (King, 2008a);
- related therapeutic jurisprudence to coronial practice (Freckelton, 2007a; King, 2008d);
- examined the significance of clinical education in developing therapeutic jurisprudence lawyering skills;[4]
- explored its relevance to the work of an administrative appeals tribunal (Toohey, 2006);
- considered it in the light of non-adversarial approaches to justice (Freiberg, 2007);
- explored the effect of legal practice on lawyers' wellbeing (Daicoff, 2004);
- critiqued the Northern Territory Emergency Response from a therapeutic jurisprudence and human rights perspective (King and Guthrie, 2008); and
- responded to criticisms raised concerning the subject at large (Freckelton, 2008c).

Therapeutic jurisprudence is especially influential in fields such as mental health law, in problem-solving courts and court diversion programs, and in associated legal practice. Although academic work in therapeutic jurisprudence extends far beyond these areas, it is less recognized as a significant concept in judging, legal practice and legal education generally. In some areas—such as civil litigation—its promise is yet to be realized in practice.

In other areas of the law, judging and legal practice there is little recognition of its relevance. In commercial law and taxation, for example, there is little or no work on the potential application of therapeutic jurisprudence (King and Wexler, forthcoming), yet in theory there is no reason why it could not be applied to such fields. As Martin CJ (2006a) observed:

> Civil lawyers are inclined to forget that corporations are really a legal fiction, and just a means of organizing people. There are always human beings at the heart of every corporation, and even corporations need therapy at times— AWB and James Hardie being two that jump to mind—and the insurance company HIH, whose demise I helped investigate, had a corporate culture which could have usefully occupied a team of therapists.

How corporations are structured, how they act and how they are regulated affects the wellbeing of employees, executives and third parties. The case of

---

4. See (2005) 17(3) *St Thomas Law Review*, a special issue devoted to the topic of therapeutic jurisprudence and clinical legal education.

James Hardie, for example, raises the issue as to whether corporations should be able to structure themselves to avoid liability for causing injury and death (Dunn, 2005).[5] While problem-solving courts and diversion programs have been a catalyst for the application of therapeutic jurisprudence in criminal law, there has as yet been no catalyst for its use in the commercial field. There is significant potential for the application of therapeutic jurisprudence to commercial law.

---

5. As to the HIH collapse, see Allan (2006). The "Report of the Inquiry into certain Australian companies in relation to the UN Oil-for-Food Programme" which investigated AWB is available at: <www.offi.gov.au/agd/WWW/unoilforfoodinquiry.nsf/Page/ Report>.

THE NATURE OF THERAPEUTIC JURISPRUDENCE

T HERAPEUTIC JURISPRUDENCE is not a theory. It has been described as "an interdisciplinary approach to law", a "research tool", a "useful lens", a "perspective", a "research program", a "project", "a framework for asking questions and for raising certain questions that might otherwise go unaddressed" and "simply a way of looking at the law in a richer way" (Winick, 1997a, p 6; Wexler and Winick, 1991b, pp 303, 308; Wexler and Schopp, 1996, p 373; Wexler, 2000c).

This research program suggests there is a dimension of the law that has not been consistently explored until recently: its impact upon the emotional and psychological wellbeing of those it affects. It does not say that this dimension of the law has been totally ignored (Wexler, 1995). After all, in some areas the effect of the law upon wellbeing is of daily concern—such as where counsel submits to a sentencing court that a term of imprisonment may reinforce criminal tendencies in a young client and inhibit his or her rehabilitation. But there has not been a conceptual umbrella through which the effect of the law upon wellbeing can be studied, nor has such a study been consistently applied across the different areas of the law. Legal actors such as judges, magistrates and lawyers have not consistently considered its implications in each aspect of their day to day work, and legal education has largely not considered such matters relevant to the training of future lawyers and members of the judiciary.

Therapeutic jurisprudence is not concerned with abstract interpretations of statute or case law but with the effect of the law in action. Like legal realism, it sees the law as a social force. Winick (1997a, p 3) observes that in "some ways law is but a casement that masks the all-important play of political, economic, and social forces . . . Law is not an artifact on display in the museum; it is a living, breathing organism". In describing the context of therapeutic jurisprudence, scholars cite that much quoted passage from Holmes: "The life of the law has not been logic; it has been experience" (for example, Winick, 1997, p 186). While other approaches to law have also focused on the effects of the law—including its effects on efficiency (law and economics) or its social effects (such as the work of Roscoe Pound)—therapeutic jurisprudence focuses on the law's effect on physical and mental health (Winick, 1997b, p 187). It can be seen as a "special application of the more general field of 'social science in law'" (Winick, 1997b, p 187).

According to this approach there can be hidden anti-therapeutic consequences arising from the law's operation. This is akin to the acknowledgment within medicine that medical treatment can in some circumstances generate disease—iatrogenic disease (Wexler, 1991b). But therapeutic jurisprudence is not confined to identifying these anti-therapeutic consequences; it is intimately concerned with the improvement of the law and its operation by seeking ways of minimising negative and promoting positive effects on the wellbeing of those affected by the law. Indeed, Winick (1997b, p 188) asserts that this is "an important objective in any sensible law reform effort".

While this approach can be applied in a remedial way by identifying problematic areas of the law in practice and suggesting solutions, it can also be applied in a preventive manner by identifying potential problems concerning wellbeing and its interface with the law and suggesting alternatives that promote more therapeutic consequences. Examples of contexts where a preventive approach could be taken include the formulation of new substantive and procedural laws, particularly those in a new or developing field, or a lawyer advising a client as to psycho-legal issues that could give rise to potential problems in the future (Stolle, Wexler and Winick, 2000).

Since Wexler and Winick's early work on anti-therapeutic consequences of mental health law provisions, therapeutic analyses have illustrated how anti-therapeutic consequences can arise in diverse circumstances, such as:

- workers' compensation schemes that inhibit workers' rehabilitation (Lippel, 1999; King and Guthrie, 2007);
- "never plead guilty" approaches to legal practice that promote clients' failure to take responsibility for their criminal conduct or for addressing its underlying causes (Wexler, 2002);

- adversarial family law processes that magnify conflict between parties in the process of trying to resolve it (Tesler, 2000; Bryant and Faulks, 2007);
- court-based schemes for the control of dangerous sexual offenders that may hinder their rehabilitation (King, 2007a); and
- insensitive judging that may promote litigants' or witnesses' disrespect for the law and the court system (King, 2006d, 2008b).

Some have questioned why therapeutic consequences should be of concern to the law in the first place (Petrila, 1996, p 686; Nolan, 2001, p 187). But, as these examples show, anti-therapeutic consequences are not simply bad for the individuals affected; they may well also inhibit the achievement of justice system outcomes such as the prevention of crime, the promotion of healing of injured workers and members of families that have broken down, and respect for the law. Therapeutic jurisprudence is normative, suggesting that anti-therapeutic consequences of the law are bad and therapeutic consequences of the law are good. In a similar vein to medicine, it asserts that the law "should strive first to do no harm" (Wexler, 1990, p 4). It resembles other schools of jurisprudence that view the law from a normative standpoint, such as feminist jurisprudence, critical race theory and law and economics (Winick, 1997a, p 5).

The above examples refer to how the law affects the wellbeing of individuals. While the bulk of work on therapeutic jurisprudence has focused on individuals, the concept also embraces the effect of the law on groups or indeed the whole society. For example, Des Rosiers (2000) examined the impact of decisions of the Supreme Court of Canada on conflicts between groups.

Therapeutic jurisprudence has interdisciplinary, non-empirical and empirical aspects. It refers to findings from behavioral science research and encourages research within the legal system to ascertain possible problem areas concerning the effect of the law on wellbeing and also in suggesting possible solutions (Wexler and Winick, 1991b). Moreover, it appeals to researchers from both law and the behavioral sciences—researchers from their own unique disciplinary perspective can study the therapeutic dimensions of a law in action to see how the behavioral sciences might promote law reform. Thus articles on therapeutic jurisprudence have been written by researchers from various disciplines and published in journals from diverse fields: law, psychology, psychiatry, social work and criminology. Interdisciplinary journals have also been an important venue for publication of work in this area.

While therapeutic jurisprudence emphasizes the importance of considering the effect of the law on wellbeing, it does not suggest it is the paramount consideration (Wexler and Winick, 1991, p xi). It recognizes that in formulating law, determining appropriate legal processes and in legal actors' work, one must consider values other than the therapeutic. Often there will be a convergence between the therapeutic and other values. In some cases, however, they will conflict. Therapeutic jurisprudence does not provide a mechanism for resolving this conflict. But the conflict of therapeutic and other values and processes for their resolution are not unknown to the justice system. For example, a common situation is a court determining that the values of deterrence and the need for preventive detention outweigh the value of rehabilitation in particular criminal cases, leading it to imprison an offender instead of imposing a non-custodial disposition. Nevertheless, therapeutic jurisprudence can still contribute to the resolution of a conflict in values: by highlighting therapeutic values, all competing values may be brought into sharper focus (Wexler and Winick, 1996b, p xvii).

Even where therapeutic values are subordinated to other values in making a legal decision, therapeutic jurisprudence may still offer suggestions for carrying out that decision more therapeutically and effectively. For example, in imprisoning an offender rather than imposing a purely rehabilitation-oriented sentence, a judicial officer could simply recite the sentence with reasons for decision or, in addition, as is done by North Liverpool Community Justice Centre Judge David Fletcher, write to the offender explaining the sentence and indicating that an officer (from the Centre) will contact them to link them with support services to assist in their rehabilitation.[6]

Court or other legal system programs need not necessarily be either therapeutic or anti-therapeutic. They may have both therapeutic and anti-therapeutic implications. Some processes may have therapeutic implications for some people and not for others. Alternatively, there may be some aspects of a program that are therapeutic but not others. Thus a drug court may be seen by therapeutic jurisprudence to promote participant wellbeing through the active interest that a judicial officer takes in participants' wellbeing, and in the respectful way in which the judicial officer interacts with participants in court, yet be seen to be anti-therapeutic in its overuse of remands in custody—a resort to coercion—for non-compliance with program rules.

---

6. Judge Fletcher described his approach in his presentation to the Third International Conference on Therapeutic Jurisprudence, Perth, 7-9 June 2006.

THERAPEUTIC PRINCIPLES AND THEIR APPLICATION

According to Wexler (1991, p 19), there are four overlapping areas of inquiry in therapeutic jurisprudence: "(1) the role of the law in producing psychological dysfunction, (2) therapeutic aspects of legal rules, (3) therapeutic aspects of legal procedures, and (4) therapeutic aspects of judicial and legal roles".

Promoting compliance with the law is a key concern of the justice system. It is also concerned with promoting behavioral change where needed to achieve that goal. Thus deterrence and rehabilitation are values to be considered in sentencing, specific performance can be ordered in particular breach of contract cases and injunctive relief can be granted in civil and family law cases where warranted. The justice system shares with psychology and other behavioral sciences an interest in ordering human behavior and in promoting behavioral change where appropriate. It is therefore understandable that a key approach of therapeutic jurisprudence is to refer to findings from the behavioral sciences in areas such as compliance with authority and the nature of, and motivation for, behavioral change in suggesting practices that courts, lawyers, justice system professionals and health professionals can use to promote a more therapeutic outcome from the law, its processes and professionals.

There has been considerable work conducted in the field of procedural justice as to the circumstances in which people will respect the actions of authority figures like judges and police officers (Tyler, 1996, 2006). The significance of procedural justice for courts and those who use them is encapsulated in this passage from social psychologist Tom Tyler (1996, pp 10-11), a principal researcher in the field:

> People value affirmation of their status by legal authorities as competent, equal citizens and human beings, and they regard procedures as unfair if they are not consistent with that affirmation. To understand the effects of dignity, it is important to recognize that government has an important role in defining people's view about their value in society. Such a self-evaluation shapes one's feelings of security and self-respect.

So what must a court (or police officer) do to affirm peoples' status as "competent, equal citizens and human beings"? It must enable people to give evidence to a tribunal (or talk to a police officer) actively interested in hearing from them (voice), ensure their case is carefully considered in the determination of the outcome (validation), and it must treat them politely and with respect for their human rights and for themselves as individuals (Winick, 2003; King, 2003a). It implies an ethic of care. A simple illustration: if a judge or lawyer does not give the litigant his or her full attention while the litigant is addressing him or her, it may create the impression of a lack of concern for the litigant. If the lawyer or judicial officer becomes angry and shouts at the person, this may also suggest a lack of care.

In terms of behavioral change, Winick (1992) has referred to findings from the behavioral sciences and wider materials from history, philosophy, politics and other fields that suggest that self-determination is important in motivating people to act and to engage in behavioral change. King (2007c) has also referred to material from economics, Eastern philosophy and Indigenous studies in support of this principle.

Coercion and paternalism have been the hallmarks of the justice system's response to behavioral change and compliance with the law. Litigants coming into the justice system place a dispute that they have not been able to resolve themselves in the hands of others—legal experts—for resolution. Unless unrepresented, their participation in and control over the process may be very limited, with lawyers and the judiciary handling the matter. The outcome may be an order or judgment that brings them little satisfaction and even less commitment to its implementation. In criminal cases, if a rehabilitation-based sentencing disposition is used, the court will commonly order the offender to take part in programs that the court and/or experts consider are in his or her best interests rather than involving the offender in the formulation of any rehabilitation plan. The sentence is backed by the coercive power of the court.

Therapeutic jurisprudence scholarship has highlighted the problems that coercive and paternalistic approaches present in motivating behavioral change. Winick (1992, p 1756) observes that "people generally do not respond well when told what to do. Unless they themselves see the merit in achieving a particular goal, they often will not pursue it, or if required to do so, will comply only half-heartedly". On the other hand, by involving people in decision-making one can tap into deep sources of motivation within. Choice "brings a degree of commitment that mobilizes the self-evaluative and self-reinforcing mechanisms that facilitate goal achievement" (Winick, 1992, p 1757). It increases the prospects of successful action (Winick, 1991). Therapeutic jurisprudence therefore suggests that in particular circumstances, promoting individual choice can promote therapeutic effects and justice system outcomes. Not that it can be applied in all circumstances. Sometimes, as noted earlier, a court must imprison offenders. Sometimes a person's mental abilities have so deteriorated that they cannot make decisions for themselves, as in cases of advanced dementia.

Therapeutic jurisprudence scholars have suggested different justice system applications of the principle of self-determination: for example, involving criminal defendants in the formulation of rehabilitation plans during defense preparation and the sentencing process (Wexler, 2001, 2005); giving defendants the choice about whether they enter a problem-solving court program (Winick, 2003; King, 2007c); promoting choice for mental health patients in obtaining treatment (Winick, 1991); involving injured workers in the formulation of their rehabilitation plans (King and Guthrie, 2007); and involving clients in the development of trial strategy (Winick, 2000c).

This discussion refers to some therapeutic principles and techniques from the behavioral sciences and their application or potential application in the justice system. Goal setting, behavioral contracts, or seizing upon the life crisis of coming to court to support motivation to change are other examples (Winick and Wexler, 2003; King, 2007c). Therapeutic jurisprudence has also highlighted how offenders can be in a state of denial concerning their criminal conduct, and how legal processes can reinforce or be used to address this dysfunctional attitude (Wexler, 2000b, 2000c; Winick, 2003; Birgden, 2004). The literature on this approach is broad in its scope.

Therapeutic jurisprudence is not static. It is an ongoing research Endeavour. It encourages researchers to think creatively as to how developments in the behavioral sciences can be used in the justice system (Wexler, 2000c). While psychology, psychiatry and counseling have been fertile sources for principles and practices by which therapeutic jurisprudence scholars have sought the enrichment of the law, increasingly scholars are turning to other disciplines, such as anthropology, architecture, criminology, public health, social work and leadership (King and Wexler, forthcoming). For example, recent Australian scholarship compared transformational leadership—which seeks to motivate individuals and organizations to higher levels of achievement and also draws on the behavioral sciences in formulating its methods—to therapeutic jurisprudence and illustrated how its principles can be applied in the context of problem-solving court judging (King, 2008a). It suggested that transformational leadership could contribute to the development of therapeutic jurisprudence.

CRITICISMS OF THERAPEUTIC JURISPRUDENCE

A LONG WITH the conceptual development and practical application of therapeutic jurisprudence over the last eighteen years have come various critiques. Some have acknowledged the value of therapeutic jurisprudence as an approach to examining the law, legal processes and the work of legal actors, but have suggested that it needs to address fundamental issues such as the need for more precise definition of its basic concepts, while others have questioned the very basis and value of therapeutic jurisprudence.

An example of the former is the suggestion that the definition of "therapeutic" in therapeutic jurisprudence is too vague. Slobogin (1995, p 196) asserts that if "therapeutic" is simply a matter of "beneficial" versus "harmful", then therapeutic jurisprudence is not distinguished from other areas of inquiry. Whether a law is good or bad has been a long-term concern of lawyers and the community generally. To address this issue, Slobogin (1995, p 196) suggested that therapeutic jurisprudence could be defined as "the use of social science to study the extent to which a legal rule or practice promotes the psychological or physical well-being of the people it affects".

This definition is precise enough to distinguish therapeutic jurisprudence from other normative approaches to law. At the same time it is broad enough to encourage researchers to "roam within the intuitive

351

and common sense contours of the concept" (Wexler, 1995; Winick, 1997) and engage in wide-ranging scholarship into the differing dimensions of wellbeing that can be affected by the law—from legal consumer satisfaction with the system, to the rehabilitation of injured workers, to the effect of court processes on child complainants giving evidence. Naturally, however, researchers need to define specific aspects of physical and/or psychological wellbeing to conduct research.

A recent example of criticisms concerning the basis and worth of therapeutic jurisprudence is Roderick and Kromholz (2006, p 211), who state that "by not specifically defining TJ, proponents have not operationalized the construct that is necessary to empirically support the theoretical principles of TJ". They say the "theory" of therapeutic jurisprudence lacks an adequate conceptual framework and operational definition.

Arrigo (2004, p 25) argues that therapeutic jurisprudence "wrongly assumes law's legitimacy, largely overlooks the ideology, power and violence embedded within legal narratives, disturbingly promotes a unitary moral (that is, good) legal subject, and unreflectively fosters a state of false consciousness among citizens". He argues that these problems arise from its "central normative stance".

Brakel (2007, p 461) rails against therapeutic jurisprudence saying that its presuming "to measure and/or structure law's impact on everyone's mental or physical health" is "even by generous intellectual standards, no concept at all". He says that its application beyond mental health law lacks intellectual coherence and intelligibility. It "contemplates a global and, therefore, meaningless interface between law and the human condition or human behavior" (p 466). Brakel asserts that therapeutic jurisprudence is pushed "not unlike mediation, as a cure for the all-too-real ills of the adversarial system" (p 467). He says that articles in *Practicing Therapeutic Jurisprudence* are bordering "on the mystical, if not occult", with some articles linking the concept to "new-age law and 'law and-' movements", citing "restorative law", preventive law and others as examples (p 468). Further, "therapeutic jurisprudence cannot deliver because it lacks content" and it "is little more than spurious verbal association" (p 467).

In considering such criticisms, it is important to note Freckelton's (2008c) observation that therapeutic jurisprudence as formulated by Wexler and Winick is rather modest in its goals. It is not a theory. It is not presented as a defense or indeed a critique of the justice system or society generally—those seeking a radical approach to the law should seek elsewhere. It is not an approach to radically restructuring the legal system or society. It is not presented as a "cure all" for the justice system. It is not a new-age movement or cult. It is not presented as a unitary, coherent body of knowledge or approach to judicial or legal practice.

Therapeutic jurisprudence simply suggests we explore the effect of the law, its processes and actors on the physical and psychological wellbeing of those affected by them and that the behavioral sciences can assist in this research. It assumes that negative effects on wellbeing are bad and positive effects are good, asserting that this approach may suggest a direction for reform. What direction that reform may take may well be guided by values that are not therapeutic within the meaning contemplated by therapeutic jurisprudence.

There is also considerable scope for difference between scholars and practitioners as to the therapeutic effect of the law and its implications for legal and court practice (Wexler, 1990, pp 14-16). An Australian example is the different conceptions of the relationship between Indigenous sentencing courts and therapeutic jurisprudence (Marchetti and Daly, 2004, 2007; King and Auty, 2005; Auty, 2006; see Chapter 11 in full text).

The criticisms that therapeutic jurisprudence cannot deliver and is devoid of content are difficult to reconcile with its influence in judicial and legal work and in legal education. It is considered sufficiently important to be included as a topic of judicial training and education for lawyers and law students; it is the fundamental philosophy behind problem-solving courts and its techniques are used in varying degrees in these courts; and it is increasingly applied to other areas, including family law and civil law.

Critics assert that therapeutic jurisprudence implications for legal system users are not as beneficial as claimed. Petrila (1996, p 688) criticizes therapeutic jurisprudence as "a conservative, arguably paternalistic, approach to mental disability law" and that "it simply reinforces the existing distribution of power in the relationship between treater and treated". He asserts that it does not include law consumers in defining what is therapeutic. Arrigo (2004) also argues that therapeutic jurisprudence does not include alternative narratives of consumers: it uncritically accepts the subject's account as being entirely their own rather than including possible narratives imposed upon them by others, such as legal authorities. Given that therapeutic jurisprudence is a research program only, the latter becomes a simple research issue: have the researchers asked the right questions and have they properly interpreted what is said to them?

As to the broader question, the therapeutic jurisprudence literature does not assert that the definition of "therapeutic" should be left solely to the judiciary, researchers, government or other authorities. It does not assert that therapeutic processes should be forced upon others, as in concepts of a therapeutic state (Wexler, 1993; Stolle, Wexler, Winick and Dauer, 2000, p 8). Indeed, as we have seen, therapeutic jurisprudence promotes therapeutic principles such as voice, validation, respect and self-determination. Therapeutic jurisprudence scholars have been highly critical of approaches that ignore autonomy and favor paternalism and coercion (Winick, 1991, 1992). Further, as Wexler and Winick (1996c, p 709) point out, therapeutic jurisprudence research has included the views of consumers and professionals. In Australia, the Geraldton Alternative Sentencing Regime has included participants in the determination of processes to be used in their rehabilitation and court program, given them voice, validation and respect, and also actively sought their input in evaluating the regime (King and Duguid, 2003; Cant, Downie and Henry, 2004).

A further criticism relates to whether therapeutic jurisprudence adds anything new, or whether it is old wine in a new bottle. As Freckleton (2008, p 584) points out "while an interesting inquiry in itself, it does little to assist resolution of the more substantive question of whether in the contemporary environment therapeutic jurisprudence scholarship has something worthwhile to offer". Winick (1997, pp 188-189) takes this issue further, questioning whether the kind of issues explored by therapeutic jurisprudence scholarship to date would have been explored without its conceptual umbrella. For example, does a fault-based tort system promote recovery better than a non-fault system? How can an appeal court's reasons for decision promote resolution for conflicting groups in the community? What is the effect of interaction between a domestic violence court judge and participants on participant respect for the system?

Some commentators take issue with the term "therapeutic jurisprudence". Some think it has new-age connotations or that it is a "mouthful" and difficult to explain (Martin, 2006a). For some, it is a matter of marketing appeal to a punitively minded public: using a term that implies a "touchy feely" approach to criminal justice in trying to promote a therapeutic court program is not likely to resonate with a punishment-oriented public (Martin, 2006a). Although the manner of presenting court programs is an important concern for maintaining public trust in the courts, the issues raised can be addressed without resort to changing the term "therapeutic jurisprudence". For example, aspects of a court program that address the "law and order" lobby's concerns could be emphasized in explaining the court's approach, such as making offenders accountable and responsible, judicial case management and preventing crime (King, 2006a). Despite these concerns, there have been no realistic alternative names suggested for a concept that extends beyond the criminal law to embrace law in general and that has been used internationally for over 15 years.

Finally, some Australian commentators have raised issues concerning the scope of therapeutic jurisprudence. Holder (2006, p 37) and Stewart (2005, pp 5, 35) have suggested that therapeutic jurisprudence is offender-oriented. As King (2008f) notes, these criticism have been made without canvassing the literature in which therapeutic jurisprudence has been applied to the situation of victims (see, for example, Simon, 1995; Winick, 2000a; Erez and Hartley, 2003). However, it is certainly the case that a prime focus in the application of therapeutic jurisprudence in Australia has been the situation of criminal defendants, and that more needs to be done in relation to its application to victims (King, 2008b, 2008f). Others have thought that therapeutic jurisprudence is court-centered (for example, Marchetti and Daly, 2007, p 438). Again, while the criticism is not correct in terms of the formulation or application of therapeutic jurisprudence (for example, Wexler and Winick, 1996; King and Guthrie, 2007, 2008) it can be considered as evidence of the need for more work in Australia on the application of therapeutic jurisprudence in legal work not directly concerning the courts.

THERAPEUTIC JURISPRUDENCE IN THE AUSTRALIAN CONTEXT

PRIOR TO 1997 therapeutic jurisprudence was largely unknown in Australia.[7] Psychologist Astrid Birgden was one of the first Australians to become aware of its implications and studied with Wexler at Puerto Rico in the late 1990s (Freiberg, 2002). Since then, she has been a leading scholar in the area, publishing important work explaining its use in corrections and in connection with the "good lives" theory of offender rehabilitation, and suggesting techniques for lawyers to use in dealing with problem criminal clients (Birgden and Vincent, 2000; Birgden, 2002a, 2002b, 2004; Birgden and Ward, 2003). In 1997 the first Australian law journal article on therapeutic jurisprudence was published that suggested a therapeutic approach to complainants in sexual assault cases who were being exposed to further

---

7. On the development of therapeutic jurisprudence in Australia, see generally Freiberg (2002) and King (2006b).

trauma by being cross-examined about their past sexual history (Kumar and Magner, 1997).

Australian academics presented papers to the First International Conference on Therapeutic Jurisprudence at Winchester (United Kingdom) in 1998 and subsequently articles drawn from some of these papers were published (Hillis and Thomson, 1999; Birgden and Vincent, 2000).

Speaking at the 24th International Congress on Psychology in San Francisco in August 1998, Eilis Magner (1998), Foundation Professor of Law at the University of New England, suggested that therapeutic jurisprudence had a toehold in Australia, with potentially wider application. In an article published in *Revista Juridica Universidad de Puerto Rico* in the same year, she identified the following attractions of therapeutic jurisprudence to Australian scholars: that it is American legal scholarship that is not tied to the United States constitutional framework which usually is of little practical relevance to Australia; its evaluative focus; its interdisciplinary nature; and that it moves the focus from appellate decision making to legal and administrative rules and procedures (Magner, 1998).

Magner (1998) suggested the following were potential put-offs: that therapeutic jurisprudence scholarship is overwhelmingly American and Australian scholars would not wish to be poor cousins in its development; that Australians may be dissuaded by the implications of the term "therapeutic" and possible paternalistic connotations; and that therapeutic jurisprudence does not purport to be comprehensive, focusing on reform at the justice system's micro level rather than its macro level—individual laws and processes rather than systems or bodies of law.[8] However, as it has transpired, a growing number of Australian scholars is involved in the development of therapeutic jurisprudence—and has suggested innovative applications of it—and their work has attracted the attention of international scholars and practitioners. While concerns about the term "therapeutic jurisprudence" have emerged in Australia (Martin, 2006a), these do not relate to paternalism and, arguably, the operation of therapeutic jurisprudence at a micro level has facilitated its use in the Australian court system through what Freiberg (2002) has described as "pragmatic incrementalism".

---

8. Therapeutic jurisprudence is not limited to microanalysis, of course. Wexler (1995) noted that although therapeutic jurisprudence scholars would generally be more interested in microanalysis, macroanalytic therapeutic jurisprudence was emerging and gave the example, amongst others, of Harrison's (1994) article asserting that the law of contract may reinforce disadvantaged consumers' low self-esteem.

Magner (1998) identified euthanasia, the Stolen Generations and complainant evidence in sexual assault cases as potential areas of application of therapeutic jurisprudence in Australia. While these are legitimate areas of its application, the emphasis in Australian therapeutic jurisprudence scholarship and practice has been elsewhere.

In the late 1990s and early 2000s, most Australian states established problem-solving courts such as drug courts and family violence courts. About that time, Hora, Schma and Rosenthal's (1999) pioneering article asserting that therapeutic jurisprudence is the underlying philosophy of drug courts and Winick's (2000a) article on applying therapeutic jurisprudence in domestic violence cases were published. Courts commonly are guided by statute law and centuries of common law in how they should conduct court processes. However, neither provides much guidance concerning court processes aimed at promoting motivation for positive behavioral change that are a key element of problem-solving courts. Therapeutic jurisprudence has filled this gap.

Consequently, the introduction of these courts inspired a greater interest in therapeutic jurisprudence in Australia. As the establishment of problem-solving courts has been almost entirely in magistrates' courts, it is natural that, amongst the judiciary, it has been magistrates who have been most active in investigating, adapting and applying the principles of therapeutic jurisprudence in their work (see, for example, King and Wilson, 2002; King, 2002, 2003b, 2006b; King and Auty, 2006; Popovic, 2002, 2006, 2007).

The concept of therapeutic jurisprudence has found ready resonance with the approach of magistrates' courts. There has been a history of magistrates, particularly those in regional areas, adopting innovative court practices to promote a more meaningful court experience and offender rehabilitation (King and Wilson, 2002; King and Auty, 2005). For example, in the 1970s then-Broome Magistrate Terry Syddall invited Aboriginal Elders to sit with him on the bench of his court. Therapeutic jurisprudence has become a convenient and powerful framework to justify and promote best practice in such projects. The therapeutic jurisprudence based projects at the Geraldton court and the Aboriginal court at Wiluna are examples (King, 2002; King and Wilson, 2002). In turn, this work has brought to light a further application of therapeutic jurisprudence: its use in judging in regional areas (King, 2003b). This work by Australian magistrates has been referred to internationally (for example, Wexler, 2004; Goldberg, 2005).

The influence of therapeutic jurisprudence on magistrates' work can be seen in the Western Australian country magistrates' 2004 resolution to apply therapeutic jurisprudence in their work (King and Auty, 2005) and in section 4M(5)(a) of the *Magistrates' Court Act 1989* (Vic) requiring the Chief

Magistrate to have regard to a magistrate's knowledge of therapeutic juris-prudence and restorative justice in assigning a magistrate to the Collingwood Neighbourhood Justice Centre.

As Freiberg (2002) noted, conferences have been a useful vehicle for the propagation of therapeutic jurisprudence in Australia. These included early conferences in Australia and New Zealand having either Wexler or Winick as a key speaker and a national conference on therapeutic jurisprudence in mag-istrates' courts in Perth in 2005.[9] By 2006 the level of interest was such that the Third International Conference on Therapeutic Jurisprudence was held in Perth in June of that year. These conferences have generated scholarship on therapeutic jurisprudence in a rapidly expanding number of areas, including family law, civil litigation, Indigenous justice issues, mediation, mental health law, judging, legal practice, legal education, ethical issues, sentencing, workers' compensation and problem-solving courts.[10]

Therapeutic jurisprudence has been slow to make any impact upon court processes applying to people other than defendants (Cannon, 2007). For example, although the value of therapeutic judging techniques in sentencing, particularly in magistrates' courts, has gained wide recognition, the potential of therapeutic jurisprudence principles to improve the situation of other court users such as witnesses and complainants has not been adequately explored.[11]

Recently the Chief Justice and Deputy Chief Justice of the Family Court of Australia presented a therapeutic jurisprudence analysis of their court that, since its creation, has endeavoured to take a more humane approach to resolv-ing family conflict (Bryant and Faulks, 2007). It has been applied to care and protection applications (King and Tatasciore, 2006). Freckelton (2007a, 2007b) has described how a therapeutic jurisprudence approach can be used in coronial procedures (see also King, 2008d; Chapter 13 in full text) and in the work of disciplinary tribunals. Carney et al (2007) have described the applica-tion of therapeutic jurisprudence to mental health tribunals. King (2008e) has suggested its use in considering the effect of the actions of legal actors on the

---

9. Key papers from the conference "At the Cutting Edge: Therapeutic Jurisprudence in Magistrates' Courts" were published as an issue of *ELaw, Murdoch University Electronic Journal of Law, Special Series* (King and Auty, 2006).

10. The agenda and some papers from the Third International Conference on Thera-peutic Jurisprudence are available at: <www.aija.org.au/TherapJurisp06/FINALPRO GRAM.pdf>.

11. A therapeutic analysis of the situation of child complainants in child sexual abuse related trials and suggestions for an appropriate judging approach are contained in King (2008b).

wellbeing of other legal actors, giving the example of the impact of appeal decisions on lower courts.

It is difficult to gauge the extent of the use of therapeutic jurisprudence in legal practice. There has been little published on the topic in Australia. What has largely deals with criminal practice in problem-solving court programs (Potter, 2006; King, 2007), aspects of criminal practice (Birgden, 2002; King, 2007, 2008g; Mugliston, 2008) or the professional conduct of barristers (Hampel, 2005; Mugliston, 2008). Some recent work considered civil legal practice (Murfett, 2006; Tapper, 2007). But it is reasonable to conclude that it has yet to make a significant impact on Australian legal practice (King, 2006b).

There have been several challenges to therapeutic jurisprudence becoming part of mainstream judging and legal practice. First, it has been commonly associated with problem-solving courts and defendants and its wider implications for judging and legal practice have not always been recognized. Secondly, when examples are given of therapeutic judging or legal practice to members of the judiciary or legal profession a common response is to say "I already do that". However, it is a mistake to equate therapeutic jurisprudence simply with imposing a sentence that favors rehabilitation without thinking about the therapeutic implications of the formulation of the sentence and the court and other legal processes involved. Therapeutic jurisprudence says that the therapeutic implications should be a factor to be considered in all aspects of judging and legal practice, not simply in particular situations.

Thirdly, legal culture has been resistant to taking a therapeutic approach. Some members of the judiciary and legal profession think that wellbeing is a matter for health professionals, not legal professionals. Some think that the more active involvement of judicial officers that a therapeutic approach often requires is contrary to how they should be acting—passively and uninvolved (King and Wager, 2005). Legal professionals have also been reluctant to undertake an approach for which they have not been professionally trained. That factor is being addressed through increased availability of materials and conferences on the subject.

Fourthly, government bureaucracy has been resistant in some cases (King and Piggott, 2007). Therapeutic approaches to judging often involve a more active judicial officer, one who is involved in judicial case management. It has been thought that in so doing, the judiciary is encroaching on areas best left to the executive that, unlike the judiciary (it is believed), has the necessary expertise. Thus in the case of innovative and successful programs such as the Geraldton Alternative Sentencing Regime, there has been a history of little government support (King and Piggott, 2007). On the other hand, in Victoria it has been suggested that mainstreaming therapeutic jurisprudence in magistrates' courts has unduly increased the executive's involvement and limited the court's control over therapeutic jurisprudence court projects (Popovic, 2007).

Still, there are signs that the judiciary has a growing interest in therapeutic jurisprudence, with its inclusion in the National Curriculum for Judicial Professional Development produced by the National Judicial College of Australia, the establishment of an Australasian Therapeutic Jurisprudence Clearinghouse by the Australasian Institute of Judicial Administration, and the latter's sponsorship of the Third International Conference on Therapeutic Jurisprudence and the 2010 conference on non-adversarial justice.[12]

---

12. The curriculum may be accessed via <www.njca.org.au>.

CONCLUSION

U<small>NTIL THE</small> introduction of therapeutic jurisprudence, the effect of the law, its processes and actors on the physical and psychological wellbeing of parties, witnesses, jurors, lawyers, the judiciary and others affected by them was often of no or very limited concern to the law and its officials. Therapeutic jurisprudence has demonstrated that this study is valuable as it can limit negative side effects of the law and promote justice system outcomes such as conflict prevention and resolution, respect for the law and offender rehabilitation. It has also usefully highlighted the contribution the behavioral sciences can make to improving legal processes and outcomes. The challenge remains for therapeutic jurisprudence to extend from specialist applications such as problem-solving courts and mental health law into mainstream legal education, legal practice and judging. That process remains in its early stages.

Dr Michael King PhD, MA, LLB (Hons), BJuris, served as a magistrate and practiced as a lawyer for Legal Aid WA, Aboriginal Legal Service (WA) and in private practice. He was the first solicitor in charge of a country office of Legal Aid WA, and served as counsel in charge of the ALS (WA) unit that represented Aboriginal families before the Royal Commission into Aboriginal Deaths in Custody.

He is an internationally recognized expert in therapeutic jurisprudence. He introduced three therapeutic jurisprudence based projects when a magistrate and served as Perth Drug Court Magistrate. His articles on diverse topics including therapeutic jurisprudence, judging, legal practice, criminology, natural law and health have appeared in peer reviewed journals in Australia, Europe and the United States.

He is researching and writing on the different modalities of non-adversarial or comprehensive approaches to justice—including therapeutic jurisprudence and restorative justice—and their application to courts, the community and legal practice.

Excerpted from *Non-Adversarial Justice* The Federation Press (2009) (with Freiberg A, Batagol B and Hyams R) Reprinted with permission of publisher and author. Citations in text of this article may be more fully explored by obtaining the book.

APPENDIX D

PRACTICING ON PURPOSE IN THE LAW FIRM: PROVIDING PRODUCTIVITY & PROFITABILITY WITH PERSONAL WELLNESS AND PROFESSIONAL VALUES

Gretchen Duhaime

INTRODUCTION/ BACKGROUND

Looking back on 2009, the legal profession saw rock bottom job satisfaction as the foundations of BigLaw shook, leaving casualties of over ten thousand lawyers and a shocking number of long-lived and previously profitable firms. This Article identifies leverage points for change and describes how one wellness program can shore up competencies required to make those changes. Part I examines the evolution of the big firm business model, with special attention to Compensation and Promotion and Billable Hours. Part II summarizes big firm responses to associates' desire for work/life balance, and the impact of generational differences on finding effective solutions. Part III reviews recent research on lawyer well-being and the relationship to job satisfaction. Part IV proposes new success measurements for big firms, based on literature from industry consultants. Part V lays out the leverage points where firms can make action plans to achieve their goals in the new measurement areas. Part VI introduces the Practicing on Purpose 7 Purposes wellness model and describes a recommended program for law firms to enhance attorney and staff well-being and the effectiveness of the identified leverage points.

EVOLUTION OF
THE BIG FIRM
BUSINESS MODEL

Abraham Lincoln found his place in the legal profession perhaps by chance. In the 1830s, admittance to the bar required no formal education, just a strong knowledge of the law. Lincoln unknowingly bartered for a copy of Sir William Blackstone's *Commentaries on the Laws of England* while working as a shop-keeper, and it gave him the opportunity, along with his strong work ethic and sharp mind, to join the ample ranks of lawyers. Lincoln made his mark on American history as the President who guided the country through the turbulence of the Civil War, but he was by his own estimation primarily a lawyer, defined not by his great oratorical skills but by his diligence and honesty.[1]

By the turn of the 20th Century, the path Lincoln took to the law had mostly closed, and the practice of law also shifted. Lawyers spent more time in the office advising clients, and less time exercising rhetorical arts in the courtroom. New printing technologies made law books more widely available, elevating case law over legal principles. States increasingly required legal education, not training alone, as a prerequisite for sitting for the bar exam. The still ample ranks of

---

1. Brian Dirck, Lincoln the Lawyer 16 (2007).

newly minted lawyers joined firms as associates of established partners, rather than practicing law as Lincoln had.[2]

These changes created opportunity for innovators like Paul D. Cravath and Louis D. Brandeis to incubate the profitable and prestigious "big law firm" structure; hiring a handful of well-pedigreed associates each year, training them and gaining efficiencies from their work on firm matters, and eventually promoting the best of each class to partnership.[3] Despite criticisms as a "law factory" that put business interests ahead of professional values, the Cravath system became the role model for corporate firms in America, and is still in use today.[4] The country's economic expansion created a greater demand for legal services, in more specialized areas, feeding the growth of big firms and formation of dedicated practice areas within them.[5]

Big firms continued relatively unchanged until the 1960s. Most big firm lawyers were white, Christian men with strong social circles. Firms had stable relationships with clients on retainer, and kept their associates until the "up or out" partnership decision.[6] These characteristics were the first components of the Cravath system to erode. Change agents emerged in the legal system in the 1970s spurring competition among firms for clients and allowing lateral mobility for both partners and associates: in-house legal departments began doing routine work, only relying on outside firms for litigation and other specialties; judicial decisions lifted the ban on communications about the inner workings of law firms, creating a legal media and dispersing information (and power) to consumers of legal services; and new technologies facilitated the spread of this information.[7] With the rise in competition for clients rose the stock-in-trade of the rainmaker, making associates only valuable as partners so much as they generate business for the firm.[8]

---

2. MARC GALANTER & THOMAS PALAY, TOURNAMENT OF LAWYERS 8-13 (1991).

3. *Id.* The policy of hiring top graduates from top schools achieved two primary goals; ensuring entering associates possessed post-secondary education (not a requirement for all law schools at the time), and enhancing the firm brand.

4. *Id.* at 16-18; The Cravath System, Cravath, Swaine & Moore, LLP, http://www .cravath.com (then follow "Law Students" link under "Career Information", then follow "Cravath System" link) (last visited Jan. 1, 2010).

5. GALANTER & PALAY, *supra* note 2, at 16-18.

6. *Id.* at 36.

7. Marc Galanter & William Henderson, *The Elastic Tournament: A Second Transformation of the Big Law Firm,* 60 Stan. L. Rev. 1867, 1894-1898 (2008).

8. George P. Baker & Rachel Parkin, *The Changing Structure of the Legal Services Industry and the Careers of Lawyers,* 84 NC L. REV. 1635, 1656 (2006).

The evolution of large law firms led to shrinking profits, as greater competition for clients and entering associates shriveled revenues and bloated starting salaries.[9] New categories of lawyer emerged, reserving full equity partner status for the rainmakers, and allowing associates to remain at a firm without ascending to partnership. Achieving partnership no longer guaranteed tenure, and firms promoted a smaller portion of associates.[10] These initiatives, intended to improve the customary barometer of success, profit per equity partner (PPP), center on cutting costs (compensation and promotion) and increasing revenue (billable hours).

COMPENSATION AND PROMOTION

One of the hallmarks of the Cravath system is its "lockstep" compensation system, where entering associates join a "class" that receives identical pay, regardless of individuals' actual contributions to the firm's profitability. Economists might call this a diversification strategy, in other words, a hedge against the risk one's human capital might not pay off as expected.[11] Despite data showing lockstep compensation to be more profitable, by the early 1990s most firms adopted marginal product-based compensation ("eat what you kill") to provide better motivation and cohesion for partners.[12] In the marginal product system, partners are credited for the business they bring to the firm, discouraging shirking and reinforcing the value of rainmaking to the firm.

A second hallmark of the Cravath system is the single-tier or "flat" partnership structure, where associates are either promoted to full partnership or

---

9. S. S. Samuelson & L. J. Jaffe, *A Statistical Analysis of Law Firm Profitability*, 70 B.U. L. Rev. 185, 189-192 (1990). As firms promote more partners, they must also hire more associates, because firm profitability hinges on billing associates' time to clients (with an enormous profit margin). Despite the constant increase in law firm graduates, even larger swelling of partnership ranks created more openings for associates, generating competition in the labor pool. Law firms thus needed to support a larger workforce despite a contracting client base.

10. Galanter & Henderson, *supra* note 7, at 1875-76.

11. Ronald J. Gilson & Robert H. Mnookin, *Sharing Among the Human Capitalists: An Economic Inquiry Into the Corporate Law Firm and How Partners Split Profits*, 37 Stan. L. Rev. 313, 341-43 (1985). As one Cravath partner notes, "In a lockstep system, the only way one partner can do better is if everyone does better, so the incentives are in the right place. It doesn't matter who gets the credit; all share in it." Paul C. Saunders, *When Compensation Creates Culture*, 19 Geo. J. Legal Ethics 295, 297 (2006) (reviewing Milton C. Regan, Jr., Eat What You Kill).

12. Gilson & Mnookin, *supra* note 11, at xx; Samuelson & Jaffe, *supra* note 9, at 207-08.

leave the firm. Like a marginal product-based compensation plan, a two-tier or "tall" structure allows firms to better align partner compensation with partners' profit contribution to the firm. Although single-tier partnerships are more profitable, most large law firms have switched to the two-tier partnership structure as a management tool to improve productivity. Equity partnership is reserved for the partners driving the business, while the lawyers with administrative skills can provide value to the firm as non-equity partners.[13]

BILLABLE HOURS

Time-based billing has been the norm for large law firms since the 1970s, as it is a discrete measurement approximating effort expended on a client's behalf.[14] In this model, increasing revenues (and profitability) is simple; bill more hours.[15] Firms expected 1,300 hours from associates in the early 1960s.[16] By the 1980s, associates' billable hours averaged about 1,850 and remained constant at that level through the 1990s, while partners' billable hours increased from about 1,500 to over 1,700 in the same timeframe.[17] After the dot-com bubble burst, associates' billable hours climbed to nearly 2,000 hours per year by 2004, and continue to rise.[18] Generally speaking, non-billable time accounts for about one-third of total hours worked.[19] Doing the math, this means that associates must work over 3,200 hours to bill just under 2,200 hours; or 12 hours every weekday, plus a half-day every weekend, leaving little time for any outside activities or responsibilities. This "time famine" creates challenges to a healthy "work-life balance."

---

13. William D. Henderson, *An Empirical Study of Single-Tier Versus Two-Tier Partnerships in the Am Law 200*, 84 N.C. L. REV. 1691, 1695-96 (2006); Baker & Parkin, *supra* note 8, at 1664-65, 1669-71.

14. The question of the value received by clients will be discussed in Part IV.

15. Samuelson & Jaffe, *supra* note 9, at 206.

16. Miguel R. Rivera, *A New Business and Cultural Paradigm for the Legal Profession*, ACC DOCKET, Oct 2008, at 66, 70.

17. Galanter & Henderson, *supra* note 7, at 1892.

18. Susan Saab Fortney, *The Billable Hours Derby: Empirical Data on the Problems and Pressure Points*, 33 FORDHAM URB. L.J. 171, 176 (2005). Associates at large firms are not only billing more hours than those at smaller firms, they also bill more hours above their required level.

19. Susan Saab Fortney, *Soul for Sale: An Empirical Study of Associate Satisfaction, Law Firm Culture, and the Effects of Billable Hour Requirements*, 69 UMKC L. REV. 239, 248 (2000).

"WORK-LIFE BALANCE" AND GENERATIONAL DIFFERENCES

STUDIES INDICATE that a majority of associates believe that they must sacrifice their personal aspirations if they wish to pursue partnership.[20] Firms responded to associate desire to create work-life balance with reduced-hours programs, which carried a stigma that participants were not serious about their work and were often derogatively referred to as "mommy-track".[21] Reduced-hours programs retain the focus on the billable hour as the metric of associates' value, reinforce the "you can't have it all" paradigm, and force associates to make difficult choices about their priorities. This diminishes the notion of "balance" to a question of optimal scheduling, ignoring the reality that differing choices are equally valid.[22] Furthermore,

---

20. *Id.* at 266; NANCER H. BALLARD, ESQ., ET AL., FACING THE GRAIL: CONFRONTING THE COST OF WORK/FAMILY IMBALANCE 4 (Boston Bar Assoc., 1999).

21. BALLARD, ET AL., *supra* note 20, at 25-26.

22. *See* Tim Batdorf, *Life Balance? Forgetaboutit!*, MICH. B.J., July 2009, at 52; *cf.* JOAN WILLIAMS & CYNTHIA THOMAS CALVERT, BALANCED HOURS: EFFECTIVE PART-TIME POLICIES FOR WASHINGTON LAW FIRMS (Project for Attorney Retention, 2nd Ed., 2001).

part-time programs usually fail at providing participants with meaningful career experiences, instead making them feel like outcasts and slackers who never get the good assignments.[23]

Proponents of reduced hours programs demonstrate improved firm profitability in support of program adoption.[24] They assert firms realize cost savings by improving recruitment and retention, and maintain revenue by keeping long-tenured, thus higher-billing, associates. The underlying assumption is that the long hours are the largest contributor to work/life imbalance and if that barrier is removed, work/life balance resolves itself.[25] In actuality, part-time programs are used almost exclusively by women to provide childcare, and have little impact on their decisions to stay with their firms.[26] In other industries, good human resources management practices (including well-aligned compensation) result in higher productivity and better work-life balance.[27] This acknowledges that time is not the only variable; transparent and effective performance evaluations are also an essential element of work/life balance.[28] A clear picture of how a firm values one's contribution allows employees to make career and life choices more effectively.

Generational differences cloud, and even exacerbate, effective work-life balance policies. The older generations (Traditionalists/Veterans and Baby Boomers) had distinct gender roles, with women as the primary caregivers for

---

23. WILLIAMS & CALVERT, *supra* note 22, at 12-15; Diane Costigan & Jamie Spannhake, *Try This: Work-Life Balance Scheduling*, LAW PRAC., Apr./May 2009, at 41.

24. BALLARD, ET AL., *supra* note 20, at 26-30; WILLIAMS & CALVERT, *supra* note 22, at 7; Darragh J. Davis, et al., *Increase Profits and Savings Through Work/Life Balance*, ACC DOCKET, Nov. 2009, at 93.

25. WILLIAMS & CALVERT, *supra* note 22, at 16. The Project for Attorney Retention's tests for a successful part-time program begin to address "softer,", less-quantifiable issues, such as assignment quality, but the majority of the measurements are hours or attrition related. *See* Brian Kropp, *Challenges to Work-Life Balance*, TALENT MGMT., Aug. 2009, *available at* http://www.talentmgt.com/departments/dashboard/2009/August/1033/index .php (claiming time management practices most important to employees' work-life balance) (last visited Jan. 3, 2010).

26. MONA HARRINGTON & HELEN HSI, WOMEN LAWYERS AND OBSTACLES TO LEADERSHIP 26-28 (MIT Workplace Center, 2007).

27. NICK BLOOM, ET AL., WORK-LIFE BALANCE, MANAGEMENT PRACTICES, AND PRODUCTIVITY (AIM Research Working Paper Series 2007). This study focused on the manufacturing industry across multiple countries, and questions about human relations included attracting talent, rewarding high performance, removing poor performers, promoting high performers, and retaining high performers.

28. *See* LAUREN STILLER RIKLEEN, ENDING THE GAUNTLET: REMOVING BARRIERS TO WOMEN'S SUCCESS IN THE LAW (Thompson/Legalworks, 2006) (arguing flex-time systems success requires change in firm management).

the children. Female lawyers either did not have children or acted more like their male counterparts in abdicating the bulk of the child-rearing to others. The younger generations (Gen X and Gen Y/Millenials) grew up as the children of the older generations, and those parents emphasized neutral gender values and the importance of a balanced family life.[29] There are not enough Gen Xers to fill the partnership ranks when Boomers retire, so Millenials have begun to realize they have bargaining power with big firms to provide better work/life balance programs.[30]

Recent economic conditions complicate finding balance. Big firms have laid off thousands of associates, and those that remain may feel fortunate to still have a job. Laid-off associates have the opportunity to re-evaluate their priorities as they find a new place in the legal profession.[31] Firms also have the opportunity to change to be more responsive to clients and associates, but it seems more likely given the long, entrenched history of the Cravath system, that those who were cut loose from big firms will lead that revolution.[32]

---

29. Joan C. Williams, *Canaries in the Mine: Work/Family Conflict and the Law*, 70 FORDHAM L. REV. 2221 (2002).

30. Galanter & Henderson, *supra* note 7, at Part III.C; Andrew Bruck & Andrew Canter, Note, *Supply, Demand, and the Changing Economics of Large Law Firms*, 60 STAN. L. REV. 2087 (2008).

31. Becky Beaupre Gillespie & Hollee Schwartz Temple, *Letting It All Hang Out: Job Jolt Could Change Your Life for the Better*, ABA J., Jul. 2009, at 33.

32. Ed Reeser, *Bring Me Another Plate of Leeches . . . Do Partners Really Want to Save Their Law Firms?*, OF COUNSEL, Aug. 2009, at 5. For one example of a revolutionary law firm, see Ralph H. Palumbo, Creating the Law Firm of the Future (2001), http://www.summitlaw.com/PalumboArticle.pdf.

LAWYER
WELL-BEING

RECENT RESEARCH confirms years of anecdotal evidence that attorneys are unhappy—in fact, twice as likely as the general population to suffer from depression or alcoholism—and dissatisfaction with work correlates strongly with their psychological distress.[33] In 1986, midlevel associates rated their work satisfaction an average of 3.7 out of 5, and twenty years later it crept up to 3.78.[34] While reported satisfaction seems satisfactory, midlevels report much lower levels of morale (2.7 out of 5 in 2009, the lowest in five years).[35] In another study, 40% of young lawyers in 1984 reported high levels of satisfaction with lawyering; six years later only 29% of the same group were very satisfied with their work.[36]

The link between lawyer distress and work satisfaction suggests that lawyers measure their self-worth in large part based on their work life. Certain personality traits and values common to lawyers help explain this. Lawyers tend to be achievement-oriented, aggressive and

---

33. Susan Daicoff, *Lawyer, Be Thyself: An Empirical Investigation of the Relationship Between the Ethic of Care, The Feeling Decisionmaking Preference, and Lawyer Wellbeing*, 16 VA. Soc. POL'Y & L. 87, 87 (2008).

34. Elizabeth Goldberg, *Midlevel Blues*, AM. LAW., Aug. 2006, at 98.

35. Rachel Breitman, *A Year to Forget*, AM. LAW., Aug. 2009, at 61.

36. Patrick J. Schiltz, *On Being a Happy, Healthy, and Ethical Member of an Unhappy, Unhealthy and Unethical Profession*, 52 VAND. L. REV. 871, 884 (1999)

competitive, preferring not to rely on social support structures.[37] When faced with ordinary stress of fast-paced law practice, many will cope by shifting their discomfort into aggression, feeding the desire to work more.[38] Unable to control their increased aggression, some then turn to alcohol as a release.[39]

These issues lurked in darkness for many years, as lawyers feared repercussions of opening up about experiencing mental health issues.[40] Continued exposure to stress, with no positive coping skills, leads to "burn-out" which is a risk factor for depression.[41] The lawyer personality type is predisposed to solving problems alone, and although firms might offer assistance for depressed employees through Employee Assistance Programs, many who need help do not take advantage of it.[42]

---

37. Susan Daicoff, *Lawyer, Know Thyself: A Review of Empirical Research on Attorney Attributes Bearing on Professionalism*, 46 Am. U. L. Rev. 1337, 1390 (1997).

38. *Id.* at 1419.

39. *Id.*

40. Sue Shellenbarger, *Even Lawyers Get the Blues: Opening Up About Depression*, Wall St. J., Dec. 13, 2007, at D1.

41. Ellen Ostrow, *Clear the Obstacles to a Balanced Life*, Trial, July 2003, at 27.

42. Nancy Spangler, *Kansas City Law Firm Looks at Results of Depression Initiative Four Years Later*, Mental Health Works, Third Q. 2008, at 3, *available at* http://www.workplacementalhealth.org/news/backissues.aspx.

HOW LAW FIRMS
SHOULD MEASURE
SUCCESS

GIVEN THE widespread dissatisfaction with lawyering, firms'
struggle to attract and retain clients, and escalating associate
salaries, it's no surprise that the Cravath model, solid for so many
years, is now little more than a Ponzi scheme.[43] To get the rewards
needed to cover expenses and boost profits, big firms took risks to get
the most profitable, "bet the company" work, creating a "winner take
all" market.[44] They also de-equitized partners to improve their rankings in the American Lawyer listings and increased partner leverage
by hiring more associates.[45]

Another disconnect in the big firm is hourly billing, which doesn't
reflect what clients are purchasing; access to legal knowledge.[46] Big
firms prefer to frame their offerings as customized legal consultation

---

43. *See* Larry E. Ribstein, *Regulating the Evolving Law Firm*, Georgetown
Law Center for the Study of the Legal Profession, Apr. 18, 2008, http://www.law
.georgetown.edu/legalprofession/ribsteinevolvinglawfirm.pdf (noting inverted
pyramid structure of law firms teeter on foundation of "highly mobile key
partners").

44. John P. Heinz, *When Law Firms Fail*, 43 SUFFOLK U. L. REV.
(forthcoming).

45. *Id.*; *A Guide to Our Methodology*, AM. LAW., May 2009, at 143.

46. Larry E. Ribstein, *The Death of Big Law*, Illinois Law and Economics Research Papers Series at 18, http://ssrn.com/abstract=1467730 (observing

rather than a commoditized service.[47] The Association of Corporate Counsel is demanding that law firms link value and cost, using metrics, tools and benchmarks.[48] Big firms would, indeed need to develop metrics to determine associate productivity and accurate billing rates for services. No longer could they rely on leverage to increase revenues and PPP.[49]

American Lawyer began including "value per lawyer," or how efficiently billings translate to compensation for all partners (not just equity partners), in its annual rankings in 2004.[50] This metric assumes that the function of the law firm is to provide wealth to its partners, but most firms claim they exist to provide legal services to clients. Ideally, firms provide lucrative profits to partners while also increasing value to their clients. One way to measure this is with a Balanced Scorecard.[51] Instead of financial performance being the sole metric, it is one of a group of measurements of a healthy firm. Other equally important measures include client service, human development, and business process.[52] Firms utilizing a Balanced Scorecard align lawyer compensation to the appropriate measurements to ensure incentives are aligned with firm goals.

---

clients not purchasing lawyer hours similar to customers not purchasing hours spent building cars); *Cisco General Counsel on State of Technology in the Law,* The Platform, Jan. 25, 2007, http://blogs.cisco.com/news/comments/cisco_general_counsel_on_state_of_technology _in_the_law/ (last visited Jan. 3, 2010). "At a famous presentation at Black and Decker, a consultant held up one of these, a drill, and asked the Black and Decker executives if this is what they sold. They all recognized the product and answered 'yes.' He then suggested to them, that from the customer's point of view, what they are selling is this, a hole in a board."

47. *See generally* RICHARD SUSSKIND, THE END OF LAWYERS? RETHINKING THE NATURE OF LEGAL SERVICES (2008).

48. Heinz, *supra* note 44, at 9.

49. Ribstein, *supra* note 46, at 20.

50. *A Guide to Our Methodology, supra* note 45.

51. John Sterling, et al., *Between a Rock and a Hard Place?. . .Clients Demand Greater Value, Partners Want More Income,* OF COUNSEL, Nov. 2009, at 5.

52. *Id.*

LEVERAGE POINTS

B ASED ON the Balanced Scorecard approach, firms can make changes at leverage points to maximize the effect of their efforts.[53] David Maister, longtime consultant to law firms and former Harvard Business School professor, identifies areas where law firms encounter unique challenges in working together: trust, skepticism about values, professional detachment, and making decisions.[54] These areas will reveal the location of the highest leverage points in each of the Scorecard domains. Big firms have long used billable hours as the proxy for assessing whether associates possessed desired values; those that traded time for money for the benefit of the firm were assumed to be committed, reliable, and solid under pressure.[55] By focusing on financial targets, associates and partners have no incentive to develop trust, values, or personal relationships, as these "soft" skills aren't rewarded.[56] Using a Balanced Scorecard to sync firm goals, associate and partner behavior, and client expectations requires firms to uphold their policies, abandoning complicated rules and processes adopted out of fear and distrust.

---

53. PETER SENGE, THE FIFTH DISCIPLINE: THE ART & PRACTICE OF THE LEARNING ORGANIZATION 64 (Random House 2006) (1990) (describing leverage points).

54. David Maister, *The Trouble With Lawyers*, AM. LAW., Apr. 2006, at 97.

55. Deborah Rhode, *Profts and Professionalism*, 33 Fordham Urb. L.J. 49, 69 (2005).

56. Maister, *supra* note 54.

CLIENT SERVICE

It's easy to find out what clients want; just ask them. According to one GC, his top priorities are "productivity and outputs," while another GC sought out diverse staff in her legal services providers (regardless of past performance and relationship duration).[57] As long as big firms bill hourly, associates have little incentive to deliver stellar client service, beyond their own self-interest to cultivate professional relationships. If clients are paying based on the value received, associates will focus on providing value instead of just ticking off entries on their timecards.[58]

HUMAN DEVELOPMENT

In the current big firm environment, associates receive little development, aside from finding or receiving a mentor and CLE. Lawyers' professional detachment results in treating each other poorly, as shown by the *American Lawyer* midlevel survey associate morale rankings. Associates want to learn, and firms need them to grow so they can continue providing value to clients. Practice areas can establish required skills and competencies for associates to level up, and provide opportunities such as formal training, outside classes, or mentoring.

BUSINESS PROCESS

Big firms have no shortage of business processes in place. The highest leverage point in this area is reexamining existing processes and removing ones that are redundant or misaligned with firm goals and values. Associates currently spend one-third of their time on administrative tasks, much of which could be reduced with streamlined business processes. Firms also need better decision-making outcomes, as endless hypothesizing and reluctance to adopt specific policies will cripple innovation and action required to make meaningful, lasting change.[59]

MAKING IT WORK

The lawyer personality type (achievement-oriented, aggressive and competitive, preferring not to rely on social support structures) combined with law

---

57. *Cisco General Counsel on State of Technology in the Law, supra* note 46; Bruck & Canter, *supra* note 30, at 2090.

58. Palumbo, *supra* note 32 at 6.

59. Maister, *supra* note 54.

school training result in the interpersonal shortcomings Maister identifies (lack of trust, skepticism about values, professional detachment, and difficulty committing to decisions). Lawyers don't need to change who they are, or alter their basic make-up to enact the change at the leverage points identified above. In fact, it is likely that trying to reduce or eliminate the hard edges of the lawyer personality type could result in psychological harm, less effective, lawyering, or both.[60]

Instead of replacing tools and skills, lawyers can enhance them by adding nuances of their opposite qualities. Competitiveness need not lead to lack of trust. The commonality to the lawyer personality type and the interpersonal shortcomings relates to decision-making style. Law school takes minds generally predisposed to analytical, "rational" decision-making and hone them to razor-sharp weapons. Self-reflection or intuitive thinking is devalued, and any inclination in that direction is obliterated by the end of the first year of law school.[61]

If lawyers can acknowledge the value of other types of thinking, and accept lessons from self-reflection, then they have a chance to overcome their interpersonal shortcomings and enact changes needed to save the big firm. Using the same sword to cut costs as slaying enemies has not worked; there are over ten thousand slain associates to vouch for that. Change is always uncomfortable, even change for the better, but adopting a smidge of introspection and a healthy dose of balance makes it easier. Starting from within, from each person's own well-being, will create the ripples and waves of transformation necessary to work the leverage points.

---

60. Susan Daicoff, *Asking Leopards to Change Their Spots: Should Lawyers Change? A Critique of Solutions to Problems with Professionalism by Reference to Empirically-Derived Attorney Personality Attributes*, 11 GEO. J. LEGAL ETHICS 547, 590 (1998).

61. This dilemma is not limited to law schools. Finance-focused MBA graduates dominate the executive ranks, and possess the same left-brained characteristics (though perhaps not so extreme) as lawyers. "Design thinking" is in vogue to help foster innovation and drive business growth using creative problem-solving. One critic asserts that this is also too limiting for ongoing success, and a more holistic approach to business (and problem-solving) is key. Peter Merholz, *Why Design Thinking Won't Save You*, HARVARD BUS. REV. BLOGS, Oct. 9, 2009, http:// blogs.hbr.org/merholz/2009/10/why-design-thinking-wont -save.html (last visited Jan. 12, 2010).

INTRODUCING PRACTICING ON PURPOSE TO THE LAW FIRM

I DEVELOPED the Practicing on Purpose 7 Purposes wellness model specifically to help lawyers improve their well-being, which results in, among other benefits, better decision-making, ethical behavior, and humane treatment of others.[62]

OVERVIEW OF THE 7 PURPOSES

The 7 Purposes wellness model is rooted in systems thinking, positive psychology, and traditional concepts of wellness. The 7 Purposes are: Physical, Inner, Analytical, Relational, External, Higher, and Reflective. Just as a prism refracts white light into a visible color spectrum, the 7 Purposes refracts a person into a visible spectrum of the aspects of self.

---

62. Gretchen Duhaime, Note, *Practicing on Purpose: Promoting Personal Wellness and Professional Values in Legal Education*, 43 SUFFOLK U. L. REV. (forthcoming).

PHYSICAL PURPOSE

The Physical Purpose is defined by self-preservation; the care we give to our bodies. Good eating, sleeping, and exercise habits create a body with stamina. We need healthy bodies to live the satisfying life the other Purposes nurture.

INNER PURPOSE

The Inner Purpose is defined by self-gratification; our passions and instinctive behaviors. Coping skills are how we integrate emotions—both positive and negative—into the decisions and actions we take. The inner purpose brings these to light and helps us adapt or create positive responses and reactions to all emotional triggers.

ANALYTICAL PURPOSE

The Analytical Purpose is defined by self-definition; the inquisitive and critical mind reasons to make sense of one's experiences. Without this sense of autonomy, the analytical mind crumbles and adopts the reasoning of others. The intellect, or ego, is necessary for independence and the ability to stand on one's own.

RELATIONAL PURPOSE

The Relational purpose is defined by self-acceptance, which generates the ability to experience love and social enrichment. It is cliché to say you must love yourself before you can love others, but that doesn't make it less true. Healthy social interactions require self-acceptance; self-confidence to be oneself and trust others to do the same.

EXTERNAL PURPOSE

The External Purpose is defined by self-expression; creating, understanding and appreciating one's part in society. Work, play, hobbies, crafts—these are self-expressions and face outward from oneself. Expressing and receiving gratitude is an indicator of a well-developed External Purpose; the converse creates a feeling of a lack of control of surroundings.

HIGHER PURPOSE

The Higher Purpose is defined by self-knowledge and involves the aspects of basic identity and life meaning, and the hope of realizing them. The Higher Purpose asks and tries to answer big questions like "Why am I here?" and "What is life?" Some might find spiritual practices helpful to make connections between current reality and the hoped-for ideal.

REFLECTIVE PURPOSE

The Reflective Purpose is defined by self-reflection and is the embodiment of the creative tension created when one sets a goal. Self-reflection is the tool for discovering and developing the other six Purposes. Introspection unveils the thoughts, beliefs, feelings, and behaviors that comprise each person and Purpose.

LAW FIRM PROGRAM

Practicing on Purpose programs help attorneys and staff improve wellness through daily reflections. The ideal program is built in to the technology systems in use by the firm already, so participants are automatically prompted to engage in that day's reflection. The actual process is very short; participants read a passage on a theme related to one or more Purposes, then spend five minutes reflecting on it, either in quiet contemplation, journal-writing, or expressive art. For example, a daily reflection might look like this:

"USA Today" tells the story of two twentieth-century innovations combining to threaten the ecosystem of the Great Lakes. The Chicago Sanitary and Ship Canal, created in 1900, reversed the flow of the Chicago River to stop the city's wastewater from entering Lake Michigan. Asian carp, large flying fish with voracious appetites and no natural predators, introduced to the US in the 1960s to fight algae overgrowth, now live in the canal and without intervention will soon enter the Great Lakes. The current solution is a combination of electric fence and fish kill when the fence is down for maintenance.

This situation reminds me of balancing the Purposes. Like the Chicago Sanitary and Ship Canal, we need an outlet for our own "wastewater" and the things that no longer serve us. But like the Asian carp, we need to be careful of what we let flow in the opposite direction.

How can I strengthen my own internal electric fence? Do I need to erect a new one?"[63]

These daily reflection exercises help participants determine their own Higher Purpose, and through development of all the Purposes, make choices that are aligned with it. Improved job satisfaction is a "side effect" of balanced Purposes, based on new skills and coping strategies that best serve each individual. The qualities that make one an excellent lawyer are enhanced, without

---

63. Adapted from Gretchen Duhaime, *Balancing Invasions*, THE DAILY PRACTICE, Dec. 1, 2009, http://www.practicingonpurpose.com/daily-practice/december12009-balancing invasions (last visited Jan. 3, 2010).

triggering Maister's laundry list of shortcomings. Individual values are identified and strengthened, allowing greater commitment to live by firm values. Lawyers can engage with others on a personal level while maintaining the appropriate level of professional detachment, fostering trust and teamwork. Having balanced Purposes also helps lawyers learn to restrain from needless argumentative posturing and mythic hypotheticals, allowing groups to reach consensus and move forward.

CONCLUSION

IN MANY ways, big law firms are unhappy, unhealthy anachronisms where associates are used as leverage for partner profits, clients have no clear picture of value received, and partners live in a state of distrust and detachment. By refocusing firm values and goals, and adopting new metrics for success, big firms can resurrect themselves from the rubble of last century's Cravath system. In order to have the best chance for achievement and change, firms can improve well-being of their attorneys and staff with the Practicing on Purpose wellness program.

RESOURCES

We hope this book will whet your appetite for more information. The following resources are not all-inclusive, but are a good place to learn more about the topics. Check www.cuttingedgelaw.com for updates and additional resources.

TABLE OF CONTENTS

ALTERNATIVE DISPUTE RESOLUTION

ARTICLES

David A. Hoffman, *The Future of ADR: Professionalization, Spirituality, and the Internet,* 14 DISP. RESOL. MAG. 4, 6 (2008).

> In this article, Hoffman addresses the following questions: (1) The Internet: How will we adapt dispute resolution methods to an electronic future in which human relationships unfold and flourish in a virtual space that our current generation can barely imagine? (2) Spirituality: How will we manage the emerging tension between those who seek to explore spiritual dimensions of dispute resolution work and those who see little, if any, place for spirituality in their ADR work? (3) Professionalization: How will we respond to the growing risk that if the ADR field does not develop its own methods of quality assurance, outsiders will do it for us?

WEB RESOURCES

The ABA database on Oregon, http://adr.uoregon.edu/aba/.

> For several years, the American Bar Association (ABA) Section on Dispute Resolution and the University of Oregon School of Law have

collaborated to maintain an online directory of alternative dispute resolution (ADR) offerings at U.S. law schools. This database provides self-reported information about courses, requirements, and certain other offerings.

APOLOGY

BOOKS

GARY CHAPMAN & JENNIFER THOMAS, THE FIVE LANGUAGES OF APOLOGY: HOW TO EXPERIENCE HEALING IN ALL YOUR RELATIONSHIPS (Northfield Publishing, 2006)

Chapman, author of the bestselling *The Five Love Languages*, teams up with psychologist Thomas to tackle the apology because, as with love, understanding it is essential for developing, maintaining, and repairing relationships. Apology applies to all varieties of relationships, from the deeply personal connection between intimate partners to the formal relationships between nations.

AARON LAZARE, ON APOLOGY (Oxford University Press, 2004)

Drawing on a vast array of literary and real-life examples, such as Agamemnon, George Patton, and Arnold Schwarzenegger, from the current pope to the machinist who approached him after a lecture, Lazare lucidly dissects the process of apology: offering an explanation; communicating remorse, shame, humility, or sincerity (according to our cultural values); making a gesture of reparation or reconciliation.

WEB RESOURCES

http://www.apologyletter.org/index.html

A wonderful site with a program for creating an apology.

www.sorryworks.net

> The Sorry Works! Coalition is the nation's leading advocacy organization for disclosure, apology (when appropriate), and upfront compensation (when necessary) after errors and mistakes in medicine, business, insurance, and the law. The coalition advocates that the litigation crisis is not a legal problem but rather a customer service crisis.

http://www.jaapa.com/Apologizing-for-adverse-outcomes/article/130982/

> Many people believe that disclosure is incomplete without an apology. An apology is an acknowledgment of responsibility together with an expression of remorse. There is an important distinction to be made between apologies and expressions of consolation. When a patient experiences an unfortunate outcome that is not the result of provider error, it is appropriate to offer consoling comments, such as "I am sorry for what happened." An apology, on the other hand, is necessary when the health care provider has harmed the patient physically or psychologically through behavior that could or should have been avoided.

Jonathan R. Cohen, Legislating Apology: The Pros and Cons, University of Florida Levin College of Law (August 2001). Available at SSRN: http://ssrn.com/abstract=283213 or doi:10.2139/ssrn.283213

> Should apologies be admissible into evidence as proof of fault in civil cases? The past year has seen a tremendous rise in "apology legislation" designed to exclude apologies from admissibility into evidence. For example, California passed a law in 2000 barring apologetic expressions of sympathy ("I'm sorry that you are hurt") but not fault-admitting apologies ("I'm sorry that I injured you") after accidents from introduction into evidence as proof of fault. Other states are now debating proposed apology legislation, including bills that would exclude fault-admitting apologies from evidence. As apologies can be central elements in preventing and settling lawsuits, such legislation has the potential to dramatically affect dispute resolution and legal practice. This article examines policy arguments that can be made supporting and opposing such legislation and offers remaining questions for future research.

Jonathan R. Cohen, Apology and Organizations: Exploring an Example from Medical Practice, University of Florida, Levin College of Law (February 25, 2000). Available at: http://papers.ssrn.com/sol3/papers.cfm?abstract_id=238330

> Abstract: In 1987, the Veterans Affairs Medical Center in Lexington, Kentucky, took a surprising step. They decided that when they made a medical error they would truly "come clean" and fully assume responsibility for the error, including apologizing for it. Over the next decade, they went from being one of the highest net-legal-cost hospitals to among the lowest net-legal-cost hospitals in the VA system. This paper uses their experience as a springboard for exploring

the potential for the use of apology by organizations. Topics discussed include (1) the impact of apology on learning to prevent future errors; (2) divergent interests toward apology stemming from principal-agents tensions in employment, risk preferences, and sources of insurance; (3) nonpecuniary benefits of apology to corporate morale, productivity, and reputation; (4) standing and scope when apologizing; and (5) the articulation of policies toward injuries to others.

Marlynn Wei, *Doctors, Apologies, and the Law: An Analysis and Critique of Apology Laws*, 39 J. HEALTH LAW 4 (Fall 2006), Harvard University, Massachusetts General Hospital; Harvard University, McLean Hospital. Also available at: http://papers.ssrn.com/sol3/papers.cfm?abstract_id=955668

This article analyzes and critiques apology laws, their potential use, and effectiveness, both legally and ethically, in light of the strong professional norms that shape physicians' reaction to medical errors. Physicians are largely reluctant to disclose medical errors to patients, patients' families, and even other physicians. Some states have passed so-called apology laws in order to encourage physicians to disclose medical errors to patients. Apology laws allow defendants to exclude statements of sympathy made after accidents from evidence in a liability lawsuit. This piece examines potential barriers to physicians' disclosure of medical mistakes and demonstrates how the underlying problem may actually be rooted in professional norms—norms that will remain outside the scope of law's influence. The article also considers other legal and policy changes that could help to encourage disclosure.

CAREER

BOOKS

DEBORAH ARRON, RUNNING FROM THE LAW: WHY GOOD LAWYERS ARE GETTING OUT OF THE LEGAL PROFESSION (Decision Books, 2003).

DEBORAH ARRON, WHAT CAN YOU DO WITH A LAW DEGREE?: A LAWYER'S GUIDE TO CAREER ALTERNATIVES INSIDE, OUTSIDE & AROUND THE LAW (Decision Books Niche Press, 5th ed., 2003).

MAUREEN F. FITZGERALD, MISSION POSSIBLE, CREATING A MISSION FOR WORK AND LIFE (Quinn Publishing (2003).

HINDI GREENBERG, THE LAWYER'S CAREER CHANGE HANDBOOK: MORE THAN 300 THINGS YOU CAN DO WITH A LAW DEGREE (HarperCollins, 1998).

CIVIL COLLABORATIVE/ COOPERATIVE PRACTICE

John Lande, *A Recent Innovation, "Cooperative" Negotiation Can Promote Early and Efficient Settlement Through Joint Case Management*, 27 ALTERNATIVES TO HIGH COST LITIG. 117 (2009).

> This article explains the concept of "cooperative practice" and "presents findings from a study the author conducted about how Divorce Cooperation Institute members handle cooperative cases. It compares cooperative practice with collaborative practice, and further discusses cooperative negotiation in business disputes.

WEBSITES

"Collaborative law" has more than 400,000 hits on Google.com.

http://www.collaborativepractice.com/

> The International Academy of Collaborative Professionals (IACP) is an international community of legal, mental health, and financial professionals working in concert to create client-centered processes for resolving conflict.

http://www.abanet.org/dch/committee.cfm?com=DR035000

> The American Bar Association's Collaborative Law Committee.

http://www.collaborativelaw.us/

> Global Collaborative Law Council (formerly Texas Collaborative Law Council) is a professional group committed to the training, education, and promotion of collaborative law.

http://www.nycourts.gov/ip/collablaw/

> The New York Collaborative Law Center is the first court-based collaborative law center in the United States.

http://www.collaborativelaw.org/

> The Collaborative Law Institute of Minnesota

BLOGS

http://www.collaborativedivorcenews.com/

> Blog written by Pauline Tesler

http://texascollaborativelaw.blogspot.com/

> Information and tips on practicing collaborative law from a Texas family lawyer.

http://www.collaborativedivorcenorthwest.com/

A look at collaborative law with insight into how it is practiced in various areas around the country and internationally.

VIDEO

http://www.youtube.com/user/IACPVideos

The YouTube Channel for the International Academy of Collaborative Professionals (IACP).

http://www.cuttingedgelaw.com/video/video-stu-webb-godfather-collaborative-law

In this three-part interview, Stu Webb, a co-founder of the collaborative law process, talks about his professional journey and the genesis of collaborative law.

http://www.cuttingedgelaw.com/video/pauline-tesler-hot-topics-collaborative-practice

Pauline Tesler, a co-founder of the collaborative law process, shares how she became a collaborative lawyer, the creation of the IACP, and the development of the interdisciplinary process.

http://www.youtube.com/watch?v=ZIXD0clcWso

A concise, illustrated introduction to the collaborative law process from Mogers Solicitors in Bath, England.

COACHING

Michael Town, *Coaches, Judges Have Much in Common,* Honolulu Advertiser, May 1, 2006. Also available at: http://the
.honoluluadvertiser.com/article/2006/May/01/op/FP605010303
.html/?print+on; reprinted for Positive Coaching Alliance: http://
www.positivecoach.org/arDisplay.aspx?SecID=130&ID=402.

http://www.cinergycoaching.com/

Conflict Coaching and Training by Cinnie Noble. As a pioneer in
the development of conflict coaching, based in Toronto, **CINERGY**®
Coaching offers conflict coaching and training programs across Canada, the United States and around the world.

COLLABORATIVE LAW

BOOKS

SHERRIE R. ABNEY, AVOIDING LITIGATION (Trafford Publishing, 2006).

FORREST MOSTEN ,COLLABORATIVE DIVORCE HANDBOOK: HELPING FAMILIES WITHOUT GOING TO COURT (Jossey-Bass, 2009).

PAULINE H. TESLER, COLLABORATIVE LAW (American Bar Association, Sep 25, 2001).

PAULINE H. TESLER, COLLABORATIVE LAW, SECOND EDITION: ACHIEVING EFFECTIVE RESOLUTION WITHOUT LITIGATION (American Bar Association, 2009).

PAULINE H. TESLER & PEGGY THOMPSON, COLLABORATIVE DIVORCE: THE REVOLUTIONARY NEW WAY TO RESTRUCTURE YOUR FAMILY, RESOLVE LEGAL ISSUES, AND MOVE ON WITH YOUR LIFE (Harper Collins, 2007).

STUART WEBB & RON D. OUSKY, THE COLLABORATIVE WAY TO DIVORCE: THE REVOLUTIONARY METHOD THAT RESULTS IN LESS STRESS, LOWER COSTS AND HAPPIER KIDS—WITHOUT GOING TO COURT (Penguin Group, 2006).

ARTICLES

Arnold D. Cribari, *Collaborative Law: Divorce Lawyer as Peacemaker*, 33 WEST-CHESTER B.J. 53 (2006).

This article claims that "An army of peacemakers is growing throughout the United States and other countries in the field of divorce law." Cribari sheds light on the benefits of collaborative law, and provides a breakdown of the collaborative case and the potential for peace-making—from the first settlement conference, through discovery, to finding peaceful solutions.

Susan Daicoff, *Collaborative Law: A New Tool for the Lawyer's Toolkit*, 20 U. FLA. J.L. & PUB. POL'Y 113 (2009).

This article discusses the emergence of collaborative law, analyzes its advantages and disadvantages, and discusses its philosophical underpinnings. The article also places collaborative law in the context of the comprehensive law movement.

Susan Gamache, *Collaborative Practice: A New Opportunity to Address Children's Best Interest in Divorce*, 65 LA. L. REV. 1455 (2005).

The article claims that collaborative practice "has the potential to fulfill children's best interest following separation and divorce." The article discusses the interdisciplinary nature of the practice groups—the collaborative lawyers, therapists, child specialists, and financial planners who pool their expertise and work together out of court to create a "post-separation family environment possible for all family members, especially the children."

David A. Hoffman, *Collaborative Law: A Practitioner's Perspective*, 12 DISP. RESOL. MAG. 1, 25 (2005).

This article provides a comprehensive response to particular criticism of collaborative law, including (1) pressure to choose collaborative law, (2) pressure to continue with collaborative law, (3) pressure to settle, (4) the sanctity of the attorney–client relationship/disqualification provision, and (5) other ethical considerations.

John Lande, *The Promise and Perils of Collaborative Law*, 12 DISP. RESOL. MAG. 1, 29 (2005).

This article describes collaborative law's promise and potential perils, focusing particularly on the *perils* to complement the literature touting the promise. Examples of "the perils" include (1) setting unrealistic expectations, (2) creating excessive settlement pressure, (3) violating rules of professional conduct, and (4) resisting choice and innovation.

Julie Macfarlane, *Experiences of Collaborative Law: Preliminary Results from the Collaborative Lawyering Research Project*, J. DISP. RESOL. 179 (2004).

Topics covered: The Decline of Cooperation; A Crisis in Family Legal Services; The Limits of Formal Procedural Change; Re-conceiving the Role of Lawyer as Agent; and The Collaborative Lawyering Research Study.

Forrest S. Mosten, *Collaborative Law Practice: An Unbundled Approach to Informed Client Decision Making*, J. DISP. RESOL. 163 (2008).

This article discusses "unbundling" (a.k.a. "limited scope" or "legal coaching")—that attorneys can "limit the scope of our services based upon the written informed decision making (i.e., consent) of the client." The article explores the commonality between the "unbundling" approach and collaborative law, and "the ways to help the client make an informed decision prior to commencing a collaborative law engagement."

Elizabeth K. Strickland, *Putting "Counselor" Back in the Lawyer's Job Description: Why More States Should Adopt Collaborative Law Statutes*, 84 N.C. L. REV. 979 (2006).

This article discusses how the collaborative method works and discusses the current state of collaborative law in the United States and abroad. Strickland argues for increased use of collaborative law and advocates the passage of a collaborative law statute to facilitate realization of its benefits and to remedy potential disadvantages arising from the practice. Finally, the article proposes "a collaborative law statute for states to adopt in order to promote the use of this alternative to traditional methods of obtaining a divorce."

Pauline H. Tesler, *Collaborative Family Law*, 4 PEPP. DISP. RESOL. L.J. 317 (2004).

This article discusses the advantages and benefits of the collaborative law model. Tesler examines the basic elements of the model, and differentiates it from "conventional settlement negotiation." She also discusses the differences between the collaborative model and mediation.

Gary L. Voegele, Linda K. Wray, & Ronald D. Ousky, *Collaborative Law: A Useful Tool for the Family Law Practitioner to Promote Better Outcomes*, WM. MITCHELL L. REV. p. 33_(2007).

"The purpose of this article is to provide family law practitioners with a brief history and an overview of the collaborative law process, as well as a description of its distinctive features. Collaborative law has been described as both a process and a model. As such, practice protocols have been developed to assist family law practitioners in the handling of collaborative law cases." Topics covered: History; Development of Collaborative Law Practice and its Current Status; The Collaborative Law Process in Family Law Cases; Ethical Considerations; Training in Collaborative Law.

Stu Webb, *Collaborative Law: A Practitioner's Perspective on Its History and Current Practice,* 21 J. AM. ACAD. MATRIM. LAW 155 (2008).

Stu Webb's personal recollection of the creation and development of collaborative law. He discusses the definition of collaborative law; its history and development; the training of settlement lawyers, and the collaborative method.

CONFLICT
RESOLUTION

BOOKS

Daniel Bowling and David Hoffman, Eds., Bringing Peace Into the Room: How the Personal Qualities of the Mediator Impact the Process of Conflict Resolution (Jossey-Bass, 2003).

Stewart Levine, Getting to Resolution: Turning Conflict Into Collaboration (Berrett-Koehler, 2000).

Stewart Levine, The Book of Agreement: 10 Essential Elements for Getting the Results You Want (Berrett-Koehler, 2002).

Douglas Noll, Peacemaking: Practicing at the Intersection of Law and Human Conflict (Cascadia Publishing House, 2003).

CONTEMPLATION AND MINDFULNESS

BOOKS

GREGORY COFFEY & MAUREEN C. KESSLER, THE REFLECTIVE COUNSELOR, DAILY MEDITATIONS FOR LAWYERS (American Bar Association, 2008).

ROGER FISHER, WILLIAM L. URY, & BRUCE PATTON, GETTING TO YES: NEGOTIATING AGREEMENT WITHOUT GIVING IN (Penguin Books, 1997).

THICH NHAT HAHN, BEING PEACE (Parallax Press, 1987).

DAVID HOFFMAN & DANIEL BOWLING, BRINGING PEACE INTO THE ROOM, HOW THE PERSONAL QUALITIES OF THE MEDIATOR IMPACT THE PROCESS OF CONFLICT RESOLUTION (Jossey-Bass, 2003).

MARSHALL B. ROSENBERG, SPEAK PEACE IN A WORLD OF CONFLICT: WHAT YOU SAY NEXT WILL CHANGE YOUR WORLD (Puddledancer Press, 2005).

MARSHALL B. ROSENBERG & ARUN GANDHI, NONVIOLENT COMMUNICATION: A LANGUAGE OF LIFE: CREATE YOUR LIFE, YOUR

Relationships, and Your World in Harmony with Your Values (Puddledancer Press, 2005).

Douglas Stone, Bruce Patton, & Sheila Heen, Difficult Conversations: How to Discuss What Matters Most (Viking Press, Harvard Negotiation Project, 1999).

Janet Smith Warfield, Shift: Change Your Words, Change Your World (Word Sculptures Publishing, 2009).

Articles

Douglas A. Codiga, *Reflections on the Potential Growth of Mindfulness Mediation in the Law*, 7 Harv. Neg. L. Rev. 109 (2002).

Codiga builds on Riskin's exposition of mindfulness meditation (below) by suggesting that "recent efforts to introduce mindfulness to the legal community" may not be effective unless "three potential misconceptions about mindfulness meditation, lawyering, and the teachings of Buddhism are firmly laid to rest." Specifically, he argues there is "nothing mystical or otherworldly about mindfulness meditation." He claims that though there is some connection with Buddhist teaching, there is no inherent conflict between mindfulness meditation and other religious orientations. He finally claims that there is more to mindfulness meditation than stress reduction and improved lawyering skills—that lawyers can establish a foundation of mindfulness meditation and "practice law from that place."

J. Patton Hyman, *The Mindful Lawyer: Mindfulness Meditation and Law Practice*, 33-SUM, Vt. B.J. 40 (2007).

In this article, Hyman discusses mindfulness meditation and its remedial use as a "stress-buster" or as a way of managing the pressures of life and how mindfulness meditation can help lawyers relate to others in the course of their practice. Topics covered: What Is Meditation?; Meditation and Stress; Beyond Stress Management; Other People; Applying Mindfulness in Law Practice; Learning to Practice Mindfulness.

Leonard L. Riskin, *The Contemplative Lawyer: On the Potential Contributions of Mindfulness Meditation to Law Students, Lawyers, and their Clients*, 7 Harv. Negot. L. Rev. 1 (2002).

An article by Leonard L. Riskin, well known for his work involving mindfulness. He addresses certain problems in the legal profession, including dissatisfaction and missed opportunities, and discusses the role mindful meditation can play in remedying those problems. Topics covered: Recent Developments, Potential Benefits Feeling Better, Dealing with Limiting Mind-Sets and Relieving

Suffering in Other Ways (listening, reacting, responding, negotiation), Roles and Places of Mindfulness Meditation in the Legal Community, and Potential Concerns.

Robert Zeglovitch, *The Mindful Lawyer*, 70 TEX. B.J. 234 (2007).

This article describes mindfulness meditation and sheds light on studies done at hospitals and laboratories that validate the link between mindfulness meditation and improved health. He highlights particular factors "inherent in law practice [that] make mindfulness and meditation particularly well suited to lawyers." (Example—lawyers suffer from stress-related health conditions; lawyers are goal oriented; lawyers are driven by time; lawyers tend to be judgmental; lawyers are trained to think their way out of problems). He then discusses how to get started in the practice of mindfulness meditation and provides some further resources that may be helpful.

COMMUNITY LAWYERING AND MINDFULNESS

A. P. Harris, J. Selbin, & L. Margaretta, *From "The Art of War" to "Being Peace": Mindfulness and Community Lawyering in a Neo-liberal Age*, 95 CALIF. L.R. 2073 (2007); 8 NYLS CLINICAL RESEARCH INSTITUTE PAPER, 1 (2009). Available at SSRN: http://ssrn.com/abstract=1024004.

WEBSITES

http://westallen.typepad.com/idealawg/2008/09/contemplative-lawyers-some-mindfulness-resources.html

Mediator, lawyer, trainer, and blogger, Stephanie West Allen maintains and updates a resource list for mindfulness and law.

http://www.imslaw.com/jurisight.html

Attorney Scott Rogers has created the Jurisight_ program for mindfulness and law. He distinguishes mindfulness practices using legal jargon such as "pain and suffering." Part of the IMS mission is to bring this "lingo" into law firms, law schools, and across a variety of legal settings so that it can provide renewed sense of community, collaboration, and support.

http://themeditationgarden.com

Attorney Sonia Gallagher is a Certified Life Coach, editor, and entrepreneur, now devoting her time to coaching professionals who want to live more fulfilled, balanced, and successful lives, sharing information about meditation through this site, and her family. This website is her way of telling the story of how meditation and the internet helped her find a new path in life, when it seemed like everything was falling apart.

CREATIVE PROBLEM SOLVING

ARTICLES

Mark Broida, *Creative Problem Solving*, THE LAW TEACHER (Spring 2001).

Debra Gerardi, *Developing Creativity and Intuition for Resolving Conflicts: The Magic of Improvisation* (Sep. 2001), available at: http://www.mediate.com/articles/geradi.cfm

WEBSITES

http://www.californiawestern.edu/main/default.asp?nav=creative_problem_solving.asp&body=creative_problem_solving/home.asp

California Western School of Law Center for Creative Problem Solving, the flagship program for the subject.

http://www.creativelearning.com/

http://www.cuttingedgelaw.com/page/creative-problem-solving-law

The Cutting Edge Law web page for creative problem solving.

MULTIMEDIA

Circle Process and Creative Problem Solving in Mediation by Professor Susan Daicoff and Elizabeth Roach (audio recording available for purchase at ConventionRecordings.com).

An interview with creative problem solving lawyer Kevin Houchin: http://www.cuttingedgelaw.com/video/kevin-houchin-creative-problem-solver

CULTURAL AND ORGANIZATIONAL TRANSFORMATION

BOOKS

PETER M. SENGE, JOSEPH JAWORSKI, C. OTTO SCHARMER, & BETTY SUE FLOWERS, HUMAN PURPOSE AND THE FIELD OF THE FUTURE(Broadway Business, 2008).

PHILIP SLATER, THE CHRYSALIS EFFECT: THE METAMORPHOSIS OF GLOBAL CULTURE (Sussex Academic Press, 2009).

FORGIVENESS

BOOKS

COLIN TIPPING, RADICAL FORGIVENESS, MAKING ROOM FOR THE MIRACLE (Quest Publications, 2005).

MULTIMEDIA

Mara Alper, *A Documentary on Forgiveness with Desmond Tutu* (Retrieved: February 8, 1010), http://www.maraalper.com/doc _forgiveness_2.html

BLOGS

http://blogcritics.org/books/article/book-review-as-we-forgive-stories/

HEALING AND LAW

Here is a list of recommended resources for learning more about law and healing. Many of the resources listed in the other sections also deal with law as a healing profession (e.g., therapeutic jurisprudence, restorative justice, etc.). Those resources have not been repeated here. A number of the resources listed here deal with the healing process generally and do not specifically address healing within the context of legal matters; however, many of the principles are equally applicable to law as a healing profession.

WEBSITES

Center for Law and Renewal, http://www.healingandthelaw.org/
A former project funded by Fetzer Institute, www.fetzer.org

Additional healing resources include the following:

Shulamit Almog, *Healing Stories in Law and Literature*, in 289 TRAUMA AND MEMORY: READING, HEALING AND MAKING LAW (Austin Sarat, Nadav Davidovich, & Michal Alberstein, Eds., 2008); http://papers.ssrn.com/sol3/papers.cfm?abstract_id=1467939

Susan Daicoff, *Law as a Healing Profession: The "Comprehensive Law Movement,"* paper presented at the 6th International Clinical Conference, UCLA/University of London (2005), available at: http://works.bepress.com/susan_daicoff/1

Healing to Wellness Courts: A Preliminary Overview of Tribal Drug Courts, http://www.tribal-institute.org/download/heal.pdf

Keeva on Life and Practice, *Once More, With Healing, Ex-Law Dean Heads Center Dedicated to Alternative Approaches to Practice,* http://www.abajournal.com/magazine/article/once_more_with_healing/

www.lawyerhealer.com

Dean David T. Link, *Healing and the Law,* http://www.consciouslawyer.org/blog/wp-content/uploads/2007/12/healing-and-the-law.pdf

Edward W. McIntyre, *The Power to Heal,* http://www.isacofflaw.com/CM/Custom/Power-to-Heal.pdf

Radical Forgiveness worksheet, which is useful in transforming the energy of a specific conflict: http://www.radicalforgiveness.com/contentnew/downloads.asp

Rachel Naomi Remen, MD, *In the Service of Life,* http://www.rachelremen.com/service.html

Marjorie Silver, ed., The Affective Assistance of Counsel: Practicing Law as a Healing Profession (Carolina Academic Press, 2007), available at: http://www.aals.org/am2006/program/balance/Silveroutline.pdf

Books

Joseph G. Allegretti, The Lawyer's Calling: Christian Faith and Legal Practice (Paulist Press, 1996).

Marc Ian Barasch, Field Notes on the Compassionate Life: A Search for the Soul of Kindness (Rodale, 2005).

Barbara Brennan, Light Emerging (Bantam Books, 1993).

Pema Chodron, Start Where You Are (Shambhala Pub., 1994).

Pema Chodron, When Things Fall Apart (Shambhala Pub., 1997).

Larry Dossey, Healing Words (Harper Collins, 1993).

Larry Dossey, Reinventing Medicine (Harper Collins, 1999).

Larry Dossey, Healing Beyond The Body, Medicine and the Infinite Reach of the Mind (Shambhala Pub., 2001).

Larry Dossey, The Extraordinary Healing Power of Ordinary Things (Crown Publishing, 2006).

Foundation for Inner Peace, A Course in Miracles (Foundation for Inner Peace, 2008).

Piero Ferrucci, The Power of Kindness (Penguin Press (2007).

Daniel Goleman, Emotional Intelligence (Bantam, 2004).

Jon Kabat-Zinn, Coming to Our Senses: Healing Ourselves and the World Through Mindfulness (Hyperion, 2006).

Byron Katie & Stephen Mitchell, Loving What Is: Four Questions That Can Change Your Life (Three Rivers, 2003).

Daniel Goleman & Dalai Lama, Destructive Emotions (Bantam Books, 2004).

Carolyn Myss, Invisible Acts of Power (Free Press, 2004).

Carolyn Myss, Defy Gravity: Healing Beyond the Bounds of Reason (Hay House Publishing, 2009).

Rachel Naomi Remen, MD, My Grandfather's Blessings (Berkeley Publishing Group, 2001).

Rachel Naomi Remen, MD, Kitchen Table Wisdom (Berkeley Publishing Group, 2006).

Eckhart Tolle, The Power of Now (New World Library, 1999).

Thomas E. Baker & Timothy W. Floyd, Eds., Can a Good Christian Be a Good Lawyer?: Homilies, Witnesses and Reflections (University of Notre Dame Press, 1999).

Philip Yancey & Dr. Phil Brand, The Gift of Pain (Zondervan Publishing, 1993).

Articles

Richard L. Halpert, *More Than One Kind of Recovery: in Personal Injury Cases, Money Does Not Always Answer the Client's Needs,* 89 A.B.A. J. 58 (2003).

Mary H. Mocine, *The Art of Listening,* Calif. Law. Mag., July 2000.

Mary H. Mocine, *Realizing Kindness,* http://www.transformingpractices.com/gc/gc.html

HOLISTIC LAW

BOOKS

STEVEN KEEVA, TRANSFORMING PRACTICES: FINDING JOY AND SATIS-
FACTION IN THE LEGAL LIFE (McGraw-Hill, 1999).

ARTICLES

Robert P. Borsody, *A New Paradigm For Lawyers?*, 74-APR N.Y. ST.
B.J. 54 (2002).

> Borsody proposes that we reexamine how we practice law. He argues
> that law practice "can often be corrosive to the soul and heart of prac-
> titioners," and this may be one reason why lawyers, as a group, "have
> some of the highest rates of divorce, heart attacks, strokes, drug and
> alcohol addiction and suicide." He discusses a new paradigm for law-
> yers that "looks for a resolution that will not inevitably involve litiga-
> tion, but rather a solution that will take the interests of all parties into
> consideration." The article characterizes holistic law as being "con-
> cerned with the whole client"—i.e., taking more time with a client "to
> understand the client's lifestyle and the client's business, going beyond
> the immediate facts of the proposed deal or the perceived conflict."

Disorder in the Courts, PSYCHOLOGY TODAY, May 1, 1993, http://www
.psychologytoday.com/articles/199305/disorder-in-the-courts

Pamela Ferdinand, *Holistic Law Tries to Make Every Case a Civil One*,
THE WASHINGTON POST, May 17, 1998.

Brooks Holland, *Holistic Advocacy: An Important But Limited Institutional Role*, 30 N.Y.U. REV. L. & SOC. CHANGE 637 (2006).

> This article is somewhat in opposition to the Steinberg article below. Talks about the *limits* of holistic practice in the office of the public defender and the *risks* that may result. Examples of limitations: Public defenders carry very high caseloads; they need to hire many lawyers, staffers—all to keep attorneys' workloads at manageable levels. If holistic public defenders hire out social workers and investigators, it means one less attorney. Extralegal holistic duties like community outreach may mean holistic lawyers have *less* time for each client's case, "increasing the already high pressure to dispose of many cases quickly." Holistic advocacy does not always address particular aspects of the trial-focused evaluation of cases (i.e., "what happened here, and can the prosecutor likely prove it." In plea bargaining, the "whole client" approach will have little impact. When it does, sometimes the "whole client" will not impress the judge/prosecutor (i.e., when there is a history of violent behavior). Examples of risks: Judges and prosecutors "may begin to think the holistic public defenders shrink from the tough task of trying cases."

Paul Peter Jesep, *Winning the Case and Healing the Soul*, 18 ME. B.J. 194(2003).

> This article discusses the holistic practice of law and its approach to remedying the effects of the "harsh, adversarial arena." Jesep sheds light on the notion that the stresses of traditional litigation severely affect not only clients but lawyers as well, and that the lawyer's "body, mind, and spirit. . .need to be nurtured in some sort of balance." Jesep discusses the holistic practice approach as it has been applied in Maine and predicts that holistic law will find its way into law school curriculum.

Elaine McArdle, *From Ballistic to Holistic*, THE BOSTON GLOBE, Jan. 11, 2004.

Robin G. Steinberg, *Beyond Lawyering: How Holistic Representation Makes for Good Policy, Better Lawyers, and More Satisfied Clients*, 30 N.Y.U. REV. L. & SOC. CHANGE 625 (2006).

> Steinberg proposes that public defenders shift from traditional advocacy to "holistic advocacy"—that zealous courtroom advocacy is not the only type of advocacy their clients need, but that, in fact, indigent clients face many more problems: "addictions to substances, joblessness, homelessness, family violence, mental illness, and the general inability to access healthcare and other social services." Steinberg suggests that holistic defense, with its emphasis on engaging the *whole* client, "has the capa[bility] to change the way justice is experienced in indigent communities." Topics covered: Traditional Public Defender Work and Holistic Advocacy; What Causes Criminality?; Some History; How Holistic Advocacy Works; Holistic Advocacy Makes Good Social Policy.

William Young, *Holistic Law's Extra Mile for the Clients*, 11 N.J. LAW. 48 (2002).

WEBSITES

International Alliance of Holistic Lawyers, http://www.iahl.org/

The seminal organization for holistic lawyers.

http://www.renaissancelawyer.com/

An organization of visionary lawyers dedicated to transforming the legal profession.

http://www.sacredrivers.neu.edu/

The website for David Hall's work on the search for sacred rivers in the legal profession.

VIDEO

http://www.cuttingedgelaw.com/video/maureen-holland

A former litigator, Maureen Holland is a pioneer in the holistic law arena as a practitioner and judge.

http://www.cuttingedgelaw.com/video/georgia-justice-project-video-series -executive-director-doug-ammar

Doug Ammar, the Georgia Justice Project executive director, discusses the integration of faith and law practice.

http://www.cuttingedgelaw.com/video/jennifer-foster-being-holistic-lawyer

Jennifer Foster shares her experience with holistic law practice in the pro-bono realm.

http://www.youtube.com/user/cuttingedgelaw

The YouTube Channel for Cutting Edge Law.

http://www.youtube.com/watch?v=g_vpuUMwDwk

Marty Reisig discusses work as a holistic lawyer.

LAWYER WELL-BEING

BOOKS

TIMOTHY D. BATDORF, THE LAWYER'S GUIDE TO BEING HUMAN: HOW TO BRING WHO YOU ARE TO WHAT YOU DO (iUniverse, 2007).

SUSAN SWAIM DAICOFF, LAWYER KNOW THYSELF: A PSYCHOLOGICAL ANALYSIS OF PERSONALITY STRENGTHS AND WEAKNESSES (American Psychological Association, 2004).

GEORGE KAUFMAN, THE LAWYER'S GUIDE TO BALANCING LIFE AND WORK (American Bar Association, 2006).

TAMA J. KIEVES, THIS TIME I DANCE! TRUSTING THE JOURNEY OF CREATING THE WORK YOU LOVE: HOW ONE HARVARD LAWYER LEFT IT ALL TO HAVE IT ALL! (Awakening Artistry, 2002).

S. LEONARD SCHEFF, THE COW IN THE PARKING LOT: A GUIDE FOR TRANSFORMING ANGER FOR A HAPPIER MORE EFFECTIVE LIFE (iUniverse, 2008). (See also www.transforminganger.com)

MARJORIE SILVER, THE AFFECTIVE ASSISTANCE OF COUNSEL: PRACTICING LAW AS A HEALING PROFESSION (Carolina Academic Press, 2006).

ARTICLES

Connie J. A. Beck, Bruce D. Sales, & G. Andrew H. Benjamin, *Lawyer Distress: Alcohol-Related Problems and Other Psychological Concerns Among a Sample of Practicing Lawyers*, 10 J.L. & HEALTH 1 (1996).

This article discusses a two-year study of postgraduate lawyers, finding that a "significant percentage of practicing lawyers are experiencing a variety of significant psychological distress symptoms" traced to law study and practice—symptoms that appeared shortly after entering law school and remained, and that go beyond that expected in a normal population. The article claims that the distress symptoms arise from traditionally effective litigation strategy. Topics covered: Alcohol-related problems, general social support, marital/relationship status and satisfaction, anger, perceived stress.

Susan Daicoff, *Lawyer, Know Thyself: A Review of Empirical Research on Attorney Attributes Bearing on Professionalism*, 46 AM. U. L. REV. 1337 (1997).

This article discusses the current state of the legal profession, characterizing a "tripartite crisis" in professionalism, public opinion, and lawyer dissatisfaction. Daicoff discusses the particular characteristics of lawyers—from early childhood to the traits of a pre-law student; from motivations for entering the field of law to attributes of a law student; from the effects of law school to lawyer attributes. Daicoff then analyzes the relationship between lawyer attributes and the tripartite crisis.

Susan Daicoff, *Lawyer, Be Thyself: An Empirical Investigation of the Relationship Between the Ethic of Care, the Feeling Decision-making Preference, and Lawyer Well-Being*, 16 VA. J. SOC. POL'Y & L. 87 (2008).

Topics covered: Lawyer Distress and Dissatisfaction (Depression, Alcoholism, General Psychological Distress, Career and Work Dissatisfaction); Decision-making Preferences ("Feeling" Decision-making Preference; The Ethic of Care; Therapeutic Jurisprudence Movement); The Instant Study.

Laurie A. Morin, *Reflections on Teaching Law as Right Livelihood: Cultivating Ethics, Professionalism, and Commitment to Public Service from the Inside Out*, 35 TULSA L.J. 227 (2000).

Morin tells her story of inner transformation—from a law professor who doubted her own abilities and the value of teaching students "who seemed to care about nothing but grades and high-paying jobs," to a law professor who believes a teacher's role should be to "guide students through the process of discovering their own truths about how the legal profession can best fulfill their need for purpose and meaning in their work." She proposes a learning process where students can learn to practice law in a way that is "consistent with their deepest held values, beliefs, and goals."

Marjorie A. Silver, *Love, Hate, and Other Emotional Interference in the Lawyer/ Client Relationship*, 6 CLINICAL L. REV. 259 (1999).

> This article is about one aspect of the need for lawyers to confront their emotional side: their relationships with their clients. Specifically, it is about how that relationship may be enhanced by the lawyer's recognition and resolution of strong emotional reactions—positive or negative—toward a client. Conversely, a lawyer's inability to come to terms with such emotions may well adversely affect the representation.

Ingrid N. Tollefson, *Enlightened Advocacy: A Philosophical Shift with a Public Policy Impact*, 25 HAMLINE J. PUB. L. & POL'Y 481 (2004).

> "This article explores how adopting the metaphorical image of the lawyer as nurturer is a cultural and conceptual tool which may help those in the legal culture find deeper meaning in their lives as lawyers and law students, and in effect, may help to restore the high regard the public once held for the legal profession." Topics covered: Current Vocational Dilemmas for Lawyers and the Impact on the Public, A Proposal for Change: The Lawyer as Nurturer, How the Lawyer as Nurturer Advances the Public Good.

LEGAL EDUCATION

William M. Sullivan et al., The Carnegie Report, Educating Lawyers: Preparation for the Profession of Law (Jossey-Bass, 2007).

Articles

Beth D. Cohen, *Helping Students Develop a More Humanistic Philosophy of Lawyering*, 12 Legal Writing: J. Legal Writing Inst. 141 (2006).

> This article discusses how "against the backdrop of the rising dissatisfaction of those entering or already in the legal profession, law faculty and administrators in general, and legal research and writing faculty specifically, have opportunities to help students develop a more satisfying way to study and practice law."

Ben W. Heineman, Jr., *Lawyers as Leaders*, 116 Yale L. J. Pocket Part 266 (2007).

Lawrence S. Krieger, *What We're Not Telling Law Students—And Lawyers—That They Really Need to Know: Some Thoughts-in-Action Toward Revitalizing the Profession from Its Roots*, 13 J.L. & Health 1 (1999).

> Topics covered: (1) How Life as a Lawyer Can Work Well (aspirations for high achievement and honors are only valuable in the context of a balanced, happy life; law students can have good lives if they act according to their conscience; they do not have to be at the top of their class, or on *Law Review*, to be successful, satisfied lawyers; good

appearances do not necessarily indicate a good life, etc.); (2) Why Law Students (and Lawyers) Surrender Their Life Satisfaction and Professional Ideals (life satisfaction requires psychological maturity; the inhibition of attorney satisfaction and sense of self; what one feels to be right; competition, the need for control, the illusion of control, etc).

Lawrence S. Krieger, *Psychological Insights: Why Our Students and Graduates Suffer, and What We Might Do About It*, 1 J. Ass'n Legal Writing Directors 259 (2002).

In this article, Krieger points to recent psychological findings "which clarify the components of a satisfying, emotionally healthy life." His purpose is to provide teachers and law faculties with the tools they need to address the problems of student and lawyer distress.

Lawrence S. Krieger, *The Inseparability of Professionalism and Personal Satisfaction: Perspectives on Values, Integrity and Happiness*, 11 Clin. L. Rev. 425, 426 (2005).

Leadership Education in the Legal Academy: Principles, Practices and Possibilities A report from the James MacGregor Burns, Academy of Leadership, University of Maryland Co-Authored by Judy Brown, PhD, and Bonnie Allen, JD. Contributing Authors: Georgia Sorenson, PhD; Carol Pearson, PhD; Richard Couto, PhD; Nina Harris, PhD (May 4, 2009): http://www.cuttingedgelaw.com/content/leadership-education-legal-academy-principles-practices-and-possibilities

Michael L. Moffitt, *Islands, Vitamins, Salt, Germs: Four Visions of the Future of ADR in Law Schools (and a Data-Driven Snapshot of the Field Today)*, Ohio St. J. on Disp. Res. (Aug. 10, 2009). Available at SSRN: http://ssrn.com/abstract=1446989

Joshua E. Perry, *Therapeutic Pedagogy: Thoughts on Integral Professional Formation*, 78 Rev. Jur. U.P.R. 167 (2009).

This is an article from the Revista Juridica Universidad de Puerto Rico. Perry proposes the creation of a more "holistic goal of legal education," that helps students "look inward during this journey of professional formation."

Joshua D. Rosenberg, *A Reply to Professor White*, 32 Ohio N.U. L. Rev. 311 (2006).

Rosenberg writes in response to Professor James White's criticism (below). He defends the work of the scholars (in particular, Professors Krieger and Sheldon) who call for humanizing legal education. He claims that Professor White's criticism is yet another example of "thinking like a lawyer."

James J. White, *Maiming the Cubs*, 32 OHIO N.U. L. REV. 287 (2006).

Professor White criticizes those scholars calling for the humanization of legal education. He is skeptical of the claim that legal education may cause students to become permanently "more anxious, more depressed, and generally mentally sicker."

LEGAL MOVEMENT

BOOKS

WALTER BENNETT, THE LAWYER'S MYTH: REVIVING IDEALS IN THE LEGAL PROFESSION (University of Chicago Press, 2002).

JOSEPH JAWORKSI, SYNCHRONCITY, THE INNER PATH TO LEADERSHIP (Berrett-Koehler Publishers, 1996).

JULIE MCFARLANE, THE NEW LAWYER: HOW SETTLEMENT IS TRANSFORMING THE PRACTICE OF LAW (UBC Press, 2008).

BENJAMIN SELLS, THE SOUL OF THE LAW (Element Books, 1994).

MEDIATION

BOOKS

ROBERT A. BARUCH BUSH & JOSEPH P. FOLGER, THE PROMISE OF
MEDIATION: RESPONDING TO CONFLICT THROUGH EMPOWER-
MENT AND RECOGNITION (Jossey-Bass, 1st ed., 1994).

R. CHARLTON, DISPUTE RESOLUTION GUIDEBOOK (Star Printery
Ltd., 2000).

R. CHARLTON & M. DEWDNEY, THE MEDIATOR'S HANDBOOK: SKILLS
AND STRATEGIES FOR PRACTITIONERS (Lawbook Co., 2004).
Called "the ultimate text for the practice of mediation" by one reviewer.

S. Rudolph Cole, C. A. McEwen, & N. Hardin Rogers, MEDIATION:
LAW, POLICY AND PRACTICE (2d ed., Trial Practice Series, West
Group, 2000–2009).
"The leading treatise in the field of mediation".

K. Domenici & S. W. Littlejohn, Mediation: Empowerment in Conflict Management (Waveland Press, Inc., 2001).

J. FOLBERG & A. TAYLOR, Mediation: A Comprehensive Guide to
Resolving Conflicts Without Litigation (Jossey-Bass, 1984).

DAVID FOSKETT, THE LAW AND PRACTICE OF COMPROMISE (6th ed.,
West Group, 2009).

D. N. FRENKEL & J. H. STARK, The Practice of Mediation: A Video-
Integrated Text (Aspen Law Publishing, 2008).

G. Friedman & J. Himmelstein, Challenging Conflict: Mediation Through Understanding (American Bar Association, 2009).

D. Golann & J. Folberg, Mediation: The Roles of Advocate and Neutral (Aspen Law Publishing, 2006).

Deborah M. Kolb, The Mediators (MIT, 1983).

Deborah M. Kolb, When Talk Works, Profiles of Mediators (Jossey-Bass, 1997).

K. Kovach, Kovach's Mediation, Principles and Practice (3d ed., American Casebook Series®, West Group, 2004).

C. J. Menkel, L. Porter Love, & A. Kupfer, Mediation: Practice, Policy, and Ethics (Aspen Law Publishing, 2006).

Christopher W. Moore, The Mediation Process; Practical Strategies for Resolving Conflict (Jossey-Bass, 1986).

N. H. Rogers, F. Sander, S. Goldberg, & S. Rudolph Cole, Dispute Resolution: Negotiation, Mediation and Other Processes (4th ed., Aspen Law Publishing, 2003).

> "One of the leading dispute resolution casebooks in the country."

Mark Umbreit, Mediating Interpersonal Conflict, http://www.colorado.edu/conflict/transform/umbreit.htm (February 8, 2010).

Articles

Robert A. Baruch Bush, *Staying in Orbit, or Breaking Free: The Relationship of Mediation to the Courts Over Four Decades*, 84 N.D. L. Rev. 705 (2008).

> Mediation has been considered a "faithful servant of the court system" and at other times has been "encouraged to 'break free' and establish itself as a separate and distinct conflict resolution process." This article presents a history and analysis of the relationship of meditation to the courts.

Dorothy J. Della Noce, Robert A. Baruch Bush, & Joseph P. Folger, *Clarifying the Theoretical Underpinnings of Mediation: Implications for Practice and Policy*, 3 Pepp. Disp. Resol. L.J. 39 (2002).

> "In this article we examine developments in explaining and understanding "the when and why" of mediation practice—from the "lay theories" that have informed much of the field, to Bush and Folger's articulation of three distinct and coherent ideologically based theoretical frameworks: the problem-solving framework, the harmony framework, and the transformative framework. We

then trace the development of the transformative framework since its articulation in 1994, and share the insights we have gained along the way regarding the impact of increasing theoretical clarity and differentiation in the mediation field. We conclude with a discussion of the implications of ideologically based theoretical distinctions for mediation practice and policy, and recommendations for a fresh, theoretically informed, approach to policy initiatives."

Joseph Folger, *Harmony and Transformative Mediation Practice: Sustaining Ideological Differences in Purpose and Practice*, 84 N.D. L. Rev. 823 (2008).

This article discusses the "harmony" and "transformative" frameworks of mediation practices, identifies the differences between the two frameworks, and "argues for the importance of sustaining a clear distinction between these two ideological approaches to conflict intervention."

David A. Hoffman, *Mediation and the Meaning of Life*, 11 Disp. Resol. Mag. 4, 3 (2005).

Hoffman illustrates the idea that reframing the particular issues in their lives can give people a sense of life meaning, that "meaning" is a fundamental interest for clients, and that mediators can help clients instill a sense of meaning into their lives even from their sad experiences.

John Lande, *Getting the Faith: Why Business Lawyers and Executives Believe in Mediation*, 5 Harv. Negot. L. Rev. 137 (2000).

Lande presents a comprehensive study "intended to examine a wide range of factors that give rise to (or at least relate to) belief in mediation," and claims that the study "shows that [an] ideology favoring use of mediation does exist and is widely held among business lawyers and executives."

John Lande, *Doing the Best Mediation You Can*, 14 Disp. Resol. Mag. 4, 43 (2008).

This article presents the findings of the Task Force on Improving Mediation Quality (Task Force) of the ABA Section of Dispute Resolution. "The Task Force findings focus on the following four aspects of mediation that the research subjects said are particularly important: (1) preparation for mediation by mediators and mediation participants, (2) case-by-case customization of the mediation process, (3) careful consideration of any "analytical" assistance that mediators might provide, and (4) mediators' persistence and patience."

Forrest S. Mosten, *Institutionalization of Mediation*, 42 Fam. Ct. Rev. 292 (2004).

Topics covered: Mediation as a Profession; Regulations of Mediators; Certification; Voluntary Standards; Mandatory Court-Connected Mediation; Courts as Institutions of Client Education; National Mediation Laws; Involvement of Lawyers in Mediation.

MEDIATION

http://www.cuttingedgelaw.com/content/many-faces-mediation

http://www.mediate.com/

> The premier site for mediation information online, featuring more than 5,000 articles on negotiation, mediation, and collaboration; a weekly newsletter (to subscribe see http://www.mediate.com/Newsletter/); and the world's most utilized mediator directory (see http://www.mediate.com/mediator/search.cfm). If you don't know where to start, start here to help you frame your search.

http://en.wikipedia.org/wiki/Mediation

> The Wikipedia entry on mediation. Extremely informative and comprehensive summary of the profession and its history.

http://www.beyondintractability.org

> Interesting conflict resolution knowledge base with writings about mediation (see, e.g., http://www.beyondintractability.org/essay/mediation).

www.nolo.com/legal-encyclopedia/mediation

> Nolo's self-help summary of mediation and mediation processes.

www.jamsadr.com/adr-mediation

> Mediation defined by JAMS, the largest private alternative dispute resolution (ADR) provider in the world, specializing in mediating and arbitrating complex commercial disputes.

www.mediationinlaw.org

> The Center for Mediation in Law is a nonprofit dedicated to integrating mediation principles into the practice of law using a collaborative understanding-based model of conflict resolution.

EDUCATION AND TRAINING PROGRAMS

California State University, http://www.humboldt.edu/isadr/training.htm

Harvard Mediation Program, http://www.law.harvard.edu/academics/clinical/hmp/

Loyola Law School, http://www.lls.edu/ccr/training/index.html

Mediation Training Institute International, http://www.mediationworks.com

National Institute for Advanced Conflict Resolution, http://www.niacr.org (provides a list of mediation training programs per state).

Northwestern University, http://www.scs.northwestern.edu/pdp/npdp/mediation

University of South Florida, http://www.crc.usf.edu/

BLOGS

Anthony Cerminaro, *Mediation Mindset*, http://mediationmindset.blogspot.com

Directory of alternative dispute resolution blogs, www.adrblogs.com

Perry Itkin, http://floridamediator.blogspot.com

Tammy Lenski, http://makingmediationyourdayjob.com

Mediation Channel, http://mediationchannel.com/ (formerly the Online Guide to Mediation)

Mediation's Place, http://www.blogcatalog.com/blog/mediations-place

Geoff Sharp, http://mediatorblahblah.blogspot.com

ORGANIZATIONS

Association for Conflict Resolution, http://www.acresolution.org

CPR Institute for Dispute Resolution, http://www.cpradr.org

National Association for Community Mediation (NAFCM), http://www.nafcm.org

Victim Offender Mediation Association (VOMA), http://www.voma.org

MEDIATION LAW

Each state has its own laws and rules governing mediation and mediators. The Uniform Mediation Act is enacted in ten states: District of Columbia, Illinois, Iowa, Nebraska, Ohio, South Dakota, Utah, Vermont, and Washington. See: www.law.upenn.edu/bll/archives/ulc/mediat/2003finaldraft.htm

The American Bar Association (ABA) also publishes Model Standards of Conduct for Mediators. See: http://www.abanet.org/dispute/news/ModelStandardsofConductforMediatorsfinal05.pdf

TOPICAL AREAS OF MEDIATION

Criminal Law

Victim Offender Mediation Association, http://www.voma.org

Employment and Labor Law

N. DOHERTY & M. GUYLER, THE ESSENTIAL GUIDE TO WORKPLACE MEDIATION AND CONFLICT RESOLUTION: REBUILDING WORKING RELATIONSHIPS (Kogan Page, 2008).

Federal Mediation and Conciliation Service (Agency of U.S. government that handles arbitration and mediation of labor disputes and contract negotiations), www.fmcs.gov

Mediation and Training Institute International, workplace dispute mediation training, http://www.mediationworks.com

National Mediation Board, http://www.nmb.gov/mediation/faq-mediation .html

Family Law

JAY FOLBERG JD (ED.), ANN L. MILNE ACSW (ED.), & PETER SALEM, DIVORCE AND FAMILY MEDIATION: MODELS, TECHNIQUES, AND APPLICATIONS (Guilford Press, 2004).

K. STONER, DIVORCE WITHOUT COURT: A GUIDE TO MEDIATION & COLLABORATIVE DIVORCE (NOLO Press, 2009).

Intellectual Property Law

World Intellectual Property Organization Mediation Resources, http://www .wipo.int/amc/en/mediation

School Law

L. SENACA, A BRIEF ANNOTATED BIBLIOGRAPHY ON MEDIATION RESOURCES FOR UNIVERSITY ADMINISTRATORS (Illinois State University, 2004), at: http://www.deanofstudents.ilstu.edu/downloads/crr/conflict-resolution -annotated-bibliography.pdf

W. C. WARTERS, MEDIATION IN THE CAMPUS COMMUNITY: DESIGNING AND MANAGING EFFECTIVE PROGRAMS (Jossey Bass, 2008).

Elder Law

J. Bertschler, L. Meyer, & L. Elder Meyer, Mediation: A New Solution to Age-Old Problems (1st ed., NCS Publishing, 2009).

Business Law

Mediation and Dispute Resolution MBA program: Colorado Technical University: http://www.coloradotech.edu/Degree-Programs/master-degree-in-business-administration-mediation-and-dispute-resolution-mba.aspx

Major Types of Mediation

R. A. Baruch Bush & J. P. Folger, The Promise of Mediation: The Transformative Approach to Conflict (Jossey-Bass, 2004)

National Association for Community Mediation, www.nafcm.org.

J. Winslade & G. Monk, Narrative Mediation: A New Approach to Conflict Resolution (Jossey-Bass, 2004).

J. Winslade & G. D. Monk, Practicing Narrative Mediation: Loosening the Grip of Conflict (Jossey-Bass, 2008).

Z. Zumeta, Styles of Mediation: Facilitative, Evaluative, and Transformative Mediation (2001), http://www.mediate.com/articles/zumeta.cfm (February 8, 2010)

International/Intercultural

D. W. Ausberger, Conflict Mediation Across Cultures: Pathways and Patterns (Westminster/John Knox Press,1992).

J. Bercovitch & S. S. Gartner, International Conflict Mediation: New Approaches and Findings (Routledge, 2001).

International Academy of Mediators, www.iamed.org

International Mediation Institute, www.imimediation.org (see also the IMI-Mediation library: http://www.imimediation.org/mediation-library.html)

PLAIN LANGUAGE

WEBSITES

http://www.sec.gov/news/extra/handbook.htm

http://www.plainlanguagenetwork.org/stephens/intro.html

http://www.plainlanguagenetwork.org/Legal/lawdefn.html

http://www.plainlanguage.gov/examples/legal/index.cfm

http://www.plainlanguagenetwork.org/stephens/biblio.html

http://www.lawfoundation.net.au/information/writing/howto

POLITICS AND PEACEMAKING

BOOKS

SHARIF M ABDULLAH, CREATING A WORLD THAT WORKS FOR ALL (Berrett-Koehler Publishers, 1999).

PETER GABEL, THE BANK TELLER AND OTHER ESSAYS ON THE POLITICS OF MEANING (Acada Books, 2000).

POSITIVE PSYCHOLOGY RESOURCES

Books Marcus Buckingham, Go Put Your Strengths to Work (Free Press, 2007).

> Marcus Buckingham, formerly with Gallup and now an independent researcher, consultant, and speaker, shows how to take the generic talents identified by Strengthsfinder and turn them into specific, powerful, and emotionally captivating personal strengths statements. He provides a step-by-step approach to recrafting your work around your strengths, thereby benefiting both yourself and your enterprise.

Cameron & Lavine, Making the Impossible Possible: Leading Extraordinary Performance: The Rocky Flats Story (Berrett-Koehler Publishers, 2006).

> Very readable and a great introduction to Cameron's work over the years looking at the four quadrants of excellence that must co-exist, despite paradoxes, for outstanding organizational success.

Jane Dutton, Energize Your Workplace (Jossey-Bass, 2003).

> The why and the how of positive human relationships at work. If you ever get an opportunity to hear Jane Dutton, jump on it!

Carol Dweck, Self-Theories: Their Role in Personality, Motivation, and Development (Psychology Press, 2000).

CAROL DWECK, MINDSET: THE NEW PSYCHOLOGY OF SUCCESS (Ballantine Books, 2006).

Both of these books detail findings from Dweck's extensive research into two particular kinds of "me" beliefs—those that are growth oriented versus those that see causes as fixed in unchanging personal qualities. (If this sounds like her work drew inspiration from Selgiman's explanatory style work, she confirms that in one of these books.) *Mindset* is more for popular audiences; it's longer, written in a more conversational style, and cheaper. *Self-Theories*, however, is very readable, and I enjoyed the deeper insights into the actual studies she and her colleagues conducted.

JOHN GOTTMAN, THE RELATIONSHIP CURE (Three Rivers Press, 2002).

Gottman is the preeminent researcher on relationships, especially marriage. This is his presentation of his research applied to a broader array of relationships. Interestingly, the 5:1 positive-to-negative ratio for excellence discovered by Losada in relation to business teams also shows up here.

LUTHANS, YOUSSEF, & AVOLIO, PSYCHOLOGICAL CAPITAL (Oxford University Press, 2007).

Introduces the PsyCap construct—a composite of self-efficacy, hope, optimism, and resilience. Includes the 24-item questionnaire and information on the "micro-intervention" the authors have developed. The authors also discuss other possible components of PsyCap and future research directions. Includes comprehensive citations.

PETERSON & SELIGMAN, CHARACTER STRENGTHS AND VIRTUES (Oxford University Press, 2004)

This is the definitive work on the VIA character strengths. The first part of the book explains the approach that was taken in identifying this set of character strengths. The rest serves as a reference resource, with a chapter on each strength about the research, measures, correlates, and possible future directions on each of the strengths.

ROBERT QUINN, BUILDING THE BRIDGE AS YOU WALK ON IT (Jossey-Bass, 2004).

Phenomenal. Outstanding on leadership, but, as the stories in the book suggest, perhaps even more important to being a parent, friend, spouse, community member.

TOM RATH, VITAL FRIENDS (Gallup Press, 2006).

This is another Gallup book. Rath, describes Gallup's discoveries concerning the various roles friends can fulfill and how to use this information to be a better friend and to strengthen the web of friendships around you.

Tom Rath, Strengthsfinder 2.0 (Gallup Press, 2007).

This book explains and provides access to the most current version of Gallup's online tool for identification of their 34 talents that underlie our strongest strengths of action.

Barry Schwartz ,The Paradox of Choice (Ecco, 2004).

Are you generally a "maximizer" or "satisficer"? Should you care? Good book not only for consumers, but for achievers. Because nothing's ever "finished," what does "do your best" mean?

Seligman, Learned Optimism (Free Press, 1991).

More depth on explanatory style as a construct and the research behind it than is provided in the more recent Authentic Happiness.

Seligman, The Optimistic Child (Harper Paperbacks, 1995).

In addition to research insights and suggestions on the question of how children develop their explanatory styles, this book has one of the best explanations of the "ABCDE" technique, a key component of moving to a more flexible, accurate style.

Shatté & Reivich, The Resilience Factor: 7 Essential Skills for Overcoming Life's Inevitable Obstacles (Broadway, 2002).

Practical, practical, practical. How to apply the insights.

George Vaillant, Aging Well (Little, Well, 2002).

Reports on multiple, longitudinal studies now under the administration of Vaillant. Science, yes, but also uplifting and hopeful. The importance of relationships is emphasized by these studies.

PREVENTIVE LAW

BOOKS

THOMAS D. BARTON, Preventive Law and Problem Solving: Lawyering for the Future (Vandeplas, 2009).

LOUIS MORRIS BROWN, PREVENTIVE LAW (Greenwood Press, 1970).

WEBSITES

The National Center for Preventive Law at California Western School of Law, http://www.preventivelawyer.org

The Nordic School of Proactive Law, http://www.proactivelaw.org/

http://www.brucewinick.com/

> This is the website for Bruce Winick, a pioneer of therapeutic jurisprudence, who also looks at the integration of preventive law with therapeutic jurisprudence concepts.

PROBLEM-SOLVING COURTS

BOOKS AND BOOKLETS

GREG BERMAN, JOHN FEINBLATT, & SARAH GLAZER, GOOD COURTS: THE CASE FOR PROBLEM-SOLVING JUSTICE (New Press, June 27, 2005).

Greg Berman, Aubrey Fox, & Robert V. Wolf, A Problem-Solving Revolution: Making Change Happen in State Courts (1st ed., Center for Court Innovation, Jan. 2004).

NATHANIEL T. W. FOLKEMER, ROADMAPS: PROBLEM SOLVING COURTS (ABA Coalition for Justice, Mar. 2008). Downloadable at: http://www.abanet.org/justice/roadmaps.html

The booklet provides information and additional contacts, resources, and websites.

Paul Higgins & Mitchell Mackinem, Eds., Problem-Solving Courts: Justice for the 21st Century? (Praeger, 2009).

This work is referenced at the Center for Court Innovation website; while not found through Google or Amazon, I did locate it on the publisher's website: http://www.greenwood.com/catalog/C35284.aspx.

C. WEST HUDDLESTON, DOUGLAS B. MARLOWE, & RACHEL CASEBOLT, PAINTING THE CURRENT PICTURE: A NATIONAL REPORT CARD ON DRUG COURTS AND OTHER PROBLEM-SOLVING COURT

PROGRAMS IN THE UNITED STATES (National Drug Court Institute, U.S. Department of Justice Bureau of Justice, May 2008).

Prepared by the National Drug Court Institute, the education, research, and scholarship affiliate of the National Association of Drug Court Professionals. Downloadable. Available at the National Drug Court Institute website: www.ndci .org/publications/publication-resources/painting-current-picture, and National Criminal Justice Reference Service site www.ncjrs.gov, administered by the U.S. Department of Justice (USDOJ). Both sites have other information and material of interest.

MICHAEL KING, ARIE FREIBERG, BECKY BATAGOL & ROSS HYAMS, NON-ADVERSARIAL JUSTICE (Federation Press, 2009).

JOANN MILLER & DONALD C. JOHNSON, PROBLEM SOLVING COURTS: NEW APPROACHES TO CRIMINAL JUSTICE (Princeton University Press, Apr. 20, 2009).

JAMES L. NOLAN, LEGAL ACCENTS, LEGAL BORROWING: THE INTERNATIONAL PROBLEM-SOLVING COURT MOVEMENT (Princeton University Press, Apr. 20, 2009).

RESEARCH STAFF, DOCUMENTING RESULTS: RESEARCH ON PROBLEM-SOLVING JUSTICE FROM THE CENTER FOR COURT INNOVATION (1st ed., Center for Court Innovation, Jan. 2007).

ARTICLES

America's Problem Solving Courts: The Criminal Costs of Treatment and the Case for Reform, 2009. National Association of Criminal Defense Lawyers Problem-Solving Courts Task Force Report (2009).

For information about the Task Force and a link to the report, see http://www .nacdl.org/drugcourts

Natasha Bakht, *Problem Solving Courts as Agents of Change*, 500 CRIM. L. Q. 224 (2005).

Pamela M. Casey & David B. Rottman, *Problem-Solving Courts: Models and Trends*, (2005). Downloadable. http://www.ncsconline.org/WC/Publica tions/COMM_ProSolProbSolvCtsPub.pdf

Michael C. Dorf & Charles F. Sabel, *Drug Treatment Courts and Emergent Experimentalist Government*, 53 VAND. L. REV. 831 (2000).

The authors argue that problem-solving courts, being experimental in nature, have the potential to reform the courts without imposing the heavy burden that usually comes from court-ordered reform, in an attempt to make the courts more efficient while still continuing to protect the constitutional values entrusted to the judiciary.

Hon. Peggy Fulton Hora, Hon. William G. Schma, & John T. A. Rosenthal, *Therapeutic Jurisprudence and the Drug Treatment Court Movement: Revolutionizing the Criminal Justice System's Response to Drug Abuse and Crime in America*, 74 NOTRE DAME L. REV.439 (1999).

The purpose of this article is to look at therapeutic jurisprudence and use it to examine drug treatment courts (DTCs). Topics covered: Therapeutic Jurisprudence (definition, history, and literature); DTC Movement; Problems and Concerns Confronting DTCs; Recommendations.

Judith S. Kaye, Delivering Justice Today: A Problem-Solving Approach, 22 YALE L. & POL'Y REV. 125 (Winter, 2004).

Michael S. King, *Non-Adversarial Justice and the Coroner's Court: A Proposed Therapeutic, Restorative, Problem-Solving Model*, 16 J. LAW MED. 442 (2008) 442.

David Rottman & Pamela Casey, Therapeutic Jurisprudence and the Emergence of Problem-Solving Courts, 240 NAT'L INST. JUST. J. 12 (July 1999).

David Rottman & Pamela Casey, *Therapeutic Jurisprudence and the Emergence of Problem-Solving Courts,* 240 NAT'L INST. JUST. J. 12–19 (July 1999). Downloadable: http://www.floridatac.org/files/document/Res_ProSol_TJ ProbSolvCrtNIJPub.pdf

Ronald J. Rychlak, *From the Classroom to the Courtroom: Therapeutic Justice and the Gaming Industry's Impact on Law*, 74 MISS. L.J. 827 (2005).

This article discusses the use of gambling treatment courts and drug courts, and the value of therapeutic jurisprudence in examining the problems that stem from the "medically-recognized mental disorder of pathological gambling."

Neil Websdale, PhD; Judge Michael Town: & Byron Johnson, PhD, *Domestic Violence Fatality Reviews: From a Culture of Blame to a Culture of Safety,* 50 JUV. & FAM. CT. JUST. J. 61 (Spring 1999). Downloadable: www.ndvfri.org (please click on publications and scroll down).

Bruce J. Winick, *Therapeutic Jurisprudence and Problem Solving Courts*, 30 FORDHAM URB. L.J. 1055 (2003).

In this article, Winick proposes that problem solving courts and therapeutic jurisprudence "can be seen as having a symbiotic relationship. Together, they can do much to transform law into an instrument of healing for both the individual and the community."

This article discusses drug treatment courts and mental health courts as solutions for the difficulties that faced the criminal justice system.

Nancy Neal Yeend, *Tips for Facilitating Problem-Solving Court Teams*, 48 THE JUDGE'S J. 2 (Spring 2009).

SPECIAL ISSUES

30 FORDHAM URB. L.J. (March 1, 2003) [Special Issue on Problem Solving Courts and Therapeutic Jurisprudence.]

Articles included:

Eric Lane, *Due Process and Problem-Solving Courts.*

Greg Berman, & Anne Gulick, *Just the (Unwieldy, Hard to Gather, But Nonetheless Essential) Facts, Ma'am: What We Know And Don't Know about Problem-Solving Courts.*

Phylis Skloot Bamberger, *Specialized Courts: Not A Cure-All.*

Jeffrey Fagan & Victoria Malkin, *Theorizing Community Justice Through Community Courts.*

Bruce J. Winick, *Therapeutic Jurisprudence and Problem Solving Courts.*

40 AM. CRIM. L. REV. (Fall 2003) [Special issue on community courts and community.]

Articles included (some available online):

James Nolan, Jr., *Redefining Criminal Courts: Problem Solving and the Meaning of Justice.*

Vicoria Malkin, *Community Courts and the Process of Accountability: Consensus and Conflict at the Red Hook Community Justice Center.*

Jane M. Spinack, *Why Defenders Feel Defensive: The Defender's Role in Problem Solving Courts.*

41 AM. CRIM. L. REV. (Summer 2003) [Special issue on community courts and community justice.]

Articles included (some available online):

Greg Berman, *Comment: Redefining Criminal Courts: Problem Solving and the Meaning of Justice.*

Michael Dorf and Jeffrey A. Fagan, *Community Courts and Community Justice: Foreword: Problem-Solving Courts: from Innovation to Institutionalization.*

Candace McCoy, *Community Courts and Community Justice: Commentary: The Politics of Problem Solving: An Overview of the Origins and Development of Therapeutic Courts.*

Laurie O. Robinson, *Community Courts and Community Justice: Commentary.*

23 LAW & PUB. POL'Y 2 (April 2001) [Special issue on drug courts.]

Articles included (available in full text through www.ebscohost.com):

Jeffrey A. Butts, *Introduction: Problem-Solving Courts.*

Greg Berman & John Feinblatt, *Problem-Solving Courts: A Brief Primer.* Downloadable. http://lawcourses.haifa.ac.il/ADR/index/main/syllabus/files/berman.pdf

OTHER ARTICLES

Articles available at the Center for Court Innovation website,

www.problemsolvingjustice.org or www.courtinnovation.org

Donald J. Farole, Jr., Nora Puffett, Michael Rempel, & Francine Byrne, *Applying Problem-Solving Principles in Mainstream Courts: Lessons for State Courts,* 2005.

Robert V. Wolf, *Breaking with Tradition: Introducing Problem Solving in Conventional Courts,* 2007.

Robert V. Wolf, *Don`t Reinvent the Wheel: Lessons from Problem-Solving Courts,* 2007.

Robert V. Wolf, *Principles of Problem-Solving Justice,* 2007.

WEBSITES

http://www.problemsolvingjustice.org

http://www.courtinnovation.org

The Center for Court Innovation site provides links to resources, fact sheets, publications, and sample documents for use in problem-solving courts to help practitioners interested in applying problem-solving techniques more widely at the local level. It is accessible at either e-address.

http://www.cuttingedgelaw.com

Cutting Edge Law explores all aspects of a "new paradigm of law practice," through a wide variety of media and resources. It has blogs, news feeds, videos, podcasts, editorials, law review articles, and links to many, many more resources.

http://www.ojp.usdoj.gov/BJA/grant/cb_problem_solving.html

The Bureau of Justice Assistance Community-Based Problem-Solving Criminal Justice Initiative website has a wealth of resources.

http://www.ncsconline.org/WC/CourTopics/ResourceGuide.
asp?topic=ProSol

The National Center for State Courts has a Resource Guide.

tjsp@topica.com

The e-mail discussion list for therapeutic jurisprudence and specialized-problem-solving courts. It is an international discussion group comprised of judges, court professionals, and researchers/academics involved with therapeutic jurisprudence and problem-solving courts.

Several law review articles are available at www.amazon.com, using "problem-solving courts" as the search terms.

The ABA site has several of ethics opinions relating to problem solving courts, primarily relating to fundraising by judges for them.

PROCEDURAL JUSTICE

BOOKS

E. ALLEN LIND & TOM R. TYLER, THE SOCIAL PSYCHOLOGY OF PROCEDURAL JUSTICE (Springer, 1988).

JOHN RAWLS, JUSTICE AS FAIRNESS: A RESTATEMENT (Belknap Press of Harvard University Press, 2001).

JOHN RAWLS, A THEORY OF JUSTICE (Belknap Press of Harvard University Press, 2005).

Websites

http://en.wikipedia.org/wiki/Procedural_justice

The Wikipedia.org page for preventive law.

BLOGS

http://lsolum.typepad.com/legaltheory/2009/08/legal-theory-lexicon-procedural-justice.html

The Legal Theory Blog's entry on procedural justice.

PURPOSE

BOOKS

KEVIN HOUCHIN, FUEL THE SPARK, 5 GUIDING VALUES FOR SUCCESS IN LAW & LIFE (MadeEasy Publishing, 2009).

TIM KELLEY, True Purpose, 12 Strategies for Discovering the Difference You Are Meant to Make (Transcendant Solutions Press, 2009).

RESTORATIVE JUSTICE

BOOKS

Kimmett Edgar, Tim Newell, & Erwin James (Foreword), Restorative Justice in Prisons: A Guide to Making It Happen (Waterside Press, 2006).

LAWRENCE W. SHERMAN, & HEATHER STRANG, RESTORATIVE JUSTICE: THE EVIDENCE (The Smith Institute, 2007); http://www.smith-institute.org.uk/publications/restorative_justice_the-evidence.htm

HEATHER STRANG & JOHN BRAITHWAITE, EDS., Restorative Justice and Family Violence, (Cambridge University Press, 2002).

D. SULLIVAN, The Handbook of Restorative Justice: A Global Perspective (Routledge International Handbooks, 2006).

HOWARD ZEHR, THE LITTLE BOOK OF RESTORATIVE JUSTICE (Good Books, 1969).

HOWARD ZEHR, CHANGING LENSES: A NEW FOCUS FOR CRIME AND JUSTICE (Herald Press, 1990).

Howard Zehr's classic work is the best introduction to the concepts of restorative justice.

There is a whole series of "Little Books" published by Good Books, http://www.goodbks.com. Written by the experts and leaders of the movement, they are short, concise, and very informative paperbacks.

> Lorraine Amstutz, The Little Book of Restorative Discipline for Schools.
>
> Lorraine Amstutz, The Little Book of Victim Offender Conferencing: Bringing Victims and Offenders Together in Dialogue.
>
> David Brubaker, The Little Book of Healthy Organizations: Tools for Understanding and Transforming Your Organization.
>
> Jayne Docherty, The Little Book of Strategic Negotiation: Negotiating During Turbulent Times.
>
> Ron Kraybill, The Little Book of "Cool Tools for Hot Topics": Group Tools to Facilitate Meetings When Things Are Hot.
>
> John Paul Lederach, The Little Book of Conflict Transformation.
>
> Allan MacRae, The Little Book of Family Group Conferences.
>
> Chris Marshall, The Little Book of Biblical Justice .
>
> Kay Pranis, The Little Book of Circle Processes: A New/Old Approach to Peacemaking.
>
> Lisa Schirch, The Little Book of Dialogue for Difficult Subjects: A Practical, Hands-On Guide.
>
> Lisa Schirch, The Little Book of Strategic Peacebuilding.
>
> Barb Toews, The Little Book of Restorative Justice for People in Prison: Rebuilding the Web of Relationships.
>
> Carolyn Yoder, The Little Book of Trauma Healing.

Articles

William Bradshaw & David Roseborough, *Restorative Justice Dialogue: The Impact of Mediation and Conferencing on Juvenile Recidivism*, 69-DEC Fed. Probation 15 (2005).

> This article analyzes the rehabilitation and retributive approaches for dealing with juvenile offenses and argues that there is little evidence that these methods reduce recidivism—and further that these methods neglect the needs of victims. The article claims that restorative justice processes hold the offender accountable and "promotes the support and reintegration of the victim and offender into the community." Topics covered: Types of Restorative Justice Dialogue Programs; Benefits of Restorative Interventions; Studies Done.

Stephen P. Carvey, *Restorative Justice, Punishment, and Atonement*, 2003 Utah L. Rev. 303 (2002).

> Discusses the role of punishment in restorative justice. Carvey argues that punishment should not be eliminated from the restorative justice approach—that it is a necessary component to repairing the wrong suffered by the victim. Rather than eliminate punishment, Carvey argues that restorative justice "insists on its transformation." He claims that when the restorative justice processes work as they are intended to, the offender "realizes the full extent of the damage he has done." "Moreover, because that burden is assumed willingly, it's no longer a punishment; it has been transformed into a secular penance, the performance of which sets the state for the reconciliation between, and the atonement of, offender and victim."

Allison Morris, *Critiquing the Critics: A Brief Response to Critics of Restorative Justice*, 32 Brit. J. Criminology 596 (2002).

> This article attempts to respond to criticisms of restorative justice and draws from research to come to the conclusion that "there are reasons to be relatively positive about the re-emergence of restorative justice."

Megan Stephens, *Lessons From the Front Lines in Canada's Restorative Justice Experiment: The Experience of Sentencing Judges*, 33 Queen's L.J. 19 (2007).

> Stephens "explores the impact of Canada's 1996 sentencing reforms, which explicitly incorporated restorative justice principles into the criminal sentencing process." She then "proposes a 'new governance' approach to facilitating the incorporation of restorative justice principles into the traditional criminal justice system."

Michael Town, *Island Voices: Restorative Justice Helps the Victim Become Whole Again*, Honolulu Advertiser, May 3, 2000, available at http://the.honoluluadvertiser.com/2000/May/03/opinion13.html

Michael Town, *Are Domestic Violence Death Reviews Consistent with Concepts of Preventive, Therapeutic and Restorative Justice?* Fatality Rev. Bull. (National Domestic Violence Fatality Review Initiative, Summer 2002), available at www.ndvfri.org; please click on newsletter link and scroll to article.

Mark S. Umbreit, Robert B. Coates, & Betty Vos, *The Impact of Victim-Offender Mediation: Two Decades of Research*, 65-DEC Fed. Probation 29 (2001).

> This article claims that 20 years of research data about victim–offender mediation has shown that participants tend to be very satisfied with the process, that they see the system as fair, that restitution plays a big role, that it decreases recidivism, and that it is less costly.

Mark S. Umbreit, Betty Vos, Robert B. Coates, & Elizabeth Lightfoot, *Restorative Justice: An Empirically Grounded Movement Facing Many Opportunities and Pitfalls*, 8 CARDOZO J. CONFLICT RESOL. 511 (2007).

This article provides an overview of the restorative justice movement in the twenty-first century. In Section II the authors offer a summary of the movement's distinguishing characteristics, its history and development, and what it looks like in practice. Section III is focused on restorative justice dialogue, the most widely practiced and extensively researched modality of the restorative justice movement. The authors present a review of current restorative justice dialogue research and an examination of public policy support for such dialogue across the United States. In Section IV the authors turn to continuing issues, including pitfalls, opportunities, and questions for the future.

Howard J. Vogel, *The Restorative Justice Wager: The Promise and Hope of a Value-Based, Dialogue-Driven Approach to Conflict Resolution for Social Healing*, 8 CARDOZO J. CONFLICT RESOL. 565 (2007).

A comprehensive introduction to restorative justice. "Part I explores the definition of restorative justice in a criminal context and beyond in order to set up the discussion of the restorative justice wager and the possibilities for healing presented by restorative justice dialogue that are taken up in Part II. In Part II, extended discussion is devoted to peacemaking circles, one of the four major forms of restorative justice. . .Part III offers a suggestion for the next step in constructing a relational theory of restorative justice and conflict resolution with the help of the principle of internal relations."

Lode Walgrave, *Restoration in Youth Justice*, 31 CRIME & JUST. 543 (2004).

This essay describes "how restorative practices have been included in existing juvenile justice systems and [explores] the potential of the restorative justice approach."

WEBSITES

http://www.restorativejustice.org/

This is the flagship of sites about restorative justice. With approximately 10,000 documents, it is a virtual library of information about restorative justice around the world. "Restorative Justice Online is a service of the Prison Fellowship International Centre for Justice and Reconciliation. Its purpose is to be an authoritative, credible, non-partisan resource of information on restorative justice."

http://www.ojp.usdoj.gov/nij/topics/courts/restorative-justice/welcome.htm

The U.S. Department of Justice overview of restorative justice.

http://ojjdp.ncjrs.org/PUBS/implementing/contents.html

>Guide for Implementing the Balanced and Restorative Justice Model, a project funded by the Office of Juvenile Justice and Delinquency Prevention (OJJDP) to Florida Atlantic University.

http://www.esmeefairbairn.org.uk/docs/RJ_exec_summary.pdf

>*Restorative Justice, The Evidence*; an independent report examining the evidence on restorative justice (RJ) from Britain and around the world.

http://www.abanet.org/crimjust/policy/my09101b.pdf

>The 2009 American Bar Association Criminal Justice Section Report to the House of Delegates Recommendation to expand mediation in criminal cases.

TRAINING PROGRAMS

Real Justice, a program of the International Institute for Restorative Practices, http://www.realjustice.org/

Just Alternatives, http://justalternatives.org/

UNIVERSITY AND LAW SCHOOL RESTORATIVE JUSTICE PROGRAMS

Campbell Law School, http://law.campbell.edu/pubs/jjp.html

Eastern Mennonite University, http://www.emu.edu/

Fresno Pacific Center for Peacemaking and Conflict Studies, http://peace.fresno.edu/

International Institute for Restorative Practices (IIRP), http://www.iirp.org/

Marquette Law School, http://law.marquette.edu/cgi-bin/site.pl?2130&pageID=1831

Northeastern University Law School Civil Rights and Restorative Justice Project, http://www.northeastern.edu/crrj/

St. Mary's Law School Restorative Justice Initiative, http://www.stmarytxrji.org/

Suffolk University the Center for Restorative Justice, http://www.suffolk.edu/college/1496.html

University of Colorado at Boulder, http://www.colorado.edu/studentaffairs/judicialaffairs/restjust.html

University of Minnesota (in collaboration with the Center for Restorative Justice and Peacemaking), http://www.cehd.umn.edu/ssw/rjp/

University of Wisconsin School of Law, http://www.law.wisc.edu/fjr/clinicals/rjp.html

BLOGS

Howard Zehr, http://emu.edu/blog/restorative-justice/

ORGANIZATIONS

Victim Offender Mediation Association (VOMA), http://www.voma.org

VIDEOS

Howard Zehr on the Continuum of Restorativeness, http://www.youtube.com/watch?v=2KXwnbsQUrI

Restorative Justice: Victim Offender Mediation Overview by Mark Umbreit, http://www.youtube.com/watch?v=IC2aBPISDno

Beyond Conviction, previously broadcast on MSNBC, an award-winning documentary, can be purchased at: http://www.beyondconviction.com/buy.htm

The Center for Restorative Justice and Mediation, University of Minnesota, has six videos available on its website. The Center can be contacted at 612/624-4923 or ctr4rjm@che2.che.umn.edu. Cost is $20 each, or all six for $100. The titles are:

- *Restorative Justice: For Victims, Communities, and Offenders*
- *Restorative Justice: Victim Empowerment through Mediation and Dialogue*
- *An Overview of Victim Offender Mediation and Conferencing*
- *Victim Offender Mediation and Conferencing: A Multi-Method Approach*
- *Complete Victim Offender Mediation and Conferencing Training: Modeling 2 Cases from Preparation to Mediation*
- *Victim Sensitive Offender Dialogue in Crimes of Severe Violence*

SPIRITUALITY
AND LAW

Books

Joseph G. Allegretti, The Lawyer's Calling: Christian Faith
and Legal Practice (Paulist Press, 1996).

J. Gary Gwilliam, Getting a Winning Verdict in My Personal Life:
A Trial Lawyer Finds His Soul (Pavior Publishing, 2007).

David Hall, The Spiritual Revitalization of the Legal Profession: A
Search for Sacred Rivers (Edwin Mellen Press, 2005).

Steven Keeva, Transforming Practices: Finding Joy and Satisfaction
in the Legal Life (McGraw-Hill, 2002).

Pat McHenry Sullivan, Work with Meaning, Work with Joy:
Bringing Your Spirit to Any Job (Sheed & Ward, 2003).

Articles

Charles Senger, Spirituality in Law School, Mich. B.J. (Dec. 2002).
http://www.michbar.org/journal/pdf/pdf4article518.pdf

Thomas Shaffer, *A Search for Balance in the Whirlwind of Law School:
Spirituality From Law Teachers*, Workshop, Association for American Law Schools (2006), http://www.aals.org/am2006/program/
balance/ShafferSpirituality.pdf.

WEBSITES

http://www.mediate.com/acrspirituality/

> The Association for Conflict Resolution's Spirituality Section: "The mission of the Spirituality Section is to transform conflict into peace through a deeper understanding of the essential unity of all beings." The section seeks to provide a professional community to supports its members in expressing their vision in their practices, their careers and their lives. The Spirituality Section's web page contains contact information and resources.

http://www.spiritlawpolitics.org/

> The Project for Integrating Spirituality, Law and Politics.

http://www.workwithmeaningandjoy.com/

> Pat Sullivan's program for balancing spirituality and the workplace.

VIDEO

http://www.cuttingedgelaw.com/video/sharif-abdullah-creating-world-works-all

> Sharif Abdullah shares his background and thoughts on how our actions affect the world.

http://www.cuttingedgelaw.com/video/peter-gabel-integrating-law-politics-and-spirituality

> An interview with Peter Gabel, co-founder of the Project for Integrating Spirituality, Law and Politics.

http://www.cuttingedgelaw.com/video/professor-rhonda-magee-challenging-norms-and-doctrines

> Rhonda Magee discusses belief systems and the law.

THERAPEUTIC JURISPRUDENCE

BOOKS

MICHAEL S. KING, SOLUTION-FOCUSED JUDGING BENCH BOOK (Australian Institute of Judicial Administration, 2010).

> Among other things, the bench book analyzes key components of therapeutic jurisprudence (TJ) and problem-solving courts; discusses nonadversarial justice in brief; analyzes the elements of solution-focused judging; has two chapters devoted to judicial communication and listening skills; covers TJ strategies to be used in court; explores the mechanisms of positive behavioral change and the stages of judicial engagement with participants in court; has a chapter on how TJ/ solution-focused judging can be applied in mainstream courts; and explores the professional and personal challenges to judging in this manner and suggests strategies that individual judicial officers and the court itself can use to address them. The Chief Justice of Australia, Robert French wrote the foreword for the bench book. A pdf copy of the bench book is available for download without charge from: http:// www.aija.org.au/Solution%20Focused%20BB/SFJ%20BB.pdf.

BRUCE J. WINICK AND DAVID B. WEXLER, EDS.,JUDGING IN A THERAPEUTIC KEY: THERAPEUTIC JURISPRUDENCE AND THE COURTS (Carolina Academic Press, 2003).

HOWARD ZEHR AND BARB TOEWS, EDS., CRITICAL ISSUES IN RESTORATIVE JUSTICE (Criminal Justice Press, June 2004).

WEB RESOURCES

http://www.law.arizona.edu/depts/upr-intj/intj-o.html
> David Wexler, one of the leading academicians on TJ wrote this introductory piece on therapeutic jurisprudence.

www.therapeuticjurisprudence.org
> This is the primary website for therapeutic jurisprudence.

The Australasian Therapeutic Jurisprudence Clearinghouse, http://www.aija .org.au/index.php?option=com_content&task=view&id=206&Itemid=103

http://www.law.arizona.edu/depts/upr-intj/
> Subscriptions to a listserv for TJ professionals.

ARTICLES

Ingrid Loreen, *Therapeutic Jurisprudence and the Law School Asylum Clinic*, 17 ST. THOMAS L. REV. 835 (2005).
> "This paper will explore how law school clinics in general, and asylum clinics in particular, can prepare students for healthier, more satisfied careers in the law by introducing them to one of the comprehensive law movements which has gained popularity in the last decades. By understanding the effects of trauma on their clients and by explicitly addressing issues of empathy, emotional intelligence, and cross-cultural communication, law school clinics, which already complement the traditional legal curriculum in significant ways, will improve and enrich the experience for both the client and the law student."

Ronald J. Rychlak, *From the Classroom to the Courtroom: Therapeutic Justice and the Gaming Industry's Impact on Law*, 74 MISS. L.J. 827 (2005).
> This article discusses the use of Gambling treatment courts, drug courts, and the value of therapeutic jurisprudence in examining the problems that stem from the "medically-recognized mental disorder of pathological gambling."

Michael Town, *The Unified Family Court: Preventive, Therapeutic and Restorative Justice for America's Families and Children*, (Spring 2001), National Center for Preventive Law (California Western School of Law); reprinted in A.B.A. CHILD LAW PRAC. 99 (September 2002) and JUV. FAM. JUST. TODAY (NCJFCJ Winter 2002). Available at http://www.preventivelawyer. org/main/default.asp?pid=essays/town.htm

Michael Town, *Court as Convener and Provider of Therapeutic Justice*, 67 UNIV. P.R. L. REV. 671 (1998) (available in English and Spanish on request).

David B. Wexler, *Reflections on the Scope of Therapeutic Jurisprudence*, 1 Psychol. Pub. Pol'y & L. 220 (1995).

> This article in therapeutic jurisprudence (the study of the role of the law as a
> therapeutic agent) looks at the appropriate scope of the terms *therapeutic* and
> *jurisprudence*. The questions considered are: What is meant by therapeutic? Ther-
> apeutic for whom? What is meant by law? What substantive areas of law should
> be involved? Should the unit of legal analysis be micro (e.g., a particular rule of
> law) or macro (e.g., a body of law)?

David B. Wexler, *Some Thoughts and Observations on the Teaching of Therapeutic Jurisprudence*, 35 Rev. Der. P.R. 273 (1996).

> This article is based on a lecture delivered at the School of Law of the Pontifi-
> cal Catholic University of Puerto Rico and discusses the concept of therapeutic
> jurisprudence; Wexler's book, Law in a Therapeutic Key: Developments
> in Therapeutic Jurisprudence; and how to structure a law school course on
> therapeutic jurisprudence.

David B. Wexler, *Two Decades of Therapeutic Jurisprudence*, 24 Touro L. Rev.
17 (2008).

> "This essay explores the therapeutic jurisprudence movement from theory to
> practice and the role of lawyers and judges as therapeutic agents. An overview
> of the history of therapeutic jurisprudence is given, followed by a discussion of
> the major developments of therapeutic jurisprudence from its inception to the
> present—a span of approximately twenty years."

Bruce J. Winick, *The Jurisprudence of Therapeutic Jurisprudence*, 3 Psychol.
Pub. Pol'y & L. 184 (1997).

> "In this essay, one of the founders of this new field offers a further elabora-
> tion of the theory of therapeutic jurisprudence and a response to the key issues
> raised by commentators and critics. This essay discusses the relationship between
> therapeutic jurisprudence and other schools of jurisprudence and analyzes the
> approach's normative focus and its limits. It also addresses how 'therapeutic'
> should be defined, whether the approach is paternalistic, whether the limits of
> social science methodology doom the enterprise, how therapeutic and other
> potentially conflicting values can be reconciled, and how the law should respond
> when such conflicts persist. Finally, the essay charts the path of therapeutic juris-
> prudence and analyzes new developments in the field."

Bruce J. Winick, *Therapeutic Jurisprudence and Problem Solving Courts*, 30
Fordham Urb. L.J. 1055 (2003).

> In this article, Winick proposes that problem solving courts and therapeutic
> jurisprudence "can be seen as having a symbiotic relationship. Together, they can
> do much to transform law into an instrument of healing for both the individual
> and the community."

TRANSFORMATIVE MEDIATION

BOOKS

R. A. B. BUSH AND J. P. FOLGER, THE PROMISE OF MEDIATION: THE TRANSFORMATIVE APPROACH TO CONFLICT (2d ed., Jossey-Bass, 2005).

MORTON DEUTSCH, PETER T. COLEMAN, & ERIC C. MARCUS, EDS., THE HANDBOOK OF CONFLICT RESOLUTION (Jossey-Bass, 2006).

J. P. FOLGER & R. A. B. BUSH, EDS., DESIGNING MEDIATION: APPROACHES TO TRAINING AND PRACTICE WITHIN A TRANSFORMATIVE FRAMEWORK (Institute for the Study of Conflict Transformation, 2001).

J. P. FOLGER & T. JONES, EDS., NEW DIRECTIONS IN MEDIATION (Sage Publications, 1994).

L. KRIESBERG, T. NORTHRUP, & S. THORSON, EDS., INTRACTABLE CONFLICTS AND THEIR TRANSFORMATIONS (Syracuse University Press, 1989).

S. KREISBERG, TRANSFORMING POWER: DOMINATION, EMPOWERMENT, AND EDUCATION (State University of New York Press, 1992).

J. P. LEDERACH, PREPARING FOR PEACE: CONFLICT TRANSFORMATION ACROSS CULTURES (Syracuse University Press, 1995).

T. PAFFENHOLZ, DESIGNING TRANSFORMATION AND INTERVENTION PROCESSES (Published in German in 2004, now available in translation at http://berghof-handbook.net/articles/preface-introduction/).

EDWARD SCHWERIN, MEDIATION, CITIZEN EMPOWERMENT, AND TRANSFORMATIONAL POLITICS (Praeger, 1995).

R. VAYRYNEN, New Directions in Conflict Theory: Conflict Resolution and Conflict Transformation (Sage Publications, 1991).

ACADEMIC PAPERS

L. Diamond, *Beyond Win/Win: The Heroic Journey of Conflict Transformation*, Occasional Paper Number 4 (The Institute for Multi-Track Diplomacy, 1994).

R. J. Donaghy, *Empowerment through Conflict: Understanding Transformative Mediation through the Theory of Partial Agency*, Paper presented at the annual meeting of the NCA 93rd Annual Convention, Chicago, IL, 2007. See: http://www.allacademic.com/meta/p192246_index.html

ARTICLES AND ESSAYS

Glenna Gerard & Linda Teurfs, *Dialogue and Organizational Transformation*, in COMMUNITY SPIRIT: RENEWING SPIRIT AND LEARNING IN BUSINESS 143–53 (New Leaders Press, 1995).

J. A. Tyson, *Victim Offender Mediation: A Field Study of the Transformative Theory of Mediation* (Dissertation Abstracts International, 2004).

WEBSITES

Beyond Intractability, Essay on Transformative Mediation: http://www.beyond intractability.org/essay/transformative_mediation

Conflict Resolution Consortium, Essay on Transformative Mediation: http://www.colorado.edu/conflict/transform/tmall.htm

Transformative Tools: A Toolkit for Transformative Mediation, Association for Conflict Resolution, http://acrnet.org/acrlibrary/more.php?id=33_0 _1_0_M

University of Colorado's Conflict Information Consortium's summary for transformative mediation, http://www.colorado.edu/conflict/transform/ tmall.htm

David C. Peterson, *Transformative Mediation Styles That Work in Ligitative and Commercial Settings*, http://www.sbcadre.org/articles/detail.asp?artID=75

S. Pope, *Transformative Mediation: Reviewing the Basics* (2005), http://www .mediate.com/articles/popeSG2.cfm

B. Spangler, *Transformative Mediation*, Beyond Intractability Knowledgebase Essay (2003), http://www.beyondintractability.org/essay/transformative _mediation

Transformative mediation in the U.S. Postal Service, http://www.usps.com/ redress/a_trans.htm

TRAINING

The Transformative Practice Institute at Hofstra Law School, http://law.hof stra.edu/academics/Programs/Skills/skills_summer_skills_institute.html

Transformative Mediation Institute, http://www.transformative-mediation .com/training

University of North Dakota, Institute for the Study of Conflict Transformation, http://www.transformativemediation.org

BLOGS

Transformative Mediation Institute Blog, http://www.transformative-media tion.com/training/mod/oublog/view.php?user=1

Dialogic Mediation Blog, http://dialogicmediation.com/2009/09/03/more-on -listening-like-a-cow/

ORGANIZATIONS

Institute for the Study of Conflict Transformation, http://law.hofstra.edu/
academics/institutesandcenters/ISCT/isct_transformative.html and http://
www.transformativemediation.org

Transformative Mediation Institute, http://www.transformative-mediation
.com

VIDEOS

Dan Simon on Transformative Mediation, http://www.cuttingedgelaw.com/
video/dan-simon-transformative-mediation

UNBUNDLING

BOOK

Mosten, F. S. *Unbundling Legal Services: A Guide to Delivering Legal Services à la Carte.* Chicago: American Bar Association, Law Practice Management Section, 2000.

Articles

Mosten, F. S. "Unbundling Legal Services: Servicing Clients Within Their Ability to Pay." *American Bar Association Judge's Journal,* Winter 2001, p. 15.

Mosten, F. S. "Peacemaking Can Be Your Day Job." *SPIDR Newsletter,* 2000, *24*(1/2), 1.

Mosten, F. S. "Unbundled Legal Services in Mediation." *ADR Report,* Nov. 1999.

Mosten, F. S. "Unbundling Your Mediation Services." *ADR Report,* 1999, *3*(25), 3–6.

Website:

http://www.unbundledlaw.org/

VICARIOUS TRAUMA

BOOKS

ELLIE IZZO & VICKI CARPEL MILLER, DAY TO DAY THE PRICE YOU
PAY: MANAGING YOUR SECOND-HAND SHOCK (Janis Publications
USA Inc., 2008).

ARTICLES

Michael Town, *Compassion Fatigue and Vicarious Trauma in Court: A
Judge's Perspective*, FATALITY REV. BULL.; reprinted in FLORIDA BAR
NEWS (June 1, 2004). Available at: http://www.floridabar.org/DIV
COM/JN/JNNews01.nsf/cb53c80c8fabd49d85256b5900678f6c/
e4fe17e7b4b9294885256ea00056c09b?OpenDocument.

Jaffe, Town, et al. *Vicarious Trauma in Judges: The Personal Challenge of
Dispensing Justice*, 54 JUV. & FAM. CT. JUST. J. 4, 1–9 (Fall 2003).
Available at National Council of Juvenile and Family Court Judges,
http://www.ncjfcj.org/images/stories/dept/fvd/pdf/journal_1
_fall_03_vicarious_trauma.pdf. Also available at: http://www
.ncjfcj.org/content/blogcategory/256/302/ (please scroll down to
article).

Blogs

http://www.ncjfcj.org/images/stories/dept/fvd/pdf/journal_1_fall_03_vicari ous_trauma.pdf

Vicarious Trauma Institute, http://www.vicarioustrauma.com/blog.html

ABOUT THE
CONTRIBUTORS

Annabelle Berrios, a graduate of Boston College Law School, has 13 years of experience in the legal field. She has trained in Sivananda Yoga and Structural and Ayurvedic Yoga Therapy and is fascinated by the service of yoga as a pain management tool. Her website is www.miamiyogatherapy.com.

Jill Breslau J.D., M.A., is a family law practitioner who took a lengthy sabbatical from the practice of law to earn a degree in Counseling Psychology. The suffering of so many individuals in the legal system, both clients and attorneys, fueled her interest in what the legal profession refers to as "work-life balance" or "stress management." Neuroscience, as well as mindfulness and other coping skills, are rich resources which help her educate lawyers and clients alike.

Sheila Boyce was a legal services lawyer for many years. For the past several years, she has put to work her degree in gerontology, experience and interest in elder law and service, by being the caretaker for her own elderly parents. A member of the Georgia bar, she lives in Asheville, NC. Sheila was also an editor of this book. Her emails were so passionate and insightful that they became part of the book.

Debra Bruce (www.lawyer-coach.com) practiced law for 18 years before becoming a professionally trained Executive Coach for lawyers. She is Vice Chair of the Law Practice Management Committee of the State Bar of Texas and the co-founder and past leader of Houston Coaches, the Houston Chapter of the International Coach Federation.

Kathleen Clark, PhD, practices law in California and is the founder and chief executive officer of ServantLawyership, a legal and health care consulting firm, based on her belief that the practice of law promotes both healing and service. In particular, the focus of her work is speaking, writing, and serving all parties involved in medical error situations through the collaborative law process.

Susan Daicoff is a Professor of Law at Florida Coastal School of Law in Jacksonville, Florida. She teaches contracts, professional responsibility, and a course on law as a healing profession.Since 1991, she has been researching and writing in the areas of the psychology of lawyers, lawyer personality, lawyer distress and dissatisfaction, professionalism, and ethical decision making by lawyers. Her book, Lawyer, Know Thyself, synthesized forty years of empirical research on lawyers' personality traits and related these findings to professionalism and lawyer well being. Her current research interests focus on "a comprehensive law movement" she perceives in the profession, which seeks a better way to resolve legal matters. She received her J.D. with honors from the

University of Florida, her LL.M. in tax from New York University, and her M.S. in clinical psychology from the University of Central Florida. In addition to her note-worthy professional career, Susan is a singer, song-writer.

Gretchen Duhaime spent ten years in Corporate America in one unhappy workplace after another. Her desire to create change and harmony in work and life led her to law school, where she decided to focus her efforts on bringing wellness to the legal community. She graduated from Suffolk University Law School in 2010 and is a certified Dream Teacher and Reiki Master. Her web site is http://www.practicingonpurpose.com/

The Rev. Eileen Epperson is a Presbyterian minister and has been a college, hospital, and hospice chaplain as well as a pastor in six churches. Eileen has been active in interfaith dialogue for over 35 years. She gave programs at both the 1993 and 1999 Parliaments of the World's Religions in Chicago and Cape Town, South Africa. She has a private practice in spiritual and life coaching with a specialty in forgiveness issues. She created *The Forgiveness Process*® and works with individuals, also leading forgiveness workshops in northwest Connecticut, Florida and New York State. www.let-resentments-go.com

Melissa Cole Essig is a writer living in Asheville, North Carolina. Her essay in the text and others about her never-ending search for mindfulness in motherhood also appear on her website, http://www.YogaMamaMe.com.

Jennifer Foster administers the Mountain Area Volunteer Lawyer Pro Bono Program through Pisgah Legal Services in Asheville, North Carolina where she has merged concepts of holistic law and attorney well-being into the pro bono culture of Western North Carolina. A 1995 graduate of The University of North Carolina School of Law, Jennifer has served as a federal judicial law clerk, an appellate public defender, a motions and appellate research and writing specialist, an expert in criminal and immigration consequences and post-conviction relief for immigrants, and private holistic attorney. Jennifer also enjoys playing and writing music, dancing, meditation practice, and yoga.

Dolly M. Garlo, RN, JD, PCC, is President of *Thrive!!*© Inc. (www.All Thrive.com) and Founder of Creating Legacy™ (www.CreatingLegacy Network.com). After 16 years of law practice (www.GarloWard.com), her current focus is business development, strategic marketing design, professional career transition, social entrepreneurism, corporate social responsibility cultivation, and making a difference that lasts for generations.

Michael Grant is a journalist, author and educator living in La Mesa, CA. He was a prize-winning columnist and essayist for The San Diego Union for

20 years and has taught college journalism and media communications since 1990. He and his wife, Karen Werve Grant, who is a lawyer, operate The Write Outsource, a professional writing resource for lawyers and other professional services firms, at www.writeoutsource.com. The latest of his several books is "Warbirds – How They Played the Game."

Gary Harper has trained thousands in conflict resolution. His students include mediators, lawyers, and police officers; counselors, diamond miners and film crews. In 2004, he authored *The Joy of Conflict Resolution* – acclaimed for its accessibility, humour and practicality. His unique blend of experience as a personal injury lawyer, general manager, insurance regulator and retail store owner, shaped his understanding of conflict and his appreciation for effective communication. See http://www.joyofconflict.com for more information.

Harvey Hyman practiced plaintiff's personal injury law for 21 years in northern California. He has begun a new career as writer, speaker and coach for lawyers wanting to learn how to decrease stress and improve their health, career satisfaction and personal happiness.

Azim N. Khamisa lost his only son, Tariq, to a senseless gang-related murder. Azim is a rare individual who not only speaks of powerful and life-changing concepts, but also walks his talk. His story and website can be found at AzimKhamisa.com or TKF.org.

Theresa Beran Kulat is a collaborative lawyer practicing in Illinois. Her work combines more than 20 years of legal training and experience with more than 30 years of personal and spiritual growth work. Visit her website at IntegralFamilyLaw.com.

Irene Leonard, a lawyer for 25 years who remembers the days of the one-line bill, is a professional development coach. Irene works with lawyers to help them value their services. Visit her website, www.CoachingForChange.com, or call her at (206) 723-9900.

Stewart Levine is the author of *The Book of Agreement* and *Getting to Resolution*. His website is www.resolutionworks.com.

Moira McCaskill, LLB, LLM/ADR, CPCC, began her career as a lawyer, obtained an LLM in alternative dispute resolution, and became a mediator; she is now a coach working with the Enneagram as a tool for personal transformation. Visit her website at http://www.moiramccaskill.com/about.html.

Forrest "Woody" Mosten is Collaborative Attorney and Mediator in Los Angeles who handles dissolutions and premarital agreements involving substantial assets and high conflict. His books include *Collaborative Divorce Handbook, Mediation Career Guide, Unbundling Legal Services*, and *Complete Guide to Mediation* and he is Adjunct Professor of Law at UCLA. He is Editor of the *Family Court Special Issue on Collaborative Law*. Mr. Mosten is a recipient of the ABA Lawyer as Problem Solver Award, Lifetime Legal Access Award, and was named 2009 Frank Sander Co-Lecturer. He is the first recipient of the Los Angeles Bar Associations Conflict Prevention Award, is a Los Angeles Super Lawyer, and Southern California Peacemaker of the Year. He is recognized internationally as the "Father of Unbundling" and serves as Keynote Speaker Conference Speaker and trains lawyers and mediators worldwide. Mr. Mosten can be reached at www.MostenMediation.com.

Alexis Martin Neely, business owner, mom, and lawyer, is the founder and chief executive officer of the Family Wealth Planning Institute, a company that is revolutionizing the way personal legal services are provided to families and small business owners in the United States. She is also a coach, a regular commentator in national broadcast media, and an author. More info can be found at http://alexisneely.com and http://www.LawBusinessRevolution.com.

Leslie Rawls is a sole practitioner in Charlotte, North Carolina concentrating on appellate advocacy. Leslie has studied Buddhism since 1970 and been actively involved in the community of practitioners in the lineage of Thich Nhat Hanh for nearly two decades. In the 1990's, she was lay coordinator for many of Thich Nhat Hanh's North American retreats. She edited the Plum Village journal, The Mindfulness Bell, from 1996 to 2001. Leslie helps maintain the online directories of Plum Village Sanghas around the world. (www.iamhome.org) She also leads retreats and Days of Mindfulness in Charlotte and the southeast, and facilitates inmate Sanghas in the North Carolina Department of Corrections. See www.charlottemindfulness.org for more information.

Scott Rogers has practiced law along with mindfulness-based contemplative techniques for 18 years. He graduated summa cum laude from the University of Florida Levin College of Law (1991) and prior to that received his Master's Degree in Social Psychology, also from the University of Florida (1988). Scott is the founder and director of the Institute for Mindfulness Studies.

carl Michael rossi is a lawyer, mediator, coach, and counselor in Chicago and can be contacted at cmr@collaborativepracticechicago.com. He is the president of the International Alliance of Holistic Lawyers: www.iahl.org.

Gretchen Rubin is the author of the New Times Best Selling book, *The Happiness Project: Or, Why I Spent a Year Trying to Sing in the Morning, Clean My*

Closets, Fight Right, Read Aristotle, and Generally Have More Fun. [Harper; December 29, 2009], an account of the year she spent test-driving studies and theories about how to be happier. Before turning to writing, she started out in law. At Yale Law School, she was editor-in-chief of the *Yale Law Journal*, and she was clerking for Justice Sandra Day O'Connor when she realized that she really wanted to be a writer. Her website is http://www.happiness-project .com/happiness_project/.

David Shearon is the Executive Director at Tennessee Lawyers' Fund for Client Protection. He received his Masters in Applied Positive Psychology from the University of Pennsylvania in 2006 , his Juris Doctor from the University of Virginia in 1979, and his Bachelor of Science in Journalism from the University of Tennessee. He and his wife, Teresa, live in Nashville where he enjoys shooting archery tournaments with his two sons.

Barbara Stahura is a freelance writer and journal facilitator. Along with writing books and magazine articles, she leads journal workshops for people with brain injury and family caregivers, as well as for others. Her website is barbarastahura.com.

Cheryl Stephens founded the Plain Language Association International in 1993. Her 4-book series Plain Language Wizardry includes Plain Language Legal Writing and the new Plain Language in Plain English. Cheryl was a pioneer in using plain language on the Internet, and created the Plain Language Online website for the Canada's Access to Justice Network in 1994 and the plain language online training site PlainTrain. Cheryl received her B.A. (with Honors) in the multi-disciplinary field of International Relations at University of the Pacific in 1970. With a JD from the University of British Columbia and law practice experience, she lead the Canadian Bar Association's BC projects on plain language and the Lawyers for Literacy Project. Since 2000, Cheryl has created 4500 plain English definitions for the Multilingual Legal Dictionary at http://legalglossary.ca, created plain language training resources for the Council of Canadian Administrative Tribunals, and assisted the Canadian Association of Chiefs of Police to develop resources for plain language and literacy awareness. She has also worked on plain language projects in the medical and social science fields and for multi-cultural and literacy programs.

Pat McHenry Sullivan is a spirit and work pioneer who helps lawyers and other professionals work with less stress, more efficiency, satisfaction and meaning. Reach Pat at www.spiritworkandmoney.com or 510-530-0284.

Kali Samaya Tara graduated from Northwestern School of Law of Lewis and Clark College in 2002 and received her Qi Dao Coaching degree from the

Academy of Qi Dao under the instruction of Lama Somananda Tantrapa in 2008. She has practiced law in Oregon and Guam and now lives in Portland, Oregon where she practices qigong daily and coaches others to manifest their life's dreams. If you are interested in learning more about Lama Tantrapa and his works, please visit his website at www.qidao.org.

Lorenn Walker JD, MPH, is a Hawai'i-based health educator with extensive legal and social service experience. Lorenn uses a public health approach with organizations and individuals in finding positive solutions for problem solving. Lorenn is an expert in designing and facilitating effective learning programs. Her recent work has focused on reentry for incarcerated people, substance abuse, violence prevention, and reconciliation for people harmed by wrongdoing and social injustice. www.lorennwalker.com

Janet Smith Warfield is the author of *Shift: Change Your Words, Change Your World*, an Amazon.com Best Seller and 2008 Indie Next Generation Book Award Winner. She is a graduate of Swarthmore College and cum laude graduate of Rutgers School of Law, Camden. She practiced law in Atlantic City for 22 years.

Jennie N. Winter is an attorney and Director of Client Services at the Pro Bono Project in San Jose, California. She oversees volunteers who help clients with family law matters, including certified law students and attorneys. Jennie holds a JD from Santa Clara University School of Law, a BA in Human Development and a Master's in Public Administration from California State University, Hayward. Before going to law school she practiced for 23 years as a Holistic Health Educator and Bodywork Therapist. She brings this background as a healer into her practice of law and her approach to helping clients solve their legal problems. Before coming to Pro Bono Project, Jennie was in private practice as a family law attorney in Santa Clara, San Mateo and Alameda counties. She serves on the Santa Clara County Bar Association Family Law Executive Committee, and the Family Law Education and Minor's Representation subcommittees. She is a member of Collaborative Practice Silicon Valley; sits on the Northern California Public Education Committee for Collaborative Practice California; is a member of the International Academy of Collaborative Professionals, the International Alliance of Holistic Lawyers, and a founding member of the Renaissance Lawyer Society.

Diane F. Wyzga has cemented a strong national presence as the only RN, JD and professionally-trained storyteller working as a trial consultant to help lawyers conceptualize and construct their case stories. Diane helps more lawyers win more cases more often by using narrative skills and techniques to develop the legal case story, strategize the trial from voir dire through closing arguments, and influence decision-makers far beyond the reach of any PowerPoint presentation. Her company, Lightning Rod Communications, is based in San Clemente, California. A motto at her Web site: "The difference between the right word and almost right word is like the difference between lightning and lightning bug" reminds us that lawyers must tell their clients' stories with power, passion, and precision. Tel: 949-361-3035; website: http://www.lightrod.net; email: diane@lightrod.net

Michael Zeytoonian is the Founding Member of the Zeytoonian Center for Dispute Resolution, and is a lawyer, mediator and ombudsman. He is a partner at Hutchings, Barsamian, Mandelcorn & Zeytoonian, LLP, in Wellesley Hills, MA and specializes in employment law, mediation, collaborative law, business law, administrative law and negligence. He is admitted to practice in the state and federal district courts of Massachusetts and New York (Southern District) and the state of Connecticut.

INDEX

ABOUT THE AUTHOR

J. Kim Wright

© Michael Matthews

J. Kim Wright is the publisher and managing editor of CuttingEdgeLaw.com. She and her business partner, Michael Matthews, have interviewed over one hundred lawyers, law professors, law students, judges, and allied professionals who are working to create a new paradigm of legal practice. She coaches lawyers on transforming their law practices and finding the right livelihood. A member of the North Carolina Bar, she occasionally practices law and has been an adjunct professor at three colleges. She develops continuing legal education programs and has published many articles and chapters in magazines and other books. She is involved in several think-tanks and support circles and is working on two primetime documentary series about law.